Legal and Geopolitical Complexity in the Arctic

This book examines the evolving geopolitical landscape of the Arctic, focusing on the impact of climate change and the war in Ukraine on regional and international relations from a legal and geopolitical perspective.

As Arctic ice melts, newly accessible natural resources and transportation routes are intensifying territorial and maritime disputes, heightening competition and tensions among regional states. The war in Ukraine has further strained relations between the West and Russia, disrupting political, economic, and scientific cooperation while accelerating the militarisation of the Arctic. In response to Russia's aggressive actions in Eastern Europe, Western states have expanded their military presence in the region, while Russia has modernised its Arctic military infrastructure. Through analysing these developments, the book highlights the interconnection between regional and global dynamics. It argues that climate change and geopolitical conflict are transforming the Arctic from the 'last frontier' into the 'first frontier', a strategic arena where states, both within and beyond the region, seek to assert their geopolitical and economic interests. Adopting an interdisciplinary approach that integrates international relations, international law, and history, this book provides a comprehensive examination of the Arctic's legal and geopolitical complexities.

The book will be of interest to researchers in the field of international relations and public international law, as well as environmental and Arctic law.

Tiziana Melchiorre is affiliated researcher at the Centre for European Law and Governance of the University of Amsterdam where she completed her Marie Skłodowska-Curie Fellowship. Previously, she held several positions such as at the NATO Energy Security Centre of Excellence in Lithuania and as consultant in consulting firms in Belgium and Italy. She holds a PhD in International Relations from the University of Stockholm, the Interdisciplinary Master in East European Research and Studies, a Laurea (old system) in International Sciences and Diplomacy with a specialisation in European Studies from the University of Bologna, and a Masters in Europlanning from the International University of Venice. She has conducted research in several countries including Sweden, France, Turkey, the Netherlands, Norway, and Lithuania. Her research interests include the Arctic and the Baltic Sea Region.

Routledge Research in Polar Law

Emerging Legal Orders in the Arctic
The Role of Non-Arctic Actors
Edited by Akiho Shibata, Leilei Zou, Nikolas Sellheim & Marzia Scopelliti

China's Role in the Arctic
Observing and Being Observed
Nong Hong

Philosophies of Polar Law

Edited by Dawid Bunikowsi and Alan D. Hemmings

Emerging Pathogens at the Poles
Disease and International Trade Law
Alexandra L. Carleton

Non-Governmental Actors in International Climate Change Law
The Case of Arctic Indigenous Peoples
Marzia Scopelliti

Legal and Geopolitical Complexity in the Arctic
The Impact of Global Crises on Regional Competition
Tiziana Melchiorre

For a full list of titles in this series, please visit https://www.routledge.com/Routledge-Research-in-Polar-Law/book-series/RRPL

Legal and Geopolitical Complexity in the Arctic

The Impact of Global Crises on Regional Competition

Tiziana Melchiorre

Routledge
Taylor & Francis Group
LONDON AND NEW YORK

First published 2026
by Routledge
4 Park Square, Milton Park, Abingdon, Oxon OX14 4RN

and by Routledge

605 Third Avenue, New York, NY 10158

Routledge is an imprint of the Taylor & Francis Group, an informa business

British Library Cataloguing-in-Publication Data
A catalogue record for this book is available from the British Library

ISBN: 978-1-032-61448-9 (hbk)
ISBN: 978-1-032-63242-1 (pbk)
ISBN: 978-1-032-63300-8 (ebk)

DOI: 10.4324/9781032633008

Typeset in Times New Roman
by Deanta Global Publishing Services, Chennai, India

To my parents

Contents

Acknowledgements

The idea for this book came up during a conversation with Professor Francesco Privitera (University of Bologna, Forlì Campus) whom I have known for about 25 years. Conversations with him are always very interesting and stimulating as there is always a lot to learn from him both because he's one of the most knowledgeable and prepared professors I have ever met and because he is able to analyse facts and events from various perspectives offering interpretations that stimulate the interlocutor's thirst for knowledge. At the end of that long conversation on the Arctic, he strongly encouraged me to write a manuscript that would be a comprehensive and original study of the geopolitical changes that occurred in the region over the last few decades. I was immediately enthusiastic about the idea to write a book, especially because this is my very first book. Of course, I have written some theses during my studies but it was not the same as writing a proper book.

Therefore, I decided to follow his suggestion and take inspiration from that conversation to structure my book. We had spoken about a number of issues that are relevant to the region, which I have tried to include in this work in the most logical and clear manner in order to provide a clear understanding of what is happening in a region that is becoming increasingly geopolitically and economically important. Thus, my gratitude certainly goes to him for the great help and support that he has always given me. This has had a huge role in the writing of this book.

I also wish to thank Dr Giacomo Tagiuri, assistant professor at the University of Amsterdam, and Dr Monica Pavese, teacher of Italian and History in Turin. They certainly are two of my closest and dearest friends. They have also had a role because they have enthusiastically supported me and advised me to embark on this journey. Additionally, Salvatore Messina has always supported and encouraged me during this journey.

Finally, I would like to thank ArcticPortal.org for very kindly allowing me to use its map on Arctic Shipping Routes, which has definitely enriched my book while also helping to clarify the text.

Preface

The Arctic 'cold' is becoming 'hot'. Climate change is transforming not only the physical environment of the Arctic but also its geopolitical setting. The increasing accessibility of natural resources and transportation routes due to ice-melting has geopolitical and legal implications involving states both inside and outside the region. The militarisation of Arctic territories, cooperation, and increased tension are some of the consequences of climate change. At the same time, the war in Ukraine is intensifying and accelerating these processes, thus contributing to demonstrate that the Arctic is not a place apart from the rest of the world and that the 'exceptionalism' of the Arctic is the wrong image of the region.

This book is an analysis of these dynamics since the Cold War until today through an interdisciplinary approach combining international relations, law, and history. The aim is to provide a comprehensive picture of the High North by discussing the main geopolitical and legal issues currently at stake in order to contribute to a better understanding of the Arctic that is emerging as one of the hottest regions in the world from a geopolitical perspective. Additionally, an important element of this book is that the analysis links the regional and the international levels because it is not possible to understand what happens regionally without taking into consideration the broader international system in which regions are embedded.

Introduction

The geopolitical resurgence of the Arctic

'Arctic exceptionalism' has never existed. Over the last few years, a number of books and articles have chorally argued that 'Arctic exceptionalism', the idea that the region has traditionally been characterised by peace and cooperation for a long time, has come to an end. By contrast, this book argues that the Arctic is not shielded from geopolitical developments elsewhere because it is a reflection of the international order. This is the main message that this book tries to give.

Like the 'end of history' from American political scientist Francis Fukuyama, 'Arctic exceptionalism' is an expression of a distorted vision of the world. 'The End of History?' is the title of an article that Fukuyama published in 1989 and was the basis of his book titled *The End of History and the Last Man* published some years later in 1992. In his work, Fukuyama defines the end of the Cold War as 'the end point of mankind's ideological evolution and the universalization of Western liberal democracy as the final form of human government' (Fukuyama, 1989, 3). Neorealist John Mearsheimer explains very well that 'this perspective suggests that great powers no longer view each other as potential military rivals, but instead as members of a family of nations, members of what is sometimes called the "international community"' (Mearsheimer, 2001, 1). Nevertheless, Mearsheimer criticises this view arguing that 'the claim that security competition and war between the great powers have been purged from the international system is wrong. Indeed, there is much evidence that the promise of everlasting peace among the great power was stillborn' (Mearsheimer, 2001, 1). In order to support his statement, Mearsheimer argues that although the Cold War is over, the United States (US) has continued to maintain about 100,000 troops in Europe and almost the same number in northeast Asia (Mearsheimer, 2001, 2). According to him, the reason is that the US 'recognises that dangerous rivalries would probably emerge among the major powers in these regions if the US troops were withdrawn' (Mearsheimer, 2001, 2). He continues saying that 'the sad fact is that international politics has always been a ruthless and dangerous business, and it is likely to remain that way. Although the intensity of their competition waxes and wanes, great powers fear each other and always compete with each other for power' (Mearsheimer, 2001, 2).

The war in Ukraine, which began in 2022 after Russia's illegal annexation of Crimea in 2014, demonstrates that Mearsheimer's perspective is right. It shows

DOI: 10.4324/9781032633008-1

that war is always possible and that the periods characterised by peace and cooperation between powers are not everlasting. This is clearly true for all the regions of the world, the Arctic included.

The analysis of the causes of the war in Ukraine is beyond the aims of this book. Instead, what this book intends to do is analyse how the interplay between the war in Ukraine and climate change affect the geopolitical dynamics in the Arctic. More specifically, the starting point of this study is that these two variables are complementary and that the war in Ukraine has accelerated a geopolitical process that had begun because of climate change some decades before. Climate change, which is making natural resources and transportation routes increasingly accessible because of ice-melting, began affecting relations among states. The Arctic states began intensifying exploration and exploitation of their territories (the coastal states also began militarising their territories) while states (e.g., China) and actors (e.g., the EU) outside the region changed their policies towards the Arctic, whose geopolitical and economic importance is growing exponentially. As a result, over the last few decades, the Arctic has become a hot region again like it was during the Cold War, when it was heavily militarised due to its peculiar geographical location that made it the shortest distance between the two superpowers (the US and the Soviet Union).

As a consequence, the false image of 'Arctic exceptionalism' has been questioned recently. Since the very last years of the Cold War until the very recent period, the Arctic has been considered an exceptional region because it has been characterised by good relations between the states belonging to it. The establishment of the Arctic Council (AC) and other cooperative links have strongly contributed to the image of the Arctic as a peaceful region where tensions or even war were unthinkable. Nevertheless, this was the wrong perception of Arctic geopolitics. Indeed, Russia's annexation of Crimea and especially the war in Ukraine as well as climate change have clearly demonstrated that the Arctic is not something apart from the rest of the world. If it is true that 'what happens in the Arctic doesn't stay in the Arctic' (which is an expression commonly used with specific reference to climate but that could be applied to geopolitics as well), it is also true that what happens in the international system also affects regions (with reference to geopolitics) because states are linked to each other in whatever part of the world they are located. States are an integral part of the international system.

Methodology

In order to add food for thought to the debate on the geopolitical changes that occurred in the Arctic over the last few decades, the methodology used in the narrative of this book is based on an interdisciplinary approach combining international relations with a focus on geopolitics, international law, and history. Taking inspiration from Colin Flint's[1] definition, this book defines geopolitics as the struggle over

1 Colin Flint is professor of Political Geography in the Department of Political Science at Utah State University.

the control of geographical entities with a regional dimension, and the use of such geographical entities for political and economic advantage (Flint, 2017). This definition well suits the aims of this book, which focuses on the Arctic region that comprises Canada, Denmark, Finland, Iceland, Norway, Russia, Sweden, and the US.

It is necessary to stress here that the definition of the Arctic region chosen in this book is a political one. A consensual definition does not exist and how the Arctic is defined depends on the chosen criteria, which can be divided approximately into political or geographical ones. An illuminating example of this is the statement that the Arctic Monitoring and Assessment Programme (AMAP) of the AC makes in its Assessment Report. The AMAP states that

> Given the different definitions of the Arctic, based on physical-geographical characteristics as described above, and those based on political and administrative considerations within different countries, no simple delineation of the Arctic region was applicable for the purposes of the AMAP assessment. To establish a geographical context for the AMAP assessment, therefore, a regional extent was defined based on a compromise among various definitions. This incorporates elements of the Arctic Circle, political boundaries, vegetation boundaries, permafrost limits, and major oceanographic features. The region covered by AMAP is, therefore, essentially the terrestrial and marine areas north of the Arctic Circle (66°32'N), and north of 62°N in Asia and 60°N in North America, modified to include the marine areas north of the Aleutian chain, Hudson Bay, and parts of the North Atlantic Ocean including the Labrador Sea.
>
> (AMAP, 2024, 10)

The problem with AMAP's definition is that it excludes parts of the territories of the Arctic states that are full members of the AC. Since this study is a political one, the definition should necessarily be coherent with its aims. Also, in this book, the two expressions 'High North' and 'Arctic' are used as synonyms.

Furthermore, although this book focuses on the Arctic region, the analysis links the regional dimension to the international because they are strictly interlinked. Indeed, it is not possible to understand what happens regionally if the international dimension is not taken into consideration and vice versa.

Furthermore, the geopolitical dynamics in the Arctic can be well understood with the help of international law, which is another branch of international studies. In fact, international law, together with geopolitics, helps explain the conduct of states in space. Additionally, international law is of particular relevance when speaking about the Arctic because this is regulated by international and regional agreements and treaties (in particular the United Nations Convention on the Law of the Sea).

Finally, history is important as well because the sequence and connection of events linking the Arctic states is of utmost importance to understanding the causality leading to the state of geopolitical dynamics in the Arctic. In particular, the analysis will start at the period of the Cold War because understanding how the relations among the Arctic states have evolved since then is crucial for conducting a consistent and clear analysis. Explaining the geopolitical dynamics in the Arctic since the Cold War, which has had an enormous impact on the relations between Eastern and Western Europe, is in fact important to understanding the very reasons for the current geopolitical situation in the region.

The combination of these academic disciplines, which are strictly intertwined, reflects the complexity of the Arctic. Such an approach to the study of this region is in fact essential if the aim is to provide a rigorous and comprehensive analysis of the reasons behind the current geopolitical and legal developments in the Arctic. In this context, the analysis is conducted by taking into account climate change and the war in Ukraine as the main variables, as explained in the previous section.

Structure

This book is divided into two parts, each of which constitutes two chapters. Thus, the book has four chapters in total. The first part analyses the geopolitical changes that occurred in the Arctic from the period of the Cold War until 2024. In order to do so, the first chapter focuses on the period between the Cold War and 2014, which is considered as a watershed as it is the year when Russia illegally annexed Crimea and the relations between the West and Russia began worsening. This chapter discusses the Arctic exceptionalism concept in the wider geopolitical context of the Cold War and explains why the Arctic can't be considered 'exceptional' even if it is compared to other regions such as the Antarctic and the Third Pole, the regions of ice, by applying a wider meaning of the term. Also, the first chapter analyses the development of cooperation in the region with particular emphasis on the AC as well as the EU's strategy towards the region. The second chapter focuses on the period between 2014 and 2024 by analysing the impact of Russia's illegal annexation of Crimea and of the war in Ukraine on the geopolitical dynamics in the region. In this context, the rapprochement between Russia and China, the militarisation of the Arctic, as well as the legal foundations of scientific cooperation, its relevance in the geopolitical and economic strategies of non-Arctic states, and the impact of the war in Ukraine on the scientific sector are also discussed.

The two chapters constituting the second part of the book focus on natural resources and infrastructure, respectively. More specifically, the third chapter discusses the geopolitical and legal implications of climate change and the war in Ukraine in the sectors of water, minerals, energy, and fishing. The fourth chapter analyses the sectors of shipping, ports, and Outer Space. Although shipping and ports are closely intertwined, they are analysed in two different sections in order to clearly explain how states pursue their geopolitical and economic interests in the broader shipping domain and in the case of ports more specifically.

Literature review

A growing number of studies on the Arctic is enriching the academic field, but a comprehensive work analysing how geopolitics in the region has changed since the Cold War by taking into consideration both climate change and the war in Ukraine and with an interdisciplinary approach has not been accomplished, yet. Most studies mainly focus on a single sector (e.g., energy, fisheries, minerals, etc.) or on how the relations among states have changed as a consequence of the war in Ukraine or climate change. Also, some books are a collection of chapters written by various authors on specific issues.

Furthermore, a growing number of works concerns Russia's strategies in the High North. The reason is certainly that Russia is one of the major actors both regionally and internationally. Thus, its policies towards the region have a great influence on Arctic geopolitical dynamics while also affecting international ones. In this context, relations between Russia and China are getting more attention in the academic field although there are still few studies focusing on their rapprochement in the Arctic. By contrast, very few works analyse the strategies of other Asian states towards the region, such as India. Given the fact that the relevance of other Asian states in the definition of geopolitical dynamics in the international system is growing, meaning that their weight in the Arctic will also grow, this book includes other Asian states in the analysis.

Furthermore, several articles about the EU's efforts to be deeply involved in Arctic affairs have been written but they usually focus on sustainable development and climate change policies towards the High North. Very few works analyse the EU's policies towards the region with a comprehensive approach aiming at studying not only its overall strategies but also its involvement in specific relevant sectors such as fisheries, energy, and minerals.

Finally, a study on a comparison between the three poles (the Arctic, the Antarctic, and the Third Pole) from a geopolitical perspective has not been accomplished, yet. Comparisons are useful for a better understanding of the object of study. Considering that the geopolitical, legal, and economic importance of the three poles is increasing because they are all rich in natural resources, better knowledge of two regions that are so different from the Arctic can help understand the place of the Arctic in world politics.

This book is an attempt to fill in these gaps in the academic discussion by providing food for thought on a number of issues concerning a region that is becoming increasingly important in everybody's lives because of its economic wealth.

References

AMAP. (2024). *Assessment Report.* Available at: https://www.amap.no/about/geographical-coverage (accessed 29 November 2024).

Flin, C. (2017). Introduction to Geopolitics. 3rd edition. Oxon Routledge.

Fukuyama, F. (1989). The End of History? *The National Interest*, 16: 3–18.

Mearsheimer, J. (2001). *The Tragedy of Great Power Politics*. New York: W. W. Norton & Company.

1 A new distribution of power in the Arctic

Introduction

This chapter discusses the geopolitical changes that occurred in the Arctic from the Cold War, which conventionally refers to the period between the aftermath of the Second World War and the disintegration of the Soviet Union in 1991 (it began at the very end of the 1980s though), until the period immediately before 2014, when Russia illegally annexed the Crimean Peninsula in the southern part of Ukraine shoring the Black Sea.

Starting from the late 1980s, the analysis focuses on the origins of the so-called 'Arctic exceptionalism' that is considered as stemming from the speech that the Soviet Union's Secretary-General Mikhail Gorbachev gave in Murmansk in 1987. Gorbachev's initiative led to a long period characterised by cooperation among states in the region and to the consequent establishment of regional bodies that have strengthened the relations among them providing a platform from where to develop their Arctic policy. The Arctic Council (AC) is the most important intergovernmental forum in the region, although it is not the only one. Nevertheless, this chapter shows that the Arctic is not exceptional as it is a reflection of the international order. What happens in the Arctic is a consequence of the geopolitical dynamics in the international system.

In this context, climate change has played a crucial role in pushing states to cooperate as the increasingly accessible natural resources and transportation routes have had an incredible geopolitical impact on the region leading to growing attention from actors both inside and outside the region. The EU is an emblematic example because its involvement in Arctic affairs has been growing over the last few decades as it is evident from the 'evolution' of its four Arctic policies adopted since 2008.

In order to analyse how the relations among states in the region have changed since the very last years of the Cold War, this chapter is divided into five sections. The first one analyses the geopolitical dynamics that occurred in the High North since the period of the Cold War by also discussing 'Arctic exceptionalism' and by linking the international and the regional level. The second section investigates the development of cooperation in the region with particular emphasis on the AC. The third section analyses the development of cooperation in the Arctic by comparing the perspective of neorealism and neoliberal institutionalism, which are the

DOI: 10.4324/9781032633008-2

two theoretical approaches that have dominated the academic debate in the field of international relations for decades. The fourth section compares the Arctic with the Antarctic and the Third Pole by using the term 'exceptionalism' in its broader meaning in order to demonstrate that each of these regions is not more exceptional than the other two although each of them has its own peculiarities. Finally, the fifth section is dedicated to the EU's geopolitical strategy towards the region.

From the Cold War to the Post-Cold War and 'Arctic exceptionalism'

During the Cold War, the Arctic played a special role in the strategic confrontation between the US and the Soviet Union both militarily and politically as they shared a maritime border along the Bering Strait and around the Arctic Ocean. Thus, the High North was the shortest distance for aircraft and ballistic missiles between the two superpowers that transformed it into a highly militarised and politically very sensitive region (Vigeland Rottem and Folkestad Soltvedt, 2020, 24; Le Mière and Mazo, 2013, 82). Additionally, the political sensitiveness of the Arctic was also increased by juridical ambiguities concerning territorial claims, which contributed to an increase in tensions between the two superpowers (Laruelle, 2014). In this context, the Soviet Union's instrumentalisation of the Central Executive Committee of the Communist Party's 1926 Decree – the Proclamation of Lands and Islands Located in the northern Arctic Ocean – serves as an emblematic case (Laruelle, 2014). The very reason behind the issuing of the decree was Canada's occupation of Wrangel Island enabling Canadian and American expeditions easy travel to Chukotka, which made the Soviet Union feel under threat in the Arctic (Laruelle, 2014). The decree stated that

> all lands and islands, both discovered and which may be discovered in the future, which do not comprise at the time of publication of the present decree the territory of any foreign state recognized by the Government of the Soviet Union, located in the northern Arctic Ocean, north of the shores of the Union of Soviet Socialist Republics up to the North Pole between the meridian 32°04′35″ E. long from Greenwich, running along the eastern side of Vaida Bay through the triangular marker on Cape Kekurskii, and the meridian 168°49′30″ W. long from Greenwich, bisecting the strait separating the Ratmanov and Kruzenstern Islands, of the Diomede group in the Bering Sea, are proclaimed to be territory of the Soviet Union.
>
> (Laruelle, 2014; Butler, 1978)

The very aim of this decree was to regulate issues over the sovereignty of the Arctic, not to lay down a general principle for the demarcation of maritime borders (Laruelle, 2014). The Soviet legal practice viewed this decree as a historical precedent and led Moscow to propose a sectoral division of all maritime borders, which was a principle to which the Soviet Union referred during its existence (Laruelle, 2014; Elferink, 1996, 1996a). Nevertheless, Soviet experts were divided on its interpretation (Laruelle, 2014; Elferink, 1996a, 1996b). According to those that strictly interpreted the decree, 'only the islands of the sectoral zone were part of the territorial contiguity of the state, not the waters between the islands and the continent', while for those that interpreted the decree more broadly, they argued that the islands, the waters, and the air space should also fall under national jurisdiction (Laruelle, 2014; Elferink, 1996a, 1996b). These views clashed with the US' views according to which those territories were international waters where it had the right to freely navigate (Laruelle, 2014; Elferink, 1996a, 1996b). The US put this claim into practice allowing its submarines to enter Soviet waters. In 1957, the USS Blackfin passed through Soviet-controlled Arctic waters and northern straits and in 1958 the USS Nautilus was the first watercraft to reach the North Pole (Laruelle, 2014; Sasgen, 2009).

In 1952, the Soviet Union issued another decree according to which the Kara Sea, the West Siberian Sea, the Laptev Sea, the East Siberian Sea, and the Okhotsk Sea were all to be considered as national Soviet territory (Araldsen, 1967). On the basis of this decree, the Soviet armed forces received orders to seize every foreign ship found in these seas and conduct them to the nearest port (Araldsen, 1967). Also, every foreign aircraft was to be requested to undertake landing and, in case of failure to comply with this request immediately, to be forced to comply by means of armed force (Araldsen, 1967). As a reaction, the US press strongly opposed this decree arguing that it was a clear violation of international law without success (Araldsen, 1967).

Nevertheless, in spite of the tensions between them, the two superpowers were able to cooperate bilaterally on some soft power issues like the protection of the environment (intended as comprising all living and non-living elements affecting human life). An example is the Agreement on Cooperation in the Field of Environmental Protection, generally known as the 'Environmental Bilateral', which was signed by the heads of state in 1972 with the aim to solve 'the most important aspects of the problems of the environment and will be devoted to working out measures to prevent pollution, to study pollution and its effect on the environment, and to develop the basis for controlling the impact of human activities on nature' (Robinson and Waxmonsky, 1988). Article II of the Agreement identified the Arctic and Subarctic Ecological Systems as one of the eleven areas of cooperation.[1] Additionally, the US and the Soviet Union also cooperated multilaterally through the Agreement on the Conservation of Polar Bears, which was signed by Canada, Denmark, Norway, the US, and the Soviet Union in 1973 in order to coordinate action pertaining to the management of polar bears throughout the circumpolar range (Polar Bear Range States, 2024). With this agreement, the 'Range States' recognised that 'the polar bear is a significant resource of the Arctic region

1 The other areas of cooperation were air pollution, water pollution, environmental pollution associated with agricultural production, enhancement of the urban environment, preservation of nature and the organisation of preserves, marine pollution, biological and genetic consequences of environmental pollution, influence of environmental changes on climate, and earthquake protection (Robinson and Waxmonsky, 1988).

that requires protection' (Polar Bear Range States, 2024). This agreement has been successful in pursuing its primary aim, namely to eliminate overharvesting (Polar Bear Range States, 2024).

It was however with the end of the Cold War that Russia (as the successor of the Soviet Union) and the US (and the West more broadly) began cooperating more intensively. The relaxation of relations between them led to a period characterised by cooperation lasting until 2014, when Russia illegally annexed Crimea. This period has been characterised by so-called 'Arctic exceptionalism'. The meaning of the expression 'Arctic exceptionalism' has changed over time. Originally, it was tied to the expression 'Arctic sublime' referring to a romantic tradition of thought that defined the Arctic in geographical terms as an area similar to a desert characterised by a combination of exotic and unique properties of physical, biological, and human systems and by a pristine and beautiful wilderness where the forces of nature challenge human capabilities to the utmost and where Indigenous Peoples live in harmony with an environment uncorrupted by the forces of modernity (Käpylä, 2015; Marland, 2021).

More recently, 'Arctic exceptionalism' has got a political meaning indicating a 'zone of peace' and a 'territory of dialogue' (Käpylä, 2015). As Professor Oran Young put it, the Arctic was seen as a 'distinctive region in international society' (Käpylä, 2015; Heininen et al., 2013; Keskitalo, 2007). Indeed, it has been usually understood 'as a unique region detached from global political dynamics and thus characterized primarily as an apolitical space of regional governance, functional co-operation, and peaceful coexistence' (Käpylä, 2015).

In her article entitled 'Can the Arctic's unique distinction as a zone of peace be maintained? "The Arctic Senator" explains what it will take', US Senator Lisa Murkowski gives a clear and effective definition of the expression 'Arctic exceptionalism'. She states that

> Arctic exceptionalism has long been the normative concept that prescribes the Arctic as a unique region with a set of unwritten rules, beliefs and history that has given it a level of immunity to many of the world's geopolitical problems. Arctic states, stakeholders and citizens exist and operate in the region and with each other largely without conflict. Arctic exceptionalism has held firm since the end of the Cold War, but in the face of today's environmental changes, it is being challenged.
>
> (Murkowski, 2021)

Indeed, the increasing accessibility to natural resources and transportation routes due to ice melting has changed the geopolitical dynamics in the Arctic by sharpening competition and tension in the region while attracting the attention of external states. Additionally, it is necessary to stress that Senator Murkowski made her statement one year before the war in Ukraine, which is the other element that is changing relations among states in the Arctic. Climate change and the war in Ukraine, the two variables taken into consideration in this book, are questioning the 'exceptional' idea of the Arctic that has prevailed globally for a long time.

The origins of Arctic 'exceptionalism' are typically traced back to the speech given by the Soviet Union's Secretary-General Mikhail Gorbachev in the Soviet polar capital Murmansk in 1987. In order to understand the very aims of this speech, it is necessary to analyse it in the wider context of Soviet foreign policy with particular reference to so-called 'New Thinking' that Gorbachev launched in 1986. The New Thinking was a radical change of Soviet foreign policy that had been essentially underpinned by the Leninist theory of international relations (Wallander, 2001)[2] although the following Soviet leaders' approach to foreign affairs naturally made significant modifications to Lenin's one.[3] The New Thinking

2 Vladimir Il'ič Lenin, the leader of the Union of Soviet Socialist Republics (USSR) from 1922 to 1924 (year of his death), aimed to realise the world proletarian revolution. He believed in the indivisibility of the international revolution meaning that 'the Russian and the Western revolutions were interdependent' (Gregor, 1967). To this aim, the Communist International (Comintern) was established in 1919. Its aim was to coordinate the action of communist parties leading to the world revolution (Wallander, 2001).

3 The world proletarian revolution conceived by Lenin did not materialise. Consequently, Joseph Stalin, who served as the general secretary of the Communist Party of the Soviet Union from 1922 to 1952, formulated 'socialism in one country'. According to this socialism, the world revolution should be temporarily postponed because capitalism had managed to stabilise itself at least for the time being. Therefore, the best path to follow was to put aside efforts to promote the revolution abroad and to focus on building the economic and military strength of the Soviet Union. Later, Georg Malenkov and Nikita Khrushev, succeeding Stalin in 1953, and from 1953 and 1964, respectively, purported that it was necessary to wait for favourable conditions for the world revolution to happen. In this period, coexistence between the Western and the Soviet blocks was necessary. This period should be used by the USSR and its allies to undertake actions to weaken the capitalist system (e.g., support wars of national liberation in the underdeveloped world, the exploitation of 'contradictions' in the Western world, and efforts to outpace the West in economic and technological sectors) Additionally, in his report to the 20th party congress in February 1956, Khrushev denounced Stalin's crimes. He also declared that the capitalist encirclement and the inevitability of wars had ended. According to this view, only socialism could prevent war as 'to abolish war and to establish everlasting peace on earth is a historic mission of communism'. Additionally, Khrushev supported the idea that the victory of communism would be facilitated by economic and technological competition and that the Soviet Union was quickly outpacing the US and other Western countries in industrial strength. Since Khruschev, 'peaceful coexistence' remained 'the fundamental basis for Soviet foreign policy in 1960s and 1970s'. However, Alexei Kosygin and Leonid Brezhnev (they held power in the so-called troika together with Nikolai Podgorny from 1964 to 1977; Kosygin remained in power until 1980 and Brezhnev until 1982) modified Khrushev's interpretation of 'peaceful coexistence' as he had been proven to be wrong in a number of the respects on which he had based his arguments. For instance, the USSR was not outdistancing the US in economics and technology and the Soviet growth rates had decelerated while those of the US accelerated. Therefore, the US was in a position to challenge the Soviet lead in the space race. Also, Khrushev had also been proven wrong in his assumptions about the durability of peace with the West (Wallender, 2001). A good example is the Cuban missile crisis of 1962 when the Soviet Union placed nuclear missiles on Cuban territory to prevent any new invasion attempt from the US (that had tried to overthrow the Castro regime with the Bay of Pigs invasion) (Wallender, 2001). It was the moment when the two superpowers came closest to nuclear conflict. The crisis ended when the US secretly indicated to the USSR that it would remove its missiles from Turkey but that this could not be announced publicly. Consequently, the USSR issued a public statement in which it announced that it would dismantle its missiles in Cuba (United States Department of State, no date). Brezhnev developed the concept of a 'restructuring of international relations' that was

served the main aim of Gorbachev's foreign policy, namely 'to make sure that the USSR [Union of Soviet Socialist Republics] faced the 21st Century as a great power' (Wallander, 2001). In order to achieve this goal, Gorbachev understood the need for political, social, and economic reforms.[4] In this context, he considered essential improving East–West relations, which were quite poor but slightly improving when he came to power in 1985 (Wallander, 2001; Van Oudenaren, 1990). Thus, Gorbachev searched for 'new policy approaches, leading to conclusions that became the core of the new thinking' (Rey, 2004). In fact, Gorbachev 'laid out a new concept of foreign policy, which was based on a vision of the world in full evolution (Wallander, 2001). As Gorbachev was 'forward thinking', he counted on 'all that unites, not all that separates' (Wallander, 2001; Van Oudenaren, 1990). Indeed, in his New Thinking, Gorbachev 'downplayed the importance of class struggle in international relations, emphasized "mutual security" and the role of politics in resolving disputes, and stressed the interdependent nature of the contemporary world' (Van Oudenaren, 1990; Rey, 2004). It is in this perspective that Gorbachev referred to the concept of a 'Common European Home' during an interview given in a television program interview on 1 October 1985 after a meeting with former French President François Mitterrand (Rey, 2004). This concept, which had been introduced by the Minister for Foreign Affairs Andrei Gromyko in a meeting with former French President Georges Pompidou in order to convince him to support the proposal for a Conference on Security and Cooperation in Europe in 1972, became part of New Thinking (Rey, 2004). Gorbachev's idea was to build a new European architecture founded on four levels, namely collective security, a peaceful resolution of conflicts, pan-European economic and trade cooperation, and a real European cultural community (Rey, 2004). Nevertheless, Marie-Pierre Rey (2004) points out that the very aims of Gorbachev's concept were essentially three. First, Gorbachev wanted to emphasise a contrast between the cultural and historical links uniting the European continent to which Russia belonged and the American civilisation perceived as alien to Europe (Rey, 2004).

based on the strengthening of the economic and military strength of the USSR. According to Brezhnev, the growing power of the USSR would ensure that socialist gains were 'irreversible', as Khrushchev had claimed. Although events showed that the prospects for a revolutionary change were still distant, Brezhnev asserted that long-term trends were favourable to the Soviet Union and that the end of capitalism was imminent (Wallender, 2001). Very importantly, Brezhnev was a strong supporter of the so-called détente, namely the 'relaxation of international relations', which he linked to peaceful coexistence and the renunciation of force to resolve conflict between socialism and capitalism. The policy of détente was reaffirmed by the Soviet leaders like Yuri Andropov, Konstantin Chernenko, and Mikhail Gorbachev, with some modifications (Garthoff, 1985).

4 Gorbachev's reforms were *glastnost* and *perestrojka*. *Glastnost* means 'openness', particularly of information, that was supposed to be realised by loosening censorship of the media. *Perestrojka* means 'restructuring', specifically of the Communist economy and political system, that should be realised by 'loosening price controls, encouraging more entrepreneurism and limited private businesses, and by making imported consumer goods easier to purchase'. These two policies went together because 'the reforms they described would make the Soviet Union more democratic and incorporate some features of capitalism to revitalize the economy' (Waxman, 2022).

Second, Gorbachev wanted to show the US that Russia was looking for other interlocutors in order to exert pressure on them to go further in European disarmament negotiations (Rey, 2004). Third, Gorbachev wanted to reach an agreement on the European missile question (Rey, 2004).[5]

Furthermore, another important element of Gorbachev's New Thinking was the fact that he wanted to return to détente while being careful not to give the impression of surrender to Western pressures (Yeşilbursa, 2019). This is why he spoke about the necessity to go 'beyond détente', which meant the establishment of a new 'comprehensive system of international security' (Yeşilbursa, 2019). This system had three main themes that were the mutuality of security in the nuclear age, the inverse relation between security and the level of nuclear and conventional weaponry, and the interdependence of the world (Wallander, 2001). All these themes departed from traditional Soviet practice in foreign policy and from Marxist-Leninist orthodoxy (Wallander, 2001). Indeed, according to Marxist-Leninist orthodoxy, the USSR should provide unilaterally for its own security and global problems were essentially due to capitalistic exploitation (Yeşilbursa, 2019).

In particular, New Thinking was based on three core propositions (Wallander, 2001). First, New Thinking refused the idea that capitalist and socialist states did not have any interests in common and that the existence of one was a fundamental threat to the security and the well-being of the other (Wallander, 2001). Second, it contested the idea that military parity was necessary for security (Wallander, 2001). Third, it supported the argument that the purpose of military policy should be to prevent war rather than defeat Soviet opponents (Wallander, 2001).

These elements were the basis of Gorbachev's Murmansk Speech in which he launched eight initiatives aiming at making the Arctic a 'pole of peace' by 'lowering the level of military confrontation' between the East and the West (Åtland, 2008; Axworthy, 2021) that long before World War II had become 'the sphere of military confrontation between the two opposing socioeconomic systems' (Vartanov and Roginko, 1990) and by establishing cooperative links among the states in the region in several areas. As Gorbachev stated, 'the main thing is to conduct affairs so that the climate here is determined by the warm Gulfstream of the European process and not by the Polar chill of accumulated suspicions and prejudices' (Gorbachev, 1987). In particular, three initiatives were related to the military sector while five concerned non-military ones (Åtland, 2008).

With regard to the military sphere, the three initiatives were the proposal for a 'nuclear weapons-free zone in Northern Europe', 'consultation between the Warsaw Treaty Organization and NATO on restricting military activity and

5 In 1976, the Soviet Union deployed a new missile, the SS-20, an intermediate-range ballistic missile (IRBM) that 'upset the balance of power in Europe'. The SS-20 was able to hit any point in Western Europe. NATO had nothing comparable. Western Europeans were alarmed, especially Germany. As a consequence, NATO deployed US missiles in Europe in 1983. This was one of the major events of the Cold War. The crisis was overcome when the Soviet Union withdrew its missiles as a result of the ratification of the Intermediate Range Nuclear Forces (INF) Treaty in 1987 (Correll, 2020; Center for Strategic and International Studies, 2021).

scaling down naval and air force activities in the Baltic, Northern, Norwegian and Greenland Seas' and the 'extension of confidence-building measures to these areas' (Gorbachev, 1987; Åtland, 2008). The first proposal aimed at reducing the nuclear threat on the northwest frontier of the Soviet Union and was mainly directed at the Nordic states (Denmark, Finland, Iceland, and Norway) (Åtland, 2008). Nevertheless, the Barents Sea was not part of this zone because it was 'the most important transit and stationing area for the Soviet Union's naval nuclear forces' (Åtland, 2008). The reason why Gorbachev's proposal did not include the whole Arctic was that both the Soviet Union and the US considered it as 'an important arena for strategic submarine operations, and neither of the two countries had plans for withdrawing their nuclear submarines from the Arctic theatre' (Åtland, 2008). The second proposal aimed at limiting Western anti-submarine warfare and naval and aerial operations in and over the Northern and the Baltic Fleets' home waters that were perceived by the Soviet Union as a threat to its nuclear deterrent (Åtland, 2008). This issue had been previously addressed by deputy Yegor Ligachev and Prime Minister Ryzhkov during official visits to the Nordic states in Finland in 1986 and in Norway and Sweden in 1988, respectively (Brodetsky, 1988). Additionally, this proposal also stemmed from Gorbachev's aim to keep military vessels out of 'mutually agreed-upon zones of international straits and intensive shipping lanes' (Gorbachev, 1987; Åtland, 2008). This was due to the fact that naval operations could jeopardise the traffic going through the Northern Sea Route (NSR)[6] and along the coasts of the Kola Peninsula where there was a number of commercial and fishing ports (Åtland, 2008). Different to these two proposals, the 'extension of confidence-building measures to these areas' did not aim at reducing military activities in the region but to create a higher level of trust between the East and the West in the region and included the Barents Sea, which was one of the most important Russian Northern Fleet's exercise areas (Åtland, 2008). These measures included 'arrangements on the limitation of rivalry in anti-submarine weapons, on the notification of large naval and airforce exercises, and on inviting observers from all countries participating in the European process to large naval and airforce exercises' (Gorbachev, 1987). Nevertheless, Gorbachev's first and second proposals were not received positively by the West that perceived them as 'intended to produce a unilateral Soviet advantage' (Hayward, 1988). The third proposal was not favourably received by the West as well, which was evident when they declined the Soviet Union's invitation to send observers to a

6 In this book, Northern Sea Route (NSR) and Northeast Passage (NEP are used as synonyms for a matter of simplicity and clearness of the reasoning although they indicate overlapping geographical areas. NEP runs from the northernmost parts of the North Sea across the icy waters of the Arctic Ocean to the Bering Strait thus reaching the North Pacific. It is also called with the Russian name (the NEP name was instead given by the Anglo-Saxon navigators – Makarov et al., 2022, 1116), the Northern Sea Route (NSR), which actually is a portion of the NEP running from the entrances to the Novaya Zemlya straits to the Bering Strait. The definition of the NSR as a separate part of the NEP and its designation as a legal entity under full Soviet jurisdiction and control were provided by the Council of People's Commissars of the USSR in 1932 (Lalonde, 2019).

Soviet exercise because of 'the lack of a mutually agreed-upon procedure for the exchange of observers at naval exercises' (Åtland, 2008).

With regard to the non-military sphere, Gorbachev launched five initiatives. The first one was cooperation on resource extraction. Gorbachev focused his speech on energy resources the exploitation of which was possible, according to him, only through a valuable 'exchange of experience and knowledge' (Gorbachev, 1987). To this aim, he proposed to reach an 'agreement on drafting an integral energy programme for the north of Europe' (Gorbachev, 1987). Cooperation on the extraction of energy resources and the formation of 'mixed firms and enterprises for developing oil and gas deposits' of the shelf of the northern seas were part of the program (Gorbachev, 1987). Furthermore, in his speech Gorbachev stressed that the Soviet Union was interested in cooperating with Western enterprises to exploit the mineral resources of the Kola Peninsula in order to modernise ore enrichment and metallurgical plants (Gorbachev, 1987; Åtland, 2008). Previously, Prime Minister Nikolai Ryzhkov proposed creating a 'special zone' in the disputed area of the Barents Sea where the Soviet Union and Norway could cooperate on offshore energy activities (Åtland, 2008). However, Norway rejected this proposal on the basis of the need to find a solution to the delimitation issue before being able to cooperate (Åtland, 2008).

The second non-military initiative concerned scientific cooperation, which Gorbachev recognised as being 'of immense importance for the whole of mankind' (1987) and was well received by Western states (Gorbachev, 1987). Until the late 1980s, cooperation between the East and the West in the scientific sector had been very limited; Soviet scientists were normally not admitted to Western conferences and seminars and communication with Western scholars was seen as suspect (Åtland, 2008).

The third non-military initiative concerned indigenous people. The relevance of this initiative depended on the fact that up to the late 1980s interaction between the indigenous people of the Soviet parts of the Arctic and the indigenous people of the Western parts of the region had not been generally allowed (Åtland, 2008). Therefore, they had been unable to discuss important issues concerning their survival for a long time (Åtland, 2008). These issues concerned in particular the negative impact of the industrialisation and the militarisation of the Arctic on their lives (Åtland, 2008). Indeed, industrial and military activities had made hunting, fishing, and reindeer herding, on which indigenous people based their livelihood, increasingly difficult because it caused the pollution of lands, rivers, and waters (Åtland, 2008). Good examples are the mining and ore processing activities on the Kola Peninsula and the nuclear tests on Novaya Zemlya that have polluted traditional fishing grounds and the life of the indigenous people more generally over a long time (Åtland, 2008). Thus, the possibility opened by Gorbachev for indigenous people to participate in the 1989 Greenland meeting of the Inuit Circumpolar Conference (ICC) was considered by the Western Arctic states as a change in its policy (Åtland, 2008).

The fourth non-military initiative was related to environmental protection. This initiative represented an important change from the traditional Soviet policy of downplaying environmental problems and the tendency to avoid cooperating with other states on this issue (Åtland, 2008; Tynkkynen and Tynkkynen, 2018). Additionally, two elements were at the basis of this initiative. The first one was the Chernobyl disaster of 1986 that had clearly shown that environmental problems have no borders and that, consequently, they can't be addressed by states individually. The second element was Gorbachev's *glasnost* that had created a political environment in which issues related to the environment could be increasingly discussed openly (Åtland, 2008; Langrind, 1990). Also, in a series of conferences held before the Murmansk Speech, a number of scientists had expressed environmental concerns like the deforestation caused by emissions from the local nickel and apatite plants asking for legislative and other measures such as the establishment of a Soviet Ministry of Ecology (Åtland, 2008). The government responded to these requests by establishing the Goskompriroda, a state committee responsible for environmental protection at the federal level and by issuing environmental legislation (Åtland, 2008; Langrind, 1990). Very interestingly, after the Murmansk Speech, in 1988, the Foreign Affairs Committee of the USSR Supreme Soviet invited the Nordic, US, and Canadian parliamentarians to attend a special meeting in Moscow to discuss environmental protection measures and arms control issues in order to make appropriate recommendations to their governments (Åtland, 2008).

The fifth non-military initiative concerns the Northern Sea Route (NSR), which is one of the three Arctic shipping routes (the other being the Northwest Passage, NP, and the Transpolar Route, TSR)[7] shortening the distance between Europe and Asia and is under Russian jurisdiction (although it is at the centre of a legal dispute with the US). In particular, Gorbachev proposed the opening of the NSR depending on the 'normalization of international relations' (Gorbachev, 1987). Russia would provide the 'services of ice-breakers' (Gorbachev, 1987). As Åtland (2008) puts it, this proposal had relevant security implications because, if implemented, the proposal would increase the presence of foreign vessels in a maritime area that was sensitive because its 'epicentre' was the Kola Peninsula. This peninsula was one of the most heavily militarised areas in the world during the Cold War (Luzin et al., 1994) and still is of utmost importance for the military defence of Russia (Boulègue, 2019). Additionally, the NSR was a potential stationing area for strategic missile submarines and an arena for land-based military surveillance activities (Åtland, 2008). Thus, the NSR has always had a military value both for the Soviet Union and later for Russia (Åtland, 2008). Furthermore, Gorbachev seemed to be aware of the commercial value of the opening of the NSR to international traffic as well as of its potential role in the exploitation of the natural resources of Siberia and the Soviet Far East (Åtland, 2008). Nevertheless, the NSR remained closed to international shipping until 1991 (Åtland, 2008).

7 The NP, which is at the centre of a dispute between the US and Canada, is considered a coastal route. By contrast, the TSR, different from the other two shipping routes, is a mid-ocean route across or near the North Pole and is the shortest route. However, the TSR is not currently navigable because it is frozen during the whole year.

Gorbachev's speech was criticised by several Western observers according to whom Gorbachev's intention was just to obtain one-sided advantages (Vartanov and Roginko, 1990). Arms control provisions in particular were considered as 'self-serving proposals that only '"repackage" or "elaborate" on previous Soviet propositions' (Vartanov and Roginko, 1990). Some others expressed instead a positive opinion on the Murmansk Speech. For instance, Canadian scholar Ronald Purver (1989) argued that Gorbachev's speech constituted 'no less than a revolution' in Soviet Arctic policies (Åtland, 2008). Similarly, Russian scholars such as Raphael Vartanov and Alexei Roginko (1990) argued that a 'striking feature' of the Murmansk Speech was Gorbachev's unified approach to Soviet Arctic policy as it brought together security, resources, and scientific and environmental issues (1990). Vartanov and Roginko (1990) also stated that 'more has been done by the Soviet Union to develop Arctic cooperation since the Murmansk speech than during the previous seventy years'. Indeed, several bilateral agreements stipulated by the USSR and some states in the Arctic since the Murmansk Speech clearly demonstrate the genuine intention of the USSR in developing international cooperation in the region (Vartanov and Roginko, 1990). Good examples are the 1990 maritime boundary US–USSR[8] and the 1989 Canada–USSR agreement concerning the prevention of incidents at sea beyond the territorial sea (UN, 1989). Other examples of the positive impact of Gorbachev's initiative on the relations among the states in the region are the establishment of the University of the Arctic[9] in Rovaniemi, Finland, in 2001 and the Northern Forum[10] in Alaska in 1991, which take the form of subnational and non-governmental forms, respectively, aiming at addressing common interests in the Arctic (Young, 2005).

Furthermore, the impact of the second non-military initiative concerning scientific cooperation on the relations among the states in the region was also relevant. This proposal led to the establishment of the International Arctic Science Committee (IASC) by the representatives of national scientific organisations of the eight Arctic countries in 1990 (Åtland, 2008). Over time, it has evolved into 'the leading international science organisation of the North' and today it comprises 23 states involved in all aspects of Arctic scientific research (IASC, no date).[11] The Soviet Union was initially against the involvement of non-Arctic

8 In the agreement the parties agreed that the line in Article 1 of the Convention Ceding Alaska, which was signed on 30 March 1867 was the maritime boundary between the US and the Soviet Union (US Senate, 1990).

9 The members of the University of the Arctic are: Canada, Denmark, the Faroe Islands, Finland, Greenland, Iceland, Norway, Russia, Sweden, the US, as well as non-Arctic universities and institutes in Europe and Asia in particular (UArctic, no date).

10 The members of the Northern Forum are: Alaska, the Chukotka Autonomous Okrug (Russia), Gangwon-do (Republic of Korea), Kamchatka Krai (Russia), the Khanty-Mansi Autonomous Okrug (Russia), Krasnoyarsk Krai (Russia), Nenets Autonomous Okrug (Russia), Sakha Republic (Yakutia, Russia), Yamalo-Nenets Autonomous Okrug (Russia) (Northern Forum Secretariat, no date).

11 The members of the IASC also include 15 non-Arctic states: Austria, China, Czechia, France, Germany, India, Italy, Japan, the Netherlands, Poland, Portugal, South Korea, Spain, Switzerland, and the UK (IASC, no date).

states but differences of perspective were sorted out and the Conference of Arctic States on Coordination of Scientific Research in the Arctic was held as planned in Leningrad (today Saint Petersburg) in 1988 (Åtland, 2008). The same year, IASC was complemented by the International Arctic Social Sciences Association (IASSA) (Exner-Pirot, 2012) and a five-year agreement was signed between the US National Academy of Sciences and the Soviet Union Academy (Archer, 1990). Additionally, several bilateral scientific agreements between the Soviet Union and its Nordic neighbours were signed (Archer, 1990). The most relevant ones were the agreement between the Soviet Union and Norway on Arctic science cooperation and the Soviet Union–Finland Academies of Science protocol (Archer, 1990). According to Kristian Åtland, 'cooperation between Soviet and Western Arctic scientists turned out to be of considerable practical and symbolic value, and it spilled over into the political and military spheres' (2008).

Furthermore, in the changed geopolitical context promoted by Gorbachev, the eight Arctic states felt free to sign a Declaration on the Protection of the Arctic Environment and to adopt an Arctic Environmental Protection Strategy (AEPS) in 1991. The so-called Rovaniemi Process was initiated by Finland as a consequence of the pollution of its northern parts by the mining industry in the Soviet Kola Peninsula (Elferink, 1992). Like the Chernobyl disaster, this showed that the cross-border character of the environmental problem can't be dealt with by states individually. Therefore, the AEPS aimed to address environmental problems affecting the region and give a collective response to pollution in the Russian part of the Arctic (Bloom, 1999). Additionally, environmental issues allowed the eight Arctic states to create a platform that could be used to build mutual trust through soft-law international cooperation given that the AEPS was non-binding (Koivurova, 2014). It was clear that 'soft-law cooperation enables better participation by the region's actors' (Koivurova, 2014). The AEPS[12] identified five key areas of cooperation: 1) protecting the Arctic ecosystem including humans; 2) contributing to the protection, enhancement, and restoration of environmental quality and the sustainable utilisation of natural resources, including their use by local populations and indigenous peoples; 3) recognising and, to the extent possible, seeking to accommodate the traditional and cultural needs, values, and practices of the indigenous peoples as determined by themselves, related to the protection of the Arctic environment; 4) reviewing regularly the state of the Arctic environment; and 5) identifying, reducing, and, as a final goal, eliminating pollution (Bloom, 1999). The AEPS had

12 The AEPS included four working groups: 1) the Arctic Monitoring and Assessment Program (AMAP) monitors and assesses the effects of anthropogenic pollutants in the Arctic; 2) the Conservation of Arctic Flora and Fauna (CAFF) Working Group facilitates the exchange of information and coordination of research on species and habitats of flora and fauna in the Arctic; 3) the Emergency Prevention, Preparedness, and Response Working Group provides a framework for cooperation aiming to respond to the threat of environmental emergencies; 4) the Protection of the Arctic Marine Environment Working Group takes preventive and other measures directly or through competent international organisations regarding marine pollution in the Arctic irrespective of origin (Bloom, 1999).

extremely relevant results like the AMAP's extensive analysis of Arctic pollution issues released in conjunction with the fourth and final AEPS Ministerial conference in Alta (Norway) in 1997 (Bloom, 1999).

Furthermore, it is necessary to stress the fact that the AEPS was the result of the combination of Gorbachev's initiative and increased interest in environmental problems at the international level that began in the late 1960s. The awareness of the urgency of the environmental problems led to the Stockholm Conference of 1972,[13] which is generally considered as the 'start of international environmental politics' (Vigeland Rottem, 2020) and the 'foundational moment of modern international environmental law' (Dupuy and Vinuales, 2019). It resulted in several environmental agreements on the conservation of endangered species, inter alia (Vigeland Rottem, 2020). In the 1970s, many treaties aiming at combating pollution were signed and in the 1980s fighting pollution became a global policy (Vigeland Rottem, 2020).

In short, after the difficult times of the Cold War, Gorbachev's initiative opened a new era in the Arctic in which cooperation prevailed over East–West tensions. This was a clear indication of a change in the Soviet Union's approach to the Arctic (Åtland, 2008) and a signal that the relations between the West and the East were opening up to new possibilities of international cooperation including in the Arctic. Indeed, since 1987 a number of 'international and regional cooperation arrangements in the Arctic' have been created, many of which are related to Gorbachev's initiative (Åtland, 2008).

Cooperation as an expression of 'Arctic exceptionalism'?

Cooperative networks in the Arctic emerged at the very end of the 1980s as a consequence of the end of the Cold War and the consequent relaxation of the relations among states in the region. In the case of the Arctic, two illuminating examples are the cooperation that emerged in the Barents region and the one that emerged in the Arctic more broadly through the establishment of intergovernmental forums. In the case of the Barents region, however, cooperation was in reality the result of historical links that can be traced back at least to the 1950s when a Nordic Passport Union was established to set up a passport-free area followed by the creation of a common

13 The Stockholm Conference was attended by delegations from more than 100 states and representatives of major international organisations. This conference resulted in three outcomes: 1) the Stockholm Declaration that consists of a preamble and 26 principles and gives the main orientations of the environmental protection. It affirms some important rights concerning the environment like the human right to 'adequate conditions of life, in an environment of a quality that permits a life of dignity and well-being', the right to a healthy environment, the importance of international cooperation for the protection of the environment, the principle of intergenerational equity, etc; 2) the Action Plan for the Human Environment including recommendations (109) organised around three fundamental axes: environmental assessment, environmental management, and supporting measures; and 3) the UN Environment Program (UNEP), established by recommendation 4 (entrust the coordination of environmental affairs to the UN, the UNEP) (Dupuy and Vinuales, 2019).

labour market in the same decade (Elenius, 2015, 337). These cooperative initiatives led to the creation of the north Calotte region, which is considered the forerunner of the Barents Euro-Arctic Region (BEAR) (Elenius, 2015, 337). Initially, it included the northern areas of Finland, Norway, and Sweden but in the 1960s it was enlarged to include the Russian Murmansk area and the Kola Peninsula (Elenius, 2015, 337). It was established in the context of the North Norwegian Plan of 1951 aimed at reducing the disparity between the more developed southern and the backward northern areas (Elenius, 2015, 338). Additionally, it was part of a process launched by various political groups in Northern Europe that began considering 'the potential of the circumpolar north as a means of re-establishing horizontal connections and functional cooperation across the Cold War political divide' (Elenius, 2015). In the 1970s and in the 1980s there were some other forms of cooperation among which the most important one is perhaps an environmental agreement between Norway and the Soviet Union that led to negotiations on the demarcation of national economic sea zones in the Barents Sea (Elenius, 2015, 338).

Nevertheless, it was only in the years immediately after the end of the Cold War that cooperation flourished in the region. Indeed, in 1993 cooperation was established at the intergovernmental and interregional levels, namely the Barents Euro-Arctic Council (BEAC) and the Barents Regional Council (BRC), respectively. At the moment of writing, the BEAC comprises five members, namely Denmark, Finland, Iceland, Norway, Sweden, and the European Commission (Russia, which was a founding member, withdrew from the forum as a consequence of the tensions with the West due to the war in Ukraine in 2003),[14] while the BRC is made up of eight subregions belonging to Denmark, Finland, Norway, and Sweden.[15] The objective of both the BEAC and the BRC is pursuing sustainable development in the region by cooperating in a number of sectors such as the environment, economic cooperation, and the forest sector, inter alia (BEAC, 2024b). In order to do so, the work of the two councils is conducted by Working Groups (WGs) with the 'aim to concretize the cooperation in the different sectors where cooperation takes place' (BEAC, 2024b).[16] They 'constitute a cross-border platform for exchange for the civil servants and professionals of the respective field both on the national and regional level' (BEAC, 2024b). In terms of project financing, the most important sources are the national and regional budgets of the Barents countries,

14 The observers of the BEAC are Canada, France, Germany, Italy, Japan, Netherlands, Poland, UK, and the US (BEAC, 2024a).

15 The eight subregions are Nordland and Troms og Finnmark in Norway; Norrbotten and Västerbotten in Sweden; Kainuu, Lapland, Oulu, and north Karelia in Finland. Russia was a founding member of the BRC with its counties of Arkhangelsk, Komi, Murmansk, and Nenets. The BRC's observer is the Council of Christian Churches in the Barents Region (BEAC, 2024a).

16 The BEAC and the BRC have established 12 thematic WGs, which are: Health and Social Issues, Education and Research, Culture, Barents Forest Sector, Tourism, Transport and Logistics, Economic Cooperation, Environment, Youth Issues, Barents Regional Youth Council, Indigenous Peoples, and Rescue Cooperation (BEAC, 2024b).

various EU programs and the Nordic Council of Ministers, but also International Financial Institutions provide economic support to cooperation projects in the region (BEAC, 2024c).

Some years later, in 1996, the eight Arctic states established the Arctic Council (AC), which can be considered as one of the major results of the geopolitical changes that occurred with the end of the Cold War and the collapse of the Soviet Union. Different from the BEAC and the BRC, the AC concerns cooperation in the whole Arctic region, broadly defined. The proposal of the establishment of the AC was essentially due to the fact that some states considered the AEPS as concerning only parts of the issues that they wanted to discuss in relation to the Arctic (Bloom, 1999). Canada proposed the establishment of an AC that would deal with a number of environmental, economic development, and maritime policy issues (Bloom, 1999). Canada proposed to transform the AEPS into a new international organisation that would subsume the existing AEPS programs but would also address the broader issue of sustainable development (Bloom, 1999). Canada's idea was to create a forum to discuss security issues, which was supported by Finland (Conde and Sánchez, 2017; Vigeland Rottem, 2020; Steinveg et al., 2023, 2). By contrast, the US preferred at first to avoid being involved in regional arrangements but was convinced by environmental disasters such as the Exxon Valdez oil spill and the sinking of the Russian nuclear-powered submarine *Komsomolets* (both occurred in 1989) to change its policy (Conde and Sánchez, 2017).[17] Very importantly, Canada aimed to support the demilitarisation process initiated at the end of the Cold War (Vigeland Rottem, 2020). Nevertheless, Canada's idea encountered some resistance because of two controversies. The first one concerned whether the forum should address hard security issues that were very sensitive political questions to which some states opposed (Vigeland Rottem, 2020). One of the most important issues that was highlighted was the risk of alienating Russia if hard security issues were included in the AC's activities, which was in fact not seen as an effective way to maintain constructive relations with Russia (Burke, 2019). The US was particularly sceptical about the possibility of including military issues also because of their 'distrust of binding cooperation on sensitive political issues and the idea that it could overshadow other important cooperation' (Steinveg et al., 2023, 2). The second controversy concerned whether the AC should be established as a forum or an international organisation (Vigeland Rottem, 2020). The differences between them are substantial as, different from a forum, an international organisation is bound by a treaty, it is established and recognised within international law, its decisions are binding, and it has a separate body operating more or less independently of the members (Vigeland Rottem, 2020). The AC does not have any of these characteristics (Vigeland Rottem, 2020). It is a consensus body where decisions are

17 In 1989, the oil tanker *Exxon Valdez* spilled 11 million gallons of oil in the Prince William Sound, Alaska, causing one of the largest environmental disasters in US history (NORR, 2023). The same year, the *Komsomolets*, a Soviet nuclear submarine, sank because of an onboard fire off Norway's northern coast, killing 41 people. In 2021, Russia sent scientists on a mission to the submarine to determine whether the wreck presents a threat to the undersea environment (Digges, 2021).

made unanimously by its members with consultation of the Permanent Participants (Arctic Council, 2023d). It does not have a budget of its own and all projects and initiatives are sponsored by one or more member states (Arctic Council, 2023e). Some projects are financed by other entities (Arctic Council, 2023e).

The eight states agreed to establish the AC as a forum and, also in this case, it was the US that preferred not to commit themselves more than necessary (Vigeland Rottem, 2020). The website of the AC states that

> 'the Arctic Council is the leading intergovernmental forum promoting cooperation, coordination and interaction among the Arctic States, Arctic Indigenous peoples and other Arctic inhabitants on common Arctic issues, in particular on issues of sustainable development and environmental protection in the Arctic'
>
> (Arctic Council Secretariat, 2023)

The AC incorporated the AEPS as well as member states,[18] observers,[19] WGs, and indigenous peoples that are Permanent Participants[20] (Vigeland Rottem, 2020). While member states have full voting rights, Permanent Participants have full consultation rights in relation to the AC's negotiations and decisions but not voting rights (Vigeland Rottem, 2020). The observers, which is a group constituted of non-governmental organisations (NGOs), international organisations, and non-Arctic states, have different interests and face different challenges (Vigeland Rottem, 2020). They observe the work of the AC and primarily interface with the WGs (Vigeland Rottem, 2020). They don't have voting rights but are invited to the meetings of the AC (Vigeland Rottem, 2020). Among the non-Arctic states

18 The members of the AC are Canada, the Kingdom of Denmark – Denmark, Greenland and the Faroe Islands – Finland, Iceland, Norway, Russia, Sweden, and the US. The Permanent Participants are the Aleut International Association, the Arctic Athabascan Council, the Gwich'in Council International, the Inuit Circumpolar Council, the Russian Association of Indigenous Peoples of the North, and the Sami Council (Arctic Council, 2023).

19 The observers can be divided into three groups: 1) non-Arctic states: France, Germany, Italy, Japan, Netherlands, China, Poland, India, Korea, Singapore, Spain, Switzerland, and UK; 2) intergovernmental and interparliamentary organisations: International Council for the Exploration of the Sea (ICES), International Federation of the Red Cross and Red Crescent Societies, International Maritime Organisation, International Union for the Conservation of Nature, Nordic Council of Ministers (NCM), Nordic Environment Finance Corporation, North Atlantic Marine Mammal Commission, OSPAR Commission, Standing Committee of the Parliamentarians of the Arctic Region, United Nations Development Program, United Nations Environment Program (UNEP), World Meteorological Organization (WMO), and West Nordic Council; and 3) non-governmental organisations: Advisory Committee on Protection of the Sea, Arctic Institute of North America, Association of World Reindeer Herders, Circumpolar Conservation Union (CCU), International Arctic Science Committee (IASC), International Arctic Social Sciences Association (IASSA), International Union for Circumpolar Health, International Work Group for Indigenous Affairs, Northern Forum (NF), Oceana, University of the Arctic (UArctic), and World Wide Fund for Nature, Arctic Program (Arctic Council, 2023).

20 Aleut International Association, Arctic Athabaskan Council, Gwich'in Council International, Inuit Circumpolar Council, Russian Association of Indigenous Peoples of the North, Saami Council (Arctic Council, 2023).

it is possible to identify two 'broad policy categories' on the basis of their Arctic policy approaches and the regional identities that are being constructed (Lanteigne, 2020, 382). The first category is *legacies*, namely 'states which have historically extensive exploration and scientific experience in the region long predating the creation of the Council, and which were often participants in Arctic meetings that were precursors of the current regional regimes' (Lanteigne, 2020, 383). Some examples are the Netherlands, Poland, and Switzerland, which have engaged in several regional exploration missions in various parts of the Arctic, as well as Italy that began exploring the Arctic in the late nineteenth century (Lanteigne, 2020, 383). The second category is *all-rounds*, namely

> states which refer to a lesser extent to their historic ties to the Arctic (and in some cases, especially observers from the Asia-Pacific region, have comparatively limited experience in Arctic engagement), and instead stress the modern economic, environmental, political and scientific 'goods' they can provide to the Council and to Arctic affairs more generally.
>
> (Lanteigne, 2020, 383)

Some examples are China, Japan, and Singapore, as they have much shorter histories in the Arctic compared to other legacies and have thus built their regional identity on their modern economic ability in sectors such as engineering, shipping, and science diplomacy (Lanteigne, 2020, 383).

In the AC, decisions are made unanimously, and the chairmanship rotates every two years (Arctic Council, 2023). Since its establishment, the amount of the work of the AC has increased enormously. In 1996, it implemented 30 projects whose number increased up to 100 in 2019 (Vigeland Rottem, 2020). From 1996 to the mid-2000s, the AC's activities focused on fighting pollution in the Arctic (Vigeland Rottem, 2020). Environmental protection was not a sensitive political issue but it was a very relevant one as the frequent international negotiations at that time clearly show (Vigeland Rottem, 2020). Also, pollution is a huge problem negatively affecting the ecosystem and the people in the region. Although the Arctic is far away from large industrialised areas, 'the environment in the high North carries the traces of human-induced pollution – from soot to plastics, from methane to pesticides' (Arctic Council, 2023a). While some pollutants originate in the Arctic (e.g., through wood combustion or oil and gas flaring), some others are transported over long distances via rivers, oceans, and the air (Arctic Council, 2023a; Vigeland Rottem, 2020).

The AC has conducted intense work to monitor environmental pollution in the Arctic whose results showed that the levels of pollutants in the Arctic were (and still are) very high thus jeopardising wildlife and local people's lives (Vigeland Rottem, 2020). In its first major report of 1998, the Arctic Monitoring and Assessment Program (AMAP), one of the most important WGs of the AC, highlighted the fact that the 'levels of many contaminants in the Arctic are likely to remain at or close to existing levels for decades because of their resistance to degradation, the slow rate of degradative processes, and the recycling of existing accumulations'

(AMAP, 1998). Much of the work of the AC concerns pollution issues such as the presence of persistent organic pollutants and mercury in the region (Vigeland Rottem, 2020).

Since the 2000s, in addition to environmental protection, climate change has become a priority in regional dialogue and cooperation (Burke, 2019), which reflects the importance of science in AC policy-making (Keskitalo, 2007; Stenlund, 2002). Actually, concerns about the impact of climate change on the Arctic date back to the 1980s and 1990s when the negotiations of the AEPS were ongoing, but it was only with the establishment of the AC that awareness about this issue grew (Burke, 2019). The Arctic Climate Impact Assessment (ACIA) Report issued by the AC in 2005 is a clear demonstration of this (Vigeland Rottem, 2020). This report, which was written by the AMAP and Conservation of Arctic Flora and Fauna (CAFF) WGs, highlights the trends of climate change in the Arctic and the implications for the rest of the world (Koivurova and Hasanat, 2009). The report stated that

> Earth's climate is changing, with the global temperature now rising at a rate unprecedented in the experience of modern human society. These climate changes, including increases in ultraviolet radiation, are being experienced particularly intensely in the Arctic. Because the Arctic plays a special role in global climate [it regulates the temperature of the Earth], these changes in the Arctic will also affect the rest of the world.
>
> (Arctic Council, 2005)

The report also stressed that it was necessary that decision-makers had 'latest and best information available regarding ongoing changes in the Arctic and their global implications' (Arctic Council, 2005). According to Vigeland Rottem, the ACIA Report 'brought the Arctic Council out of the valley of shadows into the global spotlight' as it showed the higher sensitiveness of the Arctic to climate change in comparison to the rest of the world (Vigeland Rottem, 2020). The main point of the report is that in the Arctic it is possible to see the most visible signs of climate change (Vigeland Rottem, 2020). The increase of temperature is indeed causing sea and land ice to melt thus jeopardising the delicate ecological balance of the region and people's living conditions (Vigeland Rottem, 2020). At the same time, the increasing temperature in the Arctic impacts the global climate system provoking extreme temperature events beyond the Arctic with global environmental, economic, and social implications (Arctic Council, 2023b). Climate change has been one of most relevant issues on which the Arctic Council has been working in recent years (Vigeland Rottem, 2020). Its WGs closely cooperate with the observer states, organisations, and stakeholders in order to properly address the environmental, economic, and social implications of climate change in the Arctic (Arctic Council, 2023b). The result of this work is a growing number of reports and assessments making the AC a 'knowledge broker and global advocate for Arctic topics' (Arctic Council, 2023b). Additionally, the AC has served as the place where its members draft legally binding international agreements (Vigeland

Rottem, 2020). Three examples are the 2011 Arctic SAR (search and rescue) Agreement aiming at strengthening search and rescue cooperation and coordination in the Arctic and signed with the participation of the International Civil Aviation Organization (ICAO)[21] the 2013 Agreement on Cooperation and Marine Oil Pollution Preparedness and Response in the Arctic aiming at strengthening cooperation, coordination, and mutual assistance among the parties on oil pollution preparedness and response in the Arctic in order to protect the marine environment from pollution by oil; and the 2017 Agreement on Enhancing International Arctic Scientific Cooperation aiming at facilitating access by scientists to Arctic areas, that the AC members have identified, to research infrastructure and facilities and gather data (Vigeland Rottem, 2020; IASC, 2019). All were negotiated under the auspices of the AC (Arctic Council, 2023c; Vigeland Rottem, 2013, 2020).

The fact that it has served as a venue for the discussion and negotiation of regional agreements demonstrates that the political significance of the AC has been growing over time. The work of the AC is indeed important not only regionally but also internationally because it impacts on the understanding of the Arctic as a region (Keskitalo, 2007). For instance, in the United Nations Economic Commission for Europe Meeting held in 2001 'for the first time under the Rio umbrella specific attention [was paid] to Arctic challenges and the concerns of its indigenous peoples' (Keskitalo, 2007; Stenlund, 2002), which are part of the AC's focus. Thus, the AC has become the symbol of the Arctic in northern areas but also globally (Keskitalo, 2007).

This discussion leads to two observations. The first one is that the AC is the most important intergovernmental forum fostering cooperation in the Arctic by providing a platform where the member states meet to exchange information and perspectives on relevant issues for the region. It is the most important intergovernmental forum in the High North including all eight Arctic states. In this context, the role played by the observers should not be disregarded as they contribute to the AC's projects and activities (Smieszek, 2023) although their primary role is to give ideas and opinions about projects that have already been approved (Vigeland Rottem, 2020). Vigeland Rottem points out that it is necessary to make a distinction between the Senior Arctic Officials (SAO) observers' level and the WG level (Vigeland Rottem, 2020). At the SAO level, observers have limited influence, which has translated into frustration and less interest in the work of the AC (Vigeland Rottem, 2020). At the same time, their participation in meetings helps them learn about the perspectives of AC members and engage with them (Smieszek, 2023). Involving observers in the work of the AC is important because it can increase awareness about the challenges facing the Arctic most of which are global in character like climate change, pollution, and shipping (Vigeland Rottem, 2020). These challenges can't be solved by the eight Arctic states but globally (Vigeland Rottem, 2020). Nevertheless, there are also political reasons to limit

21 ICAO is a United Nations agency, established to help countries (193 states) share their skies (UN, no date).

the number of observers (Vigeland Rottem, 2020). The first one is that Permanent Participants are afraid that a large number of observers could marginalise the influence of indigenous peoples (Vigeland Rottem, 2020). The new economic opportunities opened up by climate change have led to increasing accessibility of natural resources and shipping routes and are attracting a growing number of international actors (both state and non-state actors like the EU). Thus, international actors consider becoming AC observers as a way to be involved in Arctic affairs. The second reason is very well explained by Vigeland Rottem (2020) arguing that 'geopolitical turbulence and practical politics – Realpolitik – such as States' fear of losing power, have also affected the discussion about new observers'. For instance, several states, especially Canada and Russia, were quite sceptical about accepting China as an observer and on two occasions, namely the 2015 Iqaluit meeting in Canada and the 2017 meeting in Alaska, Russia did not agree to grant permanent observer status to the EU because of the sanctions imposed upon Russia by the West due to the war in Ukraine (Vigeland Rottem, 2020).

The second observation is that cooperation has continued precisely because the AC does not deal with security policy issues (Vigeland Rottem, 2020). The Ottawa Declaration, which established the AC, explicitly excludes military security (Arctic Council, 2023e). As argued above, the eight AC members decided to cooperate on environmental issues because these are not politically sensitive. This is why cooperation has not halted even in turbulent times (Vigeland Rottem, 2020; Clifford, 2016).

In conclusion, cooperation in the Arctic has emerged as an effect of geopolitical changes in the international system. The most important expression of cooperation in the region is the AC whose work has enormously expanded since its establishment, especially because of climate change, which is one of the most important issues on which the AC works.

New opportunities for the EU?

Although the EU is an external actor to the Arctic, it is present in the region in a number of ways. Three EU Member States, namely Denmark (although Greenland withdrew from the EU in 1985),[22] Finland, and Sweden are Arctic states. The EU is territorially part of the Arctic through its northernmost regions in Finland and Sweden, specifically Finnish Lapland and Norrbotten. These areas are part of the European Arctic (separate from the EU), which also includes the northernmost regions of Finland, Norway, and Sweden, northwest Arctic Russia, as well as the Faroe Islands, Greenland, and Iceland. As Koivurova says, this 'is the area where the EU's economic influence is the strongest, where the EU programmes operate

22 Greenland became a member of the European Community (EC) in 1973 together with Denmark, but when it obtained autonomy in 1979, it decided to leave it through an advisory referendum, which it did in 1985. By contrast, the Faroe Islands had home rule since 1948, thus it was able to opt out of the EC when Denmark became a member (Danish Parliament, 2021).

and where the pollution coming from the EU has the strongest impact' (Koivurova et al., 2019, 1). Also, the fact that Denmark, Finland, and Sweden are EU members means that the EU can indirectly influence the legislative initiatives in the region. Indeed, Denmark, Finland, and Sweden are obliged to respect the EU *acquis communautaire* when they decide to commit to international agreements to regulate certain issue-areas in the region (e.g., environmental protection, fishery, etc.). They have to respect the sincere cooperation principle contained in Article 4(3) of the Treaty of the EU stating that

> pursuant to the principle of sincere cooperation, the Union and the Member States shall, in full mutual respect, assist each other in carrying out tasks which flow from the Treaties. The Member States shall take any appropriate measure, general or particular, to ensure fulfilment of the obligations arising out of the Treaties or resulting from the acts of the institutions of the Union. The Member States shall facilitate the achievement of the Union's tasks and refrain from any measure which could jeopardise the attainment of the Union's objectives.
>
> (Eur-Lex, 2012)

In short, the EU institutions and its members are obliged to respect the treaties in order to ensure that the values, principles, and objectives of the EU are pursued.

Furthermore, the EU also indirectly influences legislation in the Arctic because Iceland and Norway belong to the European Economic Area (EEA) together with Liechtenstein. The EEA allows its members to participate in the EU Internal Market and covers the free movement of goods, services, capital, and persons as well as competition, state aid rules, and certain areas of cooperation such as consumer protection, environment, public health, and education (EFTA, 2023). The EU acts apply to the EEA European Free Trade Association (EFTA) states when the EEA Joint Committee adopts a decision to incorporate them into the EEA Agreement (EFTA, 2023). On the EFTA website it is possible to read that 'the aim is to incorporate acts as closely as possible to their date of entry into force in the EU in order to ensure that the same rules apply throughout the EEA'.[23] In fact, the EEA was set up in 1994 with the aim to extend the EU's provisions to the EFTA countries.[24]

23 The decision-making process through which EU law becomes EEA law can be divided into four stages: 1) the EEA EFTA states participate in the EC's assessment of new internal market legislation need through discussions in expert groups and committees. In this way, they contribute their technical expertise and identify possible issues for the EEA EFTA states; 2) when the EU has adopted an EEA-relevant act, the EEA EFTA states agree on a draft decision to incorporate the act after discussions with experts; 3) once the EEA EFTA states approve the draft decision, the Commission's Secretariat General (responsible for the coordination of the EEA incorporation process on behalf of the EU since 2022) coordinates the EU's part of the EEA process; and 4) the EEA Joint Committee adopts the decision (EFTA, 2023).

24 The EFTA is an intergovernmental organisation whose members are Iceland, Liechtenstein, Norway, and Switzerland. It was set up by Austria, Denmark, Norway, Portugal, Sweden, Switzerland,

Another important reason why the Arctic is geopolitically important for the EU is that Canada, Russia, and the US are traditionally strategic partners of the EU. EU–US relations are historically based on 'common history and a shared set of democratic values' (European Parliament, 2023). They cooperate in a number of foreign policy areas like security, energy, technology, and counter-terrorism and in several geographical contexts such as Russia, Ukraine, the Western Balkans, and the Middle East (European Parliament, 2023). EU–Canada relations are based on 'a vibrant and comprehensive strategic partnership founded on a common vision for a rules-based international order and a shared commitment to democratic values, peace and security, and free and fair trade' (EEAS, 2023). Before their deterioration due to Russia's illegal annexation of Crimea in 2014 and later due to the war in Ukraine that began in 2022, EU–Russia relations were based on a strategic partnership aimed at addressing common challenges like promoting a sustainable low-carbon economy and energy efficiency and fighting climate change, as well as pursuing common objectives like enhancing and deepening bilateral trade and economic relations and enhancing cooperation in a number of sectors such as research and innovation, space, and energy (Council of the European Union, 2010, 1).

Russia is part of the Northern Dimension (ND), a joint policy of the EU, Iceland, Norway, and Russia proposed by former Finnish Prime Minister Paavo Lipponen in 1997. As Finland and Sweden became EU members in 1995, the EU expanded beyond the Arctic Circle thus acquiring a 1,300km border with Russia (Ministry of Foreign Affairs of Finland, 2009, 5). The aim of the ND was to 'to support sustainable development, stability, well-being and security in the northern regions, to strengthen cooperation between Russia and the EU, and to prevent the rise of dividing lines' (Ministry of Foreign Affairs of Finland, 2009, 5). On this basis, the ND states cooperate in a number of sectors like economy, freedom, security, justice, external security, research, education, culture, the environment, nuclear safety, natural resources, social welfare, and healthcare (Ministry of Foreign Affairs of Finland, 2009, 6). Very interestingly, the ND includes regional councils that are 'the voice of the ND policy' (Ministry of Foreign Affairs of Finland, 2009, 12). They are the BEAC, the AC, the Council of the Baltic Sea States (CBSS), and the Nordic Council of Ministers (NCM) (Ministry of Foreign Affairs of Finland, 2009, 12).

The relevance of the EU in the Arctic as a geopolitical actor with some influence on Arctic affairs has been growing over time since 2008, when it adopted its first Arctic policy. Since then, the EU has been deepening and widening its engagement in Arctic affairs especially in the sectors of climate change and biodiversity, the two areas where the EU manages to have a bigger influence in the region.

While the issues discussed are more or less the same with the exception of the last Arctic policy reflecting the geopolitical changes occurring in the international system (e.g., the aggressive behaviour of Russia), the wording used in the four

and the UK in 1960 'for the promotion of free trade and economic integration between its members'. Austria, Denmark, Portugal, Sweden, and the UK left the EFTA to join the EU (EFTA, 2024).

Arctic policies issued in 2008, 2012, 2016, and 2021 has been 'evolving' over time, demonstrating a growing interest in being involved in Arctic affairs essentially for geopolitical and economic reasons. In its first Arctic Policy of 2008, for instance, the EU just states that it 'is inextricably linked to the Arctic by a unique combination of history, geography, economy and scientific achievements' (European Commission, 2008, 2). The EU Arctic Policy of 2012 still highlights that 'the EU has strong links with the Arctic: not only from historical, economic and geographical perspectives, but also as an importer of natural resources and through its wider concern and responsibility of the global environment' (European Commission, 2012, 8). At the same time, this document also stresses the fact that 'the EU should step up its engagement with Arctic partners to jointly meet the challenge of safeguarding the environment while ensuring the sustainable development of the Arctic region' (European Commission, 2012, 2). Similar to the 2012 document, the EU Arctic Policy of 2016 points out the importance of the Arctic for the EU by stating that 'a stable, safe, sustainable and prosperous Arctic is important not just for the region itself but for the EU and the world. The EU has a strategic interest in playing a key role in the Arctic region' (European Commission, 2016, 2). A real change to the wording occurs in the last document from 2021 (at the moment of writing). This is the most assertive policy as it begins by affirming that 'the European Union (EU) is in the Arctic' (European Commission, 2021, 1). This clearly demonstrates the strong commitment of the EU to affirm itself as a fully fledged Arctic actor. Indeed, it considers the EU as belonging to the region while also defining the EU as 'a geopolitical power' that has 'strategic and day-to-day interests, both in the European Arctic and the broader Arctic region' (European Commission, 2021, 1).

An element common to the four Arctic policies is the reference to the extraordinary impact of climate change on the Arctic. For instance, the 2008 document defines climate change as a 'threat multiplier' (that is an expression very much used also in several official documents of the eight Arctic states) and that

> 'the European Commission (EC) and the High Representative for the Common Foreign and Security Policy have pointed out that environmental changes are altering the geo-strategic dynamics of the Arctic with potential consequences for international stability and European security interests calling for the development of an EU Arctic Policy'
>
> (European Commission, 2008, 2)

Therefore, according to the first EU Arctic policy, the necessity of adopting a clear strategy towards the High North stems from climate change, which is 'the most comprehensive threat the Arctic is facing' as defined in the 2021 document (European Commission, 2021, 1). From the same perspective as the 2021 document, the Arctic Policy of 2012 identifies climate change as the provider of a strong rationale for the EU's commitment to fight climate change (European Commission, 2012, 2), while the 2016 document calls for 'advancing international cooperation in responding to the impacts of climate change on the Arctic's fragile environment' (European Commission, 2016, 2).

The fight against climate change, together with environmental protection, is an issue to which the EU is very sensitive because it is one of the major emitters of greenhouse gases (GHG) globally (Koivurova et al., 2019, 5). In this way, it contributes to Arctic warming by producing 8% of global greenhouse gas emissions (Koivurova et al., 2019, 5). The EU is responsible for 31% of carbon dioxide (European Commission, 2021, 10) and for about 36% of Arctic deposition of black carbon, which is transported by air to the Arctic and speeds up warming of the region and melting of snow and ice surfaces (Koivurova et al., 2019, 5). About 15% of vessels above 300 tonnes gross weight navigating Arctic waters fly EU Member States' flags or are owned by EU-based companies and are responsible for 31% of carbon dioxide and 17% of black carbon emitted by Arctic shipping (Koivurova et al., 2019, 5). Additionally, the EU is a harmful air pollutant and a considerable source of marine litter like plastic and heavy metals (Koivurova et al., 2019, 50; European Commission, 2021d). Two European sources producing microplastic particles are of particular concern, namely synthetic textiles and road traffic emissions from the wearing down of tyres and brakes (Koivurova et al., 2019, 50).

Referring to environmental protection and the fight against climate change, the EU Arctic Policy of 2021 correctly states that the EU is 'a global leader in these efforts' (European Commission, 2021, 1). Indeed, the EU is a party to major international environmental agreements like the United Nations Framework Convention on Climate Change (UNFCCC),[25] the Kyoto Protocol (adopted in 1997 and entered into force in 2005), and the Paris Agreement on Climate Change (adopted in 2015 and entered into force in 2016). Given the global character of these treaties, all of them apply to the Arctic as well. The UNFCCC, which was signed in 1992 and entered into force in 1994, is 'the main international treaty on fighting climate change' with the objective 'to prevent dangerous man-made interference with the global climate system' (European Commission, no date). It aims to reach this result by stabilising greenhouse gas concentrations 'at a level that would prevent dangerous anthropogenic (human induced) interference with the climate system' (United Nations, no date-a). In order to achieve this goal, the Kyoto Protocol, which is an international treaty too, has put into practice the UNFCCC by committing industrialised states to adopt policies and measures aimed at limiting and reducing GHG emissions in accordance with agreed individual targets as well as report their results periodically (United Nations, no date-b). Like the Kyoto Protocol, the Paris Agreement builds upon the UNFCCC and is a binding international treaty on climate change. It aims to hold 'the increase in the global average temperature to well

25 The UNFCCC has near universal membership with 198 states as parties (United Nations, no date-a). It is one of three 'Rio Conventions' together with the UN Convention on Biological Diversity and the UN Convention to Combat Desertification (United Nations, no date-a).

below 2°C above pre-industrial levels' and pursue efforts 'to limit the temperature increase to 1.5°C above pre-industrial levels' (United Nations, no date-c).[26]

In addition to being a party to these international instruments, together with its Member States,[27] in 2020 the EU approved the Green Deal (EGD), which is a package of policy initiatives aimed at defining the path to green transition in order to reach climate neutrality by 2050, delivering on the commitments made in the Paris Agreement (Council of the European Union, 2024). With the EGD, the EU aims to fight climate change and environmental degradation, which are existential threats to the EU and the world, by transforming the EU 'into a modern, resource-efficient and competitive economy, ensuring no net emissions of greenhouse gases by 2050, economic growth decoupled from resource use, no person and no place left behind' (European Commission, 2024). Thus, the EGD is a long-term strategy for carbon neutrality, sustainable growth, a circular economy, zero pollution, and the restoration of biodiversity (European Commission, 2021c, IV).

As stated in the 2021 Arctic Policy, the legislation proposals under the EGD are 'at the heart of the EU's Arctic engagement' (European Commission, 2021, 1). An example is the Fit for 55 package whose goal is to translate the objectives of the EGD into law (Council of the European Union, 2024). Its purpose is the revision of the climate-, energy-, and transport-related legislation in order to 'align EU laws with the EU's climate goals' (Council of the European Union, 2024). In particular, it aims to reduce GHG emissions by at least 55% by 2030 (Council of the European Union, 2024a).

Additionally, the 2021 Arctic Policy also emphasises the role that the EU's new approach to a sustainable blue economy, adopted in 2021 (the same year of the last Arctic Policy), has in the context of stronger EU engagement in the Arctic (European Commission, 2021, 1). The sustainable blue economy includes all sectors and industries related to the oceans, seas, and coasts based both in the marine environment (e.g., shipping, fisheries, energy generation) or on land (e.g., ports, shipyards, land-based aquaculture and algae production, coastal tourism) (European Commission, 2021, 4).

The EU's new approach to the sustainable blue economy clearly sets out the EU's agenda aiming to valuably contribute to achieve the objectives of the Green Deal (European Commission, 2021a, 2). The importance of this sustainable

26 The Kyoto Protocol and the Paris Agreement have three main differences: 1) while the Kyoto Protocol legally binds developed countries (listed in Annex I of the UNFCCC) to reduce their emissions, the Paris Agreement addresses both developed and developing countries; 2) while the approach of the Kyoto Protocol is top down because it fixes emission reduction targets, the approach of the Paris Agreement is bottom up because the countries decide internally (national pledges) how much emissions they aim to reduce; and 3) different from the Paris Agreement, the Kyoto Protocol imposes penalties for not respecting the proposed targets (Natural Resources Defense Council, 2023).

27 According to Article 4, the EU has shared competences with its Member States in a number of sectors such as, inter alia, the environment, energy, transport, space, and fisheries (except conservation of marine biological resources). 'Shared competence' means that both the EU and its Member States may adopt legally binding acts in the area concerned (Eur-Lex, 2022).

blue economy to the implementation of the EGD is also emphasised by Frans Timmermans, executive vice-president for the Green Deal, who pointed out the necessity to develop a blue economy combining environmental protection and economic activities (European Commission, 2021b). In fact, the EU's new approach offers a number of solutions aiming at achieving the EU's goal of a 90% reduction of GHG emissions from all modes of transport, including maritime transport (European Commission, 2021a, 3). Maritime transport, although generating less emissions than transport by road or air, generates carbon and other types of 'polluting emissions due to the great volumes and a heavy reliance on fossil fuels' (European Commission, 2021a, 3).

Furthermore, the resilience of the sustainable blue economy is strongly linked to the restoration and conservation of biodiversity, which is another important goal of the EGD, as mentioned above. Indeed, the 2021 Arctic Policy clearly states that biodiversity and climate change are 'two sides of the same coin' as they are interdependent (European Commission, 2021). Indeed, the sustainable blue economy 'can contribute to carbon neutrality by developing offshore renewable energy and by greening maritime transport and ports' (European Commission, 2021a).

Biodiversity loss, which is caused by climate change, pollution, over-exploitation of natural resources, and the destruction of natural habitats (European Commission, 2021a, 1), has a huge negative impact on the blue economy. Therefore, the restoration and conservation of biodiversity 'should be considered as foundational principles of maritime economic activity' (European Commission, 2021a, 6). It is a prerequisite for economic activities like fisheries, bio-technology, and tourism (European Commission, 2021a, 6). According to its communication on the 'sustainable blue economy' of 2021, the European Commission has stressed that it is necessary to shift from 'blue growth' to the 'sustainable blue economy' because the notion that environmental protection conflicts with the economy is outdated; instead they are strictly intertwined especially in the maritime industry (European Commission, 2021a). Moreover, the EU is 'a leading force' in the negotiations under the Convention on Biological Diversity (CBD), which was signed by 150 states at the United Nations Conference on Environment and Development in Rio de Janeiro in 1992 (CBD, 2000). It is a 'legally binding commitment to conserve biological diversity, to sustainably use its components and to share equitably the benefits arising from the use of genetic resources' (CBD, 2000).

Furthermore, the EU is a strong proponent of the Agreement under the United Nations Convention on the Law of the Sea (UNCLOS) on the conservation and sustainable use of marine biodiversity in areas beyond national jurisdiction (BBNJ Agreement) that was adopted by the Intergovernmental Conference on Marine Biodiversity of Areas Beyond National Jurisdiction convened under the auspices of the United Nations in 2023 (UN, 2024). The overall aim of the BBNJ is the 'conservation and sustainable use of marine biological diversity of areas beyond national jurisdiction for the present and in the long-term, through effective implementation of the relevant provisions of the Convention and further international cooperation and coordination' (UN, 2024). Also, the EU 'supports the designation of Marine Protected Areas in the Arctic Ocean, including in the Convention for the

Protection of the Marine Environment of the North-East Atlantic (OSPAR)'[28], to which it is a part through the EC (European Commission, 2021).

Additionally, the EU finances research on Arctic biodiversity. An example is the European Fisheries Inventory in the Central Arctic Ocean (EFICA) Consortium of scientists from 20 nations[29] that conducted EU-funded research into the ecosystems present in the Nansen Basins and the Fram Strait in the context of the international expedition, the Multidisciplinary Drifting Observatory for the Study of Arctic Climate (MOSAIC) (European Commission, 2022). Scientists that conducted the study between 2019 and 2020 found a deepwater layer of zooplankton and fish in the Arctic Ocean as well as evidence of continuous immigration of larger Atlantic fish to the Arctic ecosystem, much further north than expected (European Commission, 2022). This influx contributes to potential food for mammals living in the Arctic Ocean. Also, another important finding of the research is that 'the capacity of the Central Arctic Ocean ecosystem to support larger fish stocks is without doubt rather limited', as Pauline Snoeijs Leijonmalm, coordinator of the EFICA Consortium and professor in marine ecology at Stockholm University argued (European Commission, 2022). This means that 'there are no harvestable fish stocks today or in the foreseeable future' (European Commission, 2022). Thus, the MOSAIC expedition has given a valuable contribution to the study of the ecosystem of the Arctic region. Indeed, as it is possible to read on the website dedicated to the research, its goal was to 'take the closest look ever at the Arctic as the epicenter of global warming and to gain fundamental insights that are key to a better understanding of global climate change' (Alfred Wegener Institute, 2020).

The following year, in 2021, scientists from the EFICA Consortium participated in another expedition to the Central Arctic Ocean on board the Swedish icebreaker *Oden*, which is 'one of the world's most powerful non-nuclear-powered icebreakers and one of the foremost platforms for research in the polar oceans' (Swedish Polar Research Secretariat, 2023) to continue their ecosystem research (European Commission, 2022). The aim of the expedition was to investigate which fish species exist, how many fish live at a depth of 200 to 500 metres (called the mesopelagic zone), and what size fish stocks the Central Arctic Ocean can produce in terms of food availability for the fish (European Commission, 2022). Researchers managed to collect data in areas that had not been explored yet (Swedish Polar Research Secretariat, 2023). They did not manage to catch any fish, but they collected fish bones (otoliths) in the sediment and were able to tell which species it is

28 OSPAR 'is the mechanism by which 15 Governments & the EU cooperate to protect the marine environment of the North-East Atlantic'. The 15 governments are Belgium, Denmark, Finland, France, Germany, Iceland, Ireland, Luxembourg, Netherlands, Norway, Portugal, Spain, Sweden, Switzerland, and UK. The OSPAR Convention, which was adopted in 1992, 'unified, up-dated and extended' the Oslo Convention against dumping of 1972 and the Paris Convention of 1974 concerning land-based sources of marine pollution and offshore industry (OSPAR, 2024).

29 Scientists came from Austria, Belgium, Canada, China, Denmark, Finland, France, Germany, Great Britain, Italy, Japan, South Korea, Netherlands, Norway, Poland, Russia, Spain, Sweden, Switzerland, and USA (European Commission, 2022).

possible to find there (Swedish Polar Research Secretariat, 2023). This survey is important because non-icebreaking vessels including fishing vessels will be able to access these areas in about 20–30 years, which means that international agreements to protect fish species are necessary (Swedish Polar Research Secretariat, 2023).

The EU financing of research in the region is an expression of its geopolitical and economic interests in the region. By participating in research projects and joint initiatives, the EU is takes the opportunity to be involved in Arctic affairs, which serves its purpose of increasing its geopolitical leverage in the region. A good example is the EU-funded Action on Black Carbon in the Arctic, which is an initiative aiming to 'contribute to the development of collective responses to reduce black carbon emissions in the Arctic and to reinforce international cooperation to protect the Arctic environment. It provides and communicates knowledge about sources and emissions of black carbon and supports relevant international policy processes' (AMAP, 2022). It is implemented through the partnership instrument for cooperation with third-party countries that is 'the first EU's instrument designed to promote the Union's interests worldwide by reinforcing its external strategies, policies and actions' (European Commission, 2021b). Additionally, it is interesting to note here that the Action on the Black Carbon is an initiative of the Arctic Monitoring and Assessment Program, a WG of the AC. The EU is not a member or a fully fledged observer of the AC because its application for observer status has been rejected twice (in 2009 and 2011) because of opposition from Canada and Russia, although for different reasons. Canada decided to vote against the EU application because the EU regulation on the ban of seal products was against its economic interests as seal pelts are an important source of income for its Inuit population's sealers (Livernois, 2009, 42). Russia opposed the EU application because it wants to prevent the EU from increasing its involvement in Arctic affairs. However, in 2013, the AC decided that the EU could be 'an observer in principle', namely an ad hoc observer (Hossain, 2015). Later, in 2015, the AC ministerial meeting held in Iqaluit (Canada) decided in favour of two additional years of deferral for the EU's formal observer status to the Council (Hossain, 2015). Nevertheless, this possibility is not going to be realised at least in the near future.

In this context, it is interesting to note that being involved in the work of regional councils is part of the geopolitical strategies of the EU to achieve its political and economic objectives. For instance, in addition of being an ad hoc observer of the AC, the EU (through the European Commission, EC) is a fully fledged member of the BEAC and the CBSS as well as an observer of the Black Sea Economic Cooperation Organisation (BSEC).[30] It is in this geopolitical perspective that the EU strongly supports cooperation in the High North. The 2021 Arctic Policy

30 The members of the CBSS are Denmark, Estonia, Finland, Germany, Iceland, Latvia, Lithuania, Norway, Poland, Russia, Sweden, and the EU (CBSS, 2023). The BSEC members are Albania, Armenia, Azerbaijan, Georgia, Greece, Moldova, Republic of North Macedonia, Romania, Russia, Serbia, Turkey, and Ukraine (BSEC, 2023). These states (with the exception of the EC) constitute the Nordic/Baltic Region and the Black Sea Region, respectively.

states, in fact, that 'the EU will enhance its strategic foresight, mainstream Arctic matters in its external diplomacy and build on regional cooperation' (European Commission, 2021, 2). It also states that 'the EU will strengthen its Arctic engagement through contributing to maintaining peaceful and constructive dialogue and cooperation in a changing geopolitical landscape, to keep the Arctic safe and stable, by raising Arctic matters in its external contacts, intensifying regional cooperation and developing strategic foresight on emerging security challenges' (European Commission, 2021, 3).

Regional cooperation and international cooperation more broadly are part of the EU's approach to its external relations. In particular, the 2003 European Security Strategy (ESS) defines 'effective multilateralism' as one of the top priorities of the EU's external action (Council of the European Union, 2003, 36; Hewig, 2022, 3). The EU aims, in fact, to 'promote multilateral solutions to common problems, in particular in the framework of the United Nations', as stated in Article 21 of the Treaty on the EU (Council of the European Union, 2003, 36; Hewig, 2022, 3). In this context, it is important to note that the 2021 EU Arctic Policy clearly states that EU action in the region should be based inter alia on the respect of international law and the UNCLOS, in particular, as well as on rules-based multilateralism (European Commission, 2021, 2; European Parliament, 2024). The 2021 document stresses that 'the EU's policy is built upon the principles set out in UNCLOS, the UN 30 Agenda[31] and the Sustainable Development Goals' in addition to its involvement in the work of the AC, the BEAC, and the ND (European Commission, 2021, 4). In particular, the EU considers the UNCLOS 'the framework for managing the Arctic Ocean, including the peaceful settlement of disputes' (European Commission, 2021, 11). Keeping the Arctic peaceful is one of the aims of the EU whose 2021 Arctic Policy, different from the previous documents, raises concerns about the military build-up of the Russian Arctic (European Commission, 2021, 3). The document clearly stresses that this not only raises security issues, but it could also aggravate the consequences of climate change (European Commission, 2021, 3). In fact, increased military operations would increase pollution.

Thus, climate change means the EU has geopolitical and economic interests in the Arctic that emerged over the last few decades. This is why the EU has developed its own strategy for the region by progressively affirming itself as a geopolitical actor in the region. In this context, scientific cooperation offers the EU an excellent tool to increase its presence in the Arctic.

31 The UN 30 Agenda 'is a plan of action for people, planet and prosperity' aimed at 'ending poverty and hunger everywhere; to combat inequalities within and among countries; to build peaceful, just and inclusive societies; to protect human rights and promote gender equality and the empowerment of women and girls; and to ensure the lasting protection of the planet and its natural resources' (United Nations, no date-d).

Neoliberal institutionalism and neorealism in the Arctic

In order to better understand how cooperation has developed in the region, it is interesting to analyse it by comparing the perspectives of two of the most influential theoretical approaches to international relations, namely neorealism and neoliberal institutionalism, which have dominated the academic debate on international relations for decades, since the end of the Cold War. The aim here is not to propose a debate on explanations about the relations among states that they provide or to discuss their strengths or weaknesses. By contrast, the very aim is to better understand what has been happening internationally and how this has been reflected regionally, in particular, in the Arctic. Both theoretical approaches, for which the main actors are states (although neoliberals admit the existence of non-state actors in world politics), agree on the fact that the international system switched from bipolarism to unipolarism immediately after the Cold War. According to neorealist Kenneth Waltz, for instance, the structure of international politics was remade by the disappearance of the Soviet Union (Waltz, 2000). This means that the structure of the international system has remained anarchic (like neoliberal institutionalism also argues), thus changes *of* the system, which are the ones that 'would alter the international political system so profoundly that old ways of thinking would no longer be relevant', have not occurred (Waltz, 2000). By contrast, changes *in* the system have taken place (Waltz, 2000). Waltz explains that changes can occur at the unit (state) level or at the structure level (that helps identify how the relations among the units are organised, namely in an anarchic way, which is in absence of a supranational body) (Waltz, 2000). In the first case, changes can, for instance, concern the means of transportation, communication, and war fighting that strongly affect how states and other agents interact (Waltz, 2000). According to Waltz, the introduction of nuclear weaponry is the greatest change to have occurred at the unit level (Waltz, 2000). In the second case, changes can concern the polarity of the system like the reduction of great powers from two to one as happened with the collapse of the Soviet Union (Waltz, 2000). Indeed, as Waltz argues, the international system has been unipolar for some time as the US was the only great power (Waltz, 2000).

Similarly, neoliberal scholar John Ikenberry (2010) pointed out that the end of the Cold War led to the 'consolidation of the US-led postwar order'. He argued that the restructuring of the international system was a 'tale' of the two orders that coexisted during the Cold War (Ikenberry, 2010). One was the bipolar order while the other one was the American liberal hegemonic order existing 'inside' the broader bipolar one (Ikenberry, 2010). When the Cold War ended, the '"inside" order became the "outside" order, that is, its logic was extended to the larger global system' (Ikenberry, 2010). The 'inside' order has been expanding and deepening since the 1990s (Ikenberry, 2010).

Given this background, these two theoretical approaches have different views on cooperation stemming from their different approaches to the relative gains/absolute gains dichotomy, although both theories agree on the fact that anarchy constrains the willingness of states to cooperate (Grieco, 1988). Neorealists argue that states are worried about relative gains because their thinking is dominated by power calculations that are key to pursuing their interests and their survival as independent actors (Mearsheimer, 2002; Grieco, 1988). Grieco clarifies that states are concerned about both absolute and relative gains (Grieco, 1988). Waltz explains that 'when faced with the possibility of cooperating for mutual gain, states that feel insecure must ask how the gain will be divided. They are compelled to ask not "Will both of us gain?" but "Who will gain more?"' (Waltz, 1979). The consequence is that neorealists see two obstacles to cooperation. First, states fear of being cheated (Mearsheimer, 1994). Thus, they may decide to cooperate only to ensure that their partners comply with their promises and that their cooperation produces 'balanced' and 'equitable' achievements of gains (Grieco, 1988). Second, states concern about 'relative achievements of gains' (Grieco, 1988). The reason is that for neorealists states are 'positional' in character, thus they 'worry that their partners might gain more from cooperation than they do' (Grieco, 1988). As Grieco puts it,

> according to neorealists, states worry that today's friend may be tomorrow's enemy in war, and fear that achievements of joint gains that advantage a friend in the present might produce a more dangerous *potential* foe in the future. As a result, states must give serious attention to the gains of partners.
> (Grieco, 1988)

By contrast, according to neoliberals, states try to maximise their gains in absolute terms without worrying about relative gains. This difference is at the basis of their perspective over cooperation. In fact, neoliberals think that although neorealists are right to argue that anarchy constrains the willingness of states to cooperate, they can work together especially with the help of institutions (Grieco, 1988). Nevertheless, neoliberal institutionalists do not argue that achieving cooperation in world politics is easy (Axerold and Keohane, 1985, 226). Instead, they think that 'cooperation can only take place in situations that contain a mixture of conflicting and complementary interests' and that 'in such situations, cooperation occurs when actors adjust their behavior to the actual or anticipated preferences of other' (Axerold and Keohane, 1985, 226).

Cooperation is a key point to understanding the Arctic in the post-Cold War period. Indeed, the establishment of the AC was a milestone in the management of Arctic affairs in the period immediately after the end of the Cold War as a consequence of the improvement of relations among states in the region. From a theoretical perspective, the establishment of the AC[32] and its success can be more easily explained with the lens of neoliberal institutionalism because of its emphasis on institutions, other forms of power besides military force, the role of interdependence in addition to anarchy in the international system, and the relevance of both cooperation and conflict in international politics (Milner, 2009). Robert Keohane

32 The AC is an intergovernmental forum, considered here as an international institution with a regional character.

defines institutions as 'persistent and connected sets of rules (formal and informal) that prescribe behavioral roles, constrain activity, and shape expectations' (Keohane, 1989). Institutions reduce certain forms of uncertainty, provide information (through monitoring), and stabilise expectations even in the absence of hierarchical authority (Keohane, 1989). Keohane argues that institutions are expected to appear 'whenever the costs of communication, monitoring, and enforcement are relatively low compared to the benefits to be derived from political exchange' (Keohane, 1989). He also specifies that 'institutions should persist as long as, but only so long as, their members have incentives to maintain them' (Keohane, 1989). Arthur Stein clarifies that 'states find that autonomous self-interested behavior can be problematic and they prefer to construct international institutions to deal with a host of concerns' (Stein, 2008). The case of the AC is emblematic as it was established on Canada's proposal in order to face regional concerns about demilitarisation and hard security issues. As explained, member states decided not to include them as it is easier to cooperate on soft security issues such as sustainable development, which is at the core of the AC's activities. By establishing the AC, the Arctic states have reduced 'the governance costs associated with autonomous decision-making' (Stein, 2008). Over time, the work of the AC has been growing enormously because states consider cooperation in certain sectors (e.g., sustainable development) to be profitable and valuable. The AC has deepened and widened the exchange of information among states and coordination of activities concerning issues of common interest. In so doing, the AC has contributed to making the Arctic a zone where relations among states have traditionally been characterised by cooperation, which has been the distinctive characteristic of the Arctic region from the end of the Cold War until the war in Ukraine in 2022. In this region, soft power has prevailed over hard power. Joseph Nye defines soft power as 'the ability to affect others to obtain the outcomes one wants through attraction rather than coercion or payment', and power in general terms as 'the ability to affect others to obtain the outcomes you want' (Nye, 2008, 94). He also adds that 'a smart power strategy combines hard and soft power resources' (Nye, 2008, 94). The AC offers good opportunities to exert soft power as it provides a platform where states can promote their interests and priorities on a number of economic, environmental, and social issues. The same can be said for Arctic conferences such as the Arctic Frontiers and the Arctic Circle Assembly (Steinveg et al., 2023, 2–3), two of the largest, most important, and popular conferences on regional affairs. Arctic Frontiers, which was established in 2006, is held annually in Tromsø, Norway. Its purpose was to 'to contribute to sustainable social and business development in the Arctic and to fulfil the need for an arena that could promote knowledge-based policymaking and information exchange across different disciplines' (Steinveg et al., 2023, 3). Norway has exploited the conference 'to pursue its interests and priorities in the region by promoting an active Arctic strategy and positioning itself internationally after the end of the Cold War' (Steinveg et al., 2023, 3). Norway aimed to engage in business cooperation with Russia, ensure political stability and sustainable development of the northern regions, and that indigenous people would participate in decision-making processes concerning them (Steinveg et al.,

2023, 3). The relevance of Arctic Frontiers for Norway is defined in the Norwegian government's Arctic Policy of 2020 as 'one of the most important international platforms for promoting Norwegian positions in the Arctic' (Steinveg et al., 2023, 3; Norwegian Ministries, 2020). Also, the document states that the government actively uses conferences to 'have a dialogue about Nordic policy and to set the agenda regionally, nationally, and internationally' (Steinveg et al., 2023, 3; Norwegian Ministries, 2020). Similarly, the Icelandic Arctic Strategy from 2011 states that the government seeks to promote 'Iceland abroad as a venue for Arctic conferences' (Icelandic Parliament, 2011; Steinveg et al., 2023, 4). Like Norway, Iceland tries to use conferences to position itself internationally and to pursue its national interests (Steinveg et al., 2023, 4). This is the case of the Arctic Circle Assembly that Iceland launched in 2013 as a result of the US withdrawal from Keflavik air base in 2006 and the financial crisis in 2008 (Steinveg et al., 2023, 4; Ingimundarson, 2015). The Arctic Circle Assembly, which is held annually in Reykjavik, is seen as 'an open, democratic platform to include everyone with a self-declared interest in participating in the dialogue about the region's future, regardless of geographical position or institutional affiliation' (Steinveg et al., 2023, 4). Indeed, this conference gives equal visibility to both Arctic and non-Arctic states, giving them the opportunity to promote their perspectives and have more visibility (Steinveg et al., 2023, 4). In his address to the National Press Club in 2013, Iceland's former President Ólafur Ragnar Grímsson stated that 'what we [the Nordic states] thought was our Arctic has become the global Arctic with countries in faraway places wanting to have a seat at the Arctic table' (Rossi, 2017, 177). In contrast to the observer role in the AC, conferences are occasions where non-Arctic actors can have their voice heard (Steinveg et al., 2023, 4). Nevertheless, Arctic states do not appreciate this kind of conference (Steinveg et al., 2023, 4). The Arctic Frontiers conference and the Arctic Circle Assembly are in competition to attract speakers, sponsors, visibility, and participants (Steinveg et al., 2023, 4). However, they are different models of conference as Arctic Frontiers gives priority to Arctic state representatives and the organisers decide the topics to be discussed, while the Arctic Circle Assembly is organised like an 'open tent' where Arctic and non-Arctic states are considered equal participants and are involved in an open dialogue together with non-state actors (Steinveg et al., 2023, 4). This is, for instance, the case of China that actively participates in these conferences to emphasise that it is a legitimate participant in Arctic affairs (Steinveg et al., 2023, 4). In spite of their differences, both conferences help states promote their geopolitical and economic interests (Steinveg, 2022, 250; Steinveg et al., 2023, 5). Additionally, by involving different kinds of actor from different institutional affiliations and governance levels, 'conferences contribute to challenging the state-centric view of the Arctic' (Steinveg et al., 2023, 5).

Moreover, the fact that the AC is a major actor in the region leads to another consideration, namely the fact that non-state actors play a key role in the geopolitical dynamics in the Arctic, supporting neoliberal institutionalism's approach. Two cases can be mentioned here. The first one concerns the EU, which notoriously is not a state but a 'supranational organisation', which means that 'power and authority in certain policy areas are permanently given up by Member States to a higher level' (Center for European Studies, 2024). The EU's involvement in Arctic affairs is growing as its cooperation with the AC clearly demonstrates. Also, it influences the Arctic in a number of ways, in particular, its environmental impact on the region and the fact that its legislation is acquired by its Arctic Member States (Denmark, Finland and Sweden) as well as by EEA states (Iceland and Norway) are very significant in this context. Another factor is that Canada, Russia, and the US are traditionally strategic partners of the EU (although EU–Russia relations are currently very difficult).

The second case is the involvement of non-state actors in Arctic science diplomacy, which is the link between science and diplomacy and a 'subcategory of the so-called new diplomacy, as opposed to the long-standing traditional diplomacy known to date' (Łuszczuk and Szkarlat, 2022, 18). Non-state actors can be public, private, intergovernmental, or non-governmental actors (Łuszczuk and Szkarlat, 2022, 23). They can be defined as '"pivotal agenda-setters for new policy issues" because their role is not limited to advising and providing expertise, but they also introduce new concepts into international discourse, contributing to the creation of new standards' (Łuszczuk and Szkarlat, 2022, 23). However, they do not have decision-making powers and depend on governments and inter-governmental organisations (Łuszczuk and Szkarlat, 2022, 23). Indeed, it is necessary to specify here that 'the participation of states is a precondition for the occurrence of science diplomacy' (Łuszczuk and Szkarlat, 2022, 23). In short, science diplomacy is state-centric. In this sense, neorealism's approach prevails.

Furthermore, another important element of neoliberal institutionalism is interdependence, which Robert Keohane and Joseph Nye (2012, 8) define as 'mutual dependence' (Keohane and Nye, 2012, 7) where dependence is 'a state of being determined or significantly affected by external forces' (Keohane and Nye, 2012, 7). Thus, interdependence refers to 'situations characterized by reciprocal effects among countries or among actors in different countries'. Interdependence occurs when the interaction produces reciprocal costs and constraints (Özpek, 2013, 362). In the case of the Arctic region, states are strongly interdependent in a number of sectors. A good example is environmental protection, which is a transnational issue as pollution is not confined to national borders. Other examples in which Arctic states are interdependent are climate change and transportation, which are sectors where cooperation is necessary. International coordination in climate change actions and transportation activities is in fact of utmost importance to effectively deal with these issues.

This analysis seems to support the neoliberal institutionalists' idea that institutions 'markedly affect the prospects for international stability' (Mearsheimer, 1994, 1). This view is contested by neorealists that have a more negative idea of institutions. John Mearsheimer defines institutions as 'a set of rules that stipulate the ways in which the states should cooperate and compete with each other' (Mearsheimer, 1994, 1). Neorealists claim that cooperation does occur but it is difficult to achieve and to sustain (Mearsheimer, 1994, 3; Jervis, 1999, 62). In particular, there are two elements that inhibit cooperation, namely relative gains considerations and the fear of being cheated (Mearsheimer, 1994, 3). Furthermore, neorealists argue that institutions are a reflection of the distribution of power in the international system (Mearsheimer, 1994, 1). According to them, in fact, institutions are essentially based on the self-interested calculations of great powers and thus do not produce an independent effect on the behaviour of states (Mearsheimer, 1994, 1). As Mearsheimer puts it, 'the most powerful states in the system create and shape institutions so that they can maintain their share of world power, or even increase it' (Mearsheimer, 1994, 4). Thus, for neorealists 'the causes of war and peace are mainly a function of the balance of power, and institutions largely mirror the distribution of power in the system' (Mearsheimer, 1994, 4). NATO provides a good example of neorealist thought (Mearsheimer, 1994, 4; Waltz, 2000, 23). During the Cold War, NATO was an instrument in the American's hands to manage power in the face of Soviet power (Mearsheimer, 1994, 4). Waltz clarifies that 'NATO lasted as a military alliance as long as the Soviet Union appeared to be a direct threat to its members' and now it expands not because of its institutions but because the US want it (Waltz, 2000, 25).

In the case of the AC, although its establishment was proposed by Canada, which is a middle power, the US strongly influenced its work as it was against the inclusion of hard security issues in the forum's activities, as explained in the Introduction. Additionally, the AC provides a valuable platform where great powers, namely the US and Russia, can cooperate and influence Arctic affairs according to their interests and priorities. It is in fact reasonable to think that Russia has not withdrawn from the AC (at least at the moment of writing), like instead in the BEAC case (as a consequence of the worsening of the East–West relations due to the war in Ukraine), because of the increasing political leverage of the institution, which is becoming increasingly influential in defining Arctic affairs. Therefore, in order to continue asserting its influence in the region, Russia has decided to continue being part of the AC although cooperation is temporarily suspended.

Furthermore, neorealism is a better-suited theory than neoliberal institutionalism to explain why five circumpolar states (Canada, Denmark, Norway, Russia, and the US) called the Arctic 5, which are all coastal states, decided to cooperate on the adoption of the Ilulissat Declaration in 2008. Indeed, this case clearly shows that geopolitical and economic interests influence the political and economic choices of states in their relations with other states.

The overall aim of the declaration was to affirm the sovereign rights of coastal states reflecting their geopolitical and economic interests in the Arctic. The reasons behind the declaration must be found in the Russian titanium flag-planting on the Lomonosov Ridge (at a sea depth of 4,200 metres) during an exploration mission of two submarines in 2007. This ridge is a 1,800km-long ridge dividing the Eurasian basin from the Amerasia basin and it is thought to be rich in oil and gas (Hosa, 2018). Its importance is not only economic but also strategic and political because it enables control over the High North and the Northern Sea Route (NSR), which is a shipping lane from the Kara Sea in western Siberia to the Pacific Ocean. Climate change, which is making the North Pole increasingly accessible because of melting ice, is making the Lomonosov Ridge steadily important from a geopolitical and economic perspective.

Russian officials gave several interpretations of the event (Dodds, 2013, 47–48). Some of them gave a technical-scientific interpretation stating that Russia's aim was just to collect scientific data necessary to a Russian submission to the Commission on the Limits of the Continental Shelf (Dodds, 2013, 47). Other officials gave a territorial consolidation or a cultural-symbolic interpretation aimed at asserting that the North Pole was an extension of the Russian land mass or part of the Russian tradition (Dodds, 2013, 47). For instance, Russian expedition member Artur Chilingarov, who also was a member of the Russian Duma, noted that 'the Arctic is Russian. We must prove the North Pole is an extension of the Russian land mass' (Dodds, 2013, 47). Other senior scholars compared the Russian flag-planting in the Arctic with the US flag-planting on the Moon, but this reference was confusing as the US did not make any territorial claim to this planet (Dodds, 2013, 47). Moreover, it is interesting to note here that in addition to Russia, also Canada and Denmark claim that the Lomonosov Ridge is a prolongation of their continental shelf comprising the prolongation of the land territory of a state up to 200 nautical miles from the baseline against which the continental shelf is measured (Dodds, 2013, 47). However, the Russian flag-planting did not have any legal consequences, but its political significance was huge (Dodds, 2013, 47), as the Ilulissat Declaration demonstrates.

The Arctic 5 met in Ilulissat upon Greenland's invitation to discuss climate change in the region. The result of this meeting was 'an eight paragraph soft power statement on Arctic Ocean management with *Realpolitik* implications' (Rossi, 2017, 45). In this document, the Arctic 5 reinforced the principle according to which 'the land dominates the sea' that was stated by the International Court of Justice (ICJ) in its 1969 North Sea Continental shelf judgement (Papanicolopulu, 2018, 39). The Arctic 5 asserted their 'unique position' (Arctic Portal, 2021) to address issues affecting the Arctic environment for which much needed to be done, as well as issues relating to indigenous communities and natural resources exploitation (Rossi, 2017, 170). Furthermore, a fundamental issue that the Arctic 5 addressed was the key role played by UNCLOS, which they considered the international legal framework within which issues concerning the Arctic would be addressed (Rossi, 2017, 171). The reference to UNCLOS was foundational as without it the meeting would have not been possible (Dodds, 2013, 49). This is very surprising when it comes to the US as they have never been a party to UNCLOS. They refused to sign it because of their objection to the limits that it imposes on seabed mining (Gwertzman, 1982), which means that the US want to preserve their sovereignty over natural resources contained in its territory. The US, like other industrialised democracies, rejected the Deep Seabed Mining Provisions of UNCLOS because they perceived them as contrary to the economic and political philosophy of Western capitalist states (Remy, 1992, 1217), which means that those provisions were against their economic and security interests.

Furthermore, by stressing their commitment to UNCLOS, the eight Arctic states marginalised the proposals of some parliamentarians of the Parliament of the EU that called for an Arctic treaty modelled on the basis of the 1959 Antarctic Treaty (Dodds, 2013, 49) and the criticism that the Arctic had been 'caught in a legal void' (Dodds, 2013, 49). Therefore, they affirmed the vision that the Arctic is not a *terra nullius* (Dodds, 2013, 53), namely a land that is not under the sovereignty or the control of any state, but a region belonging to the coastal states.

The Ilulissat Declaration was criticised by Iceland, Finland, and Sweden, who had been excluded from the meeting because they are not coastal states (Rossi, 2017, 171), although they are Arctic states and also members of the AC, the most important organisation guiding cooperation in the region. In its Parliamentary Resolution on its Arctic policy of 2011, for instance, Iceland stressed that 'if consultation by the five States develops into a formal platform for regional issues, it can be asserted that solidarity between the eight Arctic states will be dissolved and the Arctic Council considerably weakened' (Althingi, 2011, 5). Additionally, Iceland very interestingly stresses in the document that its interests are shaped by its geographical position and access to natural resources and that it aims at being included in those group of states that 'have the greatest influence on the future development of the region' (Althingi, 2011, 5). Nevertheless, criticism from Iceland, Finland, and Sweden was raised again in 2010 when Canada organised a meeting in 'furtherance of commitments in the 2008 Ilulissat Declaration' (Ministry of Foreign Affairs of the Russian Federation, 2010). This made even clearer that the Arctic 5 preferred to establish a dialogue among themselves to discuss maritime jurisdiction and security issues that they considered unsuitable to be decided in the framework of the AC (Rossi, 2017, 171).

On the one hand, both neoliberal institutionalism and neorealism can explain the fact that cooperation among the Arctic 5 occurred just because they aimed to protect their national interests. On the other hand, the Ilulissat Declaration did cause tensions between the Arctic 5 and those Arctic states that had been excluded from it. This supports the neorealist perspective according to which cooperation does not guarantee peace and stability.

Furthermore, another element concerning Arctic cooperation deserves to be discussed from the perspectives of neorealism and neoliberalism, namely the involvement of states external to the region in Arctic affairs. In 2008, namely one year after the Russian flag-planting, two geopolitically oriented French analysts, Richard Labévière and François Thual, published a book titled *La Bataille du Grand Nord a Commencé* (The struggle for the High North has begun), in which they say that the 2007 episode is 'a token of the continued game for economic, environmental and strategic positions in the Arctic, intensified by climatic and technological changes' (Vigeland Rottem, 2020, 37). They also argue that these changes attract the interest of states external to the region aiming at participating in the exploitation of natural resources and shipping routes of the region (Vigeland Rottem, 2020, 37), which ice-melting due to climate change is making increasingly accessible. Consequently, states like China, India, Singapore, and South Korea are becoming more active players in the region trying to be increasingly involved in the Arctic affairs. This is why, for instance, they are observers in the AC. Thus, climate change has played a key role in this process bringing the Arctic to the political agenda of these states.

As Taisaku Ikeshima puts it, 'they may be seen as stakeholders in Arctic matters because they intend to participate in the process of decision-making and law-making in any region where global interests are affected' (Ikeshima, 2019, 391). Global interests are, for instance, the fight against climate change and environmental protection, which are very sensitive issues in the Arctic. As 'what happens in the Arctic does not stay in the Arctic' (NATO Parliamentary Assembly, 2017), ice-melting and environmental problems may affect the world environment, ecosystem, and natural resources (Ikeshima, 2019, 390; Pahuja, 2012, 401). Therefore, the entire world has realised that 'it has a community interest in a peaceful and stable situation in the Arctic region as a whole, since global environmental problems have brought about the concept of "common concern" with legal significance. This interest may also be called a public interest of the international community' (Ikeshima, 2019, 390). At the same time, the idea of 'global responsibility', meaning that 'the states which are engaged in any activities are responsible for their conduct in relation with the international community as a whole', has been gradually emerging (Ikeshima, 2019, 391). This idea empowers states external to the region to have a significant voice on the environmental and ecological conditions of the Arctic Ocean also because they are affected by these natural conditions irrespective of their geographical location (Ikeshima, 2019, 391). In particular, they can exert their influence on international agreements, treaties, and conventions dealing with climate change and environmental protection that are applied to the Arctic region as well. Some examples are the Kyoto Protocol and the Paris Agreement. Both of them are fundamental instruments to reduce greenhouse gas emissions at the global level and are legally binding. Thus, they also apply to the Arctic. China and India, for instance, which are the two emerging powers internationally, are parties to both the Kyoto Protocol and the Paris Agreement. It is interesting to note here that states do or do not commit to a specific international law instrument because of their geopolitical and economic interests. This means that states commit themselves to international law only when it is beneficial to them. They calculate the absolute and relative gains that they can eventually obtain from participation. For instance, the decision of the US not to ratify UNCLOS to preserve their sovereignty as well as their economic and security interests clearly demonstrates the validity of this reasoning. Similar considerations can be made in the case of the Kyoto Protocol concerning both the US and Russia. The US decided not to be a party to the Kyoto Protocol because 'it exempts 80 percent of the world, including major population centres such as China and India, from compliance, and would cause serious harm to the US economy', as former US President George Bush explained in 2001 (Hovi et al., 2010, 130). By contrast, Russia has ratified the Kyoto Protocol but only in 2004 because of political and economic incentives in engaging in environmental protection internationally (Tynkkynen, 2010, 180). More precisely, in exchange for its ratification, Russia received the EU's support for its membership in the World Trade Organization (WTO) (Tynkkynen, 2010, 180).

In this context, two factors are relevant from a theoretical perspective. First, the interest of states external to the Arctic in participating in the exploitation of natural resources and shipping routes of the region. Second, their interest in participating in the process of decision-making and law-making in any region where global interests are affected. While the first factor can be easily explained through a neoliberal institutionalist lens, the second one can be better explained from a neorealist perspective. Indeed, in the first case, states try to maximise their gains in absolute terms because, being external to the region, the maximum reward that they can have is not to be excluded from the exploitation of natural resources and shipping routes in order to have the opportunity to obtain some of the geopolitical and economic advantages coming from it. By contrast, the second factor can be better explained from a neorealist perspective because states can have their voice heard as much as the other states when being party to international agreements. Of course, external states are excluded from multilateral agreements regulating a specific issue-area stipulated by states belonging to the region at stake.

In conclusion, the end of the Cold War has brought about significant changes in the Arctic essentially due to the interplay of two elements, namely the redistribution of power among states in the international system and climate change. These two factors have reshaped relations among states internationally by impacting those at the regional level while also attracting, geopolitically and economically, some states external to the region like China and India. Also, the two theoretical approaches provide explanations of the redistribution of power in the Arctic from different angles. Of course, there are some issues that can be better explained from the lenses of one or the other theory. The reason is that theories can explain only parts of the reality.

The Arctic, the Antarctic, and the Third Pole: is there anything exceptional about the Arctic?

This section analyses Arctic exceptionalism by using the word 'exceptionalism' in more general terms, departing from the strict meaning usually given to it as discussed. The reason is that a comparison with the Antarctic and the Third Pole in broad terms is useful for a deeper understanding of the geopolitical dynamics of the Arctic and its geographical peculiarities. More specifically, this word is intended as simply meaning unusual or extraordinary. The aim is to show that the Arctic is exceptional in its own way, characterised by geographical, historical, and political features that are unique but that the other two poles, the Antarctic and the Third Pole, the other two polar systems of the Earth, are unique as well in their own way. Indeed, the Arctic is not exceptional if compared to the Antarctic and the Third Pole or at least it is not more exceptional than them. The Arctic is often compared to the Antarctic but in reality they are very different both geographically and geopolitically, although some similarities can be identified. While the Arctic is an ocean covered by a thin layer of perennial sea ice and surrounded by land (the term 'perennial' refers to the oldest and thickest sea ice), the Antarctic is land covered and surrounded by ice (NASA, 2023). The Antarctic, different from the Arctic, is a continent, the world's largest, driest, coldest, and highest continent (Brady, 2014). It is covered by a very thick ice cap and surrounded by a rim of sea ice and the Southern Ocean (NASA, 2023). The Arctic Ocean is more sensitive to climate change than the Antarctic because it is very deep and closely linked with the climate systems around it (NASA, 2023). Geopolitically, the relations among states are also very different because of two main reasons. First, the Arctic territory belongs to the Arctic coastal states (Canada, Denmark/Greenland, Norway, Russia, and the US/Alaska) also called the Arctic 5, while the Antarctic is no man's land. Second, Arctic governance is legally based on the United Nations Convention on the Law of the Sea, as explicitly stated in the Ilulissat Declaration of 2008, while the Antarctic is legally based on the Antarctic Treaty System (ATS) signed in Washington in 1959 and entered into force in 1961. In this regard, it is interesting to note a paramount difference between the Arctic and Antarctic from a historical perspective. The confrontation between the Soviet Union and the US during the Cold War had in fact a different impact on the two areas. In the Arctic it prevented states from cooperation as explained above, while in the Antarctic it led to cooperative links among states through the ATS. Thus, the Antarctic could be considered even more 'exceptional' than the Arctic according to the meaning of 'exceptionalism' discussed. The ATS was signed by the 12 states[33] (today the signatories of the treaty are 56[34]) whose scientists had been active in and around Antarctica during the International Geophysical Year (IGY) of 1957–1958 (Secretariat of the Antarctic Treaty, 2023). The successful international cooperation achieved during the IGY gave great impetus to the negotiation of the treaty (Brady, 2014). However, the success of the initiative to sign a treaty was also due to another crucial element that was the so-called Standstill Proposal, namely the agreement not to pursue territorial claims during the IGY (Brady, 2014). Additionally, like in the case of the establishment of the AC, the involvement of the Soviet Union was another important factor taken into consideration but that raised some concerns that Australia's Foreign Minister helped to overcome by playing a key role in ensuring the participation of the Soviet Union and its support for the treaty (Brady, 2014).

Furthermore, another similarity with the Arctic case is the exclusion of military issues from cooperation. Indeed, the ATS is based on the two pillars of peace and science, explicitly stipulating that the Antarctic should be used exclusively for peaceful purposes, basically for scientific research, and that military activities (e.g., the establishment of military bases and weapons testing) are prohibited, except those in support of science (Scientific Committee on Antarctic Research, 2020). By contrast, different from the Arctic case, territorial sovereignty cannot be claimed in Antarctica. In particular, Article IV stipulates that

33 The 12 states were Argentina, Australia, Belgium, Chile, France, Japan, New Zealand, Norway, Russia, South Africa, UK, and US (Secretariat of the Antarctic Treaty, 2023a).

34 The other 58 parties to the ATS are: Argentina, Australia, Austria, Belarus, Belgium, Brazil, Bulgaria, Canada, Chile, China, Colombia, Costa Rica, Cuba, Czechia, Denmark, Ecuador, Estonia, Finland, France, Germany, Greece, Guatemala, Hungary, Iceland, India, Italy, Japan, Kazakhstan, Malaysia, Monaco, Mongolia, Netherlands, North Korea, New Zealand, Norway, Pakistan, Papua New Guinea, Peru, Poland, Portugal, Romania, Russia, San Marino, Saudi Arabia, Slovakia, Slovenia, South Africa, South Korea, Spain, Sweden, Switzerland, Turkey, UK, Ukraine, United Arab Emirates, US, Uruguay, Venezuela (Secretariat of the Antarctic Treaty, 2023a).

> no acts or activities taking place while the present Treaty is in force shall constitute a basis for asserting, supporting or denying a claim to territorial sovereignty in Antarctica or create any rights of sovereignty in Antarctica. No new claim, or enlargement of an existing claim to territorial sovereignty in Antarctica shall be asserted while the present Treaty is in force.
>
> (Secretariat of the Antarctic Treaty, 2023)

Also, Articles I, II, and IV and the statement in the Preamble to the ATS clearly stipulate that the Antarctic 'shall not become the scene or object of international discord' (Brady, 2014).

Nevertheless, the treaty, whose Secretariat is located in Buenos Aires, Argentina, will become modifiable in 2048 (Dodds, 2018). In particular, it is the protocol on environmental protection to the Antarctic Treaty that could be amended. Article 25 of the protocol stipulates that 'if, after the expiration of 50 years from the date of entry into force of this Protocol, any of the Antarctic Treaty Consultative Parties so requests by a communication addressed to the Depositary, a conference shall be held as soon as practicable to review the operation of this Protocol' (Dodds, 2018; Secretariat of the Antarctic Treaty, 2023). The protocol can be amended by a majority of the parties, including three of the four states that are Antarctic Treaty Consultative Parties at the time of the protocol's adoption (Secretariat of the Antarctic Treaty, 2023). This protocol came into effect in 1998 (seven years after having been signed) with the aim to 'enhance protection of the Antarctic environment and dependent and associated ecosystems' (Dodds, 2018; Secretariat of the Antarctic Treaty, 2023). Article 7 of the protocol stipulates that 'any activity relating to mineral resources, other than scientific research, shall be prohibited' (Dodds, 2018; Secretariat of the Antarctic Treaty, 2023). Thus, it clearly states that the resources of the Antarctic, whatever they are (e.g., minerals),[35] must not be touched, at least for now (Dodds, 2018). The amendment of the protocol could have geopolitical implications because several states could claim territories in the Antarctic, making mining possible with serious environmental implications. Thus, the geopolitical situation and environmental challenges could become similar to those in the Arctic. Also, states from South Asia like China, India, and South Korea, are involved in both Arctic and Antarctic affairs. They are AC observers and parties to the ATS. Their increased engagement in the Arctic and the Antarctic over the last few decades can be explained both with the geopolitical rise of Asia in the international system and the global increasing need for food and natural resources. Indeed, it is estimated that in the future there will be a shortage of food, commodities, energy/oil, water, and clean environment and that climate change will aggravate these problems (Chaturvedi, 2014).

35 It is estimated that the Antarctic contains minerals like manganese nodules, geothermal energy, coal, petroleum, and natural gas. Water and fish are other important resources of the Antarctic (Wright and Williams, 1974; Britannica, 2023).

The Arctic is more different from the Antarctic than from the Third Pole although many differences can be identified also in this case, of course. An important difference is a geographical one as the Arctic and the Antarctic are at high latitudes while the Third Pole is at a high altitude (Marsden, 2016). The Third Pole encompasses the Tibetan Plateau and surrounding areas including the Pamir-Hindu Kush Mountain ranges in the west, the Hengduan mountains in the east, the Tienshan and Qilian mountains in the north, and the Himalayas in the south (UNEP, 2022). The states involved are Afghanistan, Bangladesh, Bhutan, Cambodia, China, India, Kazakhstan, Kyrgyzstan, Laos, Myanmar, Nepal, Pakistan, Tajikistan, Thailand, Uzbekistan, and Vietnam (The Third Pole, 2023). It is very sensitive to climate change and is considered the place to observe for early warning signs of global warming (World Meteorological Organization, 2020). It contains the largest ice mass outside the polar regions and after them it offers the largest freshwater resources sustaining more than ten major river systems and approximately 2 billion people in Southern Asia (UNEP, 2022; Europe Asia Foundation, 2023). Water, most of which is in frozen form (glaciers, snow, permafrost, rivers and lake ice), is essential for the survival of humans, livestock, and wildlife as well as agriculture and energy generation (Europe Asia Foundation, 2023). The presence of transboundary watercourses is an important similarity between the Arctic and the Third Pole as well as national territory and the presence of a human population (approximately 4 million in the Arctic and 2 billion in the Third Pole) that is instead totally absent from the Antarctic (apart from scientists that are only temporarily there). In addition to water, the Third Pole is also rich in water, energy, minerals, and forest and agricultural products (World Meteorological Organization, 2020). Furthermore, the Third Pole's governance is more similar to the Arctic than to the Antarctic because of the presence of organisations guiding and fostering cooperation among states in the region. Nevertheless, none of them covers the whole region like in the case of the AC, as it includes only some of the states of the region. Two examples are the South Asia Cooperative Environment Program (SACEP) and the South Asian Association for Regional Cooperation (SAARC) that have the same members, namely Afghanistan, Bangladesh, Bhutan, India, the Maldives, Nepal, Pakistan, and Sri Lanka (Marsden, 2016; SACEP, 2022; SAARC, 2023). SACEP aims to promote 'regional cooperation in South Asia in the field of environment, both natural and human in the context of sustainable development' (SACEP, 2022) while SAARC aims to promote the welfare of the peoples of South Asia and their quality of life while also accelerating economic growth, social progress, and cultural development in the region (SAARC, 2023). Thus, the areas of cooperation of SAARC and SACEP overlap with the AC with a focus on environmental protection in general, water management, energy development, climate change, and sustainable development more generally (Marsden, 2016). Nevertheless, the status of SAARC and SACEP are different from that of the AC the SAARC is an association while SACEP is an intergovernmental organisation. Additionally, another difference with the AC is of a geopolitical nature as the 'Third Pole regime must contend with the interests of states traditionally in conflict for land and resources; these include India and Pakistan, and India and China, where boundary disputes are a continuing issue' (Marsden, 2016). Moreover, it is worth noting the presence of China and India, included in the Arctic and Antarctic geopolitical system as well, and the fact that the EU has an observer status in the SAARC and an ad hoc observer status in the AC, as will be discussed in Chapter 2.

Therefore, the Arctic, the Antarctic, and the Third Pole are three different geopolitical systems, each with its own peculiarities. In spite of this, the Arctic has more similarities with the Third Pole than with the Antarctic.

Conclusion

The Arctic has emerged as a geopolitically and economically important region only during the last few decades as a consequence of the new economic opportunities opened up by ice-melting due to climate change. Nevertheless, while during the Cold War the region had a military value for the two superpowers, this dimension was reduced with the collapse of the Soviet Union. The consequent relaxation of relations among states in the region led them to strengthen their links by cooperating in a number of sectors through the establishment of intergovernmental forums such as the AC, the BEAC, and the BRC. Cooperation, which is the keyword to understanding geopolitics in the Arctic in this period, is strictly linked to the so-called concept of 'Arctic exceptionalism'. Nevertheless, the analysis has shown that while it is undoubtably a case of successful cooperation, the High North is not exceptional because it is not detached from the rest of the world. By contrast, the Arctic is a reflection of the international order. In fact, cooperation in the region flourished immediately after the end of the Cold War when relations among states radically changed. In this context, Gorbachev's foreign policy, which was based on the so-called 'New Thinking', played a key role as it aimed to improve East–West relations. Therefore, Gorbachev's Murmansk Speech, specifically concerning the Arctic, can be fully understood only if it is considered in relation to his foreign policy aims. Since then, the eight Arctic states have created a well-functioning cooperation system through the establishment of the AC, which can be considered as one of the most important products of the new geopolitical situation brought about by the end of the Cold War. Since the 2000s, the AC has been working not only on environmental protection, which is the issue on which cooperation in the region was established, but also on climate change. This latter issue is a problem that can only be faced globally because it is global in character. Climate change has had an enormous geopolitical impact on the region because it is making natural resources and transportation routes increasingly accessible. This is why it has been attracting a growing number of international actors interested in being involved in Arctic affairs: they want to take advantage of these new economic opportunities. A good example is the EU that has adopted four Arctic policies since 2008, increasing its presence in the region over time. The EU has taken the opportunity to study the impact of climate change on the region as a way to get more involved in Arctic affairs.

Furthermore, this chapter has extended the meaning of the term 'exceptionalism' by using it in general terms in order to compare the Arctic with the Antarctic and the Third Pole. The discussion demonstrates that the Arctic is not exceptional in comparison with the other two regions and that each of them has its own peculiarities. Additionally, an interesting result is the fact that the High North can be considered more similar to the Third Pole than to the Antarctic from a governance perspective in spite of the deep geopolitical differences among them.

References

Alfred Wegener Institute. (2020). *MOSAIC*. Available at: https://mosaic-expedition.org/ (accessed 25 February 2024).

Althingi. (2011). *A Parliamentary Resolution on Iceland's Arctic Policy*. Available at: https://www.government.is/media/utanrikisraduneyti-media/media/nordurlandaskrifstofa/A-Parliamentary-Resolution-on-ICE-Arctic-Policy-approved-by-Althingi.pdf (accessed 3 February 2024).

AMAP. (1998). *AMAP Assessment Report: Arctic Pollution Issues*. Available at: https://www.amap.no/documents/download/100/inline (accessed 8 September 2023).

AMAP. (2022). *An EU Initiative to Support International Policy to Reduce Black Carbon*. Available at: https://eua-bca.amap.no/ (accessed 30 March 2024).

Araldsen, O.P. (1967). *The Soviet Union and the Arctic*. Available at: https://www.usni.org/magazines/proceedings/1967/june/soviet-union-and-arctic (accessed 26 March 2024).

Archer, C. (1990). Arctic Cooperation: A Nordic Model. *Bulletin of Peace Proposals*, 21(2): 165–174.

Arctic Council. (2005). *Arctic Climate Impact* Assessment (ACIA). New York: Cambridge University Press.

Arctic Council. (2023). *Organization*. Available at: https://arctic-council.org/about/states/ (accessed 30 July 2023).

Arctic Council. (2023a). *Addressing Arctic Pollution*. Available at: https://arctic-council.org/explore/topics/pollutants/ (accessed 4 September 2023).

Arctic Council. (2023b). *The Arctic in a Changing Climate*. Available at: https://arctic-council.org/explore/topics/climate/#:~:text=The%20temperatures%20in%20the%20Arctic,and%20the%20global%20climate%20system. (accessed 9 September 2023).

Arctic Council. (2023c). *Celebrating 25 Years of Arctic Cooperation*. Available at: https://arctic-council.org/news/arctic-council-celebrates-25-years-of-arctic-cooperation/#:~:text=Three%20legally%20binding%20agreements%20were,and%20the%202017%20%E2%80%9CAgreement%20on (accessed 5 October 2023).

Arctic Council. (2023d). *How We Work*. Available at: https://arctic-council.org/explore/work/ (accessed 10 October 2023).

Arctic Council. (2023e). *About the Arctic Council*. Available at: https://arctic-council.org/about/ (accessed 12 October 2023).

Arctic Portal. (2021). *The Ilulissat Declaration*. Available at: chrome-extension://efaidnbmnnnibpcajpcglclefindmkaj/https://arcticportal.org/images/stories/pdf/Ilulissat-declaration.pdf (accessed 24 January 2024).

Åtland, K. (2008). Mikhail Gorbachev, the Murmansk Initiative, and the Desecuritisation of Interstate Relations in the Arctic. *Cooperation and Conflict*, 43(3): 289–311.

Axerold, R., Keohane, Robert. (1985). Achieving Cooperation Under Anarchy. Strategies and Institutions. World Politics, 38(1), 226-254.

Axworthy, T. (2012). A Proposal for an Arctic Nuclear-Weapon-Free Zone. *Yearbook of Polar Law*, 4(1): 87–139.

BEAC. (2024a). *Members of the Barents Euro-Arctic Council and the Barents Regional Council*. Available at https://barents-council.org/barents-euro-arctic-council/members-of-the-beac-and-the-brc (accessed 21 January 2024).

BEAC. (2024b). *Cooperation in the Barents Euro-Arctic Region.* Available at: https://barents-council.org/about-us/cooperation-in-the-barents-euro-arctic-region (accessed 25 January 2024).
BEAC. (2024c). *Project Finding.* Available at: https://barents-council.org/working-groups/project-funding#:~:text=EUR%201%20million%20(total%20budget). (accessed 25 January 2024).
Bloom, E. (1999). Establishment of the Arctic Council. *American Journal of International Law*, 93(3): 712–722.
Boulègue, M. (2019). *Russia's Military Posture in the Arctic. Managing Hard Power in a 'Low Tension' Environment. Russia Eurasia Programme.* Research Paper, Chatham House.
Brady, A. M. (ed.) (2014). *The Emerging Politics of Antarctica.* London and New York: Routledge.
Britannica. (2023). *Economic Resources.* Available at: https://www.britannica.com/place/Antarctica/Discovery-of-the-Antarctic-poles (accessed 12 October, 2023).
Brodetsky, V. (1988). Alternative for the Arctic. (Interview with Major General Yuri Lebedev, spokesman for the General Staff of the Armed Forces of the USSR). *Moscow News*, 17 January.
BSEC. (2023). *Member States.* Available at: https://www.bsec-organization.org/member-states (accessed 14 December 2023).
Burke, D. C. (2019). *Diplomacy and the Arctic Council.* Montreal: McGill-Queen's University Press.
Butler, W. E. (1978). *International Straits of the World: Northeast Arctic Passage.* Alphen aan den Rijn: Sijthoff & Noordhoff.
CBD. (2000). *Convention on Biological Diversity.* UNEP. Available at: chrome-extension://efaidnbmnnnibpcajpcglclefindmkaj/https://www.cbd.int/doc/publications/cbd-sustain-en.pdf (accessed 31 March 2024).
CBSS. (2023). *About Us.* Available at: https://cbss.org/about-us/ (accessed 14 December 2023).
Center for European Studies. (2024). *Chapter 4. What is the European Union.* Available at: https://europe.unc.edu/toolkits/chapter-3/#:~:text=The%20EU%20is%20what%20is,areas%20to%20the%20higher%20organization. (accessed 13 December 2024).
Center for Strategic and International Studies. (2021). *RSD-10 Pioneer (SS-20).* Available at: https://missilethreat.csis.org/missile/ss-20-saber-rsd-10/ (accessed 1 August 2023).
Chaturvedi, S. (2014). India and Antarctica. Towards Post-Colonial Engagement? In Brady, A. M. (ed.) *The Emerging Politics of Antarctica.* London and New York: Routledge.
Clifford, R. (2016). *How Has Cooperation in the Arctic Survived Western-Russian Geopolitical Tension?.* Available at: https://polarconnection.org/cooperation-arctic/ (accessed 12 October 2023).
Conde, E., Sánchez, S. I. (2017). *Global Challenges in the Arctic Region.* London and New York: Routledge.
Correll, J. (2020). The Euromissile Showdown. *Air and Space Forces Magazine.* Available at: https://www.airandspaceforces.com/article/the-euromissile-showdown/#:~:text=Deployment%20of%20the%20Soviet%20SS,medium%2Drange%20%E2%80%9CEuromissiles.%E2%80%9D (accessed 1 August 2023).
Council of the European Union. (2003). *European Security Strategy. A Secure Europe in a Better World.* Brussels: General Secretariat of the Council.
Council of the European Union. (2010). *Joint Statement on the Partnership for Modernisation EU-Russia Summit 31 May-1 June 2010.* Available at: chrome-extension://efaidnbmnnnibpcajpcglclefindmkaj/https://www.consilium.europa.eu/uedocs/cms_data/docs/pressdata/en/er/114747.pdf (accessed 31 March 2024).
Council of the European Union. (2024). *European Green Deal.* Available at: https://www.consilium.europa.eu/en/policies/green-deal/ (accessed 21 March 2024).

Danish Parliament. (2021). *Greenland and the Faroe Islands*. Available at: https://www.thedanishparliament.dk/en/eu-information-centre/greenland-and-the-faroe-islands (accessed 27 March 2024).

Digges, C. (2021). Russia Launches Mission to the Sunken Komsomolets Nuclear Submarine. *Bellona*. Available at: https://bellona.org/news/nuclear-issues/2021-05-russia-launches-mission-to-the-sunken-komsomolets-nuclear-submarine (accessed 3 September 2023).

Dodds, K. (2013). The Ilulissat Declaration (2008): The Arctic States, "Law of the Sea", and Arctic Ocean. *SAIS Review of International Affairs*, 33(2): 45–55.

Dodds, K. (2018). In 30 Years the Antarctic Treaty Becomes Modifiable, and the Fate of a Continent Could Hang in the Balance. *The Conversation*. Available at: https://theconversation.com/in-30-years-the-antarctic-treaty-becomes-modifiable-and-the-fate-of-a-continent-could-hang-in-the-balance-98654 (accessed 12 October 2023).

Dupuy, P. M., Vinuales, J. (2019). *International Environmental Law*. Cornwell: Cambridge University Press.

EEAS. (2023). *EU-Canada Relations*. Available at: https://www.eeas.europa.eu/eeas/eu-canada-relations_en#:~:text=The%20European%20Union%20(EU)%20and,and%20free%20and%20fair%20trade. (accessed 27 March 2024).

EFTA. (2023). *How EU Law Becomes EEA Law*. Available at: https://www.efta.int/eealaw (accessed 23 March 2024).

EFTA. (2024). *History*. Available at: https://www.efta.int/about-efta/european-free-trade-association/history (accessed 26 March 2024).

Elenius, L. (2015). *The Barents Region*. Pax Forlag: Oslo.

Elferink, A. G. (1992). Environmental Protection in the Arctic-the Rovaniemi Process. *Marine Pollution Bulletin*, 24(3): 128–130.

Elferink, A. G. (1996a). The Law and Politics of the Maritime Boundary Delimitation of the Russian Federation, Part II. *The International Journal of Marine and Coastal Law*, 11(1): 5–35.

Elferink, A. G. (1996b). The Law and Politics of the Maritime Boundary Delimitation of the Russian Federation, Part I. *The International Journal of Marine and Coastal Law*, 10(4): 525–561.

Eur-Lex. (2012). *Consolidated Version of the Treaty on European Union - TITLE I COMMON PROVISIONS - Article 4*. Available at: https://eur-lex.europa.eu/legal-content/EN/TXT/?uri=CELEX%3A12012M004 (accessed 14 March 2024).

Eur-Lex. (2022). *Division of Competences within the European Union*. Available at: https://eur-lex.europa.eu/EN/legal-content/summary/division-of-competences-within-the-european-union.html (accessed February 23, 2024).

Europe Asia Foundation. (2023). *The Third Pole: How Is Climate Change affecting Himalayas and the Tibetan Plateau?*. Available at: https://europeasiafoundation.org/insights/the-third-pole-how-is-climate-change-affecting-himalayas-and-the-tibetan-plateau (accessed 15 October 2023).

European Commission. (2008). *Communication from the Commission to the European Parliament and the Council. The European Union and the Arctic Region*. COM(2008) 763 Final, Brussels.

European Commission. (2012). *Joint Communication to the European Parliament and the Council. Developing a European Union Policy towards the Arctic Region: Progress since 2008 and Next Steps*. JOIN(2012) 19 Final, Brussels.

European Commission. (2016). *Joint Communication to the European Parliament and the Council. An integrated European Union Policy for the Arctic Region*. JOIN(2012) 19 Final, Brussels.

European Commission. (2021a). *Communication to the European Parliament, the Council, the European Economic and Social Committee and the Committee of the Regions on a New Approach for a Sustainable Bleu Economy in the EU Transforming the EU's Blue Economy for a Sustainable Future*. COM(2021)240 final.

European Commission. (2021b). *European Green Deal: Developing a Sustainable Blue Economy in the European Union.* Press release. Available at: https://ec.europa.eu/commission/presscorner/detail/en/ip_21_2341 (accessed 28 February 2024).

European Commission. (2021c). *The EU Blue Economy Report 2021.* Luxemburg: Publications Office of the European Union.

European Commission. (2021d). *Questions and Answers on the EU's Arctic Strategy.* Available at: https://ec.europa.eu/commission/presscorner/detail/en/qanda_21_5164 (accessed 3 March 2024).

European Commission. (2021e). *Joint Communication to the European Parliament, the Council, the European Economic and Social Committee and the Committee of the Regions. A Stronger EU Engagement for a Peaceful, Sustainable and Prosperous Arctic.* JOIN(2021) 27 Final, Brussels.

European Commission. (2021f). *Partnership Instrument for Cooperation with Third Countries.* Available at: https://ec.europa.eu/info/sites/default/files/about_the_european_commission/eu_budget/db_2021_programme_statement_partnership_instrument_for_cooperation_with_third_countries_pi.pdf (accessed 30 March 2024).

European Commission. (2022). *Arctic Biodiversity: EU-funded Research Reveals New Life in the Arctic Ocean.* Available at: https://oceans-and-fisheries.ec.europa.eu/news/arctic-biodiversity-eu-funded-research-reveals-new-life-arctic-ocean-2022-02-21_en (accessed 25 February 2024).

European Commission. (2024). *The European Green Deal.* Available at: https://commission.europa.eu/strategy-and-policy/priorities-2019-2024/european-green-deal_en (accessed 24 February 2024).

European Commission. (no date). *Global Climate Action.* Available at: https://climate.ec.europa.eu/eu-action/international-action-climate-change/global-climate-action_en (accessed 28 February 2024).

European Parliament. (2023). *Transatlantic Relations: The US and Canada.* Available at: https://www.europarl.europa.eu/factsheets/en/sheet/174/transatlantic-relations-the-us-and-canada (accessed 30 March 2024).

European Parliament. (2024). *Recommendation on the Draft Council Decision on the Conclusion, on Behalf of the European Union, of the Agreement under the United Nations Convention on the Law of the Sea on the Conservation and Sustainable Use of Marine Biological Diversity of Areas Beyond National Jurisdiction.* A9-0177/2024. Available at: https://www.europarl.europa.eu/doceo/document/A-9-2024-0177_EN.html (accessed 31 March, 2024).

Exner-Pirot, H (2012). How Gorbachev Shaped Future Arctic Policy 25 Years Ago. *Anchorage Daily News.* Available at: https://www.adn.com/arctic/article/how-gorbachev-shaped-future-arctic-policy-25-years-ago/2012/10/01/ (accessed 21 July 2023).

Garthoff, R. (1985). *Détente and Confrontation. American-Soviet Relations from Nixon to Reagan.* Washington: The Brookings Institution.

Gorbachev, M. (1987). *Mikhail Gorbachev's Speech in Murmansk at the Ceremonial Meeting on the Occasion of the Presentation of the Order of Lenin and the Gold Star to the City of Murmansk.* https://www.barentsinfo.fi/docs/Gorbachev_speech.pdf (accessed 24 June 2023)

Gregor, R. (1967). Lenin, Revolution, and Foreign Policy. *International Journal*, 22(4): 563–575.

Grieco, J. (1988). Anarchy and the Limits of Cooperation: A Realist Critique of the Newest Liberal Institutionalism. *International Organisation* 42(3): 485–507.

Gwertzman, B. (1982). U.S. Will not Sign Sea Law Treaty. *The New York Times,* July 1982. https://www.nytimes.com/1982/07/10/world/us-will-not-sign-sea-law-treaty.html

Hayward, D. (1988). Gorbachev's Murmansk Initiative: New Prospects for Arms Control in the Arctic?. *Northern Perspectives*, 16(9): 15–36.

Heininen, L., Exner-Pirot, H., Plouffe, J. (2013). *From Regional Transition to Global Change: Dualism in the Arctic*. Arctic Yearbook.
Hewig, N. (2022). *The EU's Strategic Multilateralism. Global Engagement in an Era of Great-Power Competition*. Helsinki: Finnish Institute of International Affairs.
Hosa, J. (2018). *Strategy on Ice: Has Russia Already Won the Scramble for the Arctic?*. European Council of Foreign Relations. Available at: https://ecfr.eu/article/commentary_strategy_on_ice_has_russia_already_won_the_scramble_for_the_arct/ (accessed 18 January 2024).
Hossain, K. (2015). EU Engagement in the Arctic: Do the Policy Responses from the Arctic States Recognise the EU as a legitimate Stakeholder?. *Arctic Review on Law and Politics*, 6(2): 89–110.
Hovi, J., Sprintz, D. F., Bang, G. (2010). Why the United States did not become a party to the Kyoto Protocol: German, Norwegian, and US perspectives. *European Journal of International Relations*, 18(1): 129–150.
IASC. (2019). *Arctic Science Agreement*. Available at: https://iasc.info/cooperations/arctic-science-agreement (accessed 3 October 2023).
IASC. (no date). *IASC History*. Available at: https://iasc.info/about (accessed 26 June 2023).
Icelandic Parliament. (2011). *A Parliamentary Resolution on Iceland's Arctic Policy*. Available at: https://www.government.is/media/utanrikisraduneyti-media/media/nordurlandaskrifstofa/A-Parliamentary-Resolu tion-on-ICE-Arctic-Policy-approved-by-Althingi.pdf (accessed 16 January 2024).
Ikenberry, J. (2010). The Restructuring of the International System after the Cold War. In Leffleer, M., Westad, O. (eds).*The Cambridge History of the Cold War, The Cold War*, vol. III. Cambridge: Cambridge University Press.
Ikeshima, T. (2019). Geopolitical Dynamics in the Arctic: Arctic and Global Interests. In Conde, E., Sanchez, I. (eds.) *Global Challenges in the Arctic Region*. New York: Routledge.
Ingimundarson, V. (2015). Framing the National Interest: The Political Uses of the Arctic in Iceland's Foreign and National Policies. *Polar Journal*, 5(1): 82–100. Available at: https://doi.org/10.1080/2154896X.2015.1025492 (accessed 16 January 2024).
Jervis, R. (1999). Realism, Neoliberalism, and Cooperation: Understanding the Debate. *International Security*, 24(1): 42–63.
Käpylä, J., Mikkola, H (2015). *On Arctic Exceptionalism. Critical Reflections in the Light of the Arctic Sunrise Case and the Crisis in Ukraine*. FIIA Working Paper.
Keohane, R., Nye, J. (2012). *Power and Interdependence*. London: Longman.
Keohane, R. (1989). International Institutions and State Power. Essays in International Relations Theory. London. Routledge.
Keskitalo, C. (2007). International Region-Building: Development of the Arctic as an International Region. *Cooperation and Conflict: Journal of the Nordic International Studies Association*, 42(2): 187–205.
Koivurova, T. (2014). *Increasing Relevance of Treaties: The Case of the Arctic. AIJL Unbound 108*. Cambridge University Press.
Koivurova, T., Hasanat, M. W. (2009). The Climate Policy of the Arctic Council. In Koivurova, T., Keskitalo, C., Bankes, N. (eds.) *Climate Governance in the Arctic*. Dordrecht: Springer, pp. 51–75.
Koivurova, T., Hoel, H., Humpert, A., Kirchner, M., Raspotnik, S., Śmieszek Małgorzata, A., Stępień, A. (2019). *Overview of EU Actions in the Arctic and Their Impact. Final Report*. Poland: European Commission.
Lalonde, S. (2019). The Northwest Passage and Northern Sea Route. In Conde, E., Sànchez, I. (2019). Global Challenges in the Arctic Region. Sovereignty, environment and geopolitical balance. London> Routledge.
Langrind, P. (1990). An Overview of Environmental Law in the USSR (Practicing Law and Doing Business in the Soviet Union). *NYLS Journal of International and Comparative Law*, 11(3): 482–498.

Lanteigne, M. (2020). Inside, Outside, Upside Down? Non-Arctic States in Emerging Arctic Security Discourses. In Spohr, K., Hamilton, D. (eds.) *The Arctic and World Oder*. Washington: Johns Hopkins University, pp. 379–404.

Laruelle, M. (2014). *Russia's Arctic Strategies and the Future of the Far North*. New York: Routledge.

Le Mière, C., Mazo, J. (2013). *Arctic Opening Insecurity and Opportunity*. London: Routledge.

Livernois, J. (2009). The Economics of Ending Canada's Commercial Harp Seal Hunt. *Marine Policy,* 34: 42–53.

Łuszczuk, M., Szkarlat, M. (2022). The International Arctic Science Committee (IASC) in the Changing Arctic. Between International Scientific Cooperation and Science Diplomacy. In Sellheim, D., Menezes, R. (eds.) *Non-State Actors in the Arctic Region*. Cham: Springer.

Luzin, G., Pretes, M., Vasiliev, V. (1994). The Kola Peninsula: Geography, History and Resources. *Arctic*, 47(1): 1–15.

Marland, L. (2015). *Savage Beauty: The Arctic Sublime*. Available at: https://medium.com/@lauramarland/the-arctic-sublime-89c964d13d1 (accessed 7 October 2023).

Marsden, S. (2016). *From the High North to the Roof of the World: Arctic Precedents for Third Pole Governance*. The Yearbook of Polar Law, pp. 56–75.

Mearsheimer, J. (1994). The False Promise of International Institutions. *International Security,* 19(3): 1–27.

Mearsheimer, J. (2002). *Realism, the Real World and the Academy*. Realism and Institutionalism.

Milner, H., Moracvsik, A. (2009). Power, Interdependence, and Non-State Actors in World Politics. Princeton. Princeton University Press.

Ministry of Foreign Affairs of Finland. (2009). *Northern Dimension.* Available at: chrome-extension://efaidnbmnnnibpcajpcglclefindmkaj/https://www.europarl.europa.eu/meetdocs/2009_2014/documents/deea/dv/0209_/0209_05.pdf (accessed 30 March 2024).

Ministry of Foreign Affairs of the Russian Federation. (2010). *The Arctic Ocean Foreign Ministers' Meeting, Chelsea, Canada.* Available at: https://www.mid.ru/en/sovet-gosudaW[srstv-barenceva/evroarkticeskogo-regiona-sber-/-/asset_publisher/0vP3hQoCPRg5/content/id/257162 (accessed 16 February 2024).

Murkowski, L. (2021). Can the Arctic's Unique Distinction as a Zone of Peace Be Maintained? "The Arctic Senator" Explains What It Will Take. *The Foreign Service Journal*. Available at: https://afsa.org/arctic-exceptionalism (accessed 30 July 2023).

NASA. (2023). *Arctic and Antarctic Sea Ice: How Are They Different?* NASA. Available at: https://climate.nasa.gov/explore/ask-nasa-climate/2861/arctic-and-antarctic-sea-ice-how-are-they-different/ (accessed 12 October 2023).

NATO Parliamentary Assembly. (2017). *What Happens in the Arctic, Does Not Stay in the Arctic" - Climate Change in the Arctic Will Have Global Consequences and Cannot Be Ignored.* Available at: https://www.nato-pa.int/news/what-happens-arctic-does-not-stay-arctic-climate-change-arctic-will-have-global-consequences (accessed 21 February 2024).`

Natural Resources Defense Council. (2023). *Paris Climate Agreement: Everything You Need to Know.* Available at: https://www.nrdc.org/stories/paris-climate-agreement-everything-you-need-know#sec-whatis (accessed 21 February 2024).

NORR. (2023). *Exxon Valdez*. Available at: https://darrp.noaa.gov/oil-spills/exxon-valdez (accessed 3 September 2023).

Northern Forum Secretariat. (no date). *Members*. Available at: https://www.northernforum.org/en/members (accessed 31 July 2023).

Norwegian Ministries. (2020). *The Norwegian Government's Arctic Policy. People, Opportunities and Norwegian Interests in the Arctic*. Oslo: Ministry of Foreign Affairs,

Ministry of Local Government and Regional Development, Ministry of Trade, Industry and Fisheries, Office of the Prime Minister. Available at: https://www.regjeringen.no/en/dokumenter/arctic_policy/id2830120/ (accessed 15 January, 2024).

Nye, J. (2008). Public Diplomacy and Soft Power. *Annals, AAPSS,* 616: 94–109.

OSPAR. (2024). *OSPAR Commission.* Available at: https://www.ospar.org/about (accessed 31 March 2024).

Özpek, B. B. (2013). Securing Energy or Energising Security: The Impact of Russia's Energy Policy on Turkey's Accession to the European Union. *Journal of International Relations and Development,* 16: 358–379.

Pahuja, S. (2012). Conserving the World's Resources?. In Crawford, J., Koskenniemi, M. (eds.) *The Cambridge Companion to International Law.* Cambridge: Cambridge University Press, pp. 398–420.

Papanicolopulu, I. (2018). The Land Dominates the Sea (Dominates the Land Dominates the Sea). *Questions of International Law Journal,* 47: 39–48.

Polar Bear Range States. (2024). *The 1973 Agreement on the Conservation of Polar Bears.* Available at: https://polarbearagreement.org/about-us/1973-agreement (accessed 12 February 2024).

Purver, R. (1989). Arctic Security. The Murmansk Initiative. In Purver, R. (ed.) Soviet Foreign Policy. New Dynamics, New Themes. New York. St. Martin's press, pp. 182-203.

Remy, C. E. (1992). U.S. Territorial Sea Extension: Jurisdiction and International Environmental Protection. *Fordham International Law Journal,* 16(4): 1208–1252.

Rey, M. P. (2004). 'Europe Is our Common Home': A Study of Gorbachev's Diplomatic Concept. *Cold War History*, 4(2): 33–65.

Robinson, N A., Waxmonsky, G. R. (1988). The U.S.-U.S.S.R. Agreement to Protect the Environment: 15 Years of Cooperation. *Environmental Law*, 18(3): 403–448.

Rossi, C. (2017). *Sovereignty and Territorial Temptation. The Grotian Tendency.* Cambridge: Cambridge University Press.

SAARC. (2023). *About SAARC.* Available at: https://www.saarc-sec.org/index.php/about-saarc/about-saarc (accessed 15 October).

SACEP. (2022). *SACEP Member Countries.* Available at: http://www.sacep.org/ (accessed 15 October).

Sasgen, P. (2009). *Stalking the Red Bear: The True Story of a US Cold War Submarine's Covert Operations Against the Soviet Union.* New York: St Martin's Press.

Scientific Committee on Antarctic Research. (2020). *The Antarctic Treaty System.* Available at: https://www.scar.org/policy/antarctic-treaty-system/ (accessed 14 October 2023).

Secretariat of the Antarctic Treaty. (2023a). *Parties.* Available at: https://www.ats.aq/devAS/Parties?lang=e (accessed 12 October 2023).

Secretariat of the Antarctic Treaty. (2023b). *The Antarctic Treaty.* Available at: https://www.ats.aq/e/antarctictreaty.html (accessed 12 October 2023).

Smieszek, M. (2022). What Effects Has the Ukraine war Had on the Arctic Council?. *High North News*, 30 March 2023. Available at: https://www.highnorthnews.com/en/what-effects-has-ukraine-war-had-arctic-council (accessed 10 October 2023).

Stein, A. (2008). Neoliberal Institutionalism. In Reus-Smit C., Snidal, D. (eds.) *The Oxford Handbook on International Relations*. New York: Oxford University Press.

Steinveg, B. (2022). Arctic Conferences as Arenas for Power Games and Collaboration in International Relations. *The Polar Journal*, 12(2): 240–260.

Steinveg, B., Vigeland Rottem, S., Andreeva, S. (2023). Soft Institutions in Arctic Governance – Who Does What?. *Polar Record*, 60(1): 1–7.

Stenlund, P. (2002). Lessons in Regional Cooperation from the Arctic. *Ocean & Coastal Management*, 45(11): 835–839.

Swedish Polar Research Secretariat. (2023). *Icebreaker Oden.* Available at: https://www.polar.se/en/research-support/icebreaker-oden/ (accessed 27 February 2024).

The Third Pole. (2023). *Countries*. Available at: https://www.thethirdpole.net/en/countries/ (accessed 15 October, 2023).
Tynkkynen, V., Tynkkynen, N. (2018). Climate Denial Revisited: (Re)contextualising Russian Public Discourse on Climate Change during Putin 2.0. *Europe-Asia Studies*, 70(7): 1103–1120.
Tynkkynen, N. (2010). A Great Ecological Power in Global Climate Policy? Framing Climate Change as a Policy Problem in Russian Public Discussion. Environmental Politics, 19(2), 179-195.
UArctic. (no date). *Members*. Available at https://www.uarctic.org/members/member-profiles/ (accessed 31 July 2023).
UN. (1989). *USSR and Canada Agreement Concerning the Prevention of Incidents at Sea Beyond the Territorial Sea*. Available at https://treaties.un.org/doc/Publication/UNTS/Volume%201568/volume-1568-I-27323-English.pdf (accessed 16th July 2023).
UN. (2024). *United Nations Convention on the Law of the Sea. Agreement under the United Nations Convention on the Law of the Sea on the Conservation and Sustainable Use of Marine Biological Diversity of Areas Beyond National Jurisdiction*. Available at: https://www.un.org/depts/los/bbnj.htm (accessed 30 March 2024).
UN. (no date). *About ICAO*. Available at: https://www.icao.int/about-icao/Pages/default.aspx (accessed 9 October 2023).
UNEP. (2022). *A Scientific Assessment of the Third Pole Environment*. Available at: https://www.unep.org/resources/report/scientific-assessment-third-pole-environment (accessed 12 October 2023).
United Nations. (no date-a). *What Is the United Nations Framework Convention on Climate Change?*. Available at: https://unfccc.int/process-and-meetings/what-is-the-united-nations-framework-convention-on-climate-change (accessed 19 February 2024).
United Nations. (no date-b). *What Is the Kyoto Protocol?*. Available at: https://unfccc.int/kyoto_protocol (accessed 21 February 2024).
United Nations. (no date-c). *The Paris Agreement*. Available at: https://unfccc.int/process-and-meetings/the-paris-agreement (accessed 21 February, 2024).
United Nations. (no date-d). *Transforming Our World: The 2030 Agenda for Sustainable Development*. Available at: https://sdgs.un.org/2030agenda#:~:text=We%20resolve%2C%20between%20now%20and,protection%20of%20the%20planet%20and (accessed 30 March 2024).
United States Department of State. (no date). *The Cuban Missile Crisis, October 1962*. Available at: https://history.state.gov/milestones/1961-1968/cuban-missile-crisis (accessed 7 July 2023).
US Senate. (1990). Agreement with the Union of Soviet Socialist Republics on the Maritime Boundary. *Treaty Document*: 101st Congress, 2nd session, 101–22.
Van Oudenare, J. (1990). *Understanding Soviet Foreign Policy, McNair Papers 7, National Defense University*. Washington, DC: The Institute for National Strategic Studies, pp. 1–44.
Vartanov, R.V., Roginko, A. Y. (1990). New Dimensions of Soviet Arctic Policy. Views from the Soviet Union. The Annals of the American Academy of Political and Social Science, 512(1), 69-78.
Vigeland Rottem, S. (2013). The Arctic Council and the Search and Rescue Agreement: The Case of Norway. *Polar Record*, 50: 284–292.
Vigeland Rottem, S. (2020). *S The Arctic Council. Between Environmental Protection and Geopolitics*. Singapore: Palgrave MacMillan.
Vigeland Rottem, S., Folkestad Soltvedt, I. (2020). *Arctic Governance. Law and Politics*. London: I.B.Tauris.
Wallander, C. (2001). Lost and Found: Gorbachev's 'New Thinking'. *The Washington Quarterly*, 25(1): 117–129.

Waltz, K. (1979). *Theory of International Politics.* Addison-Wesley Publishing Company: Reading.
Waltz, K. (2000). Structural Realism after the Cold War. *International Security,* 25(1): 5–41.
Waxman, O. (2022). Mikhail Gorbachev Championed 'Glasnost' and 'Perestroika'. Here's How They Changed the World. *Time.* Available at https://time.com/5512665/mikhail-gorbachev-glasnost-perestroika/ (accessed 11th July 2023).
World Meteorological Organization. (2020). Third Pole Climate Warming and Cryosphere System Changes. *Bulletin,* 69(1). Available at: https://public.wmo.int/en/resources/bulletin/third-pole-climate-warming-and-cryosphere-system-changes (accessed 15 October 2023).
Wright, N. A., Williams, P. L. (1974). *Mineral Resources of Antarctica, Geological Survey Circular 705.* Reston: US Department of Interior.
Yeşilbursa, B. K. (2019). Understanding Soviet Foreign Policy (1917–1991). *Journal of International Eastern European Studies,* 1(1): 215–234.
Young, O. (2015). Governing the Arctic. From Cold War Theatre to Mosaic of Cooperation. Global Governance, 11(1), 9-15.

2 The impact of the Ukraine war on the Arctic

Introduction

The year 2014 was a watershed in the history of the Arctic region. Russia's illegal annexation of Crimea had a negative impact on the relations among states in the High North as a reflection of the deterioration of East–West relations at the international level. Later on, the war initiated by Russia against Ukraine on 24th February 2022 further worsened East–West relations leading to a complete halt to cooperation and causing the end of a period characterised by a good neighbourhood.

These events have led many scholars to speak about a 'new' Cold War in the international arena and in the Arctic as well. Robert Legvold, professor emeritus at Columbia University, was the first one to speak about a 'new Cold War' in an article published on Foreign Affairs in 2018, originally published in 2014 (Achcar, 2023, 12). He argued that 'the collapse in relations between Russia and the West does indeed deserve to be called a new Cold War' (Achcar, 2023, 12). According to Gilbert Achcar, professor at the School of Oriental and African Studies of the University of London, in reality, the new Cold War began with the war in Kosovo in 1998–1999, which, after having caused tensions between East and West, was solved with the armed intervention of NATO.[1] By contrast, some other scholars

1 The war in Kosovo saw opposition between ethnic Albanians and ethnic Serbs and the government of Yugoslavia because Slobodan Milošević, then president of the Serbian Republic, decided on the abrogation of Kosovo's constitutional autonomy. Milošević's government and the Serbian minority of Kosovo had always affirmed that Muslim Albanians were in demographic control of an area held sacred by the Serbs. In 1996, the Kosovo Liberation Army (KLA), the ethnic Albanian Kosovar militant group, emerged in the effort to obtain Kosovo's independence from Serbia. After the conflict erupted between the two factions, diplomatic negotiations began in February 1999, but they broke down the following month. In March that year, NATO began a bombing campaign lasting 11 weeks. In response, Yugoslav and Serbian forces drove out all of Kosovo's ethnic Albanians, obliging hundreds of thousands of people to move to Albania, Macedonia (now North Macedonia), and Montenegro. In June, NATO and Yugoslavia signed a peace accord envisaging a troop withdrawal and the return of nearly one million ethnic Albanians. (Britannica, no date).

According to Achcar, the military intervention of NATO caused tensions with Russia, which translated into an 'arm-wrestling' contest between them. For instance, Russian troops seized the airport of Pristina in order to plant their flag in Kosovo before NATO. The Russian troops had come from Bosnia without informing the local NATO command (Achcar, 2023, 119). Russia and NATO disagreed on the future of Kosovo. While NATO (and the EU) wanted to grant it de jure sover-

DOI: 10.4324/9781032633008-3

argue that in reality the 'old' Cold War has never ended. For instance, Rob Huebert argues that 'it is not about an appearance of a new Cold War, it is simply the resurfacing of the "old" Cold War' (Huebert, 2019, 4). Referring to the High North in particular, Huebert argues that the Arctic has never ceased to be a 'critical point of competition' because of geographical proximity, which makes Russia and the US connected by the Arctic region, and because of 'the existing weapon systems', which makes the Arctic 'the best staging location for strikes against each other' (Huebert, 2019, 1).

This study agrees with Huebert's assertion because while 'temporary decreases of the power of either the US or Russia may have the impact of making the region appear less significant', an event or a technological breakthrough may make the tensions between the West and Russia emerge again (Huebert, 2019, 4). For instance, when the Cold War ended, the relations between the US (and the West more broadly) and Russia improved also as a consequence of the diminished power of Russia. Nevertheless, Russia's illegal annexation of Crimea and the war in Ukraine (with a strengthened Russia) made the old rivalry between them emerge again. Additionally, another point is that the Arctic has always 'remained the core region of their [of Russia and the US] ultimate security defence policy for the deployment of their nuclear weapon deterrent' (Huebert, 2019, 4).

In order to analyse the geopolitical changes that occurred in the High North as a consequence of Russia's annexation of Crimea and the war in Ukraine, this chapter is divided into five sections. The first section analyses the impact of these two variables on governance in the region with a focus on the Arctic Council (AC) and the Barents Euro-Arctic Council (BEAC), the two main intergovernmental forums guiding cooperation in the Arctic. The second section investigates the rapprochement between Russia and China as an effect of the deterioration of the relations between Russia and the West. The third section investigates the increased militarisation of the region. The fourth section focuses on scientific cooperation, which is of utmost importance to understand climate change and its effects not only regionally but also globally. While the involvement of the EU in scientific cooperation in the Arctic has been discussed in the previous chapter, this chapter analyses the legal foundations of scientific cooperation, its relevance in the geopolitical and economic strategies of non-Arctic states, and the impact of the war in Ukraine on the scientific sector. Finally, the fifth section analyses the geopolitical situation in the Arctic from the two perspectives of neorealism and neoliberal institutionalism.

eignty, Russia insisted that no decision could be taken without Serbia's consent. Serbia's defeat was considered Russia's defeat as well by many and as one of the darkest chapters of former Russian President Boris Yeltsin's foreign policy (Antonenko, 2007, 7).

Arctic governance revisited

The first issue published immediately after 24th February 2022 by *Limes*,[2] an authoritative Italian journal on geopolitics, was entirely dedicated to the war in Ukraine. This issue was titled 'Russia changes the world' meaning not only that Russia has destroyed the geopolitical equilibrium on which its relations with the West had been based for a long time, since the very last years of the Cold War, with global implications, but also that the invasion of Ukraine was a shock for the entire international community. According to Andrej Kortunov (2022, 35), Director General for the Russian International Affairs Council, 'in the future historians will very probably describe the period between 2014 and 2022 as a break in the evolution of the European geopolitics of the twenty-first century'. He also argues that 'many of the processes and of the tendencies initiated or delineated in 2014 have assumed their definitive shape eight years later' and that this eight-year period has been characterised by a truce during which the West and Russia have been preparing for a new phase of their confrontation (Kortunov, 2022, 35). Russia accelerated the modernisation of its military forces, has diversified its import sources, increased its currency reserves, widened its trade relations with China, and deepened its geopolitical and military cooperation with its partners from the Collective Security Treaty Organization (CSTO)[3] (Kortunov, 2022, 35–36). At the same time, the West strengthened NATO's eastern flank, increased geopolitical coordination within the Alliance and the EU, increased technical-military assistance to Ukraine, and imposed sectoral sanctions[4] on Russia (Kortunov, 2022, 36).

Russia's illegal annexation of Crimea inevitably had consequences at the regional level as well, especially in the sectors affected by Western sanctions (defence, energy, finance). Nevertheless, as the reaction of the West was weaker then than in 2022, Arctic governance was preserved. In fact, the AC continued fulfilling its duties and cooperation was not interrupted although the relations between Russia and the West worsened internationally (Vigeland Rottem, 2020; Clifford,

2 Limes was founded in 1993.

3 The CSTO originates from the conclusion of the Collective Security Treaty, which was signed in Tashkent (Uzbekistan) in 1992 by the heads of Armenia, Kazakhstan, Kyrgyzstan, Russia, Tajikistan, and Uzbekistan. In 1993, Azerbaijan, Belarus, and Georgia joined the organisation. The treaty entered into force upon completion of the national ratification procedures in 1994. The aim of the CSTO is contained in Article 4 stating that 'if one of the States Parties is subjected to aggression by any state or group of states, then this will be considered as aggression against all States Parties to this Treaty'. Article 4 also states that in case of aggression 'all other participating States will provide him with the necessary assistance, including military, and will also provide support at their disposal in exercising the right to collective defense in accordance with Article 51 of the UN Charter' (CSTO, 2024).

4 Sanctions on Russia were directed at three Russian strategic sectors, namely defence, energy, and finance. Defence sector sanctions included an arms embargo, restrictions on exports of dual use (civil and military) goods, and secondary sanctions against third countries purchasing Russian weapons. Energy sector sanctions imposed restrictions on cooperation and the cancellation of joint projects. In the financial sector, sanctions concerned the interdiction of access to Western financing. The EU and the US have been cooperating in order to make sanctions more effective. Since 2014, they have added various other restrictive measures (Russell, 2022, 1).

2016). In this context, the fact that the AC did not deal with hard security played a key role. As Vigeland Rottem argues, if the AC had dealt with security policy issues, it would have happened the same as in the case of cooperation between NATO and Russia (Vigeland Rottem, 2020). Indeed, as a consequence of the Crimea annexation, the Alliance suspended practical cooperation with Russia but decided to keep channels of communication open in the NATO–Russia Council (NRC)[5] and the Euro-Atlantic Partnership Council (EAPC)[6] at the ambassadorial level and above in order to allow the exchange of views, especially on the crisis in Ukraine (NATO, 2023). In this regard, it is interesting to mention a statement made by a Nordic Arctic researcher who suggested that Arctic military discussions could be held within the NRC since the AC members repeatedly argued that talks on this kind of issue could be held elsewhere (Burke, 2019).

Therefore, in spite of the Russian annexation of Crimea, in the High North cooperation with Russia continued at least on the so-called soft power issues (Clifford, 2016). For instance, coastguard cooperation remained untouched as it is vital to the interests of states and is therefore an essential part of their actions in the region especially because access to Arctic waters is increasing (Clifford, 2016). However, instead of increasing cooperation, all efforts within the AC were concentrated on limiting the impact of the crisis in Ukraine on the relations among states in the region and trying to consolidate past achievements (SIPRI, 2015). However, some meetings like the annual meetings of the chiefs of staff of the Arctic states, the only circumpolar platform for discussing security cooperation, were cancelled in 2014 (SIPRI, 2015). Also, important confidence-building measures, such as bilateral and multilateral military exercises, were suspended for an indefinite period of time (SIPRI, 2015).

Cooperation in the Arctic definitely deteriorated when the relations between the West and Russia further worsened because of the war initiated by Russia against Ukraine on the 24th February 2022. Since then, the Arctic became a place where it was extremely difficult to cooperate (Koivurova and Shibata, 2023). This became even more evident since the 3rd March 2022, when seven Arctic states (Canada, Kingdom of Denmark, Finland, Iceland, Norway, Sweden, and the US) announced that they would pause their participation in all meetings in the AC

5 The NRC was established by the Declaration on NATO–Russia Relations: a New Quality at the NATO–Russia Summit in Rome in 2002 (NATO, 2022). It was conceived as 'a mechanism for consultation, consensus-building, cooperation, joint decision, and joint action for the member states of NATO and Russia on a wide spectrum of security issues in the Euro-Atlantic region' within which NATO and Russia would work as equal partners (NATO, 2022). It aimed at advancing relations between NATO and Russia and operated on the principle of consensus (NATO, 2022). The declaration stated that it would be chaired by the Secretary General of NATO and would meet at the level of foreign ministers and defence ministers twice annually, and at the level of heads of state and government when necessary (NATO, 2002).

6 The EAPC, established in 1997, 'is a 50-nation multilateral forum for dialogue and consultation on political and security-related issues among Allies and partner countries'. Its goal is to provide a framework to strengthen the relations between NATO and its partners, facilitating dialogue and exchange of views on current political and security-related issues (NATO, 2023).

(Smieszek, 2022). In their official statement, they affirmed to strongly 'condemn Russia's unprovoked invasion of Ukraine and note the grave impediments to international cooperation, including in the Arctic, that Russia's actions have caused' (Government of Canada, 2022). The pause was intended to be temporary, until the circumstances would improve (Smieszek, 2022). However, in June 2022, when it was clear that the war would continue, the seven states decided to resume the AC work that does not involve Russia's participation (Smieszek, 2022). Russia defined this decision as 'regrettable' and announced that it would refocus the program of its chairmanship (2021–2023)[7] on domestic events and needs in the region (Smieszek, 2022). In May 2023, the chairmanship passed to Norway in the 13th AC meeting held in Salekhard (Russia) and online (Arctic Council, 2023a). During the meeting, the eight members issued a common statement 'recognizing the historic and unique role of the Arctic Council for constructive cooperation, stability and dialogue between people in the Arctic region [...] It further recognizes the rights of Arctic Indigenous Peoples, their special relations to the Arctic and the importance of cross-border and people-to-people cooperation in the region' (Arctic Council, 2023a). Very significantly, the statement stressed the commitment of the AC members 'to work to safeguard and strengthen the Arctic Council' (Arctic Council, 2023a). Morten Høglund, the new Chair of the Senior Arctic Officials (SAO) and Norway's Arctic Ambassador, pointed out that Russia is giving positive signals meaning that it is interested in resuming the work of the AC and this is 'the best basis for movement' (Edvardsen, 2023). In an interview to Russian News Agency TASS, Russia's Arctic ambassador, Nikolay Korchunov said that 'Russia will continue to participate in the Arctic Council's work, like the other countries. We are interested in effective work within this body' (Edvardsen, 2023a). Indeed, the AC resumed the work of its Working Groups (WGs) virtually in particular issue areas and specific projects thanks to the hard work of Morten Høglund (Edvardsen, 2024; Andreeva et al., 2024). He argued that 'the decision to resume virtual working group meetings was the result of productive consultations with all Arctic states and permanent participants that have taken place over the last months' (Edvardsen, 2024). Also, he stated that 'without functioning Working Groups, we don't have an Arctic Council', thus 'allowing working groups to virtually meet and advance their work is critical in meeting that commitment and the responsibility the council has to play a leading role in addressing issues of emerging concern as it relates to environmental protection and sustainable development in the Arctic' (Edvardsen, 2024).

This is a relevant and meaningful achievement considering that Finland's and Sweden's NATO membership has increased tensions in the Arctic. Russia has in fact considered Finland's and Sweden's NATO membership as an aggressive

7 The program of the Russian AC chairmanship focused on promoting collective action on sustainable development through multilateral cooperation in four priority areas, namely people of the Arctic (including indigenous people), environmental protection (including climate change), socioeconomic development, and strengthening of the AC (Arctic Council, 2023f).

move. At a press briefing in February 2024, Russia's Foreign Ministry spokeswoman Maria Zakharova said that Russia would 'closely monitor what Sweden does in the aggressive military bloc, how it will implement its membership in practice' (The Moscow Times, 2024). She also added that Russia's

> military and technical retaliation would depend on the types of NATO weapons and units Sweden deploys, as well as the types of drills and strategies it adopts as a member of the military alliance. Based on that, we'll develop our response policy, as well as military and technical steps, to stop the threats to Russia's national security.
>
> (The Moscow Times, 2024)

Seven out of the eight AC members belong to the Alliance, leaving Russia apart. Finland's and Sweden's NATO membership, acquired in 2023 and 2024, respectively, is one of the major consequences of the war in Ukraine. However, this could be considered the event that has pushed Finland and Sweden to become members of the Alliance, not the real reason behind their decision. The very reason might be their fear of Russia, which has historical roots. Both states applied for NATO membership in March 2022, just three months after the beginning of the war in Ukraine (Moyer, 2024). Additionally, in December 2021 the Russian Ministry of Foreign Affairs wrote down an eight-point draft treaty with a list of security issues that it wanted to be agreed upon with the Alliance (Forsberg and Moyer, 2022). In particular, Article 4 envisages that

> the Russian Federation and all the Parties that were member States of the North Atlantic Treaty Organization as of 27 May 1997, respectively, shall not deploy military forces and weaponry on the territory of any of the other States in Europe in addition to the forces stationed on that territory as of 27 May 1997. With the consent of all the Parties such deployments can take place in exceptional cases to eliminate a threat to security of one or more Parties.
>
> (Ministry for Foreign Affairs of Russia, 2021)

According to Article 6, 'all member States of the North Atlantic Treaty Organization commit themselves to refrain from any further enlargement of NATO, including the accession of Ukraine as well as other States' (Ministry for Foreign Affairs of Russia, 2021). The US responded that this treaty was unrealistic because this would imply the removal of several Eastern European countries from NATO and capitulate to Russia's desire for a greater sphere of influence over its neighbours (Forsberg and Moyer, 2022). As a response, Russia positioned an estimated 100,000 troops along its border with Ukraine and subsequently it invaded its neighbour (Forsberg and Moyer, 2022).

Renewed debates over NATO's Eastern European enlargement ambitions, the potential for further Russian aggression, and uncertainty over Ukraine's future pushed Finland and Sweden to reconsider their non-alignment[8] and their engagement with NATO (Forsberg and Moyer, 2022). This is clear from Finland's and Sweden's official statements. In a speech given at Selwyn College in Cambridge on 16 April 2024, Minister for Foreign Affairs Tobias Billström argued that 'two years ago, Russia launched its full-scale invasion of Ukraine – an irreversible turning point, for Swedish, British, European and global security. Although Sweden's cooperation with NATO began decades earlier, the Swedish membership of NATO is a direct result of Russia's illegal, unprovoked and indefensible war of aggression' (Government of Sweden, 2024a). He also added that 'becoming a NATO member is a paradigm shift in Swedish foreign and security policy, but it is also the natural and final step of a journey Sweden has made in recent decades. Sweden's NATO accession is the culmination of a long farewell to the policy of neutrality and non-alignment' (Government of Sweden, 2024a). In his speech in parliament held on the 1 March 2024, President of the Republic of Finland Sauli Niinistö stated that

> Russia's cruel invasion of Ukraine in the early years of this decade dramatically changed the security situation in the whole of Europe. Finland responded by joining NATO and continued by negotiating the Defence Cooperation Agreement (DCA) with the United States. Even though the agreement is bilateral, it has clear interactions with other similar agreements.
> (President of the Republic of Finland, 2024)

Moreover, another consequence of the war in Ukraine is the fact that for indigenous peoples the paralysis of the AC has meant the loss of their most important platform for multilateral engagement in the region (Andreeva et al., 2024). The AC has indeed always been an important forum for the six permanent participants representing indigenous peoples, which are associated with certain territories, especially because they struggle to have their voice heard at the national level (Andreeva et al., 2024). Indigenous peoples represent about 10-12% of the

8 Finland's and Sweden's neutrality had different characteristics. In Wilhelm Agnell's words, the non-aligned states 'by definition [did] not constitute a homogenous group'. Finland's and Sweden's neutrality had different points of departure. After the Second World War, Finland's territory had been reduced, its land had been partly burned or destroyed, it had lost a huge number of military and civilians, and it had to pay a lot for war reparations to the Soviet Union in terms of goods and money. Sweden was the only Nordic state that had not been involved in the war directly. Its institutions and industry were intact, its populations had been harmed only marginally, and its defence capability was effective. When the Cold War broke out, Sweden had more room for manoeuvre when it decided to stay out of NATO while Finland was forced to stipulate the Friendship, Cooperation, and Mutual Assistance Treaty with the Soviet Union in 1948 (it remained in force until 1992). According to this treaty, Finland and the Soviet Union were obliged to give mutual defence and Finland was forbidden to join any organisation considered hostile to the USSR. Nevertheless, Finland's and Sweden's neutrality was seen with suspicion from both Western and Eastern bloc countries because they were located between the two blocs. After the end of the Cold War, Finland's and Sweden's position changed dramatically, allowing them to join the EU in 1995 while continuing to stay outside of military alliances, although they established a close partnership with NATO (Kramer et al., 2021, 515; Pakkasvirta and Tuominen, 2024).

4 million inhabitants of the Arctic and their largest part amounts to approximately 250,000 people that reside in the Russian Far North (Andreeva et al., 2024). In addition, a high number of men from small indigenous communities in the Russian Arctic have died in Ukraine because Russia has targeted them in its conscription policy (Andreeva et al., 2024). Despite the devastating consequences for their own peoples, the representatives of the Russian Association of Indigenous Peoples of the North, Siberia, and the Far East (RAIPON) have not criticised or protested against the government's policy because RAIPON has been coopted by the Kremlin at least since 2014 and supports Russia's aggression towards Ukraine (Andreeva et al., 2024). However, in March 2022 a group of prominent Russian indigenous activists founded the International Committee of Indigenous Peoples of Russia (ICIPR) that in several open letters condemned the war against Ukraine and called upon international organisations to suspend their recognition of and cooperation with RAIPON (Andreeva et al., 2024). However, ICIPR is an organisation acting from abroad, thus it does not have any influence on developments in Russia (Andreeva et al., 2024).

Furthermore, the case of the BEAC,[9] another forum working on sustainable development, is different from that of the AC. As Russia withdrew from it in 2023, all its members are NATO allies. The website of the Ministry for Foreign Affairs of Russia (2023) reports the official reason for Russia's withdrawal, namely that

> through the fault of the Western members (Denmark, Iceland, Norway, Finland, Sweden, the EU), the Council's activities have been effectively paralysed since March 2022. The Finnish presidency failed to confirm the transfer of the BEAC presidency to Russia, scheduled for October 2023, in violation of the principle of rotation thus disrupting the necessary preparations. [Therefore] under these circumstances, we [the Russians] are compelled to announce the withdrawal of the Russian Federation from the Barents Euro-Arctic Council [and Russia] is convinced that the fleeting political situation, which our northern European neighbours are guided by, does not correspond to the long-term interests of the people of the Arctic region. The responsibility for breaking down the architecture of Barents cooperation rests entirely with our 'partners'.
>
> (Ministry for Foreign Affairs of Russia, 2023)

Although the BEAC plays an important role in fostering cooperation in the High North, the AC remains the most important political forum in the region. As former Norwegian Minister of Foreign Affairs Anniken Huitfeldt has recently stated, 'it is vital that the Arctic Council maintains its role as the most important multilateral

9 The BEAC is one of two structures established in 1993 to foster cooperation in the Barents Region (a sub-Arctic region). Its members are Denmark, Finland, Iceland, Norway, Sweden, and the European Commission (BEAC, 2023). The second structure is the Barents Regional Council, an inter-regional forum whose members are Lapland, Oulu Region, Kainuu, and North Karelia in Finland; Nordland and Troms og Finnmark in Norway; and Norrbotten and Västerbotten in Sweden (BEAC, 2023a).

forum for addressing issues relating to the Arctic' (Government of Norway, 2023). Similarly, Morten Høglund, the new Chair of the SAO, has argued that it is his clear understanding that 'everyone wants the Arctic Council to continue as the main body for Arctic issues and that's a good starting point for the upcoming years' (Arctic Council, 2023b).

The relevance of the AC is very often discussed in annual conferences held in the High North like the Arctic Frontiers conference in Tromsø (Norway), the Arctic Circle conference in Reykjavík (Iceland), and the Arctic Circle Greenland conference in Nuuk (Greenland). I participated in these conferences in 2022 and in all these circumstances the participants (experts, politicians, analysts) agreed that the exclusion of Russia from common projects, which is supposed to be temporary, is not a reason to establish an institution where only the seven Western Arctic states would be the members. The reason is that the involvement of Russia, which is the largest state in the region and a key actor both regionally and internationally, in Arctic cooperation is of utmost importance for the implementation of projects on issues of common interest like coastguard cooperation. Also, the future of the AC has been discussed in a number of debates in which the participants have stressed the resilience and usefulness of this institution, the role of soft law, the severity of environmental threats in the Arctic, and the value of international scientific cooperation (Andreeva et al., 2024).

The importance of preserving the work of the AC has been highlighted by Huitfeldt. Indeed, the website of the Ministry of Foreign Affairs of Norway quotes Huitfeldt's words. She has said that the aim of the Norwegian chairmanship is to resume the work of the AC by exploring together with the member states how this can be done (Government of Norway, 2023). She has also argued that 'political contact with Russia is not possible, but we [the Norwegian chairmanship] will continue to be predictable in our dealings with Russia in the Arctic Council' (Government of Norway, 2023). In short, Norway announced that the survival of the AC is its priority essentially for three reasons: 1) the potential dissolution of the AC would weaken the ability of the Arctic indigenous groups to contribute to decision-making processes; 2) the AC has played a crucial role in raising global awareness of Arctic climate and environmental issues through the work of its WGs. Thus, if the AC would collapse, the networks built since its establishment and the knowledge accumulated would be difficult to reconstruct. At the same time, the reputation of Norway as an environmental leader (despite its commitment to exploiting oil and gas) would be jeopardised if the primary cooperative effort on Arctic environmental and climate matters would disintegrate; 3) the AC plays a fundamental role in addressing shared challenges (Andreeva et al., 2024).

Thus, the Norwegian chairmanship has identified four priority areas on which it will focus until 2025, namely the oceans, climate and environment, sustainable economic development, and people in the north (particular attention will be given to the Arctic youth and indigenous peoples) (Government of Norway, 2023). Espen Barth Eide, current Minister of Foreign Affairs of Norway and Chair of the Arctic Council, has recently stated the overall objective of the Norwegian chairmanship of the AC is to promote stability and constructive cooperation in the region (Arctic Council, 2023c). Climate change is the element common to the four priorities as it negatively affects the ecosystem in the region and in the oceans, and, consequently, the living conditions of people.

Given the relevance and the urgence of the issues which the AC deals with, cooperation is of utmost importance for all the Arctic states. Cooperation in the Arctic, which is based both on treaties and soft law arrangements, and the impact of the war in Ukraine on it have been analysed by several scholars. In an interesting article titled 'After Russia's invasion of Ukraine in 2022: Can we still cooperate with Russia in the Arctic?', Timo Koivurova, professor at the Arctic Centre of the University of Lapland (Finland), and Akiho Shibata, professor at the Polar Cooperation Research Centre of Kobe University (Japan) argue that Arctic cooperation based on treaties is more resilient than that on soft law (Koivurova and Shibata, 2022, 2). Indeed, they demonstrate that 'most treaty-based cooperative frameworks are still legally in force, with Russia remaining as a state party' (Koivurova and Shibata, 2022, 7). According to them, the reason is that 'terminating or suspending the operation of a cooperative framework established by a treaty regarding Russia would require high-threshold legal justifications in conformity with the relevant rules of international law' (Koivurova and Shibata, 2022, 7). Therefore, Koivurova and Shibata (2022, 7) argue that treaties have a stabilising effect even in a 'geopolitically contentious area' like the Arctic. After clarifying that cooperation with Russia occurs at the global, regional, and bilateral level, they discuss some examples to demonstrate their hypothesis. At the global level, the United Nations Framework Convention on Climate Change (UNFCCC) and the International Maritime Organisation (IMO) are two cases in point. The UNFCCC, which is the UN climate regime, is very important in the region (Koivurova and Shibata, 2022, 4). Indeed, in the *Arctic States Statement for UNFCCC COP 19* of 2013, the AC members clearly state that

> within the Arctic Council, we know that we can learn from each other, and cooperate to contribute to global solutions. This is why Arctic Council States remain firmly committed to work alongside other countries under the UNFCCC to reach – as a matter of urgency – an ambitious, inclusive, durable and flexible protocol, other legal instrument or an agreed outcome with legal force under the Convention, applicable to all Parties by 2015 which will meet the long term goal aimed at reducing greenhouse gas emissions so as to hold the increase in global average temperature below 2°C above pre-industrial levels.
>
> (Arctic Council, 2024)

Additionally, the AC actively cooperates with the IMO, which is the UN specialist agency aiming to ensure the safety and security of shipping and the prevention of marine and atmospheric pollution by ships (IMO, 2019). The AC's Protection of the Arctic Marine Environment Working Group works together with the IMO on these issues as well as to encourage the implementation of the Polar Code[10] (Arctic Council, 2020). Koivurova and Shibata point out that

> the overall atmosphere for developing the Code has deteriorated after the invasion and that the only impact of the war in Ukraine on these institutions are the speeches by Russia and Ukraine in the plenary sessions and the strong condemnation of Russia's aggression especially from the European and North American states.
>
> (Koivurova and Shibata, 2022, 4)

In spite of this, the work on the Polar Code moves forward (Koivurova and Shibata, 2022, 5). In fact, Russia continues to participate in the meetings of both the UNFCCC and IMO (Koivurova and Shibata, 2022, 5).

At the regional level, emblematic examples are the three legally binding agreements negotiated under the auspices of the AC (Koivurova and Shibata, 2022, 5). They are the SAR (search and rescue) Agreement of 2011, the Spills (oil spill preparedness and response) Agreement of 2013, and the Science Cooperation Agreement (international scientific cooperation) of 2017 (Koivurova and Shibata, 2022, 5). All these agreements are still in force, but they are not being implemented (Koivurova and Shibata, 2022, 5). Another regional agreement is the Polar Bear Agreement, which was concluded by Canada, Denmark (Greenland), Norway, the US, and Russia in 1973 with the aim to protect the polar bear and its habitat, namely the sea ice (Koivurova and Shibata, 2022, 5).

In the same way, bilateral treaties also continue to be in force and are functioning even after the invasion of Ukraine. This is the case of the 1964 agreement on frontier watercourses stipulated between Russia (then the Soviet Union) and Finland in order to regulate the use and management of transboundary waters (Koivurova and Shibata, 2022, 6). A similar type of technical cooperation was established between Finland, Norway, and Russia through a 1959 agreement on the regulation of Lake Inari situated in Finland in the Arctic region by means of a dam in Russia (Koivurova and Shibata, 2022, 6). The agreement envisages Russia's right to regulate the lake by means of the Kaitakoski hydroelectric power station and dam within a specified water level of the lake, Finland's obligation not to carry out measures affecting the regime of Lake Inari, and Norway's role as a neutral monitoring party (Koivurova and Shibata, 2022, 6).

Nevertheless, an exception is the International Council for the Exploration of the Sea (ICES)[11] that was established in 1902 with the aim to 'advance and share

10 The International Code for Ships Operating in Polar Waters (Polar Code) 'covers the full range of design, construction, equipment, operational, training, search and rescue and environmental protection matters relevant to ships operating in the inhospitable waters surrounding the two poles'. It entered into force in 2017 and is mandatory under both the International Convention for the Safety of Life at Sea (SOLAS) and the International Convention for the Prevention of Pollution from Ships (MARPOL) (IMO, 2019a).

11 ICES' members are Belgium, Canada, Denmark, Estonia, Finland, France, Germany, Iceland, Ireland, Latvia, Lithuania, the Netherlands, Norway, Poland, Portugal, Russia, Spain, Sweden, the UK, and US (ICES, no date).

scientific understanding of marine ecosystems and the services they provide and to use this knowledge to generate state-of-the-art advice for meeting conservation, management, and sustainability goals' (ICES, no date). ICES has been closely cooperating with the AC and its observers since 2017 and has provided scientific information during the discussion on the Joint Program of Scientific Research and Monitoring under the Central Arctic Ocean Fisheries Agreement (discussed in the next chapter). In March 2022, the ICES Council of Delegates held a vote to place 'a temporary suspension of all Russian Federation delegates, members and experts from participation in ICES activities' (Koivurova and Shibata, 2022, 5). Thus, with a short time announcement, a number of the ICES members instructed their scientists and representatives to boycott or avoid engagement in activities where Russian representatives are present (Koivurova and Shibata, 2022, 5).

In conclusion, cooperation in the Arctic has been heavily affected by the war in Ukraine, much more than by Russia's illegal annexation of Crimea. In the case of soft-law arrangements, such as the AC and the BEAC, this is particularly evident. By contrast, cooperation based on treaties is still continuing although with some difficulties in some cases like the ICES.

Russia and China's rapprochement in the Arctic

The war in Ukraine has played a key role in the rapprochement between Russia and China both internationally and in the Arctic. Nevertheless, in this context the relevance of climate change should not be disregarded as China's interest in the economic opportunities opened up by ice melting in the High North had previously pushed China to get involved in Arctic affairs and in closer relations with Russia as well. As Nong Hong puts it, 'climate change has increased accessibility to potential Arctic resources. This is changing the geopolitical landscape and broadening the international focus on the Arctic to include more geographically distant countries such as China, Japan, South Korea, India and Singapore' (Hong, 2020, 16). These Asian states were simultaneously granted observer status in the AC in 2013 (Hong, 2020, 16). Japan and South Korea very quickly issued their Arctic strategies in the following years, while India launched its Arctic policy in 2022 (Hong, 2020, 5). Singapore has always been more concerned with the potential competition for its port industry arising from the future increase of Arctic shipping (Hong, 2020, 9). China released its White Paper in 2018 in order to respond to international skepticism about its real intentions by aligning its objectives in the region with Western multilateral principles (Hong, 2020, 9). Also, this document clearly demonstrates the utmost importance that the Arctic has in China's global strategies aiming at being considered as part of the great powers' circle (Hong, 2020, 5). China has not released a policy document for all the regions where it wants to be a key player (Hong, 2020, 5); however, it has released one for the Arab and Asia-Pacific regions but not for Central America and Antarctica (Hong, 2020, 5). The White Paper contains the four key principles of China's policy in the Arctic, namely 'respect, cooperation, win-win result and sustainability', which are necessary to pursue its policy goals on the Arctic that are 'to understand, protect, develop and participate in the governance of the Arctic' (The State Council of China, 2018). As for 'respect', which is the 'key basis for China's participation in Arctic affairs', the White Paper states that respect should be reciprocal and that it is in China's interest to utilise Arctic resources in a lawful and rational manner by abiding by international treaties such as the UN Charter, the United Nations Convention on the Law of the Sea (UNCLOS), and general international law (The State Council of China, 2018; Hong, 2020, 5). Also, the document stresses the importance of respecting the sovereign rights of the Arctic states, the culture, and the tradition of indigenous peoples, and the right of other non-Arctic states to carry out activities in this region in accordance with the law, and respecting the overall interests of the international community in the Arctic (The State Council of China, 2018). 'Cooperation' is, according to China, an effective means to participate in Arctic affairs as it implies that it should occur through global, regional, multilateral, and bilateral channels through which all stakeholders (the document defines China as 'an important stakeholder in Arctic affairs')[12] should take part in cooperation on climate change, scientific research, environmental protection, shipping route development, resource utilisation, and cultural activities (The State Council of China, 2018). Cooperation should have a 'win-win result' meaning that all stakeholders 'should pursue mutual benefit and common progress in all fields of activities' (The State Council of China, 2018). Finally, 'sustainability' is a fundamental goal of China in the region, which means that it is necessary to promote sustainable development in the Arctic through environmental protection, resource utilisation, and human activities (The State Council of China, 2018).

These key principles serve China's four policy goals that are 'to understand, protect, develop and participate in the governance of the Arctic' (The State Council of China, 2018). In order to achieve these aims, China engages in promoting scientific research, protecting its fragile environment, improving its capacity and capability in using applied Arctic technology, strengthening technological innovation, and participating in the regulation and management of Arctic affairs on the basis of rules and mechanisms (The State Council of China, 2018).

However, China has been trying to get a voice in the region through multilateral and bilateral means for several years before releasing its White Paper leading the Arctic 5 to be suspicious of its intentions (Hong, 2020, 8). In particular, Russia and Canada have always been especially vigilant because they seek to control the Northern Sea Route (NSR) and the Northwest Passage (NP), respectively, and China has not yet recognised their rights over these shipping routes (Hong, 2020, 8; Jakobson, 2013). In the case of Canada, officials have not openly shown vigilance or suspicion regarding China while the academic community has (Hong,

12 By 'all stakeholders' China intends 'states from both inside and outside the Arctic, intergovernmental organizations, and non-state entities (The State Council of China, 2018).

2020, 8). Indeed, Professors David Wright and Rob Huebert from the University of Calgary and Victor Suthren from the Canadian War Museum argue that 'China believes that the Arctic is open to the international community and that it does not acknowledge Canadian sovereignty over northwestern sea lanes' (Hong, 2020, 8). Therefore, Canada and the other Arctic states as well have always been reluctant to 'open' the High North to China as it has not hidden its aim of being involved in the definition of the future in the region (Hong, 2020, 16). In order to achieve this goal, for several years China has been trying to become an observer in the AC, which it considered a relevant body for governance and cooperation (Hong, 2020, 16). This is why, since 2007, China has been regularly attending the AC's sessions as an ad hoc observer in order to better understand its functioning (Hong, 2020, 16). China officially expressed its intentions to become a fully fledged observer of the AC in 2008, but its application was rejected three times because of the wariness of the Arctic states, before finally being accepted in 2013.[13] In particular, while Canada and the US neither supported nor opposed China's application, Russia's concerns about China's emerging global status was the principal impediment to its observer status aspirations that obstructed the process for seven years (Hong, 2020, 17–18; Flake, 2013, 2). In the end, Russia accepted to confer upon China permanent observer status because of two elements. The first one was considerable pressure from the Nordic states that see the growing interest of China in the region as an opportunity (Hong, 2020, 18; Flake, 2013, 2). A good example is the fact that Iceland has been strengthening its relations with China over the last few decades mainly for economic reasons. In particular, China began strengthening its relations with Iceland in 2008 when 'the global financial crisis hit the heavily finance-dependent Icelandic economy, creating a geostrategic and commercial void that China was able to fill'.[14] In 2012, they signed the Framework Agreement on Arctic Cooperation (concerning scientific research in particular), which was 'the first intergovernmental agreement on Arctic issues between China and an Arctic state' (Hong, 2020, 207).

Nevertheless, it is necessary to stress here that in recent years the Nordic states have become more cautious towards China's political and economic strategies in the region (Dams et al., 2020, 2). A case in point is Greenland. China is particularly interested in its polar research, natural resources, and infrastructures (Dams et al., 2020, 2). At the same time, Greenland is interested in Chinese investments in its territory in order to diversify its economy and become less dependent on Denmark.[15] Nevertheless, Denmark tries to limit China's presence in the territory.

13 The AC accepted the application of four other Asian states, namely Japan, South Korea, Singapore, and India (Hong, 2020, 8).

14 In 2008, the financial crisis led Iceland into a deep economic depression. In 2009 Iceland applied for EU membership but in 2013 it withdrew its application because of a fishing quota issue. Consequently, Iceland was not eligible for recovery financing from the EU's structural funds. The same year, Iceland became the first state to sign a free trade agreement with China (Dams et al., 2020, 2).

15 China began increasing its strategic presence in Greenland since the adoption of the Self-Government Act of 2008, which gave it a higher level of autonomy including the ability to conclude agreements with other states (Dams et al., 2020, 2).

For instance, when a Chinese company tried to buy a privately owned former military base in 2018, Denmark immediately bought it back in order to prevent them from owning it (Hong, 2020, 151; Irvig, 2022).

The second element that convinced Russia to accept China's application for observer status in the AC was a 2011 change in the AC's rules to accept new observers (Criteria for Admitting Observers) that required them to 'recognize Arctic states' sovereignty, sovereign rights and jurisdiction in the Arctic' (Flake, 2013, 2). However, following the decision, former Russian Prime Minister Dmitry Medvedev clearly reminded China that the 'Arctic states lay down the rules here' (Flake, 2013, 2). The acceptance of its observer status was obviously received with enthusiasm by the Chinese media commenting that China would continue cooperating with the AC and contributing to the response to climate change and to the necessity to protect the Arctic environment (Sun, 2014, 46).

Nevertheless, in spite of its wariness towards China, Russia is China's strongest partner among the eight Arctic states (Flake, 2013, 2). Their economic trade has increased over the last few decades reaching the highest amount of all times of 240 billion dollars in 2023 (Fong and Maizland, 2024). At the same time, they have strengthened their political relations especially since the beginning of the war in Ukraine in 2022. On 16 May 2024, the leaders of the two great powers, Vladimir Putin and Xi Jinping, concluded their 43rd visit, which is much more often than with any other world leader (Fong and Maizland, 2024). This visit has marked the 75-year anniversary of China–Russia diplomatic relations while also confirming their 'strategic comprehensive partnership in a new era', which had already been emphasised during the meeting held in Moscow in 2019 (Saxena, 2024; Ji, 2023, 35). Every word of this statement has a specific meaning: 'strategic' means large investments in the security and defence sector; 'comprehensive' defines the scope of cooperation; 'partnership' stresses that it is not an alliance; the expression 'new era' highlights the increasing confrontation between the US and China, on the one hand, and the US and Russia, on the other, after American President Donald Trump had identified Russia and China as the main strategic US adversaries (Ji, 2023, 35). Moreover, during the 2024 meeting, China and Russia also expressed their mutual contempt for the 'closed-door military and political alliances' led by the West (Saxena, 2024). During the meeting, China and Russia also discussed the trajectory that their relationship should follow, namely the alignment of international interests given the fact that they have a common idea of how the future global order should be, that is to say a multipolarism, where they should be considered as the most important actors in the international system (Saxena, 2024; Ji, 2023, 36). Also, their relationship should aim at contributing to the 'renovation' of global economic governance and providing more tourism to each other and better people-to-people ties (Saxena, 2024). Additionally, China and Russia discussed the war in Ukraine and agreed 'that the central node of tension is the existence of an unsustainable security architecture in the EU, which requires a political solution with Russia and China on the table' (Saxena, 2024). Also, this meeting emphasised that the China–Russia relationship is not a 'marriage of convenience' but a 'no limits partnership' and that 'there are no "forbidden" areas of cooperation', which was announced for the first time in the Joint Statement of their February 2022 meeting on the sidelines of the Beijing Winter Olympics, just some weeks before the Russian invasion of Ukraine (Saxena, 2024). During that meeting, China and Russia agreed that 'the world is entering a new phase of fluidity and transformation, [with] multiple challenges and crises facing humanity' and that it is going through an evolutionary phase (Saxena, 2024). In this context, the two partners' cooperation aims at shaping global governance by pursuing their mutual interests, 'creating viable economic and military alternatives to the international "rules-based order" propagated by the US-led West, and undertaking "responsible action" vis-a-vis pandemic management, incentivization of economic growth and tackling of climate change' (Saxena, 2024). China and Russia, in fact, coordinate their position and action within and across international institutions against the 'norms of the US-led world order' (Fong and Maizland, 2024). An example is the UN Security Council,[16] where China and Russia back each other or at least do not oppose each other (Fong and Maizland, 2024). For instance, China was one of the 35 states that abstained from signing the 2022 UN resolution deploring the 'aggression' committed by Russia against Ukraine.[17]

In addition to this, cooperation between China and Russia is also evident in the current Israeli–Palestinian conflict, especially in relation to the confrontation between Israel and Iran recently emerged (Saxena, 2024). While the US are an important ally of Israel, China and Russia have backed Iran's counterattack (Saxena, 2024). Additionally, China, which has positioned itself as a 'comprehensive strategic partner' for Iran, is its largest trading partner and an importer of 90% of its oil (Saxena, 2024). At the same time, Russia has become Iran's largest military backer since 2022 (Saxena, 2024). On its side, Iran has been supporting Russia in its war against Ukraine, both diplomatically and militarily (Saxena, 2024). As a consequence, China, Russia, and Iran have created an anti-Western axis that has become important in their attempt to shape the global order in their favour (Saxena, 2024).

Like Iran, China has expressed its sympathy for Russia in relation to the war in Ukraine and its support has grown over time (Bohman et al., 2024). This has been clear on the occasion of the peace conference organised upon Ukraine's request in Lucerne, Switzerland, on 15 and 16 June 2024. Of the 160 states invited by Switzerland from all around the world, excluding Russia, 68 states declined the invitation, including China, that pointed out very clearly that it would not

16 China is a permanent member of the UN Security Council together with France, Russia, Great Britain, and the US. The other non-permanent members are Algeria, Ecuador, Guyana, Japan, Malta, Mozambique, Republic of Korea, Sierra Leone, Slovenia, and Switzerland. The primary responsibility of the UN Security Council is 'the maintenance of international peace and security' (UN, no date).

17 The vote resulted in 141 in favour, 5 against, and 35 abstained (UN, 2024).

participate if Russia would be absent (Bohman et al., 2024). On this occasion, 80 of the 92 present states did not sign the joint declaration that resulted from the conference and that reaffirmed the territorial integrity of Ukraine while stressing that 'dialogue between all parties is necessary to end' the conflict.[18]

In spite of the support that China gives Russia on the war issue, the two great powers do not completely agree on all the aspects of the war (Bohman et al., 2023, 2024). China recognises that Ukraine is a sovereign state, does not consider it as a 'Nazified Western puppet', has spoken out against Russian nuclear threats, and has not publicly supported the invasion (Bohman et al., 2024). Additionally, China has vaguely argued that 'the sovereignty of all countries' must be respected, thus suggesting that the invasion is not justifiable (Bohman et al., 2024). However, the two great powers agree on some key points (Bohman et al., 2024). For instance, China shares with Russia its 'legitimate security concerns' about NATO's eastward expansion arguing that the US are the culprit of the conflict as it has unleashed a confrontation in the region (Bohman et al., 2024). China's skepticism of NATO began with US bombing of the Chinese embassy in the former Yugoslavia in 1999 and over time has evolved into aversion (Bohman et al., 2024; Caracciolo, 2019, 7). Moreover, the fact that NATO's Strategic Concept of 2022 lists China as a security challenge highlighting that China's 'stated ambitions and coercive policies challenge our [namely of NATO] interests, security and values' (NATO, 2022a), is interpreted by China as confirmation of its suspicions that the Alliance aims at expanding its geographical scope and contain China (Bohman et al., 2024).

Thus, China will support Russia until it will be a necessary partner to struggle against US global hegemony (at least in the short or medium term) (Bohman et al., 2023, 2024). According to some experts, the alignment between China and Russia is more due to their common rivalry with the US than to their natural affinity (Fong and Maizland, 2024). China sees the US as the only state able to hamper its global ambitions because of its strategic and economic power although there are also other powers like Japan, India, and Russia that could prevent it from achieving its goals (Rudd, 2023, 22). This element influences China's geopolitical strategies and explains its rapprochement with Russia both internationally and in the Arctic. In fact, China's geostrategic and economic cooperation with Russia is functional to its plans to geopolitically, economically, and militarily compete with the US in order to affirm itself as a great power in the international system. China's global strategy consists in increasing its influence on the economics, foreign policy, and security of all regions (Rudd, 2023, 281).

Thus, China and Russia are not allies, but partners that share a common enemy, the US. Their relations have indeed been defined as a 'marriage of convenience' although several experts have recently emphasised that it is now possible to speak about a true partnership (Oliphant and Child, 2024; Legarda, 2024). Indeed, their

18 Armenia, Brazil, Colombia, the Vatican, India, Indonesia, Libya, Mexico, Saudi Arabia, South Africa, Thailand, and the United Arab Emirates did not sign the final communiqué (Bohman et al., 2024).

relations have been characterised by periods of both cooperation and fierce strategic rivalry (Fong and Maizland, 2024). While border issues[19] have caused stress in China–Russia relations, recently these have improved substantially (Fong and Maizland, 2024). In addition to strengthening their trade relations, the two great powers have increased joint security exercises (Fong and Maizland, 2024). An example is the joint military exercise conducted in the Sea of Japan in 2023 which, from the Russian perspective, should have taught China's People's Liberation Army 'how to respond to the undesired presence of US military aircraft in the neighbourhood' (Yu Lin, 2023).

Thus, China is increasingly shaping its place in the Arctic. On the one hand, the worsening of West–Russia relations and the sanctions imposed by the West on Russia have pushed Russia to turn to the East in order to compensate for the loss of the EU market, which is traditionally essential for its economy, with new ones in Asia, especially the Chinese market. On the other hand, China has taken the chance to calm its appetite for natural resources on the Russian market. In this context, the Russian Arctic plays a crucial role as it is rich in a number of natural resources like energy and fish, in addition to providing viable shipping routes. Furthermore, the Arctic is useful to China's aim to affirm itself as a great power internationally. As François Perreault, adjunct research associate at the Institute of Defence and Strategic Studies in Singapore, puts it, China 'wants to restore and heighten its status within the world's hierarchy by participating in regional issues worldwide. The Arctic is a "convenient location to demonstrate this new status" and thus a necessary adjunct to China's overall strategic posture or grand strategy' (Perrault, 2019, 427). Perreault also points out that unlike Canada, Norway, and Russia, China can't count on geography to get recognition in the Arctic (Perrault, 2019, 427). Canada, Norway, and Russia are in fact coastal states, which gives them 'a de facto elevated status in the region' (Perrault, 2019, 428). Moreover, Canada and Russia are using the Arctic to increase their importance in the world's hierarchy (Perrault, 2019, 428). Consequently, Chinese academics and policy makers use geography to define China as a 'near Arctic state' in order to justify its involvement in Arctic affairs (Perrault, 2019, 428; Sun, 2014, 48; The State Council of China, 2018). This label makes China more tied to Arctic environmental changes and economic development, which is important in order to be considered a 'legitimate Arctic stakeholder' (Perrault, 2019, 428). Additionally, as it is a global player, China claims 'to provide public goods in Arctic governance' arguing that the High North should be globally governed' (Perrault, 2019, 428). Also, China affirms to

19 The border between China and Russia is 2,600 miles long (4,209.3 kilometres) (Martin et al., 2021, 1). In 2023, when China released its map, Russia rejected Beijing's claim to all of Bolshoi Ussuriysky Island (known as Heixiazi or Black Bear in Chinese), which sits at the confluence of two border rivers, the Ussuri and Amur. These territories had been the object of a century of territorial dispute before Russia ceded roughly half of the island to the People's Republic of China in 2008. Russia also abandoned its army base there and handed over nearby Tarabarov Island. In exchange, China agreed not to claim more territory from Russia (Indo-Pacific Defence Forum, 2023; Reuters, 2008).

have positively affected 'the interactions between Arctic and non-Arctic States in relations to Arctic governance' (Perrault, 2019, 428).

At the same time, the changed geopolitical environment emerging in the Arctic is making the US increasingly worried and concerned about the Russia–China rapprochement. The US and China are the two largest economies in the world and command the two strongest militaries but they are part of a multipolar world where other powers, middle and small, can influence the policies and behaviour of the great, especially if they work collectively (Patey, 2020). Thus, the cooperation between China and the other great power, Russia, is not seen positively by the US. In particular, the US fears that those two great powers' partnership could dominate the Arctic (Hong, 2020, 11). As the Arctic is part of China's global long-term strategic vision (which is mainly based on economic development and scientific understanding), it is crucial for the US to understand how that vision impacts on its interests and on Arctic institutions and governance (Hong, 2020, 11).

In October 2022, the US adopted a new Arctic strategy that marked 'a strong and clarifying shift in the US' focus in the Arctic over recent years' (Coninsx, 2022). American Arctic experts had criticised the previous Arctic strategy from 2013 considering it 'largely rhetorical and underwhelming at advancing American Arctic capabilities, particularly if Russia and China pursue closer strategic and military cooperation in the future' (Patey, 2020). In this respect, the US recognised already in 2019 the fact that 'great power competition' characterises Arctic geopolitics (Conley and Melino, 2020, 7). That year, former US Secretary of State Mike Pompeo gave a speech in Rovaniemi proclaiming that it was 'America's moment to stand up as an Arctic nation' and that 'the region has become an arena of global power and competition' (Conley and Melino, 2020, 7).

The new strategy addresses the challenges that the US have been increasingly facing in the Arctic over the last decade and gives new impetus to US involvement in Arctic issues (Coninsx, 2022). Given the geopolitical changes due to the war in Ukraine that have occurred in the region, the US Arctic strategy identifies security as a top priority (Coninsx, 2022). Indeed, the strategy states that the US' 'highest priority [is] to protect the American people and our sovereign territory and rights' (Coninsx, 2022; The White House, 2022, 3). Indeed, according to the text, the US will deter threats to its territory and its allies by enhancing the capabilities required to defend their interests in the Arctic (The White House, 2022, 3). Additionally, the strategy addresses climate change with great urgency and envisages the need to increase investments in sustainable development in order to improve the livelihoods of indigenous people while protecting the environment at the same time (The White House, 2022, 3). Moreover, another important point stressed in the strategy is international cooperation and governance in the Arctic. This means that although there are challenges to cooperation resulting from the war in Ukraine, the US will work to sustain institutions such as the AC (The White House, 2022, 3).

In conclusion, Arctic geopolitics is being deeply affected by the war in Ukraine and it is causing a change in the relations among states at the international level, which is reflected at the regional level. Russia's turning to the East (China) is the most emblematic example of the huge impact of the war in Ukraine on the relations among states internationally and regionally. Nevertheless, the war in Ukraine is complementary to climate change that had previously pushed Russia and China to strengthen their relations for geopolitical and economic reasons.

From militarisation to re-militarisation

Following the geopolitical changes occurring at the international level, the Arctic has passed from being militarised to being demilitarised and then to being militarised again. During the Cold War, the Arctic was a very highly militarised region because of its peculiar geographical location that made it an area of strategic confrontation between the Soviet Union and the US of the utmost importance. Given the fact that it was the shortest distance between the two superpowers, the Arctic was an excellent location for aerial threats via strategic bombers and intercontinental ballistic missiles (ICBMs) traveling over the pole, and maritime threats by ballistic missile submarines and hunter-killer submarines operations under the Arctic sea ice (Huebert, 2019; Teeple, 2021). The North American Aerospace Defense Command (NORAD), a binational partnership between the US and Canada that celebrated its 66th anniversary on 10 May 2024 (NORAD, 2024), provided air defence and an early warning system (Teeple, 2021). The US began heavily investing in Alaskan military defence during World War II, 'when the combination of increased international tensions and advances in long-range aviation made Alaska important for both defense and power projection' (US Army, 2021, 5). The importance of military activities in Alaska reached their high point during the Cold War because its proximity to the Soviet Union, its harsh climate made it the front line of defence for the US, and as a vital training ground for Arctic operations (US Army, 2021, 5). In 1947, the US established the Alaskan Command with the task to protect its territory through Alaska (US Army, 2021, 5). Additionally, NATO established a robust defensive presence in the region (Donnelly, 2024). For instance, it deployed early warning systems, military bases, and surveillance efforts 'designed for Soviet deterrence, safeguarding NATO's interests in the Arctic, and securing transatlantic supply lines critical for Western defense' (Donnelly, 2024).

Also, since the 1950s, the Soviet Union built key industries and infrastructure related to the Russian nuclear deterrent like installations on the Kola Peninsula (Laruelle, 2014, 113). This has always had a role of utmost importance in the Soviet Union's (and later Russia's) military strategies because of its peculiar geographical position making it convenient for launching ballistic missiles, missile defence systems, missile early warning systems, and other elements of strategic deterrence systems (Laruelle, 2014, 113). In this context, the Severomorsk air base, protecting the Soviet Union's northern flank and providing air protection for both navy facilities on the Kola Peninsula and Allied supply convoys destined for the port of Murmansk, is particularly important (Melino et al., 2020, 1). During the Cold War, indeed, Severomorsk-1's strategic importance increased as well as that of its two sister air bases, Severomorsk-2 and Severomorsk-3 (Melino et al., 2020, 1). Other military means and weapons, such as strategic bombers (e.g., Tu-16/-95), strikes (e.g., Su-24), and patrol aircraft (e.g., Il-38) were based there to protect the Soviet

Union's northwestern Arctic flank and to provide strategic strike capability against the US (Melino et al., 2020, 1). Also, Severmosrk on the Kola Peninsula was the base of the Soviet Northern Fleet that an interesting declassified CIA document from 1968 defines as 'the source of ballistic missiles submarines which pose an increasingly significant portion of the Soviet strategic threat to NATO, including the continental United States' (CIA, 1968, 1). According to this quite detailed document, the 'Northern Fleet long range attack and cruise missile submarines provide the Soviets with a considerable capability against Free World merchant shipping and naval surface units in the Norwegian Sea, Atlantic and Mediterranean' (CIA, 1968, 1). A substantial part of the Soviet naval forces were located on the Kola Peninsula posing 'a strategic threat to NATO's transatlantic sea lines of communication via the Norwegian and Greenland seas and the Greenland–Iceland–UK gap, making the defence of this region critical for the Allies and providing a key role of the Royal Navy' (Le Mière and Mazo, 2013). Moreover, an important reason why Russia highly militarised the Kola peninsula was that the Arctic Ocean has always been vital to Russia as it guarantees access to the Atlantic Ocean (Laruelle, 2014, 113). The importance of the Arctic for Russia has even increased after the end of the Cold War and the collapse of the Soviet Union as Russia lost several ports like the Estonian port of Paldiski on the Baltic Sea (Laruelle, 2014, 113). This port was one of the most important military bases of the Soviet Union hosting one of only three nuclear submarine training centres in the USSR (equipped with a mock-up of a nuclear submarine) since the 1960s (Military Heritage, no date). Consequently, Russia began leasing the port of Sevastopol in Ukraine 'leaving the main Russian military port on the Black Sea subject to the multiple upheavals in Russian-Ukrainian relations and reinforcing the importance of access to the open sea through the Arctic region' (Laruelle, 2014, 113).

The post-Cold War period was characterised by the demilitarisation of the Arctic meaning that Russia was not considered militarily dangerous, at least temporarily, essentially for two elements. First, the process initiated by Gorbachev's Murmansk speech led to the improvement of East–West relations and to cooperation between them. Second, the fact that after the collapse of the Soviet Union, Russia was politically, economically, and financially weak meant that investing in the military sector was not a priority for Russia. Indeed, as Marlene Laruelle, research professor of International Affairs and Political Science at The George Washington University, puts it, 'the Russian army was one of the major forgotten institutions during the economic liberalization of the 1990s; the Russian state spent almost nothing on it for almost a decade' (Laruelle, 2014, 113). When Vladimir Putin came to power, Russia was in 'a state of misery and turmoil', as Masha Lipman, a Moscow-based political analyst correctly argued in an interview with *The New Yorker* in 2020 (Chotiner, 2020). At that time, Putin's priorities were to consolidate his power in the Kremlin, to bring back stability, and to ensure national development and economic growth (Chotiner, 2020). Consequently, Russia's defence expenditure drastically declined (but so did the defence spending of all the other Arctic states) because of lack of funding, which meant that vessels, submarines, and aircraft, of the Northern Fleet were not maintained and there were no resources or staff to ensure regular patrols (Le Mière and Mazo, 2013, 83). For instance, the number of patrols by Northern Fleet nuclear-powered submarines fell from 80 per year in 1985 to 18 in 1995 while the number of submarines patrols fell from 230 in 1984 to fewer than 10 in the early 2000s (Le Mière and Mazo, 2013, 84). In the years after 1991, the Northern Fleet was cut by more than 50% (Elenius, 2015). Thus, the strategic importance of the Kola Peninsula and the Murmansk area more generally was dramatically reduced (Elenius, 2015, 256). At the same time, Alaska's military significance was also reduced (US Army, 2021, 5). During the 1990s, the US Army deactivated the 6th Infantry Division and resurrected the US Army Alaska as a component of a newly re-established US Alaskan Command (US Army, 2021, 5).

%%The situation began changing in the 2000s when Russian economic growth dramatically improved especially thanks to an increase in resource availability (Laruelle, 2014, 114). Indeed, the increase in oil prices in those years allowed Russia to base its economic transition on the capitalist system and get rid of its external financial dependence (Trenin, 2019). Consequently, in the years 1999–2000, Russia's military expenditure was extraordinary, increasing from 2.6% of the gross domestic product (GDP) in 1999 to 2.75% in 2000 (SIPRI, 2001). Between 2000 and 2008, the Russian military budget increased by 500%, especially in sectors like weaponry, the navy, and missiles (Laruelle, 2014, 114). However, the financial crisis of 2008 hindered Russia's ambition to strengthen and modernise its military sector (Laruelle, 2014, 114). Nevertheless, in 2013, Russia was the third country in the world by volume of spending on the armed forces, rising from fifth in 2010 and ninth in 2005 (Cooper, 2013, 6). Over time, Russia's expenditure has been increasing and in 2023 it tripled compared to the period before the war in Ukraine (Grozovski, 2023). At the end of 2023, the budget proposed by the government for the year 2024 included military expenditures equal to 6% of GDP for the first time in history, and defence spending exceeded social spending (Luzin and Prokopenko, 2023). Russia has increased its military expenditure the most in the world, together with the US and China (SIPRI, 2024a). Generally speaking, world military expenditure has risen for the ninth consecutive year reaching the highest level of all time (SIPRI, 2024a). Additionally, it is interesting to add here that since the beginning of the Russian invasion of Ukraine, the ground forces of the Northern Fleet have been used in the war (Aliyev, 2022; Staalensen, 2022; Bye, 2022b). In particular, the troops from the 200th Motorised Rifle Brigade and marines from the 61st Naval Infantry Brigade were deployed near Kharkiv in Ukraine to prepare for landing operations near Black Sea cities (Staalensen, 2022). According to Norway's Chief of Defence Eirik Kristoffersen, 'Russia believes that the area is stable and that they do not need any more ground forces here now – precisely because there is no threat to the country. At the same time, they know that the deterrence [which lies in the nuclear weapon arsenal, journalist's note] is working' (Bye, 2022b). This is interesting since, while it is true that a conflict is not currently contemplated in the Arctic, tensions and competition in the region emerged about a couple of decades before the war in Ukraine, following the Russian flag-planting on Lomonosov Ridge in 2007 (Heinine and Exner-Pirot, 2020). Since then, the Arctic has been considered to be at risk of a 'new Cold War' and one of the geographical areas (the others being Africa and, very probably in the near future, the Antarctic, and possibly the Third Pole) where there is a 'scramble' for natural resources (Exner-Pirot, 2019). Thus, the very reason behind the militarisation of the Arctic are not the tensions between the West and Russia due to the illegal annexation of Crimea or the war in Ukraine, but the enormous increased interest in the natural resources of the Arctic and non-Arctic states that are becoming increasing accessible because of climate change. This is an important element in the geopolitical strategies of the Arctic states and an important variable in the relations between them. For instance, already in 2019, in his article titled '20 Years of Vladimir Putin: How Russian Foreign Policy Has Changed', Dmitri Trenin, director of the Carnegie Moscow Centre, wrote that 'as a result of climate change, [the Arctic] has turned into a new arena for the development of relations with the outside world and a new front for confrontation with its [of Russia] rivals' (Heinine and Exner-Pirot, 2020). Although the reference here is to Russia and its historical enemy (that is the US), this statement could be applied to the other Arctic states as well as the increasing accessibility to natural resources impacting relations among the Arctic states as well as their relations with states external to the region. Additionally, in the case of Russia in particular, the wealth of its Arctic territories is an excellent opportunity for Russia to economically develop and modernise, contributing to its goal of keeping its great power status both regionally and internationally. As Trenin (2019) correctly points out, 'a great power is essentially a military-political concept'. The economic exploitation of the natural resources of the Arctic serves exactly Russia's purpose to increase its military power, which is also necessary to protect its sovereignty in the Arctic and, consequently, the territories where natural resources are located. A good example is the case of the air-launched ballistic missile Kh-47M2 Kinzhal whose deployment by the Northern Fleet in 2021 (thus before the war in Ukraine) 'is consistent with Russia's ongoing and persistent efforts to strengthen its military presence in the Arctic' (Lavikainen, 2021). This is explicitly written in Russia's *Strategy of development of the Arctic Zone of the Russian Federation and the provision of national security for the period to 2035*, adopted in 2020. Indeed, this document states that the Russian armed forces must increase their combat potential in the Arctic as the possibility that a conflict might occur in the region has increased (Lavikainen, 2021). Furthermore, over the last decade Russia has been systematically expanding and strengthening its Arctic military through bases, airfields, large-scale radar installations, as well as defensive and offensive weapons systems (Humpert, 2022). For instance, Russia has fortified and expanded its radar stations at the Olenegorsk site on the Kola Peninsula, at Vorkuta north of the Arctic circle as well as one of five Rezonans-N radar systems at Ostrovnoy on the Barents Sea, near Norway and Finland in Russia's west (Walsh and Dean, 2022). In particular, the Kola Peninsula 'is the crux of Russia's military establishment in the western Arctic, and its air and maritime capabilities are essential to Russia's homeland defense, Arctic dominance, and global power projection capabilities' (Conley and Melino, 2020, 1). Thus, Russia is modernizing and expanding its Severomorsk-1 air base, Gadzhiyevo submarine base, and Okolnaya submarine support base, which have significantly improved Russia's operational readiness and its ability to control the surrounding maritime space in the Arctic (Conley and Melino, 2020, 1). Moreover, Russia has positioned on the Kola Peninsula systems such as the RS-24 YARS, located at the Plesetsk Cosmodrome, that pose a significant challenge to the US and its allied defence systems (Conley and Melino, 2020, 1).

Russia has reactivated and renovated more than 50 military bases from the Soviet era and has invested in fighter jets and missile defence systems to strengthen its defensive and deterrent capabilities (Winkel, 2023). In addition to this, the Northern Fleet is equipped with nuclear submarines, aviation capabilities, coastal forces, ground forces, and surface ships with missile and anti-submarine capabilities (Winkel, 2023). The Northern Fleet 'possesses a large arsenal of dual-capable, high-precision weapons that Nordic countries cannot compete with, even if they combined their forces in the Arctic' (Lavikainen, 2021). Thus, it strongly contributes to Russia's military superiority in the Arctic (Lavikainen, 2021).

Of course, the war in Ukraine pushed the Arctic states to further militarise the Arctic and to dramatically increase their military expenditure in general terms. The case of the Nordic states is emblematic. Between 1991 and 2011, defence spending as a percentage of the GDP also diminished in the Nordic states with drastic decreases in Norway and Sweden passing from 3.3% to 1.4% and from 2.5% to 1.1% ,respectively (Le Mière and Mazo, 2013, 87). Nevertheless, after 2008, the Nordic states began increasing their military expenditure. Norway, which had not been seriously constrained from the 2008 financial crisis due to its resource wealth, was the most active state to modernise its military (Le Mière and Mazo, 2013, 88). Norway increased the capability of its navy surface combatants by adding five Fridtjof Nansen-class frigates and six fast Skjold-class patrol craft thereby greatly improving its ability to defend its coastline, although these vehicles are not ice-capable (Le Mière and Mazo, 2013, 87). Additionally, in 2009, Norway moved its National Joint Headquarters, which has the overall command and control of all military activity, and commands military personnel abroad as well, from Jåttå in the south to Bodø in the north (Forsvaret, 2020; Le Mière and Mazo, 2013, 88). Moreover, in general terms and as a consequence of the war in Ukraine, Norway has enormously increased its defence budget in 2024 envisaging investment of 13 billion NOK in defence of which 6 billion is supposed to be spent on military support for Ukraine and 7 billion to increase the operational capability of the Norwegian Armed Forces (Government of Norway, 2024). In this regard, Defence Minister Bjørn Arild Gram stated that

> this is a significant increase, and it means that we will reach NATO's two per cent goal already this year. It also means that we can start several initiatives we have planned in the long-term plan on defence earlier, which involves strengthening the foundation of the Armed Forces. Both support for Ukraine and investment in our own Armed Forces are crucial in the current security situation.
>
> (Government of Norway, 2024)

Like Norway, Denmark has increased its military expenditure in order to face the new threat represented by the war in Ukraine. Danish Minister of Defence Troels Lund Poulsen explained the government's decision by arguing that

> the security situation in Europe has worsened since we decided the Danish Defence Agreement last summer. Russia is preparing for a long-term war and could pose a potential threat to NATO Allies within a few years. It is vital that we react now, together with our Allies, in order to deter a resurgent Russia. Therefore, we must fast-track investments in key military capabilities.
>
> (Danish Ministry of Defence, 2024)

To this aim, the government has increased funds to build-up the Army's First Brigade, for the acquisition of land-based air defence systems and to strengthen the Navy's anti-submarine warfare capabilities (Danish Ministry of Defence, 2024). Like Norway, before 2014 it embarked on a very large procurement program with the purchase of three Iver Huitfeldt-class frigates and the commissioning of two Knud Rasmussen-class patrol vessels in 2008 and 2009, which should be added to four Thetis-class frigates commissioned in the early 1990s (Le Mière and Mazo, 2013, 88).

Iceland does not a military of its own, but it is a NATO member. As such, in 2022 former Prime Minister Katrín Jakobsdóttir announced that Iceland would increase its NATO funding especially on cyber security, which is one of the areas of emphasis within the Alliance, in consequence of the war in Ukraine (Tómas, 2022).

As members of NATO, Finland and Sweden, which are not coastal states, have decided to increase their military expenditure. Finland's defence budget, ratified in October 2023, is to be increased by 5% in 2024 compared to that of the previous year (O'Dwyer, 2023). This increase is due to both its accession to NATO, which fixes military spending targets for member nations at two% of national gross domestic product, and to Russia's invasion of Ukraine (O'Dwyer, 2023), which increases insecurity in the Arctic also considering that Finland shares a border of 1,340 kilometres with Russia. Indeed, Finland will spend part of its defence budget on the construction of 125 miles of so-called smart fencing supported by advanced sensors and drones operated by the Finnish Border Guard in order to reinforce its border (O'Dwyer, 2023). Finnish Defence Minister Antti Häkkänen explained the defence budget increase stating that it is 'fundamental to national security and enhancing defense capability' and that Finland

> cannot ignore how the war instigated by Russia has changed the security landscape in our Nordic region and in the wider neighborhood. The world around Finland is becoming an increasingly dangerous place. Despite Finland's economic challenges, we are now part of NATO and with membership comes added costs and responsibilities.
>
> (O'Dwyer, 2023)

Finland's NATO membership has pushed Russia to erect buildings for its Arctic Motor Rifle Brigade in its Alakurtti military base, about 50 kilometres from the

Finnish border, east of the municipality of Salla in Finnish Lapland (O'Dwyer, 2023; Mäkeläinen, 2023). In addition to this, Russia has built a new large military storage site in Petrozavodsk, a town located 175 kilometres from the border, east of the Finnish town of Kitee (O'Dwyer, 2023; Mäkeläinen, 2023). Russia amassed its troops at the border with Finland because of the tensions with NATO, which were due to the war in Ukraine (Mäkeläinen, 2023). Also, it seems that Russia is also using its storage site in Petrozavodsk as a regional depot to deliver equipment to Russian front-line motorised brigade forces attacking Ukraine (Mäkeläinen, 2023). Thus, the 'calm' situation in the Arctic described by Norway's Chief of Defence Eirik Kristoffersen has completely disappeared with NATO's expansion eastward in 2023 and 2024.

Like most Western states, Sweden reduced its military expenditure after the end of the Cold War but it began ramping it up again as a consequence of Russia's illegal annexation of Crimea in 2014 (Reuters, 2024). Additionally, as a new NATO member, Sweden has doubled its appropriations for military defence since 2020 and has reported defence expenditures corresponding to 2.2% of GDP at the beginning of 2024 (Government of Sweden, 2024). This huge increase is also due to the war in Ukraine that has led Sweden to rethink its security policy (Reuters, 2024). Sweden has decided to rapidly expand its army, to increase its investments in defence against air attack, in civil defence, and expansion of its navy as well as increasing conscription from 2032 (Reuters, 2024). With Finnish and Swedish membership, NATO has increased its military capabilities thus decreasing the military advantage that Russia has had for decades in the Arctic (Preve, 2024). According to Nima Khorrami, research associate at the Arctic Institute in Lapland, 'this membership enables them to develop shared threat perceptions in the Arctic, which, in turn, facilitates better and quicker coordination. NATO can enhance its stance and deploy its resources more swiftly, thereby becoming a significant security presence in the Arctic' (Preve, 2024).

Acknowledging sovereignty challenges in the Arctic, Canada as well has announced an increase in its investment in the country's defence (Martinussen, 2024). Indeed, in a speech at the Halifax International Security Forum in November 2023, Prime Minister Justin Trudeau pointed out that 'here at home, our [of Canada] Arctic sovereignty is being increasingly challenged by Russia and China' (Edvardsen, 2024a). In 2023, Canada began modernising NORAD, which it considered essential for the defence of the population, and is now charged with the missions of aerospace warning, aerospace control, and maritime warning for North America (Edvardsen, 2023a; Bye, 2022a). During the Halifax Forum, in fact, Canadian Defence Minister Bill Blair said that 'just nine months ago, NORAD played a key role when a Chinese high-altitude surveillance balloon violated the sovereignty of Canada and the United States – reminding us of NORAD's centrality to the security of our peoples' (Edvardsen, 2023a). Thus, Canada is investing in underwater surveillance capabilities and Arctic defence infrastructure that matter to NORAD, tactical aviation capabilities essential in responding to emergencies, as well as in long-range precision strike capabilities that are essential to NATO (Edvardsen, 2023a). Canada considers NATO essential for the security of the

Northern Atlantic area including the security of Europe (Edvardsen, 2023a). The words of Canadian Defence Minister Bill Blair are clear in this regard. He argued that 'even though we are across the Atlantic, we are under no illusions: Europe's security is our security too. And given the threats we currently face, we believe that NATO is more important than ever' (Edvardsen, 2023a). Furthermore, Canada is modernising its navy, which also operates in the Arctic (Edvardsen, 2023a). Four new Arctic and offshore patrol ships for the navy have been built and two more are under construction (Edvardsen, 2023a).

The US had the highest military expenditure in 2023, corresponding to over 40% of the total military spending worldwide that year, most of which is dedicated to the navy and air force (Statista, 2024). Like all the other Arctic states, the US has increased its military presence in the Arctic (Speak, 2023). It is investing hugely in the expansion of the port of Nome, Alaska, which could be transformed into a deepwater hub servicing Coast Guard[20] and Navy vessels navigating into the Arctic Circle (Baker, 2022). The Coast Guard currently has only two operational icebreakers (the 48-year-old heavy icebreaker *Polar Star* and the 25-year-old medium icebreaker *Healy*) but it expects to deploy three new icebreakers (Lopez, 2022; Baker, 2022; Humpert, 2024). The US acknowledge the fact that they need more icebreakers than they have and their importance in the Arctic (Lopez, 2022). For instance, Randy Kee, a senior advisor for Arctic security affairs at the Ted Stevens Center for Arctic Security Studies in Anchorage, Alaska, argues that 'strategically, icebreakers provide persistent presence in a way that's not met by anything else in the maritime region. Remember, the Arctic is a maritime region, and icebreaking provides you year-round access to be able to go in the region' (Lopez, 2022). Nevertheless, the construction of these icebreakers is facing a delay due to the fact that the Coast Guard did not request additional funding for the Polar Security Cutter icebreaker program in 2025 (Humpert, 2024). The reason is that the Coast Guard has decided to 'rebaseline' the program, 'which will result in a new program schedule that is expected to be completed "later this year and will be critical to informing future budget requests"' (Park, 2024). In order to bridge the icebreaker gap in the short term, the Coast Guard is planning to eventually buy a commercial vessel (Humpert, 2024b). Nevertheless, the suitability for the Coast Guard has been questioned by its leadership doubting that the vessel would be 'suitable for military service without a substantial refit' (Humpert, 2024a, 2024b). Additionally, the vessel is considered to be less capable than the medium icebreaker *Healy* (Humpert, 2024a). Also, the US Air Force has transferred dozens of F-35 fighter jets to Alaska, announcing that the state will host 'more advanced fighters than any other location in the world' (Baker, 2023). In 2021, the US Army released its first strategic plan titled 'Regaining Arctic Dominance' that highlights the fundamental role played by the Army in the Arctic, stating that it 'is an essential key to ensur-

20 The Coast Guard is 'a branch of the U.S. Armed Forces and the principal Federal agency responsible for maritime safety, security, and environmental stewardship in U.S. ports and inland waterways' (US Department of Homeland Security, 2024).

ing land dominance in support of the joint force in the all-domain environment' (US Army, 2021, 50). Additionally, this document stresses the fact that the Arctic has the potential to become a great powers competition area where the interests of the US can be jeopardised. In particular, it states that the Arctic could 'become a contested space where United States' great power rivals, Russia and China, seek to use military and economic power to gain and maintain access to the region at the expense of US interests' (US Army, 2021, 15). This is why the US Army must generate forces able to face the challenges stemming from increased competition in the region (US Army, 2021, 15). Another element that the document stresses is climate change impacting security in the region. This is why the Department of Defense (DoD) takes into consideration this element in every mission it conducts (Speak, 2023). Joe Bryan, special climate adviser to the US DoD, said that 'the DoD recognizes that climate change is a climate multiplier for instability in fragile regions of the world [...] and it is reshaping the way we need to construct our force posture to be able to mitigate risk from the changing climate' (Speak, 2023). The 2016 DoD Directive specifies that the 'DoD must be able to adapt current and future operations to address the impacts of climate change in order to maintain an effective and efficient U.S. military' (US Department of Defense, 2016, 3). To this aim, its tasks are the 'identification and assessment of the effects of climate change on the DoD mission; taking those effects into consideration when developing plans and implementing procedures; anticipating and managing any risks that develop as a result of climate change to build resilience' (US Department of Defense, 2016, 3). In fact, climate change has a huge impact on military operations. Thus, the Corps of Engineers Research and Development Center's Cold Regions Research and Engineering Laboratory (ERDC-CRREL) is studying the impacts of climate change on Alaskan ecosystems because it affects military operations for the Strategic Environmental Research and Development Program (SERDP) and the Environmental Security Technology Certification Program (ESTCP) (SERDP-ESTCP, 2024).[21] For instance, the landscape around Fairbanks where multiple military bases and vast training lands are situated is characterised by discontinuous permafrost, or a mix of permafrost and pockets of unfrozen ground (SERDP-ESTCP, 2023). Permafrost thaw can undermine military infrastructure, ports, and runways and represents a challenge for resources (personnel, equipment, and finances) 'given the necessity to respond to the compounding effects of climate change on domestic and/or regional environments (i.e. search and rescue and disaster response)' (Arctic Centre, 2024). Thus, the very harsh climate conditions in the Arctic can potentially restrict military mobility, survivability, and sustainability (Arctic Centre, 2024). At the same time, climate change is making multinational

21 The Strategic Environmental Research and Development Program (SERDP) and the Environmental Security Technology Certification Program (ESTCP) are the Department of Defense's environmental, resilience, and installation energy and water research programs, harnessing the latest science and technology to improve the DoD's environmental performance, reduce costs, and enhance and sustain mission capabilities (SERDP-ESTCP, 2024).

forces cooperate, which is essential due to global warming and increasing geopolitical competition in the Arctic, more difficult, complex, and costly because it increases environmental challenges such as difficult ice conditions, small breakaways from icebergs and glaciers threaten to damage ships, and permafrost thaw (Arctic Centre, 2024). The dangers for military operations coming from climate change are acknowledged by states. For instance, in its Climate Adaptation Plan, the US Department of Defense clearly stresses that it is necessary to take 'bold steps to accelerate adaptation to reduce the adverse impacts of climate change' in order to ensure that the US 'military can deter aggression and defend the nation under all conditions' (US Department of Defense, 2021, 3).

Furthermore, in order to face the challenges imposed by climate change, a number of collaborations and efforts are underway in order to address the implications of climate change in the region (Arctic Centre, 2024). For instance, the Climate Change and Arctic Security – Military Implications (CLIMARCSEC) project has been launched within the NATO Multinational Capabilities Development Campaign series, which is an initiative 'led by the United States designed to collaboratively develop and assess concepts and capabilities to address the challenges associated with conducting joint, multinational and coalition operations' (NATO, 2023a). CLIMARCSEC is led by the Norwegian Ministry of Defence and Norwegian Institute of International Affairs and includes the contributing nations of Austria, Canada, Finland, France, Germany, Poland, Romania, Sweden, the UK, and the US as well as a number of observers (e.g., the Netherlands and the EU) (Arctic Centre, 2024). CLIMARCSEC's goal is to examine the challenges that climate change and competitive activity in the Arctic pose to military operations as well how gaps in military capability and governance can be closed (Arctic Centre, 2024). Within the wide range of military challenges and capabilities, the project focuses primarily on command, control, communication, and coordination capabilities necessary to lead effective Multinational Forces Arctic operations (Arctic Centre, 2024).

The growing relevance of climate change in NATO's activities is also demonstrated by the establishment of its Climate Change and Security Centre of Excellence (CCASCOE) in Montreal, Canada, in 2021. Its goal is to 'support the implementation of the NATO Climate Change and Security Action Plan and contribute to NATO's overall 'military readiness, deterrence and defence posture' in order to 'be an internationally recognized hub of expertise on climate change and security for military and civilian experts and decision-makers' (CCASCOE, 2024). Canada, which is the framework nation, was joined in its effort to establish a new Centre of Excellence by Denmark, France, Germany, Greece, Italy, Latvia, Luxembourg, Norway, Romania, Turkey, and the UK, which are the sponsoring nations (CCASCOE, 2024). On the CCASCOE's website, it is possible to read that

> climate change will have severe impacts on Allied security and collective defence. It acts as a threat multiplier by increasing instability, geostrategic competition, insecurity and conflict. The resilience and efficiency of our military infrastructure and equipment and the way that we conduct operations

> will be affected by changes in climate that include extreme temperatures, changes in water acidity, air density, and Atlantic Meridional Overturning Circulation (AMOC), thawing permafrost, sea level rise, changes in precipitation patterns, and extreme weather events.
>
> (CCASCOE, 2024)

Over the last few years, NATO has strengthened its presence in the Arctic acknowledging that 'the High North remains a critical focal point in safeguarding collective defence, fostering cooperation, and addressing emerging challenges in the Arctic region' (NATO, 2023b). As some of its members are Arctic states, NATO has considered the region 'as a crucial frontier for security interests from the outset' (Donnelly, 2024). Also, at the Arctic Circle Assembly held in Iceland in 2023, Admiral Rob Bauer, Chair of NATO's Military Committee, expressed concerns for the growing threat coming from the strengthened relationship between Russia and China arguing that 'the increasing competition and militarization in the Arctic region, especially by Russia and China, is worrying. The melting ice in the Arctic allows for new sea routes that make sailing easier for larger vessels and shorten the time it takes to navigate' (Edvardsen and Molid Martinussen, 2023). He also raised concerns about Russia, which he considered as 'the largest and most direct threat against the alliance's security' (Edvardsen and Molid Martinussen, 2023). Thus, NATO has reaffirmed (since the end of the Cold War) its commitment to the defence and security of its members in the Arctic (Donnelly, 2024).

Between 2015 and 2020, NATO has doubled its Arctic military activities (Evans, 2021). In fact, the changed security environment has led NATO to boost its exercise program, which is essential to 'enable militaries and civilian organisations deployed on the ground to work together to identify "best practices" (what works) and "lessons learned" (what needs improving)' (NATO, 2023c). More specifically, exercises are fundamental 'to prepare commands and forces for operations in times of peace, crisis and conflict' (NATO, 2023c).[22] NATO has been conducting exercises since 1951 (NATO, 2024). During the Cold War, NATO conducted a number of exercises across multiple domains like air, land, maritime, and cyberspace helping the Allies to operate within an integrated military force under a single centralised command (NATO, 2024). An example is the Return to Forces to Germany (REFORGER), which was a series of exercises that tested the ability of North American troops to rapidly deploy to Europe (NATO, 2024). During the

22 NATO exercises can be executed in three forms:

> a) a live exercise (LIVEX) in which forces actually participate; b) a command-post exercise (CPX), which is a headquarters exercise involving commanders and their staffs, and communications within and between participating headquarters; c) an exercise study, which may take the form of a map exercise, a war game, a series of lectures, a discussion group or an operational analysis.
>
> (NATO, 2023c)

1970s and the 1980s, NATO maintained an intensive training program of exercises, considered 'an essential part of the Alliance's deterrence posture and helped to ensure that forces were prepared for potential aggression throughout the Cold War' (NATO, 2024). In 1994, the Alliance launched the Partnership for Peace initiative that has at its core objectives such as the promotion of closer military cooperation and interoperability between NATO and non-NATO countries in the Euro-Atlantic area (NATO, 2024). In 2002, NATO created the Response Force, which is a highly ready and technologically advanced multinational force that the Alliance can deploy quickly and effectively in a number of various situations (NATO, 2024). In 2004, the Istanbul Cooperation Initiative was introduced with the goal to strengthen cooperation between NATO and countries from the broader Middle East in areas such as education and training and to engage in joint training for terrorism (NATO, 2024). Since 2010, the introduction of the 2010 Strategic Concept (setting flexible guidelines for NATO's evolution and strengthening) and the new partnerships policy opened NATO exercises to all partners (NATO, 2024). In 2012, NATO launched the Connected Forces Initiative ensuring that the high level of interoperability Allied forces gained during their operational experience in Afghanistan, Libya, the Horn of Africa, and the Balkans was maintained (NATO, 2024). Since Russia's illegal annexation of Crimea of 2014, NATO has increased the number of exercises that focus on collective defence scenarios, which were further increased immediately after the war initiated by Russia against Ukraine in 2022 (NATO, 2024). At the extraordinary summit held in Brussels on 24 March 2022 the Allies agreed on a strengthened deterrence and defence posture based on all the tools at NATO's disposal, including military exercises (NATO, 2024). A good example is the Cold Response training exercise, a long-standing military operation conducted by NATO members and partner nations, led by Norway, and held in the second part of March 2022;[23] 35,000 military personnel from 23 out of the 30 NATO states as well as from Finland and Sweden (as a combined brigade) that were NATO partners at that time participated in this two-week exercise (Elfar, 2022). Russia declined the invitation to participate because of the war in Ukraine that, together with the death of four US marines that were killed in a transport plane crash during the exercise, clearly showed the seriousness of the circumstances that characterised the event that year (Elfar, 2022). This exercise raised questions about how militarisation in the Arctic may affect regional cooperation and future relations between NATO members and Russia (Elfar, 2022), especially with Finland and Sweden being part of the Alliance. Also, although the exercise had been planned before the war in Ukraine began, there were some concerns whether moving forward with the already scheduled Cold Response would cause any reactions from Russia (Elfar, 2022). Nevertheless, NATO members decided to conduct the exercise as this could deter Russia from invading a greater swath of land (Elfar, 2022). Also, Russia conducted a military exercise in the Arctic just before invading

23 The Cold Response exercise is typically conducted every two years but it was cancelled because of the coronavirus pandemic of 2020 (Elfar, 2022).

Ukraine, which was seen as a 'warning to the West' (Elfar, 2022). In March 2024, the Cold Response exercise was expanded to a Nordic Response because Finland and Sweden became NATO members (Norwegian Ministry of Defence, 2024). This exercise aimed at validating the Regional Plan North-West (RPNNW)[24] and demonstrating the integration of Finland and Sweden in NATO operations (Ministry of Defence of Italy, 2024). In this way, the exercise aimed to reinforce troops up north by training a defensive joint operation in arctic conditions in areas of Finland, Norway, and Sweden (Finnish Defence Forces, 2024). The military exercise was conducted on land, at sea, and in the air and convened altogether up to about 20,000 soldiers from 13 countries.[25] Another important military exercise conducted in 2024 is Steadfast Defender, which is the largest military exercise since the Cold War, running between January and May and involving more than 90,000 troops across the Atlantic and up to the Arctic (NATO, 2024). General Christopher G. Cavoli, Supreme Allied Commander Europe, has commented that this exercise is 'a clear demonstration of our [of NATO] unity, strength and determination to protect each other, our values, and the rules-based international order (NATO, 2024).

Moreover, in 2007 NATO accredited a Centre of Excellence-Cold Weather Operations (COE-CWO),[26] sponsored by Norway where it is located (Elverum, southern Norway). It 'acts as the main provider and coordinator of expertise and capabilities in the area of Cold Weather Operations in NATO' in order to 'provide NATO and partner nations the necessary competence in order to operate under Arctic, sub-Arctic and Cold Weather conditions' (Ministry for Foreign Affairs of Norway, 2024). The Education and Training branch (E&T) of the COE provides training and education in order to increase combat preparedness and effectiveness as well as general knowledge on how to operate in an arctic or cold weather environment (Ministry for Foreign Affairs of Norway, 2024). The importance of this COE is not only on increased tensions in the region and geopolitical changes but also on threats coming from climate change that has a 'multiplier effect' on a number of 'security phenomena, including conflicts and competition for scarce resources' (NATO, 2024b). Thus, 'increased occurrence of natural disasters and climate-related crises will require the more extensive deployment of armed forces and a wider adoption of dual-use and autonomous platforms such as unmanned underwater vehicles' (Carniel et al., 2024).

Nevertheless, in an interesting article titled 'NATO Is Unprepared for Russia's Arctic Threats', Liselotte Odgaard, a non-resident senior fellow at Hudson Institute

24 The RPNNW specifically deals with the Atlantic and the European Arctic and aims at making Arctic defence more cohesive (Edvardsen and Molid Martinussen, 2023).

25 The states that participated in the exercise were Belgium, Canada, Denmark, Finland, France, Germany, Italy, the Netherlands, Norway, Spain, Sweden, the UK, and the US (Norwegian Ministry of Defence, 2024).

26 Centres of Excellence (COEs) are defined by NATO as 'international military organisations that train and educate leaders and specialists from NATO member and partner countries'. Currently, NATO has 30 COEs (NATO, 2024a).

in Washington, argues that although the exercise 'suggests that NATO has a strong and capable defense presence in the region [...], a closer look at the capabilities of the Arctic states—which are all NATO members except Russia—reveals otherwise' (Odgaard, 2024). According to her, while Finland's and Sweden's recent NATO membership has been defined as 'a turning point in deterrence against Russia in the north', in reality their proximity to Russia means that their strategic focus is primarily targeted at the Baltic Sea region 'where Russia has pursued a military buildup directed toward NATO's eastern flank' (Odgaard, 2024). Additionally, NATO members have always prepared for other theatres, such as the Indo-Pacific and the Baltic Sea regions (Odgaard, 2024). For instance, they don't have ice-strengthened ships with both anti-aircraft and anti-submarine capabilities; Iceland only operates coastguard vessels and Norway has ice-strengthened coastguard vessels that are however not designed for military operations (Odgaard, 2024). Thus, Odgaard points out that NATO's defence posture has big gaps as 'Russia's nuclear submarines, which are capable of launching an attack on North America, can travel from the Barents Sea through the Bear Gap between Scandinavia and Svalbard, Norway, and under the ice along the coast of eastern Greenland without being detected' (Odgaard, 2024). In 2019, Russia conducted its largest strategic nuclear exercise in the Arctic, Grom or Thunder-2019, and a month later tested a hypersonic cruise missile from the White Sea (Conley and Melino, 2020, 2). Thunder-2019 involved 12,000 troops, 213 missile launchers, 105 aircraft, 15 surface warships, and 5 nuclear submarines (Conley and Melino, 2020, 2). At a briefing for foreign military attachés held before the exercise, Yevgeny Ilyin, acting chief of the Ministry's Directorate for International Military Cooperation, pointed out that test launches would be conducted from air, land, and sea (Litvinova, 2019). Ilyin stresses that the exercise was purely defensive in nature, aimed at training troops to deter a potential enemy and that it was not directed against any state (Litvinova, 2019).

Additionally, Odgaard also argues that the war in Ukraine has led Russia to organise coastguard cooperation and joint naval exercises with China (Odgaard, 2024). Russia's naval strategy of 2022 has raised the Arctic to its highest priority, building 475 military facilities between 2014 and 2019 (Odgaard, 2024). These capabilities are protected by a multilayered network of sensors, missile systems, coastal defence systems, electronic warfare technology, and strategic submarines (Odgaard, 2024). Being a partner of Russia, China can use its military facilities in the Arctic, including icebreakers and semi-submersible vessels (Odgaard, 2024). However, China is not interested in becoming a military power in the region, but it benefits from Moscow maintaining a strong force posture toward NATO in order to contrast the US (Odgaard, 2024). As mentioned above, the partnership between Russia and China will work as long as they have a common enemy, namely the US. Moreover, it is expected that China will have expanded its maritime presence in the Arctic (both subsurface and surface assets) under the guise of its dual military and scientific purposes (Conley and Melino, 2020, 2). It is clear that a more significant Chinese naval presence in the Arctic would need the assistance of Russia, which will translate into strengthened cooperation between the two states (Conley and Melino, 2020, 2). Thus, Russia would accept China's greater economic and military activity in the Arctic in exchange for an anti-Western partnership in the Arctic (Conley and Melino, 2020, 2).

Furthermore, another aspect that needs to be taken into account is the impact that militarisation has on the Arctic environment. A study conducted by the International Peace Bureau of Geneva (2002), Switzerland, highlights that 'military activities place a number of stresses on the physical environment' both in direct and indirect ways. Direct ways are 'pollution of the air, land, and water in peacetime; the immediate and long-term effects of armed conflict; militarisation of outer space; nuclear weapons development and production; land use' (International Peace Bureau of Geneva, 2002, 3). As for the pollution of the air, land, and water in peacetime, the study states that 'the world's military forces are responsible for the release of more than two thirds of CFC113 [chlorotrifluoromethane] into the ozone layer' (International Peace Bureau of Geneva, 2002, 3). It also states that during the Cold War, the US and Soviet armed forces produced enormous amounts of hazardous waste and that there are at least 50 nuclear warheads and 11 nuclear reactors littering the ocean floor as a result of naval accidents (International Peace Bureau of Geneva, 2002, 3). The study also stresses that the nuclear weapons industry is partly responsible for environmental contamination caused by the whole nuclear chain due to the link between the nuclear arms industry and civil nuclear power generation (International Peace Bureau of Geneva, 2002, 3). Murmansk, like many other sites (e.g., Chelyabinsk, La Hague, Yucca Mountain, Hanford, and Sellafield) contain huge amounts of nuclear material (International Peace Bureau of Geneva, 2002, 3). The military is responsible for climate change because of its greenhouse gas emissions, especially from aircraft (International Peace Bureau of Geneva, 2002, 3). As for the immediate and long-term effects of armed conflict, some very well-known consequences on the environment are radiation from nuclear explosions (Hiroshima, Nagasaki), agricultural degradation due to landmines (many African and Asian countries), unexploded 'remnants of war' impeding agriculture like cluster bombs (Kosovo, Afghanistan), and chemical agents and burning of oil wells (Gulf War) (International Peace Bureau of Geneva, 2002, 3). In the case of the militarisation of outer space, the risk of contamination of space through conventional or nuclear explosions in warfare is real since the militarisation of outer space is increasing (International Peace Bureau of Geneva, 2002, 7). As for nuclear weapons development and production, the manufacturing, storage, transport, disposal, etc., all place strains on the environment and impact human health (International Peace Bureau of Geneva, 2002, 7). Finally, land use is another critical direct way in which the military affect the environment and human health. Indeed, sometimes people are displaced when the military take over the land that is necessary to people for their survival in order to construct bases or to use it for target ranges, weapons stores, training grounds, etc. (International Peace Bureau of Geneva, 2002, 7). A good example is Thule in Greenland where Indigenous Inuit were displaced for the US base (International Peace Bureau of Geneva, 2002, 7). Among the indirect effects of military activities there is resource diversion, namely the fact that states spend huge amounts of money on military security (International Peace Bureau of Geneva, 2002, 7).

Since the 1970s, the military dimension has been addressed on several international occasions. The first one was the 1972 Stockholm Conference, the first global event to focus on environmental issues, in particular those concerning environmental degradation and transboundary pollution (International Peace Bureau of Geneva, 2002, 7). The Stockholm Declaration and Action Plan for the Human Environment resulting from the conference called for 'the elimination [and] complete destruction of such weapons' (UN, 1972). In 1987, the Brundtland Report titled 'Our Common Future: The World Commission on Environment and Development', which was the first international report on environmental issues to stress the new concept of sustainable development (defined as 'meeting the needs of the present without compromising the ability of future generations to meet their own needs'), dedicated an entire chapter to 'Peace, Security, Development and the Environment' (International Peace Bureau of Geneva, 2002, 9; UN, 2024a). This chapter states that 'a comprehensive approach to international and national security must transcend the traditional emphasis on military power and armed competition' and that 'the real sources of insecurity encompass unsustainable development. Armed competition and conflict create major obstacles to sustainable development. They stimulate an ethos that is antagonistic towards cooperation amongst nations' (International Peace Bureau of Geneva, 2002, 9). In 1992, the Rio Declaration stemming from the UN Conference on Environment and Development, also called the Earth Summit and held in Rio de Janeiro, Brazil, included two principles pertaining to the military sector, both of which reflect the insights of the Brundtland Report (International Peace Bureau of Geneva, 2002, 9). Principle 24 states that 'warfare is inherently destructive of sustainable development. Nations shall respect international laws protecting the environment in times of armed conflict, and shall cooperate in their further establishment' (International Peace Bureau of Geneva, 2002, 9). Principle 25 states that 'peace, development and environmental protection are interdependent and indivisible' (International Peace Bureau of Geneva, 2002, 9). In 2002, the World Summit on Sustainable Development held in Johannesburg, South Africa, paid little attention to the military (International Peace Bureau of Geneva, 2002, 9). Nevertheless, the draft outcome document of the Preparatory Committee contains a reference to it in its fifth paragraph stating that 'warfare is inherently destructive of sustainable development' (International Peace Bureau of Geneva, 2002, 9). Since then, a number of initiatives have been taken that 'either address the military dimension of environmental issues, or aim to create the opportunity to do so' (International Peace Bureau of Geneva, 2002, 10).

Interestingly, military activities were instead excluded from the 1997 Kyoto Protocol upon US insistence (International Peace Bureau of Geneva, 2002, 3; Hermann, 2022). Behind this request was Pentagon officials' claim, like the one of former Deputy Undersecretary of Defence for Environmental Security Sherri W. Goodman, that the protocol would negatively affect 'military readiness' with serious implications for military training, operations, and fuel use (Hermann, 2022). Under the 2015 Paris Agreement, states can voluntarily report their military emissions, but many states with large militaries do not report anything at all (Weir, 2024).

More recently, the war in Ukraine has reinforced the debate on the link between the military and environment. In early 2022, some journalists began investigating how Russia's aggression towards Ukraine was affecting the climate crisis, but data on emissions were not available (Weir, 2024). The war in Ukraine has highlighted once again that 'national security choices, such as military spending or warfighting, can have an impact on the climate, and so undermine our collective security' (Weir, 2024). Also, Russia's war in Ukraine 'has seen the first attempt to comprehensively document the emissions from any conflict, and researchers have had to develop their methodologies from scratch' (Weir, 2024). The analysis has shown that the emissions caused by the war are equal to the annual emissions of a state like Belgium (Weir, 2024). These calculations do not include the increased military activities in the Arctic as a consequence of the war in Ukraine.

In conclusion, the militarisation of the Arctic and climate change are complementary elements that deeply affect geopolitics in the region. It began after Russian flag-planting in 2007 and has intensified as a consequence of the war in Ukraine.

Scientific cooperation

Science is certainly one of the most crucial sectors in the cooperative efforts of Arctic states because it provides essential information to help understand how our climate has changed over millions of years, what we should expect in the near future, and what measures it is necessary to take in order to face the environmental, economic, and social challenges brought about by climate change. It is perhaps the sector where cooperation among the Arctic states (and non-Arctic states as well) has been more successful not only because of its importance in the study of the environment but also because it is a soft power issue on which it is easier to cooperate.

Scientific research, which in the case of the Arctic mainly refers to marine scientific research, is mainly regulated through the legal framework provided by UNCLOS in its Part XIII (from Article 34 to Article 45) with the goal to promote international cooperation (Yaxin, 2020, 4). UNCLOS does not contain a definition of 'marine scientific research', which refers to a variety of scientific disciplines such as biology, biotechnology, geology, chemistry, physics, geophysics, hydrography, physical oceanography, and ocean drilling and coring, which are dedicated to the study of the oceans, the marine environment (flora and fauna), as well as to the physical boundaries with solid earth and the atmosphere (Pavliha and Martínez Gutiérrez, 2010, 115). Marine scientific research is expressly listed as one of the freedoms of the high seas[27] (Pavliha and Martínez Gutiérrez, 2010, 119). In particular, Article 238 concerning the right to conduct marine scientific research stipulates that 'all States, irrespective of their geographical location, and competent interna-

27 According to Article 86 of UNCLOS, high seas are 'all parts of the sea that are not included in the exclusive economic zone, in the territorial sea or in the internal waters of a State, or in the archipelagic waters of an archipelagic State' (United Nations, 1982).

tional organizations[28] have the right to conduct marine scientific research subject to the rights and duties of other States as provided for in this Convention' (UNCLOS, 1982). This can occur only 'for peaceful purposes and for the benefit of mankind as a whole' and provided that states and international organisations make known all pertinent information about their research and make the results available, as Article 242 and Article 244 clearly say (UNCLOS, 1982). Additionally, according to Article 143, international organisations are obliged to actively promote the flow of information and scientific data and the transfer of knowledge resulting from research (UNCLOS, 1982). Also, Article 241 provides that marine scientific research activities may not serve as the legal basis for a claim 'to any part of the marine environment or its resources' (UNCLOS, 1982). Furthermore, UNCLOS gives coastal states, in the exercise of their sovereignty, the exclusive right to regulate, authorise, and conduct marine scientific research in their territorial sea (Article 245). By analogy, this right is also extended to internal waters of a coastal state or in the archipelagic waters of an archipelagic state (Article 245) (Pavliha and Martínez Gutiérrez, 2010, 121). Marine scientific research can be carried out only if the coastal state has given its explicit consent and if the conditions that it establishes are rigorously followed (Article 245) (UNCLOS, 1982). For instance, ships can't conduct research or survey activities while exercising the right of innocent passage because this would make the passage non-innocent (Article 19) (UNCLOS, 1982). When the territorial sea forms part of a strait used for international navigation or an archipelagic sea lane, Article 40 of UNCLOS provides that while exercising the right of transit passage, 'foreign ships, including marine scientific research and hydrographic survey ships, may not carry out any research or survey activities without the prior authorization of the States bordering straits' (UNCLOS, 1982). Article 246 provides that coastal states can conduct marine scientific research in their exclusive economic zone and on their continental shelf (UNCLOS, 1982). The same article also provides that, under normal circumstances (that is to say in the absence of an imminent danger of an armed conflict), 'coastal states must give consent to other States or international organizations to conduct research projects exclusively for peaceful purposes and in order to increase scientific knowledge of the marine environment for the benefit of all mankind' (UNCLOS, 1982; Pavliha and Martínez Gutiérrez, 2010, 121). Nevertheless, Article 246 of UNCLOS also provides that coastal states can refuse to give their consent if the proposed marine scientific research project is of 'direct significance for the exploration and exploitation of natural resources, whether living or non-living, [if it] involves drilling into the continental shelf, [or if it requires] the use of explosives or the introduction of harmful substances into the marine environment' (UNCLOS, 1982; Pavliha and Martínez Gutiérrez, 2010, 122). Coastal states can withhold their consent also 'if the proposed research project will require that artificial islands be constructed or used, if the coastal State receives inaccurate information about the goal of the

28 UNCLOS does not define 'competent international organizations', which it uses in general terms as opposed to other parts (Pavliha and Martínez Gutiérrez, 2010, 118).

project, or if the "researching State or competent international organization has outstanding obligations to the coastal State" from a previous project' (Pavliha and Martínez Gutiérrez, 2010, 122).

Over the last few decades, scientific research in and on the Arctic has increased, especially as a consequence of climate change that, according to scientific studies, will probably make the Arctic largely ice-free by the summer of 2040 (The Economist, 2017). Indeed, the melting of Arctic glaciers has caused a 30% sea level rise between 1992 and 2017.[29] Climate change causes continued loss of sea ice, melting of glaciers and of the Greenland ice cap, and influences atmospheric circulation, vegetation, and the carbon cycle, negatively affecting the ecosystem both inside and outside the Arctic (Norwegian Polar Institute, no date). This has environmental, social, cultural, economic, and political consequences that are interlinked (Arctic Centre, 2024a). Plants and animals are very sensitive to environmental changes and different species respond differently to them (Arctic Centre, 2024a). For instance, low-growing Arctic plants are threatened by higher species spreading further south, and the small-sized Arctic fox cannot compete with foxes spreading from the south (Arctic Centre, 2024a). Also, new species moving from the south to the north thus jeopardise the indigenous species in the region and terrestrial flora and fauna cannot move much further north because they are facing the Arctic Ocean (Arctic Centre, 2024a). Moreover, environmental changes deeply affect indigenous people's livelihoods that are often linked to nature (Arctic Centre, 2024a). In fact, hunting, fishing, reindeer herding, and tourism are very dependent on the environment and weather conditions (Arctic Centre, 2024a). The unpredictability of ice conditions is making the travel of hunters using dogsleds or snowmobiles dangerous and melting ice and rising sea levels are exposing indigenous people to destructive coastal erosion and damages to infrastructure (Government of Canada, 2019, 20). Additionally, climate change forces indigenous people to change their diet while also increasing health risks related to water quality and increased chemical and microbial contaminants, health risks to reindeer and reindeer herders through greater threat of accidents from changes in ice and snow stability, and risks to physical health and cultural well-being through shifts in livelihoods (Coggins and Ford, 2021). On top of this, the melting of permafrost[30] and the fact that the sea is without ice cover longer than before are threatening many indigenous villages with shoreline collapse (Arctic Centre, 2024a). For instance, in Canada, many villages have voted in favour of relocating but have not received sufficient funding for the relocation (Cunliffe et al., 2019).

All these changes are at the centre of the controversial debate whether climate change is a consequence of man's economic activities (Anthropocene) or of the richest part of mankind (the Western part of the world) that has altered the sustainable

29 It is not the melting of sea ice that raises the sea level, but the melting of the ice sheet (Arctic Centre, 2024a).

30 Permafrost is defined as rock or soil that remains at or below the freezing point of 32°F (0°C) for two or more years (United States Environmental Protection Agency, 2022).

development principle with its capitalist system (Capitalocene). According to this second theory, the West should pay the highest price for the negative impact that climate change has on the environment and should help less developed states face the consequences of this problem as they have less resources at disposal. This debate is well discussed in the book titled *Anthropocene or Capitalocene?: Nature, History and the Crisis of Capitalism* by Jason Moore (2016, 7) that collects a number of chapters suggesting that the Anthropocene theory emphasises the risks and the consequences of climate change but that it does not explain the very causes of it as it does not take into consideration several issues like capitalism, power and class, the dualist framings of 'nature' and 'society', as well as the role of states and empires. The Arctic, which is warming four times faster than the rest of the world and regulates the temperature of the earth, is crucial in the climate change issue and, consequently, in this debate. Considering that most of the states belonging to the region are among the most developed states in the world, this debate is particularly relevant. Consequently, scientific cooperation is of utmost importance in order to study the causes, the scope, and the environmental impact of climate change on the Arctic. Also, scientific cooperation is essential for scientists' access to geographical areas under different jurisdictions, as well as transport of scientific equipment to collect data, conduct experiments, and attend conferences (Tsui, 2019).

The relevance of scientific cooperation led to the establishment of the International Arctic Science Committee (IASC) in 1990, a non-governmental international scientific organisation founded by the eight Arctic states that were observers in the Arctic Environmental Protection Strategy and in the AC since 1998 (IASC, no date; Arctic Council, 2024a). According to the Founding Articles, IASC was founded 'to encourage and facilitate international consultation and cooperation for scientific research concerned with the Arctic' and 'the committee [...] provides a forum for discussion, exchange of information and cooperation' (IASC, 1990). As Łuszczuk and Szkarlat explain, 'the main declared reasons for the establishment of IASC were then the unpolitical needs related to the need for better coordination of the existing research cooperation and developing it in an institutional framework guaranteeing durability and efficiency (Łuszczuk and Szkarlat, 2022, 27).

Additionally, the document stressed the fact that the Arctic is environmentally very sensitive and that it 'has a major influence on global systems of climate, weather, ocean circulation and other important environmental issues' (IASC, 1990). Additionally, already at that time the founding states acknowledged the fact that 'there has been a growing national and international interest in the Arctic, stimulated largely by the recognition of the scientific and political importance as well as its economical potential' (IASC, 1990). Over time, the IASC has become 'the leading international science organization of the North' (IASC, no date). Today, it includes 23 countries involved in all aspects of Arctic research, including 15 non-Arctic countries (Austria, China, Czechia, France, Germany, India, Italy, Japan, the Netherlands, Poland, Portugal, South Korea, Spain, Switzerland, and the UK) (IASC, no date). Nowadays, the establishment of IASC is considered as an indirect result of Gorbachev's Murmansk Speech of 1987 (Łuszczuk and Szkarlat, 2022, 27). However, it is also true that IASC 'evolved through a series of developments' (Rogne et al., 2015), which 'were embedded in the rich history of the discovery and scientific exploration of the region in which particular political-economic national interests intertwined with purely scientific international collaboration (Łuszczuk and Szkarlat, 2022, 27). In this context, particularly relevant are the so-called 'international polar years' (IPYs), which are multinational research projects organised in 1882–1883, 1932–1933, 1957–1958, and 2007–2008 (Łuszczuk and Szkarlat, 2022, 27; Barr and Lüdecke, 2010, 24). As stated in the Initial Concept Note of October 2023, the fifth IPY will be held in 2032–2033, whose aim is

> to provide a vital opportunity to close outstanding major knowledge gaps through targeted attention and globally-coordinated action enabling polar researchers, knowledge holders, rights holders and stakeholders to achieve major breakthroughs in the knowledge required to protect the global environment, develop effective national and local strategies to mitigate and adapt to environmental changes, and accelerate progress towards achieving the UN Sustainable Development Goals.
>
> (IASC, 2023)

Later, in 2017, the eight Arctic states adopted the legally binding Agreement on Enhancing International Arctic Scientific Cooperation ('Science Agreement' or 'Agreement'). This was the first legally binding agreement to promote Arctic scientific research across the entirety of the Arctic region and one of only three agreements stipulated under the auspices of the AC, the other two being the 2011 Agreement on Cooperation on Aeronautical and Maritime Search and Rescue in the Arctic and the 2013 Agreement on Cooperation on Marine Oil Pollution Preparedness and Response in the Arctic (Tsui, 2019) that also aim at strengthening cooperation among the eight Arctic states in the respective areas.

The crucial aim of the Science Agreement is 'to enhance cooperation in Scientific Activities in order to increase effectiveness and efficiency in the development of scientific knowledge about the Arctic', as clearly stated in Article 2 (Arctic Council, 2017). In order to pursue this goal, according to Article 4, 'each Party shall use its best efforts to facilitate entry to, and exit from, its territory of persons, research platforms, material, samples, data, and equipment of the Participants as needed to advance the objectives of this Agreement' (Arctic Council, 2017). More specifically, Article 5 regulates access to research infrastructure, facilities, and logistical services (transportation, storage of equipment, and material) 'for the purpose of conducting Scientific Activities in Identified Geographic Areas' (Arctic Council, 2017). Access to such areas is regulated by Article 6 envisaging that

> the Parties shall facilitate access by the Participants to terrestrial, coastal, atmospheric, and marine areas in the Identified Geographic Areas, consistent with international law, for the purpose of conducting Scientific Activities. The Parties shall facilitate the processing of applications to conduct marine

> scientific research under this Agreement consistent with the 1982 United Nations Convention on the Law of the Sea.
>
> (Arctic Council, 2017)

Article 6 also adds that 'the Parties also shall facilitate joint Scientific Activities that require airborne scientific data collection in the Identified Geographic Areas, and that are subject to specific implementing agreements or arrangements concluded between the Parties or Participants pertaining to those activities' (Arctic Council, 2017). Article 7 regulates access to scientific information stating that

> the Parties shall support full and open access to scientific metadata and shall encourage open access to scientific data and data products and published results with minimum time delay, preferably online and free of charge or at no more than the cost of reproduction and delivery. The Parties shall facilitate the distribution and sharing of scientific data and metadata by, as appropriate and to the extent practicable, adhering to commonly accepted standards, formats, protocols, and reporting.
>
> (Arctic Council, 2017)

Additionally, Article 17 stipulates that the parties can continue to 'enhance and facilitate cooperation with non-Parties' but that 'nothing in this Agreement shall affect the rights and obligations of the Parties under agreements with non-Parties, nor preclude cooperation between the Parties and non-Parties' (Arctic Council, 2017).

The Science Agreement has huge potential to encourage states to reduce barriers to scientists' access because it identifies four crucial areas for coordination, namely entry and exit of persons, research infrastructure, research areas, and data (Tsui, 2019). Nevertheless, the effectiveness of the Science Agreement to enhance international scientific cooperation is questionable because it depends substantially on individual states' interest as it gives significant deference to states to implement their policies. Indeed, Article 7 clearly stipulates that the 'Agreement makes it a legal obligation for states to facilitate access to data, but leaves it up to the state to decide how they would like to do so' (Arctic Council, 2017; Tsui, 2019). Indeed, the flexibility for states to act could 'increases the unpredictability of the Agreement's potential to facilitate access' because it could have two opposite effects (Tsui, 2019). It could lead a state to ambitiously implement the Science Agreement by even changing its national laws in order to make it easier for scientists to enter and exit their jurisdiction, access research infrastructure and research areas, and data or it could also mean that a state would not do anything to implement the Agreement because this Agreement does not envisage any minimum standard to be respected (Tsui, 2019).

The Science Agreement clearly shows the importance of the AC in coordinating and fostering cooperation among the Arctic states and between these and non-Arctic states. As already stated, the AC's work focuses on sustainable development, environmental protection, and climate change. The AC's WGs developed several projects that address these issues. For instance, the WG on Conservation of Arctic Flora and Fauna works on the development of mechanisms to develop common responses on issues concerning the Arctic ecosystem in order to preserve and protect biodiversity in the region (Arctic Council, 2024b). The WG on the Protection of the Arctic Marine Environment (PAME) focuses on the protection and sustainable use of the Arctic marine environment (Arctic Council, 2024c). In particular, PAME identifies the marine policy measures necessary to respond to environmental change from both land and sea-based activities (Arctic Council, 2024c). In order to do so, PAME develops and coordinates strategic plans, programs, assessments, and guidelines that complement existing legal arrangements aimed at protection of the Arctic marine environment (Arctic Council, 2024c). The themes that PAME addresses are Arctic Shipping, Marine Protected Areas, Resource Exploration and Development, Ecosystem Approach to Management, and Arctic Marine Pollution (Arctic Council, 2024c). The WG on Arctic Contaminants Action Program (ACAP) works to prevent and reduce pollution and environmental risks in the Arctic (Arctic Council, 2024d). It aims to raise awareness and show ways to reduce pollution in the Arctic by carrying out demonstration projects that encourage nations to strengthen their policies in regards to reducing pollutants and mitigating associated environmental, human health, and socioeconomic risks (Arctic Council, 2024d). ACAP's projects especially focus on persistent organic pollutants (POPs) (e.g., mercury), waste management on shore to prevent marine litter, plastics, and microplastics, as well as hazardous substances (e.g., obsolete pesticides, solvents and pharmaceuticals, and chemicals), and short-lived climate pollutants (e.g., black carbon, methane, and hydrofluorocarbons currently covered in international conventions) (Arctic Council, 2024d). Finally, the WG on Arctic Monitoring and Assessment Program (AMAP), which is probably the most relevant WG, aims to measure and monitor pollutants and climate change effects on ecosystems and human health in the Arctic (Arctic Council, 2024e). It has numerous tasks like documenting the sources and pathways of pollutants, trends in key climate indicators and their environmental implications, examining the impact of pollution and climate change on Arctic ecosystems and people, and giving advice to ministers on priority actions needed to improve Arctic conditions (Arctic Council, 2024e). Additionally, AMAP also supports international processes aiming at reducing global threats from contaminants and climate change like the UNFCCC, the UN Environment Stockholm Convention on Persistent Organic Pollutants,[31] Minamata Convention on Mercury,[32]

31 The Stockholm Convention on Persistent Organic Pollutants of 2001 'is a global treaty to protect human health and the environment from chemicals that remain intact in the environment for long periods, become widely distributed geographically, accumulate in the fatty tissue of humans and wildlife, and have harmful impacts on human health or on the environment' (UN Stockholm Convention, 2019).

32 The Minamata Convention on Mercury of 2013 is a global treaty to protect human health and the environment from the adverse effects of mercury (UNEP, 2021).

and the United Nation's Economic Commission for Europe (UNECE) Convention on Long-range Transboundary Air Pollution[33] (Arctic Council, 2024e).

In this context, the role played by AC observers should not be disregarded because they valuably contribute to the work of WGs, especially through knowledge sharing (e.g., experience in polar science and observation, research icebreakers, and scientific research stations) or financial support (Bowman, 2017; Kim, no date). Observers provide a fresh perspective and bring resources critical to the implementation of projects (Bowman, 2017). For instance, observers can contribute to the Álgu Fund (Álgu means 'beginning' in the Saami language), which is meant to provide financial support to permanent participants in order to foster greater participation on projects and programs in their communities (Bowman, 2017). It is a charitable foundation based in Sweden set up by Aleut International Association, Arctic Athabaskan Council, Gwich'in Council International, Russian Association of Indigenous Peoples of the North (RAIPON), and the Saami Council (Gwich'in Council, no date). Many observers consider it as an opportunity to directly support the needs of indigenous peoples of the region (Bowman, 2017). In fact, the Álgu Fund is very much focused on the indigenous communities as it contributes to the work of the AC by facilitating the inclusion of traditional indigenous knowledge, the understanding and respect for this knowledge and for Indigenous cultural traditions (Gwich'in Council, no date). Additionally, the Álgu Fund provides experts, facilitates the involvement of local people, and promotes cross-border cooperation amongst indigenous peoples and the jurisdictions in which they live (Gwich'in Council, no date). Another possibility for observers to strengthen their engagement in the AC's work is the Arctic Economic Council (AEC), which was established by the AC in late 2014 (Bowman, 2017). At present, it is an independent organisation aiming to foster circumpolar business partnerships and whose members represent a wide range of businesses operating in the Arctic, from mining and shipping companies to reindeer herding and indigenous economic development corporations (Bowman, 2017; Arctic Economic Council, 2020). One of the AEC WGs[34] is the Blue Economy WG, which combines knowledge, expertise, and funding instruments to encourage product development and economic growth in the sector (Arctic Economic Council, 2020). Its tasks include the application of scientific and engineering principles to the processing of materials by marine biological agents to provide goods and services, and the use of technologies for the safe use, exploitation, protection of, and intervention in the marine environment (Arctic Economic Council, 2020).

While they provide knowledge and resources to the work of the AC, observers also benefit from contributing to it. They can participate in the WGs' meetings,

33 The Convention on Long-range Transboundary Air Pollution of 1979 aims 'to limit, to gradually prevent and to reduce their discharges of air pollutants in order to combat the resulting transboundary pollution' (Eur-Lex, 2020).

34 The WGs of the AEC are the Maritime Transportation WG, the Investments and Infrastructure WG, the Responsible Resource Development WG, the Connectivity WG, and the Blue Economy WG (Arctic Economic Council, 2020).

grasping important information that can help them formulate effective policies or strategies for the region (if the observer is a state/regional body) or identifying the type of projects that they should pursue (if the observer is an NGO) (Bowman, 2017). Moreover, access to high-level government officials gives observers the possibility to form relationships that can continue outside the confines of the AC (Bowman, 2017). Finally, obtaining observer status is considered by many as 'a legitimising stamp of approval' to have Arctic interests and to act within the norms set by the Arctic community (Bowman, 2017).

In this context, the role played by China, an AC observer, in scientific research in the region is growing in importance. The reason why China is intensifying its scientific presence in the region is that this gives it the 'right to speak' on Arctic affairs, which is functional to its ambitions to become 'a polar great power' by 2030, as it is written in its 2018 White Paper (Funaiole et al., 2023). China has two research stations in the Arctic. China's Arctic Yellow River Station is the first Chinese scientific station in the region and was established in 2004 in Ny-Alesund, Svalbard, a Norwegian archipelago in the Arctic Ocean (CGTN, 2024). Over 20 years, the Yellow River Station has supported more than 250 scientific research projects and hosted over 660 expedition members (CGTN, 2024). Chinese scientists have carried out a range of operational surveys and scientific research projects in the fields of glaciology, terrestrial and marine ecology, and space physics and have undertaken studies on environmental pollutants in the Arctic jointly with Norwegian scientists (China Daily, 2024). Also, China has successfully carried out several Arctic scientific expeditions using platforms such as the polar icebreakers *Xuelong* and *Xuelong 2* (China Daily, 2024). The second Chinese scientific station is the Iceland–China Science Observatory, which was established in Karholl in northern Iceland in 2018 with the aim to support 'multi-disciplinary observation and research on aurora and space weather, atmospheric science and meteorology, biology and ecology, oceanography, glaciology, geophysics and geology, climate change and environmental science' (Polar Research Institute of China, 2018). The observatory was initially intended to serve as an aurora observatory but it is now also used to research satellite remote sensing, raising some concerns about the possibility that China's presence in Iceland might have long-term security implications (Dams et al., 2020, 6).

Moreover, China has launched international initiatives that affect Arctic science cooperation. An example is the establishment in 2013 of the China–Nordic Arctic Research Centre (CNARC), which is an international consortium created by the Polar Research Institute of China in collaboration with respective institutes in the Nordic states (Denmark, Finland, Iceland, Norway, and Sweden) and China in order to promote and facilitate China–Nordic cooperation for Arctic research (CNARC, 2024). To this aim, CNARC works to increase awareness, understanding, and knowledge of the Arctic and its global impacts and promote cooperation to ensure the sustainable development of the Arctic and the development of China in the global context (CNARC, 2024). It mainly focuses on three research themes, namely Arctic climate change and its impacts; Arctic resources, shipping, and economic cooperation; and Arctic policy-making and legislation (Nielsson, 2023).

Generally speaking, CNARC has the purpose of 'building the bridge' and 'filling in gaps of knowledge' between the Nordic states and China so that the two parties can enhance their understanding of each other (Beixi and Jian, 2014). From China's perspective, it is useful to understand major issues concerning Arctic governance, figure out the main concerns of the Arctic states, get knowledge about the region, and construct an innovative cooperative model between Arctic and non-Arctic states (Beixi and Jian, 2014). CNARC has accelerated and intensified exchange between the Nordic states and China through, for instance, the organisation of international symposiums like the Asian Countries and the Arctic Future symposium held in Shanghai in April 2014, which was the very first (Beixi and Jian, 2014). In particular, it was jointly organised by Shanghai Institute of International Studies and Fridtjof Nansen Institute with the support of CNARC, with the aim to address the topics of Arctic governance and the engagement of Asian stakeholders in Arctic trans-regional cooperation (Beixi and Jian, 2014). Asian states like Japan, Korea, India, and Singapore were also invited to participate (Beixi and Jian, 2014). Moreover, CNARC has also undertaken concrete activities like the fellowship program that every year grants two Nordic and two Chinese candidates a fellowship to advance their own research project falling under CNARC's research priorities for a one-month period in an institute within CNARC's network (Beixi and Jian, 2014).

Furthermore, in 2004, China established the Asian Forum for Polar Sciences (AFoPS), a non-governmental organisation 'encouraging and facilitating cooperation for the advance of polar sciences among countries in the Asian region' (AFoPS, 2004). The forum consists of its six members that are national polar research institutions representing China, Japan, South Korea, India, Malaysia, and Thailand, and four observers, namely Indonesia, Philippines, Sri Lanka, and Vietnam (AFoPS, 2004). None of these states has territory north of the Arctic Circle, but all of them are interested in Arctic resources, thus they are trying to get involved in polar affairs (Arctic and Antarctic). Science is a good way to achieve this goal. For instance, China, India, Japan, Singapore, and South Korea have engaged in scientific projects led by the AC's Working Groups, Task Forces, and Expert Groups (e.g., the Black Carbon and Methane Expert Group is tasked with developing a biennial 'Summary of Progress and Recommendations' based on national reports and other relevant information on the impact of black carbon and methane on the warming of the atmosphere) (Arctic Council, 2024f). All of them but Singapore have released white papers outlining their Arctic policies and all but India have appointed official Arctic ambassadors or envoys (Heng and Freymann, 2023). Also, China, India, Japan, Singapore, and South Korea are AC observers since 2013 but they have developed different strategies and approaches to the Arctic (Heng and Freymann, 2023). Chinese state officials and academics consider environmental research a useful tool to advance China's long-term ambitions without rousing too much suspicion from Arctic states (Heng and Freymann, 2023). For instance, in an interview given to state-owned new agency Xinhua in 2009, Deputy Director of the State Oceanic Administration Chen Lianzeng suggested that China could use Arctic climate science to lay the groundwork for broader presence in the future (Heng and Freymann, 2023). In his interview, Chen outlined a three-stage strategy for achieving China's gradual expansion in the Arctic (Heng and Freymann, 2023). The first step is to deepen China's understanding of climate change and the status of resources in the poles; the second step is to 'further strengthen its substantive presence'; while the third step is to 'actively participate in international polar affairs' and 'establish [a] strategic position' near both the Arctic and the Antarctic (Heng and Freymann, 2023).

Moreover, in 2016 China established the Trilateral High-Level Dialogue on the Arctic together with Japan and South Korea (Heng and Freymann, 2023). It is an informal forum held annually (it has been suspended for four years because of the global pandemic that began in 2020) with the aim to cooperate on scientific matters and share scientific data (Heng and Freymann, 2023). Historically, the forum has focused on non-sensitive issue like marine pollution, but it has also framed the Arctic as a global issue in order to legitimise non-Arctic states' participation in regional issues (Heng and Freymann, 2023). However, the conclusion of the Dialogue often includes other important issues such as fisheries, resources, and trade routes that are defined as 'opportunities' and notes that climate change creates both opportunities and challenges (Heng and Freymann, 2023). Also, the Dialogue might be expanded to include India and Singapore (Heng and Freymann, 2023).

In 2022, India's government published a document titled *India's Arctic Policy: Building a Partnership for Sustainable Development* demonstrating ambitions similar to China's (Heng and Freymann, 2023). The emphasis that this document puts on India's scientific expertise in glaciology nurtured from extensively studying the Himalayas seems to justify an 'interlinked polar programme' combining Indian activities in the Arctic, Antarctic, and Alpine regions (Heng and Freymann, 2023). Also, this document includes the Arctic in a broader global narrative that 'would be incomplete without India' (Heng and Freymann, 2023).

Singapore is the only AC observer not to have an Arctic policy (Heng and Freymann, 2023) and, unlike many other Asian states, it does not have a historic tradition of polar science (The Arctic Institute, 2024). However, since 2019, Singaporean scientists have been conducting research in the region especially on the acoustics of tidewater glaciers in Svalbard, Norway (The Arctic Institute, 2024). Singapore's scientific interest is essentially due to its interests in shipping, energy resources, and climate change (The Arctic Institute, 2024). In particular, its interest in the Arctic stems from the challenge posed by the NSR to its role as a global shipping hub, as well as from the consequences of the melting sea ice (The Arctic Institute, 2024).

Japan's involvement in Arctic science began with the creation of the Arctic Environment Research Center in 1990, which led the National Institute of Polar Research to establish a Japanese research station in Ny-Ålesund, Svalbard to conduct research on atmospheric physics, glaciology, meteorology, oceanography, and terrestrial biology (The Arctic Institute, 2024a). In the 1990s, Japan was invited to join IASC and participate in the founding of the International Northern Sea Route Program, a six-year project between Japan, Norway, and Russia to study the viability of Arctic shipping lanes (The Arctic Institute, 2024a). Currently, the program is called the Japan Northern Sea Route Program and is still dedicated to

Arctic shipping research (The Arctic Institute, 2024a). Furthermore, after applying for observer status in the AC in 2009, the Japanese Ministry of Foreign Affairs established an Arctic Task Force within the Ocean Division 'in order to make a cross-sectorial approach towards foreign policy on the Arctic including the aspect of International Law' (The Arctic Institute, 2024a). When it obtained permanent observer status in 2013, Japan adopted the Basic Plan on Ocean Policy that lays out its priority areas in the Arctic, namely international cooperation and trans-Arctic shipping (The Arctic Institute, 2024a).

Like Japan, South Korea also began engaging in the Arctic in the 1990s through a number of unilateral and multilateral scientific studies such as a scientific study conducted between 1993 and 1995 and joint research with Japan (The Arctic Institute, 2024a). In 2001, South Korea organised the Korea Arctic Science Council to continue Korea's scientific endeavours in the region while also pursuing research on the potential of the sea routes, which is its real interest in the region (The Arctic Institute, 2024a). Through the Council, South Korea conducted marine research in cooperation with the Geological Survey of Japan and dispatched two researchers to a Chinese icebreaker to explore the Bering and Chukchi Seas (The Arctic Institute, 2024a). In 2002, South Korea became an IASC member and inaugurated its first research station in Svalbard at the Arctic Dasan Station (The Arctic Institute, 2024a). In 2009, South Korea completed *Araon*, its first research icebreaker that has continued conducting annual research activities in the Arctic between July and August every year and resupplies South Korea's two Antarctic research stations (The Arctic Institute, 2024a). Furthermore, it has a proactive stance towards the so-called Asian Arctic Club (consisting of South Korea, China, and Japan) that demonstrates a clear and strong interest of these states in the Arctic (mainly for economic reasons) by promoting 'a distinct Asian view on Arctic affairs' (The Arctic Institute, 2024a).

Although scientific cooperation is unanimously considered crucial, the war in Ukraine has had a strong negative impact on it because many projects involving Russian scientists have been stopped. Some Arctic states have imposed severe restrictions (Finland is one of the strictest ones) on researchers to prevent them from cooperating with the Russian government or institutions, while some other states like the US and Canada have a lighter position (Arctic Portal, 2024).

As most data can be collected in Russia, the largest state in the Arctic with the longest coast, this makes Russia key to understanding climate change both regionally and globally; excluding Russia from cooperation means that international Arctic scientists will not have the necessary information to conduct scientific research. In fact, they are cut off from over 60% of their research region, and exchange of data with Russian scientists is impossible (Orphal, 2024). As Stephanie Orphal points out, 'the long-term consequences of this could be drastic, as Arctic warming is an important indicator for global climate developments, and without data exchange it will be impossible to model the broader impacts of climate change' (Orphal, 2024). In their report titled *New Arctic realities. Between conflicting interests and avenues for cooperation* published by the Centre for East European and International Studies in 2024, Andreeva et al. quote the words of

German oceanographer Heidemarie Kassens according to whom 'research in the Arctic, and in particular climate research, relies on international collaboration, access, and continuous monitoring and data sharing among all regional actors of the Arctic, to understand and effectively respond to the climate crisis in the Arctic' (Andreeva et al., 2024). She also argues that if the UN Commission on the Limits of the Continental Shelf recognises that the Lomonosov Ridge is the continuation of the Russian continental shelf in its pending final recommendation, international scientific expeditions into the international waters of the Arctic Ocean might become more difficult (Andreeva et al., 2024).

Russian scientists have been affected by the war in Ukraine as well (Andreeva et al., 2024). For example, they can't access international academic journals or publication databases like Elsevier (Andreeva et al., 2024). Additionally, the Russian Arctic station Snowflake on the Yamal Peninsula, which is expected to be open in late 2024 and was originally conceived as a hub for international Arctic scientists, will very probably be used for joint Russian–Chinese projects (Andreeva et al., 2024).

Nevertheless, as Andreeva et al. correctly point out, 'unlike former times, there is no time to wait for an international research strategy to emerge' because 'the pace of climate change is too fast' (Andreeva et al., 2024). The necessity to re-establish cooperation between East and West is being discussed in several fora. For instance, on 21 February 2024 the Belfer Center for Science and International Affairs of the Harvard Kennedy School hosted the second meeting of its Cooperation or Conflict in the Arctic: What to Do About Russia During a Climate Crisis? study group (Wandenfels and Williams, 2024). After stressing that the war in Ukraine has halted fruitful cooperation on biology and nature conservation research, stopping the flow of data across boundaries, the group has highlighted 'the necessity of working across political boundaries to fully understand Arctic ecosystems' (Wandenfels and Williams, 2024). For instance, one scientist described an international expedition that traversed the maritime boundary from Alaska into Russian waters of the Chukchi Sea in which she participated in the early 1990s as an opportunity to get a clear understanding of the ecosystem she was studying (Wandenfels and Williams, 2024). She explained that before that expedition that boundary was like a curtain but after that she and other biologists could see how completely different the ecology and physical oceanography are in the western Chukchi compared to the eastern Chukchi (Wandenfels and Williams, 2024). Another scientist spoke about the role played by binding agreements in the continuation of cooperation (Wandenfels and Williams, 2024). A good example is the *Agreement on the Conservation and Management of the Alaska Chukotka Polar Bear Population* stipulated by the US and Russia in 2000 where scientists and the native Alaskan people and indigenous Chukchi participated in joint research and management (Wandenfels and Williams, 2024). This agreement also demonstrates the key role played by indigenous communities in working across political boundaries (Wandenfels and Williams, 2024). Furthermore, the cooperation between the Alaska Eskimo Whaling Commission and the Alaska Walrus Commission with the indigenous hunters and subsistence whaling communities in Chukotka (Russia) is another example of this (Wandenfels and Williams, 2024). In the same vein, the *Agreement on the Conservation of Polar Bears* that was stipulated by Canada, Denmark (Greenland), Norway (Svalbard), the United States, and the Soviet Union in 1973 still allows scientists to exchange information and data about polar bears, a climate-imperiled species (Wandenfels and Williams, 2024).

Some solutions to re-establish cooperation in the Arctic have been proposed such as the intermediation of non-Arctic states between regional actors to foster scientific collaboration (Andreeva et al., 2024). Other possibilities are the UN Intergovernmental Panel on Climate Change (UNIPCC),[35] which provides governments with scientific information on climate change, or the International Council for the Exploration of the Sea (ICES),[36] which is 'a leading scientific forum for the exchange of information and ideas on the sea and its living resources, and for the promotion and coordination of marine research by scientists within its member countries' (European Environment Agency, no date). Since the beginning of the war in Ukraine, scientists have been trying to find a solution to continue their research without the exchange of data with Russia (Andreeva et al., 2024). As the Cold War has taught, efforts to restore scientific cooperation could help build trust (Andreeva et al., 2024; Arctic Portal, 2024).

In short, science, a sector of utmost importance in order to study and understand climate change and its challenges, is instrumentalised by non-Arctic states to pursue their own geopolitical and economic interests. Nevertheless, the war in Ukraine has negatively affected this sector halting cooperation with devastating consequences for research.

The Arctic strategies of the eight Arctic states: a comparison

Given the increasing geopolitical and economic relevance of the High North, the governments of the eight Arctic states have formulated clear Arctic strategies by identifying their main national priorities in the region. The Arctic states began releasing their strategy documents in 2008 and they have updated them since then essentially because of the changing geopolitical scenario of climate change and increased tensions with Russia. The documents of the eight Arctic states include more or less the same sectors in which the state intends to work. In spite of this, the relevance that the eight states give to those sectors varies according to their

35 The UNIPCC was created in 1988 by the World Meteorological Organization (WMO) and the United Nations Environment Program (UNEP). It has the task 'to prepare comprehensive Assessment Reports about the state of scientific, technical and socioeconomic knowledge on climate change, its impacts and future risks, and options for reducing the rate at which climate change is taking place'. It also produces special reports on topics agreed to by its member governments, and methodology reports that provide guidelines for the preparation of greenhouse gas inventories (IPCC, 2024).

36 ICES was established in 1902 but it currently operates under the terms of the 1964 Convention for the International Council for the Exploration of the Sea. The area of competence of the council is the Atlantic Ocean (broadly defined) and its adjacent seas, with an emphasis on the North Atlantic (which is not precisely defined) (European Environment Agency, no date).

geopolitical and economic interests. These sectors are security and defence (Denmark, Norway, Russia, and the US), human/social development and indigenous rights (Canada), sustainable economic development (Iceland), and international cooperation (Finland and Sweden). Climate change is discussed in all documents because it is given much more relevance due to its impact on the Arctic environment and geopolitics. Thus, the necessity to cooperate to effectively face the challenges brought about by climate change is emphasised in the strategies of the eight Arctic states. At the same time, it should also be considered a cross-cutting sector underpinning all others.

The Arctic strategies of Denmark, Norway, Russia, and the US are very much focused on security and defence as they consider their military presence in the Arctic of utmost importance in order to protect their sovereignty. Denmark's strategy points out that the increase in activity in the region due to climate change also means an increase in the need to enforce sovereignty, which 'is exercised by the armed forces through a visible presence in the region where surveillance is central to the task' (Kingdom of Denmark, 2011, 20). Similarly, Norway's document stresses that the role played by the Norwegian Armed Forces in exercising sovereignty and authority is a very important element of the government's Arctic policy and that NATO is the cornerstone of Norway's security, defence, and deterrence policy (Government of Norway, 2021, 17). Also, Norway's strategy explicitly refers to Russia's aggression towards Ukraine that has obliged Norway to suspend bilateral military cooperation with the exception of cooperation in areas of particular importance like maritime safety, airspace security, and stability in the North (Government of Norway, 2021, 19). Russia's Basic Principles introduces the concept of 'ensuring sovereignty and territorial integrity' as the top national interest in the Arctic, which is also included in the Foundations of the Russian Federation State Policy in the Arctic for the Period up to 2035 (Davis and Vest, 2020, 3; Klimenko, 2020). In this context, the increase in Russia's military capabilities to enforce its sovereignty over Arctic territories and waters is of utmost importance (Klimenko, 2020).

Likewise, the US' strategy indicates security as its first pillar (the others being climate change and environmental protection, sustainable economic development, and international cooperation and governance) (The White House, 2022, 3). More specifically, the US document states that it aims to deter threats to its territory and to that of its allies by enhancing its military capabilities and coordinating shared approaches with its allies and partners (The White House, 2022, 3). In doing so, the US intends to protect its sovereignty and people in the Arctic (The White House, 2022, 3). By contrast, sovereignty is not mentioned in Finland's and Sweden's documents very probably because they do not own territories in the Arctic. In spite of this, both states link the importance of the military dimension to the increased tensions in the Arctic due to the economic opportunities opened up by climate change. In particular, Finland stresses its commitment to engage in 'continuous dialogues on foreign policy, security policy and defence cooperation on the Arctic security situation, both bilaterally and multilaterally' (Finnish Government, 2021, 18). For instance, the Finnish Defence Forces participates in research cooperation and conducts military exercises at both the national and international level (Finnish Government, 2021, 18). Additionally, Finland links the security of the Arctic region to the security situation in the Baltic Sea region and the rest of Europe (Finnish Government, 2021, 19).

Sweden's strategy links the necessity to strengthen military cooperation with both 'the greater strategic importance of the Arctic' and 'military strategic developments' in the neighbourhood, referring to Russia's aggressive behaviour against Ukraine (Government Offices of Sweden, 2020, 24). In fact, the document states that 'the Government intends to work for the further development and deepening of Nordic and Euro-Atlantic security and defence policy cooperation focusing on the European part of the Arctic, the Cap of the North and the North Atlantic region' (Government Offices of Sweden, 2020, 24).

In the case of Canada, its strategy states that the armed forces play a key role in demonstrating Canada's sovereignty over its Arctic territory (Government of Canada, 2019, 20). Sovereignty is seen as centred on indigenous peoples and based on history. Canada's policy document, in fact, says that 'Canada's sovereignty over the region is long-standing, well-established and based on historic title, and found in part on the presence of Inuit and First Nations since time immemorial' (Government of Canada, 2019, 20). Additionally, the relevance of the armed forces is also seen in the context of the 'increased safety and security challenges' (including search and rescue and human-created disasters) brought about by the increased commercial and tourism interests due to climate change (Government of Canada, 2019, 20). Moreover, in 2024 Canada published its Arctic Foreign Policy White Paper in which Russia is seen as a threat to the international order because 'its full-scale invasion of Ukraine has fundamentally changed the geopolitical landscape, with spillover effects in the Arctic. It is an attack not only against Ukraine, but also on the fundamental principles of international relations, including respect for sovereignty, territorial integrity and international law' (Government of Canada, 2024). The security of the state is seen as a priority by Canada that, consequently, considers strengthening its partnership with its Arctic allies (the US and the Nordic states) of utmost importance (Government of Canada, 2024).

Finally, the position of Iceland in relation to security and sovereignty is quite peculiar as it sees the AC as the right forum where sovereignty issues should be dealt with while the militarisation of the Arctic should be diminished in favour of cooperation with other states of the region to maintain peace and stability in the region (Government of Iceland, 2021, 5).

Human/social development and indigenous rights are the top priorities of the Arctic strategy of Canada. Recognising that the work done until now has not closed the gaps in well-being between Arctic and northern people and the rest of the country, the Canadian government aims to build stronger communities[37] through sus-

37 The indigenous peoples in Canada are Inuit, Métis, and First Nations. The Inuit primarily inhabit the northern part of the country and their homeland is Nunangat, which includes much of the land, water, and ice contained in the Arctic region. The Métis live mostly in the Prairie provinces and

tainable resource development, job creation, and building infrastructures in the region (Government of Canada, 2019, 20). Moreover, Canada has committed to protect the right of indigenous people to self-determination and cooperate with them on matters that affect them such as climate change (Government of Canada, 2019, 52; Barclay, 2021, 14).

Furthermore, indigenous peoples are mentioned also in the strategies of the other Arctic states that recognise the importance of protecting and supporting them. The US considers regular consultation with indigenous peoples as crucial to ensure that Alaska native communities are involved in issues affecting them because their experience and knowledge are essential for the success of its Arctic strategy (The White House, 2022, 7). Sweden intends to work to preserve and develop the identity, the culture, the language, and the traditional livelihoods of indigenous people (Government Offices of Sweden, 2020, 53). Finland aims to promote the rights of the Saami,[38] the indigenous people living in its Arctic territory, through active participation in international cooperation and their involvement in dealing with issues affecting them (like Canada and Sweden) (Finnish Government, 2021, 18). Russia[39] commits to protect its indigenous peoples especially by bringing them health and education services, creating the conditions for providing education (that is envisaged also by the strategy of other Arctic states like Finland because it is considered an important tool for social inclusion), and by developing and implementing a state support program for traditional economic activities of indigenous peoples (Barclay, 2021, 15). Norway, where the majority of the Saami live,[40] aims to foster dialogue between business actors, outline ethical guidelines for resource extraction, and promote the development of Saami industries (e.g., ecologically, economically, and culturally sustainable reindeer husbandry) in order to safeguard the interests of the indigenous peoples (Government of Norway, 2021, 17; Barclay, 2021, 14). Iceland wants to promote the involvement of the indigenous peoples in decision-making impacting their political, social, economic, cultural, or environmental interests (Government of Iceland, 2021, 6; Barclay, 2021, 15). In addition, Iceland aims to protect their language and cultural heritage (Government of Iceland, 2021, 6). Denmark will contribute to reinforce the rights of indigenous peoples in negotiations for a new international climate agreement by promoting the visibility of their conditions and ensuring that the UN Declaration on the Rights of Indigenous Peoples of 2007 is respected (Kingdom of Denmark, 2011, 44).

Ontario while the First Nations mainly occupy the territories south of the Arctic (The Canadian Encyclopedia, 2023).

38 The Saami constitute 3% of the entire Finnish population (180,000 out of 5.5 million people) (Finnish Government, 2021; Eurydice, 2024).

39 Fourty groups of indigenous people live in Russia, 11 of which live around or above the Arctic Circle. The largest groups include Dolgan, Nganasan, Nenets, Saami, Khanty, Chukchi, Evenk, Even, Enets, Eskimo (Yupik), and Yukagir. They are 250,000 people in total (Arctic Council, 2024h).

40 The Saami live in Sápmi, an area that stretches across the northern parts of Finland, the Russian Federation, Norway, and Sweden. The precise number of Saami people is not known but it is estimated that over 100,000 Saami people live in Sápmi (Arctic Council, 2024g).

The strategy of Iceland, which relies on the fragile resources of the Arctic, is very much focused on economic development especially in the sectors of fishing, energy production, and tourism (Government of Iceland, 2021, 5; Barclay, 2021, 3). Also, Iceland intends to exploit possible economic opportunities by paying attention to sustainability and the responsible use of resources (Government of Iceland, 2021, 4; Barclay, 2021, 14). Similarly, Canada's document stresses that all investments must be conducted in a sustainable manner and that Northern economic development is challenged by high operating costs for businesses due to the region's small and sparse population and infrastructure as well as high energy and connectivity costs (Government of Canada, 2019, 6). Like Canada, Sweden intends to contribute to sustainable trade and investments and the increase in economic activity in the Arctic benefits local peoples (Government Offices of Sweden, 2020, 43). Norway's strategy puts the accent on the importance of promoting job creation and value creation while Finland mentions economic development in reference to the circular economy and the UN Sustainable Development Goals that underpin all Finnish priorities in the region (Government of Norway, 2021, 9; Finnish Government, 2021, 14). The circular economy is at the core of Russia's plan to implement a special economic regime in the Arctic based on the extraction of gas, oil, and solid minerals in a sustainable manner (Barclay, 2021, 10). Denmark stresses the link between economic development and maritime activity and its commitment to involve Greenland's citizens in tasks of maritime safety like surveying, buoying, and search and rescue at sea (Kingdom of Denmark, 2011, 14; Barclay, 2021, 10). The US aims to work closely with its allies and partners to foster sustainable development and high-standard investment in the region where it intends to invest in infrastructure, improve access to services, and support the development of industries expanding economic opportunities for the local communities (The White House, 2022, 11).

The strategies of Finland and Sweden are very much focused on international cooperation. Both Finland and Sweden see constructive cooperation as a priority crucial to ensuring that the Arctic remains a peaceful region (Finnish Government, 2021, 15; Government Offices of Sweden, 2020, 9). However, while Finland stresses the importance and the necessity of involving indigenous people in active collaboration, Sweden emphasises cooperation in the framework of international law (Finnish Government, 2021, 15; Government Offices of Sweden, 2020, 11). Denmark also commits to constructive cooperation with an emphasis on the UNCLOS (Kingdom of Denmark, 2011, 13). Norway commits to cooperation in the region as well through various bodies like the AC and the BEAC (Government of Norway, 2021, 18). Similarly, Iceland's commitment to international cooperation mainly focuses on the AC and respect of the UNCLOS (Government of Iceland, 2021, 12). The US, whose strategy is the most updated as it was released in 2022, points out that Russia's aggression towards Ukraine has made cooperation in the Arctic very difficult but that it is necessary to collaborate with the NATO Allies in order to achieve their objectives in the region (The White House, 2022, 13). Canada's document states that the government will continue supporting the cooperative and rule-based international order that fosters peace and stability

(Government of Canada, 2019, 5). Similarly, Russia aims to conduct mutually beneficial cooperation and peaceful settlement of all disputes in the Arctic on the basis on international law (Davis and Vest, 2020, 4).

In short, the eight Arctic states have released documents that identify the same sectors in which it is necessary to work and often have similar views on, but each of them gives prominence to one sector or another according to their national interest.

Neoliberal institutionalism and neorealism in the Arctic

The war in Ukraine raises questions concerning the redistribution of power and the role of institutions in the Arctic. As for the redistribution of power, it is clear that all states have tried to increase their military sector through the militarisation of their territories, which actually had previously began because of the increasing accessibility of natural resources and shipping routes due to climate change. The war in Ukraine, which highlighted Russia's aggressive behaviour, led all Arctic states to increase their military strength in the region. This can be associated with the 'security dilemma', which was first coined by realist John Herz in 1950 and then used by other scholars such as neorealists Robert Jervis and Charles Glaser. Herz explains the concept of 'security dilemma' by saying that groups and individuals are concerned about their security as they fear being attacked or annihilated by some other groups or individuals (Herz, 1950, 157). In order to escape the power of others, they acquire more and more power (e.g., building armaments, putting military forces on alert, forming new alliances), which makes others insecure and pushes them to prepare for the worst (Herz, 1950, 157; Walt, 2022). Consequently, nobody can feel entirely secure and the competition for power goes on in a vicious circle of security and power accumulation (Herz, 1950, 157). According to John Mearsheimer, a state stops pursuing power only when hegemony is achieved (Mearsheimer, 2001, 34). He argues that

> even if a great power does not have the wherewithal to achieve hegemony (and that is usually the case), it will still act offensively to amass as much power as it can, because states are almost always better off with more rather than less power. In short, states do not become status quo powers until they completely dominate the system.
>
> (Mearsheimer, 2001, 35)

It is clear that Russia does not have the military and economic strength to become a hegemon especially in the current international system given the fact that the international system is characterised by emerging powers such as China and India, in addition to the US that is a military superpower. In spite of this, Russia is still a great power, namely it is one of those states that 'through their great economic, political and military strength, are able to exert power over world diplomacy' (Flemes, 2010, 25). Power is very well defined by Waltz pointing out that the power of a state can be measured in terms of its territory, its population, its human resources, economic capability, military power, political stability, and political competence (Waltz, 1979, 35).

Furthermore, the 'security dilemma' reflects the logic of offensive realism, namely for that strand of neorealism that see states as power-maximiser revisionists (Mearsheimer, 2001, 35). For offensive realists such as John Mearsheimer and Robert Gilpin, states care about relative power, which means that they try to gain as much power as possible as they are concerned with the distribution of material capabilities (Mearsheimer, 2001, 36). They aim to have more power than their rivals because this is the only means to survive in a dangerous world (Mearsheimer, 2001, 36). By contrast, for defensive realists such as Kenneth Waltz and Robert Grieco, states are concerned with absolute power because they aim to defend their position in the international system (Mearsheimer, 2001, 36). Consequently, states cooperate only if the agreement at the basis of the cooperation 'roughly maintains pre-co-operation balances of capabilities', which means that states cooperate only if there is a balanced distribution of gains (Grieco, 1990, 47).

In the case of the war in Ukraine, it is possible to argue that Russia has acted as a revisionist power because it aimed at gaining more power in the international system (Zachary, 2023, 539) and has established a partnership with China, the US' other rival. But this can't be said in the case of the Arctic since a military battle has not occurred there, at least at the moment of writing. By contrast, apart from the factor of the militarisation of the region, the case of the Arctic can be read through the lenses of defensive realism or neoliberal institutionalism. From the defensive realism perspective, it can be argued that Russia still feels quite safe in the Arctic because its territories in the region have become very much militarised over the last few decades, more than other states. According to some experts, 'it would take the West at least 10 years to catch up with Russia's military in the region, if it chose to do so' (Gronholt-Pedersen and Fouche, 2022). Although the NATO membership of Finland and Sweden has been a destabilising factor from a security perspective because it has divided the Arctic into seven NATO members on the one hand and one non-NATO member (Russia) on the other, Russia is the most powerful state in the region militarily. As argued above, NATO is still weaker than Russia in the High North.

Moreover, from a neoliberal institutionalist perspective, the successful attempt of the Norwegian chairmanship to resume the work of the AC, although only partially, could be read as the neoliberal institutionalism view that 'the presence of international institutions can contribute to patterns of security and peace that rest on specific power distributions by improving the information environment and encouraging cooperation toward common or complementary goals' (Geller and Travlos, 2019, 19). According to this perspective, 'such managerial coordination of foreign policies moderates the need for defensive policies driven by the security dilemma' (Geller and Travlos, 2019, 19). However, Russia has withdrawn from the BEAC, that is, the other intergovernmental forum in the region. However, it is necessary to stress that, as argued above, the AC is the most important forum guiding cooperation in the region. Indeed, the historical and political role played by the AC in the region is widely recognised. Thus, for states it would be unthinkable to dismiss such a crucial platform for dialogue and cooperation. Russia also recognises the significance of the AC considering its membership essential to exert influence on Arctic affairs. Thus, the AC serves the political interests of Russia. Consequently, neorealists are right when they say that institutions are useful to powers to 'maintain their share of world power, or even increase it' (Mearsheimer, 1994, 4).

In conclusion, defensive realism and neoliberal institutionalism seem to offer a better interpretation of the geopolitical dynamics in the Arctic. However, tension in the Arctic is still very high and cooperation in vital sectors such as science and energy is still halted. Thus, the possibility that military confrontation might occur in the Arctic can't be excluded.

Conclusion

The war in Ukraine has clearly demonstrated that the Arctic is not a place apart from the rest of the world. In fact, like it has happened internationally, the war has had a huge impact on the geopolitical dynamics in the region by negatively affecting the relations among the Arctic states. More specifically, it is possible to identify three main consequences of the war in Ukraine on the region. First, Arctic governance has been heavily affected because cooperation has halted. In 2022, the AC, which can be considered the symbol of good relations and cooperation in the region, suspended its work. However, its political relevance in the region is so huge that its work has recently resumed, at least partially. In this regard, the work of the Norwegian chairmanship has had excellent results, demonstrating that 'storming' events with a dramatic impact on the relations among international actors like the war in Ukraine have not destroyed one of the major outcomes of the end of the Cold War. The continuation of the AC's life is out of question. States agree that it is necessary and that another political forum will not be established. Moreover, the negative consequences of worsened state relations for scientific cooperation deserve to be mentioned given its importance for the fight against climate change. The loss of accessibility to Russian data makes scientific analysis impossible, making the fight against climate change ineffective. Additionally, as the climate change problem has no borders, cooperation among states is vital for scientific research.

Second, the war in Ukraine has determined the increase and the acceleration of militarisation, which had begun because of climate change. The most militarised state is Russia. Therefore, the region has gone through three stages since the Cold War. During the Cold War, it was highly militarised (the Russian Kola Peninsula was the most militarised area in the Arctic). With the end of the Cold War, the High North was de-militarised due to the relaxation of relations (in this context, a weakened Russia played a role) among states. During the last few decades, the war in Ukraine has increased and accelerated the militarisation process of the Arctic.

Third, the war in Ukraine led to a rapprochement between Russia and China. However, as argued above, their partnership (that is not an alliance) began because of climate change that increased the geopolitical and economic interests of China in Arctic natural resources and transportation routes.

References

Achcar, G. (2023). *The New Cold War. The United States, Russia and China from Kosovo to Ukraine*. London: The Westbourne Press.

Aliyev, N. (2022). *Russia's Icebreakers, North Sea Route, and Invasion of Ukraine*. Ponars Eurasia. Available at: https://www.ponarseurasia.org/russias-icebreakers-north-sea-route-and-invasion-of-ukraine/ (accessed 8 April 2022.

Andreeva, S., Dodds, K., Douglas, N., Humrich, C., Nawrath, T. (2024). *New Arctic Realities. Between Conflicting Interests and Avenues for Cooperation*. Report 1. Berlin: Centre for East European and International Studies.

Antonenko, O. (2007). *Russia and the Deadlock over Kosovo*. Paris: Russia/NIS Center.

Arctic Centre. (2024a). *How Is the Arctic Region Changing?*. Available at: https://www.arcticcentre.org/EN/arcticregion/climatechange (accessed 29 April 2024).

Arctic Centre. (2024b). *Climate Change in the Arctic, the Military Consequences and Security Implications*. University of Lapland. Available at: https://www.arcticcentre.org/blogs/Climate-Change-in-the-Arctic,-the-Military-Consequences-and-Security-Implications/41286/ac5cd7d0-e45a-473e-805b-d3f739056914 (accessed 10 April 2024).

Arctic Council. (2017). *Agreement on Enhancing International Arctic Scientific Cooperation*. Available at: https://oaarchive.arctic-council.org/items/9d1ecc0c-e82a-43b5-9a2f-28225bf183b9 (accessed 29 April 2024).

Arctic Council. (2020). *Navigating Arctic Waters with the Arctic Council and the International Maritime Organization*. Available at: https://arctic-council.org/news/navigating-arctic-waters-with-the-arctic-council-and-imo/ (accessed 3 April 2024).

Arctic Council. (2023a). *Arctic States and Indigenous Permanent Participants Convened for the 13th Arctic Council Meeting and Issued statement*. Available at: https://arctic-council.org/news/13th-arctic-council-meeting-salekhard/ (accessed 14 October 2023).

Arctic Council. (2023b). *Q&A with Morten Høglund, the New Chair of the Senior Arctic Officials*. Available at: https://arctic-council.org/news/q-a-with-morten-hoglund-chair-of-the-senior-arctic-officials/#:~:text=15%20May%202023&text=On%2011%20May%2C%20Norway%20took,during%20the%20next%20two%20years (accessed 15 October 2023).

Arctic Council. (2023c). *Norway's Chairship, 2023–2025*. Available at: https://arctic-council.org/about/norway-chair-2/ (accessed 15 October 2023).

Arctic Council. (2023d). *Russian Chairmanship 2021–2023*. Available at: https://arctic-council.org/about/previous-chairmanships/russian-chairmanship-2/ (accessed 11 October 2023).

Arctic Council. (2024). *Arctic States Statement for UNFCCC COP 19*. Available at: https://arctic-council.org/news/arctic-states-statement-for-unfccc-cop-19-november-20-2013/ (accessed 3 April 2024).

Arctic Council. (2024a). *IASC*. Available at: https://arctic-council.org/about/observers/iasc/ (accessed 30 April 2024)

Arctic Council. (2024b). *Conservation of Arctic Flora and Fauna*. Available at: https://arctic-council.org/about/working-groups/caff/ (accessed 30 April 2024).

Arctic Council. (2024c). *Protection of the Arctic Marine Environment*. Available at: https://arctic-council.org/about/working-groups/pame/ (accessed 30 April 2024).

Arctic Council. (2024d). *Arctic Contaminants Action Program*. Available at: https://arctic-council.org/about/working-groups/acap/ (accessed 2 May 2024).

Arctic Council. (2024e). *Arctic Monitoring and Assessment Programme*. Available at: https://arctic-council.org/about/working-groups/amap/ (accessed 2 May 2024).

Arctic Council. (2024f). *Black Carbon and Methane*. Available at: https://arctic-council.org/about/task-expert/egbcm/ (accessed 7 May 2024).

Arctic Council. (2024g). *Saami Council*. Available at: https://arctic-council.org/about/permanent-participants/saami-council/#:~:text=About%20the%20S%C3%A1mi

%20People&text=The%20majority%20of%20the%20S%C3%A1mi,fishing%2C%20livestock%20farming%20and%20hunting. (accessed 27 May 2024).
Arctic Council. (2024h). *The Russian Federation.* Available at: https://arctic-council.org/about/states/russian-federation/#:~:text=Of%20the%2040%20Indigenous%20Peoples,reindeer%20herding%2C%20fishing%20and%20hunting. (accessed 27 May 2024).
Arctic Economic Council. (2020). *About.* Available at: https://arcticeconomiccouncil.com/about/ (accessed 3 May 2024).
Arctic Portal. (2024). *Arctic Collaboration in Crisis: The Impact of Geopolitical Tensions on Scientific Research.* Available at: https://arcticportal.org/ap-library/news/3592-arctic-collaboration-in-crisis-the-impact-of-geopolitical-tensions-on-scientific-research (accessed 9 May 2024).
Asian Forum for Polar Sciences. (2004). About AFOPS. Available at: www.afops.org&home&about
Baker, M. (2022). With Eyes on Russia, the U.S. Military Prepares for an Arctic Future. *The New York Times.* Available at: https://www.nytimes.com/2022/03/27/us/army-alaska-arctic-russia.html (accessed 9 April 2024).
Barclay, J. (2021). *A Comparison of Strategies and Policies of the Eight Arctic States.* Peterborough: North American and Arctic Defense and Security Network.
Barr, S., Lüdecke, C. (2010). *The History of the International Polar Year (IPYs) (from Pole to Pole).* Cham: Springer.
BEAC. (2023a). *About the Regional Council.* Available at: https://barents-council.org/barents-regional-council/about-the-council (accessed 15 October 2023).
Beixi, D., Jian, Y. (2014). *Asian-Arctic Cooperation: A Briefing on the China-Nordic Arctic Research Center (CNARC).* Arctic Yearbook.
Bohman, V., Andersson, P., Von Essen, H. (2023). *China's and Russia's Narratives on the War against Ukraine: Examining the Boundaries of Political Alignment.* Swedish National China Centre. Available at: https://kinacentrum.se/publikationer/chinas-and-russias-narratives-on-the-war-against-ukraine-examining-the-boundaries-of-political-alignment/ (accessed 5 April 2024).
Bohman, V., Andersson, P., Von Essen, H. (2024). *Final Blow to Chinese 'Neutrality' on Ukraine War.* Politico. Available at: https://www.politico.eu/article/xi-jinping-vladimir-putin-ukraine-war-swiss-peace-summit/ (accessed 5 April 2024).
Bowman, L. (2017). *Observers to the Arctic Council and Their Benefits.* Available at: https://polarconnection.org/arctic-council-observers-benefits/ (accessed 3 May 2024).
Britannica. (no date). *Kosovo Conflict.* Available at: https://www.britannica.com/event/Kosovo-conflict (accessed 1 April 2024).
Burke, D. C. (2019). *Diplomacy and the Arctic Council.* Montreal: McGill-Queen's University Press.
Bye, H.-G. (2022a). *Canada to Spend Billions on Modernizing Air Defense in the Arctic.* Available at: https://www.highnorthnews.com/en/canada-spend-billions-modernizing-air-defense-arctic (accessed 9 April 2024).
Bye, H.-G. (2022b). Chief of Defence to HNN: Russian Military Activity is Unusually Low in the High North. *The High North News.* Available at: https://www.highnorthnews.com/en/chief-defence-hnn-russian-military-activity-unusually-low-high-north (accessed 8 April 2024).
Caracciolo, L. (2019). Finché America non ci separi. *Limes*, 11: 7–33.
Carniel, S., Lissi, F., Blanco, A., Russo. A. (2024). *Climate Change Threatens NATO's Readiness and Resilience at Sea.* NATO. Available at: https://www.nato.int/docu/review/articles/2023/11/30/climate-change-threatens-natos-readiness-and-resilience-at-sea/index.html (accessed 27 April 2024).
CCASCOE. (2024). *Our History.* Available at: https://ccascoe.org/our-story/ (accessed 3 December 2024).

China Daily. (2024). *Chinese Researchers Start 2024 Arctic Expedition at Yellow River Station.* Available at: https://www.chinadaily.com.cn/a/202405/01/WS66319adfa31082fc043c4fc0.html (accessed 5 May 2024).

Chotiner, I. (2020). *How Putin Controls Russia.* The New Yorker. Available at: https://www.newyorker.com/news/q-and-a/how-putin-controls-russia (accessed 6 April 2024).

CGTN. (2024). *Chart of the Day: 20 Years of China's Arctic Yellow River Station.* Available at: https://news.cgtn.com/news/2024-07-28/Chart-of-the-Day-20-years-of-China-s-Arctic-Yellow-River-Station-1vB0AhkBdxm/p.html (accessed 4 May 2024).

CIA. (1968). *The Soviet Northern Fleet.* Available at: chrome-extension://efaidnbmnnnibpcajpcglclefindmkaj/https://www.cia.gov/readingroom/docs/CIA-RDP79B00972A000100220005-2.pdf (accessed 7 April 2024).

Clifford, R. (2016). *How Has Cooperation in the Arctic Survived Western-Russian Geopolitical Tension?.* Available at: https://polarconnection.org/cooperation-arctic/ (accessed 12 October 2023).

CNARC. (2024). *China-Nordic Arctic Center.* Available at: https://www.cnarc.info/ (accessed 6 May 2024).

Coggins, S., Ford, J. D. (2021). Indigenous Peoples and Climate Justice in the Arctic. *Georgetown Journal of International Affairs.* Available at: https://gjia.georgetown.edu/2021/02/23/indigenous-peoples-and-climate-justice-in-the-arctic/ (accessed 30 April 2024).

Coninsx, M. (2022). *The New US Arctic Strategy. Welcome Back, America!.* Egmont Institute. Available at: https://www.egmontinstitute.be/the-new-us-arctic-strategy-welcome-back-america/ (accessed 6 April 2024).

Conley, H., Melino, M. (2020). *America's Arctic Moment. Great Power Competition in the Arctic to 2050.* Washington: Center for Strategic and International Studies.

Cooper, J. (2013). *Russian Military Expenditure: Data, Analysis and Issue.* Stockholm: Swedish Defence Research Agency.

CSTO. (2024). *History of Creation, Fundamentals of Activity, Organizational Structure.* Available at: https://en.odkb-csto.org/25years/ (accessed 2 April 2024).

Cunliffe, A., Tanski, G., Radosavljevic, B., Palmer, W. F., Sachs, T., Lantuit, H., Kerby, J. T., Myers-Smith, I. H. (2019). *Rapid Retreat of Permafrost Coastline Observed with Aerial Drone Photogrammetry.* Available at: https://tc.copernicus.org/articles/13/1513/2019/ (accessed 28 April 2024).

Dams, T., van Schaik, L., Stoetman, A. (2020). *Presence before Power. China's Arctic Strategy in Iceland and Greenland.* The Hague: Clingedael Institute.

Danish Ministry of Defence. (2024). *The Danish Government Proposes to Fast-Track Key Investments in Defence and Security.* Available at: https://www.fmn.dk/en/news/2024/the-danish-government-proposes-to-fast-track-key-investments-in-defence-and-security/ (accessed 7 April 2024).

Davis, A., Vest, R. (2020). Foundations of the Russian Federation State Policy in the Arctic for the Period up to 2035. *RMSI Research*, 5. Available at: https://digital-commons.usnwc.edu/rmsi_research/5?utm_source=digital-commons.usnwc.edu%2Frmsi_research%2F5&utm_medium=PDF&utm_campaign=PDFCoverPages (accessed 17 May 2024).

Donnelly, E. (2024). *NATO in the Arctic: 75 Years of Security, Cooperation, and Adaptation.* Available at: https://www.wilsoncenter.org/blog-post/no-26-nato-arctic-75-years-security-cooperation-and-adaptation (accessed 17 April 2024).

Edvardsen, A. (2023a). Canada With Defense Policy Update on the Horizon. *The High North News.* Available at: https://www.highnorthnews.com/en/canada-defense-policy-update-horizon (accessed 9 April 2024).

Edvardsen, A. (2023b). Light at the End of the Tunnel for the Arctic Council. *The High North News.* Available at: https://www.highnorthnews.com/en/light-end-tunnel-arctic-council (accessed 15 October 2023).

Edvardsen, A. (2024a). Canada With Defense Policy Update on the Horizon. *The High North News*. Available at: https://www.highnorthnews.com/en/canada-defense-policy-update-horizon (accessed 9 April 2024).
Edvardsen, A. (2024b). The Arctic Council with New Decisive Step Forward. *The High North News*. Available at: https://www.highnorthnews.com/en/arctic-council-new-decisive-step-forward#:~:text=%E2%80%93%20Norway%20took%20over%20the%20chairship,activities%20based%20on%20written%20procedure. (accessed 6 April 2024).
Edvardsen, A., Molid Martinussen, B. A. (2023). *NATO's Military Leader: "We Must Be Prepared for Military Conflicts Arising in the Arctic"*. Available at: https://www.highnorthnews.com/en/natos-military-leader-we-must-be-prepared-military-conflicts-arising-arctic (accessed 20 April 2024).
Elenius, L. (2015). *The Barents Region*. Pax Forlag.
Elfar, A. (2022). *NATO's Cold Response and the Implications of Militarization in the Arctic*. Columbia Climate School. Available at: https://news.climate.columbia.edu/2022/06/08/natos-cold-response-and-the-implications-of-militarization-in-the-arctic/ (accessed 20 April 2024).
Eur-Lex. (2020). *Geneva Convention on Long-Range Transboundary Air Pollution*. Available at: https://eur-lex.europa.eu/EN/legal-content/summary/geneva-convention-on-long-range-transboundary-air-pollution.html (accessed 2 May 2024).
European Environment Agency. (no date). *International Council for the Exploration of the Sea*. Available at: https://www.eea.europa.eu/help/glossary/eea-glossary/international-council-for-the-exploration (accessed 10 May 2024).
Eurydice. (2024). *Finland*. Available at: https://eurydice.eacea.ec.europa.eu/national-education-systems/finland/population-demographic-situation-languages-and-religions (accessed 24 May 2024).
Evans. (2021). *The History and Future of Arctic State Conflict: The Arctic Institute Conflict Series*. Available at: https://www.thearcticinstitute.org/the-history-and-future-of-arctic-state-conflict-the-arctic-institute-conflict-series/ (accessed 17 April 2024).
Finnish Defence Forces. (2024). *Nordic Response 2024*. Available at: https://puolustusvoimat.fi/en/nordic-response-en (accessed April 20 2024).
Finnish Government. (2021). *Finland's Strategy for Arctic Policy*. Helsinki.
Flake, L. (2013). Russia and China in the Arctic: A Team of Rivals. Commentary. *Strategic Analysis*, 37(6): 681–687.
Flemes, D. (2010). *Regional Leadership in Global System, Ideas, Interests, and Strategies of Regional Powers*. Farnham: Ashgate.
Forsberg, R., Moyer, J. (2022). *Sisters But Not Twins: Prospects of Finland and Sweden's NATO Accession*. Available at: https://www.wilsoncenter.org/article/sisters-not-twins-prospects-finland-and-swedens-nato-accession (accessed 23 April 2024).
Forsvaret. (2020). *The Norwegian Joint Headquarters*. Available at: https://www.forsvaret.no/en/organisation/norwegian-joint-headquarters (accessed 7 April 2024).
Funaiole, M., Hart, B., Bermudez Jr., J. S., Powers-Riggs, A. (2023). *China's Great Power Ambitions in the Polar Regions*. Center for Strategic and International Studies. Available at: https://features.csis.org/hiddenreach/china-polar-research-facility/ (accessed 4 May 2024).
Geller, D., Travlos, K. (2019). *Integrating Realist and Neoliberal Theories of War: Peace Economics, Peace Science and Public Policy*. Berlin and Boston: Walter de Gruyter GmbH.
Government of Canada. (2019). *Canada's Arctic and Northern Policy Framework*. Ottawa: Government of Canada.
Government of Canada. (2022). *Joint Statement on Arctic Council Cooperation Following Russia's Invasion of Ukraine*. Available at: https://www.canada.ca/en/global-affairs/news/2022/03/joint-statement-on-arctic-council-cooperation-following-russias-invasion-of-ukraine.html (accessed 10 October 2023).

Government of Canada. (2024). *Canada's Arctic Foreign Policy.* Available at: leHRuA2FlbQIxMQABHQCXe8eC0ZBGHIR-iq1lpQ5TyJGWut3qfpaMei1zG3IuphXMB6l6AZImuw_aem_dHHAUESO8-e_YY62j97gIw#a3_1 (accessed 13 December 2024).
Government of Iceland. (2021). *Iceland's Policy on Matters Concerning the Arctic Region.* Reykjavik: Government of Iceland.
Government of Norway. (2021). *The Norwegian Government's Arctic Policy. People, Opportunities and Norwegian Interests in the Arctic.* Oslo.
Government of Norway. (2023). *Norway Takes Over as Chair of the Arctic Council.* Available at: https://www.regjeringen.no/en/aktuelt/norway-takes-over-as-chair-of-the-arctic-council/id2976965/ (accessed 15 October 2023).
Government of Norway. (2024). *The Norwegian Defence Boost Begins Now.* Available at: https://www.regjeringen.no/en/aktuelt/no-startar-forsvarsloftet/id3038972/ (accessed 7 April 2024).
Government of Sweden. (2024a). *Speech by Tobias Billström. Why Sweden Joined NATO - a Paradigm Shift in Sweden's Foreign and Security Policy.* Available at: https://www.government.se/speeches/2024/04/why-sweden-joined-nato---a-paradigm-shift-in-swedens-foreign-and-security-policy/ (accessed 25 April 2024).
Government of Sweden. (2024b). *Military Budget.* Available at: https://www.government.se/government-policy/military-budget/ (accessed 7 April 2024).
Government Offices of Sweden. (2020). *Sweden's Strategy for the Arctic Region.* Stockholm.
Grieco, J. (1990). *Cooperation among Nations: Europe, America, and Non-Tariff Barriers to Trade.* New York: Cornell University Press.
Gronholt-Pedersen, J., Fouche, G. (2022). Dark Arctic. NATO Allies Wake up to Russian supremacy in the Region. *Reuters.* Available at: https://www.reuters.com/graphics/ARCTIC-SECURITY/zgvobmblrpd/ (accessed 5 December 2024).
Grozovski, B. (2023). *Russia's Unprecedented War Budget Explained.* Wilson Center. Available at: https://www.wilsoncenter.org/blog-post/russias-unprecedented-war-budget-explained (accessed 7 April 2024).
Gwich'in Council. (no date). *The Álgu Fund.* Available at: https://gwichincouncil.com/%C3%A1lgu-fund (accessed 3 May 2024).
Heinine, L, Exner-Pirot, H. (2020). Climate Change and Arctic Security: Searching for a Paradigm Shift. London: Palgrave McMillan.
Heng, C., Freymann, E. (2023). Outsiders Wanting In: Asian States and Arctic Governance. Policy Brief. In *Belfer Center for Science and International Affairs, Harvard Kennedy School.* Available at: https://www.belfercenter.org/publication/outsiders-wanting-asian-states-and-arctic-governance (accessed 6 May 2024).
Hermann, B. (2022). *National Security and Climate Change: Behind the U.S. Pursuit of Military Exemptions to the Kyoto Protocol.* Available at: https://nsarchive.gwu.edu/briefing-book/environmental-diplomacy/2022-01-20/national-security-and-climate-change-behind-us (accessed 20 April 2024).
Herz, J. (1950). Idealist Internationalism and the Security Dilemma. *World Politics*, 2(2): 157–180.
Hong, N. (2020). *China's Role in the Arctic. Observing and* Being Observed. New York: Routledge.
Humpert, M. (2022). From Ukraine to the Arctic: Russia's Capabilities in the Region and the War's Impact on the North. *The High North News.* Available at: https://www.highnorthnews.com/en/ukraine-arctic-russias-capabilities-region-and-wars-impact-north (accessed 8 April 2024).
Humpert, M. (2024a). *U.S. Coast Guard Looking to Acquire Commercial Icebreaker 'Aiviq'.* QCaptain. Available at: https://gcaptain.com/u-s-coast-guard-looking-to-acquire-commercial-icebreaker-aiviq/# (accessed 8 April 2024).
Humpert, M. (2024b). U.S. Coast Guard Icebreaker Faces Delays with No Funding Request for 2025, Aims to Acquire Commercial Icebreaker. *The High North News.*

Available at: https://www.highnorthnews.com/en/us-coast-guard-icebreaker-faces-delays-no-funding-request-2025-aims-acquire-commercial-icebreaker (accessed 8 April 2024).
IASC. (1990). *Founding Articles for an International Arctic Science Committee.* Available at: chrome-extension://efaidnbmnnnibpcajpcglclefindmkaj/https://iasc.info/images/about/iasc-founding-articles.pdf (accessed 30 April 2024).
IASC. (2023). *Initial Concept Note. International Polar Year 2032–2033.* Available at: https://iasc.info/cooperations/international-polar-year-2032-33 (accessed 30 April 2024).
IASC. (no date). *IASC History.* Available at: https://iasc.info/about (accessed 30 April 2024).
ICES. (no date). *Who We Are.* Available at: https://www.ices.dk/about-ICES/who-we-are/Pages/Who-we-are.aspx (accessed 3 April 2024).
IMO. (2019a). *International Code for Ships Operating in Polar Waters.* Available at: https://www.imo.org/en/ourwork/safety/pages/polar-code.aspx#:~:text=The%20International%20code%20of%20safety,waters%20surrounding%20the%20two%20poles. (accessed 3 April 2024).
IMO. (2019b). *Introduction to IMO.* Available at: https://www.imo.org/en/About/Pages/Default.aspx (accessed 3 April 2024).
Fong, C., Maizland, L. (2024). *Exploring Ties with Two Authoritarian Powers.* Council on Foreign Relations. Available at: https://www.cfr.org/backgrounder/china-russia-relationship-xi-putin-taiwan-ukraine (accessed 5 April 2024).
Huebert, R. (2019). *A New Cold War in the Arctic? The Old One Never Ended!.* Arctic Year Book – Commentaries. Available at: https://arcticyearbook.com/arctic-yearbook/2019/2019-commentaries/325-a-new-cold-war-in-the-arctic-the-old-one-never-ended. (accessed 6 Appril 2024).
Indo-Pacific Defense Forum. (2023). *PRC-Russia 'No Limits' Friendship Has Disputed Boundaries.* Available at: https://ipdefenseforum.com/2023/10/prc-russia-no-limits-friendship-has-disputed-boundaries/ (accessed 6 April 2024).
International Peace Bureau of Geneva. (2002). *The Military's Impact on the Environment: A Neglected Aspect of the Sustainable Development Debate. A Briefing Paper for States and Non-Governmental Organisations.* Geneva: International Peace Bureau of Geneva.
IPCC. (2024). *About the IPCC.* Available at: https://www.ipcc.ch/about/ (accessed 10 May 2024).
Irvig, D. (2022). *What Does China's Arctic Presence Mean to the United States?.* RAND. Available at: https://www.rand.org/pubs/articles/2022/what-does-chinas-arctic-presence-mean-to-the-us.html (accessed 5 April, 2024).
Jakobson, L. (2013). *China and the Arctic: What's the Fuss?.* Available at: https://www.lowyinstitute.org/the-interpreter/china-arctic-what-s-fuss (accessed 3 April 2024).
Ji, You. (2023). Alleanza Militare? Non così in fretta. Limes, 11: 35–42.
Kim, J. (no date). *Observer States in the Arctic Council: A Way Forward to Better Cooperation.* University of the Arctic. Available at: https://old.uarctic.org/shared-voices/shared-voices-magazine-2016-special-issue/observer-states-in-the-arctic-council-a-way-forward-to-better-cooperation/ (accessed 2 May 2024).
Kingdom of Denmark. (2011). *Strategy for the Arctic 2011–2020.* Copenhagen.
Klimenko, E. (2020). *Russia's New Arctic Policy Document Signals Continuity Rather Than Change.* SIPRI. Available at: https://www.sipri.org/commentary/essay/2020/russias-new-arctic-policy-document-signals-continuity-rather-change (accessed 17 May).
Koivurova, T., Shibata, A. (2022). After Russia's Invasion of Ukraine in 2022: Can We Still Cooperate with Russia in the Arctic?. *Polar Record*, 59(12): 1–9.
Kortunov, A. (2022). Voci dalla Russia e dall'Ucraina. *Limes*, 2: 35–40.
Kramer, M., Makko, A., Ruggenthaler, P. (eds.) (2021). *The Soviet Union and Cold War Neutrality and Nonalignment in Europe.* Lanham, MD and London: Lexington Books.

Laruelle, M. (2014). *Russia's Arctic Strategies and the Future of the Far North.* Routledge: New York.
Lavikainen, J. (2021). *Strengthening Russia's Nuclear Forces in the Arctic: The Case of the Kinzhal Missile.* Available at: https://www.csis.org/analysis/strengthening-russias-nuclear-forces-arctic-case-kinzhal-missile (accessed 8 April 2024).
Le Mière, C., Mazo, J. (2013). *Arctic Opening Insecurity and Opportunity.* London: Routledge. Available at: https://www.routledge.com/Arctic-Opening-Insecurity-And-Opportunity/LeMiere-Mazo/p/book/9781138776692 (accessed 6 April 2024).
Legarda, H. (2024). *From Marriage of Convenience to Strategic Partnership: China-Russia Relations and the Fight for Global Influence.* Mercator Institute for China Studies. Available at: https://merics.org/en/comment/marriage-convenience-strategic-partnership-china-russia-relations-and-fight-global (accessed April 5 2024).
Litvinova, D. (2019). *Russia Kicks off Huge War Games to Test Its Nuclear Arsenal.* Available at: https://www.cbsnews.com/news/russia-war-games-thunder-2019-test-strategic-nuclear-weapons-today-after-inf-collapse-2019-10-15/ (accessed 21 April 2024).
Lopez, T. (2022). *U.S. Needs More Icebreakers for Arctic.* US Department of Defence. Available at: https://www.defense.gov/News/News-Stories/Article/article/2928402/us-needs-more-icebreakers-for-arctic/ (accessed 8 April 2024).
Łuszczuk, M., Szkarlat, M. (2022). The International Arctic Science Committee (IASC) in the Changing Arctic. Between International Scientific Cooperation and Science Diplomacy. In Sellheim, N., Menezes, D. R. (eds.) *Non-state Actors in the Arctic Region.* Cham: Springer.
Luzin, P., Prokopenko, A. (2023). *Russia's 2024 Budget Shows It's Planning for a Long War in Ukraine.* Carnegie Politika. Available at: https://carnegieendowment.org/russia-eurasia/politika/2023/09/russias-2024-budget-shows-its-planning-for-a-long-war-in-ukraine?lang=en (accessed 7 April 2024).
Mäkeläinen, M. (2023). *Satellite Images: New Buildings Appear at Russian Military Bases Near Finnish Border.* Available at: https://yle.fi/a/74-20049340#:~:text=Satellite%20images%20obtained%20by%20Yle,for%20the%20war%20against%20Ukraine.&text=Three%20large%20buildings%20have%20been,wilderness%20near%20the%20Finnish%20border (accessed 7 April 2024).
Martin, D., Ryzhova, N., Rippa, A., Reeves, M. (2021). *The Russia/China Border. Where Geographies, Histories, and Hegemonies Meet.* Book Symposium. Berghahn Open Anthro.
Martinussen, B. (2024). Canada's New Billion-Dollar Defense Investment: Strong Arctic Focus. *The High North News.*
Mearsheimer, J. (1994) The False Promise of International Institutions. *International Security,* 19(3): 1–27.
Mearsheimer, J. (2001). *The Tragedy of Great Power Politics.* New York: Norton & Company.
Melino, M., Conley, H., Bermudez, J. (2020). *The Ice Curtain. Bringing Transparency to the Arctic.* Washington: Center for Strategic and International Studies.
Military Heritage Tourism. (no date). *Paldiski – Soviet-era Closed City.* Available at: https://militaryheritagetourism.info/en/military/sites/view/322?0&a=od; (accessed 6 April 2024).
Ministry of Defence of Italy. (2024). *Nordic Response 2024.* Available at: https://www.marina.difesa.it/cosa-facciamo/per-la-difesa-sicurezza/esercitazioni_maggiori/Pagine/Nordic-Response.aspx (accessed 20 April 2024).
Ministry for Foreign Affairs of Norway. (2024). *Centre of Excellence-Cold Weather Operations.* Available at: https://www.forsvaret.no/en/organisation/centre-of-excellence-cold-weather-operations (accessed 21 April 2024).
Ministry for Foreign Affairs of Russia. (2021). *Agreement on Measures to Ensure the Security of The Russian Federation and Member States of the North Atlantic Treaty*

Organization. Available at: https://mid.ru/ru/foreign_policy/rso/nato/1790803/?lang=en&fbclid=IwAR1e94yIg69YpOZ1KtSscwFyo6DQfiaD1IMD-2trxN6bJ-TELxq_Zxryxqk. (accessed 24 April 2024).

Ministry for Foreign Affairs of Russia. (2023). *Foreign Ministry Statement on Russia's Withdrawal from the Barents Euro-Arctic Council*. Available at: https://mid.ru/en/foreign_policy/rso/1904899/ (accessed 19 September 2023).

Moore, J. (2016). *Anthropocene or Capitalocene? Nature, History and the Crisis of Capitalism*. London: PM Press.

Moyer, J. (2024). *Finland's Remarkable First Year in NATO*. Available at: https://www.wilsoncenter.org/article/finlands-remarkable-first-year-nato (accessed 23 April 2024).

NATO. (2022a). *NATO 2022 Strategic Concept*. Available at: https://www.nato.int/cps/en/natohq/topics_210907.htm (accessed 5 April 2024).

NATO. (2022b). *NATO-Russia Council*. Available at: https://www.nato.int/cps/en/natohq/topics_50091.htm (accessed 2 April 2024).

NATO. (2023). *Euro-Atlantic Partnership Council*. Available at: https://www.nato.int/cps/en/natohq/topics_49276.htm (accessed 2 April 2024).

NATO. (2023a). *Joint Force Development Experimentation & Wargaming Branch 2023 Fact Sheet – Multinational Capability Development Campaign*. Available at: chrome-extension://efaidnbmnnnibpcajpcglclefindmkaj/https://www.act.nato.int/wp-content/uploads/2023/05/2023_Fact_Sheet_MCDC.pdf (accessed 15 April 2024).

NATO. (2023b). *The Evolving Dynamics of the High North and NATO's Strategic Imperatives*. Available at: https://www.act.nato.int/article/evolving-dynamics-high-north/ (accessed 15 April 2024).

NATO. (2023c). *NATO Exercises*. Available at: https://www.nato.int/cps/en/natohq/topics_49285.htm (accessed 18 April 2024).

NATO. (2024a). *Centres of Excellence*. Available at: https://www.nato.int/cps/en/natohq/topics_68372.htm (accessed 22 April 2024).

NATO. (2024b). *History of NATO Exercises*. Available at: https://www.nato.int/cps/en/natohq/222847.htm (accessed 17 April 2024).

Nielsson, E. T. (2023). *The China-Nordic Arctic Research Center: One decade in*. Arctic Yearbook.

NORAD. (2024). *NORAD Celebrates 66 Years of Excellence*. Available at: https://www.norad.mil/Newsroom/Article/3772192/norad-celebrates-66-years-of-excellence/ (accessed 6 April 2024).

Norwegian Polar Institute. (no date). *Climate Change in the Arctic*. Available at: https://www.npolar.no/en/themes/climate-change-in-the-arctic/#toggle-id-3 (accessed 28 April 2024).

Odgaard, L. (2024). *NATO Is Unprepared for Russia's Arctic Threats*. Available at: https://www.hudson.org/defense-strategy/nato-unprepared-russia-arctic-threats-liselotte-odgaard (accessed 20 April 2024).

O'Dwyer, G. (2023). *Finland's 2024 Defense Budget Targets Arms Restocking, Border Security*. Available at: https://www.defensenews.com/global/europe/2023/10/13/finlands-2024-defense-budget-targets-arms-restocking-border-security/#:~:text=The%20budget%2C%20which%20is%20on,budget%20with%20amendments%20in%20September. (accessed 7 April 2023).

Oliphant, R., Child, D. (2024). Xi and Putin: The Marriage of Convenience That Is Reshaping the World Order. *The Telegraph*. Available at: https://www.telegraph.co.uk/world-news/2024/05/18/vladimir-putin-xi-jinping-allies/ (accessed 5 April 2024).

Orphal, S. (2024). *Arctic Cooperation at a Standstill because of Russia's War in Ukraine*. Centre for East European and International Studies. Available at: https://www.zois-berlin.de/en/press/press-releases/arctic-cooperation-at-a-standstill-because-of-russias-war-in-ukraine

Pakkasvirta, J., Tuominen, H. (2024). *From Cold War 'Neutrality' to the West: Finland's Route to the European Union and NATO*. E-International Relations. Available at: https://

www.e-ir.info/2024/07/12/from-cold-war-neutrality-to-the-west-finlands-route-to-the-european-union-and-nato/#google_vignette (accessed 26 April 2024).

Park, A. (2024). *JUST IN: Coast Guard Reevaluating Polar Security Cutter Schedule.* National Defense. Available at: https://www.nationaldefensemagazine.org/articles/2024/3/20/just-in-coast-guard-reevaluating-polar-security-cutter-schedule (accessed 8 April 2024).

Patey, L. (2020). *Managing US-China Rivalry in the Arctic.* Available at: https://www.diis.dk/en/research/managing-us-china-rivalry-in-the-arctic (accessed 5 April 2024).

Pavliha, M., Martínez Gutiérrez, N. A. (2010). Marine Scientific Research and the 1982 United Nations Convention on the Law of the Sea. *Ocean and Coastal Law Journal,* 16(1): 115–133.

Perrault, F. (2019). The Role(s) of China in the Arctic: Regional Governance and Foreseeable Challenges-. In *Global Challenges in the Arctic Region.* Conde, E., Sànchez, S. I. (eds). Baskerville: Routledge.

Polar Research Institute of China. (2018). *China-Iceland Arctic Science Observatory.* Available at: https://en.pric.org.cn/index.php?c=category&id=99 (accessed 5 May 2024).

President of the Republic of Finland. (2024). *Speech by President of the Republic of Finland Sauli Niinistö in Parliament on 1 March 2024.* Available at: https://www.presidentti.fi/niinisto/en/speeches/speech-by-president-of-the-republic-of-finland-sauli-niinisto-in-parliament-on-1-march-2024/ (accessed 25 April 2024).

Preve, C. (2024). What Does Finland and Sweden's Membership to NATO Mean for Race to Arm the Arctic?. *Euronews.* Available at: https://www.euronews.com/my-europe/2024/05/31/what-does-finland-and-swedens-membership-to-nato-mean-for-race-to-arm-the-arctic#:~:text=Their%20accession%20into%20NATO%20%E2%80%94%20in,are%20in%20the%20military%20alliance. (accessed 25 April 2024).

Reuters. (2008). *China Signs Border Demarcation Pact with Russia.* Available at: https://www.reuters.com/article/us-china-russia-border/china-signs-border-demarcation-pact-with-russia-idUKPEK29238620080721/ (accessed 5 April 2024).

Reuters. (2024). *Sweden Should Hike Military Budget to 2.6% of GDP, Defence Committee Says.* Available at: https://www.reuters.com/world/europe/sweden-should-hike-military-budget-26-gdp-defence-committee-says-2024-04-26/#:~:text=The%20Nordic%20country's%20defence%20spending,gross%20domestic%20product%20(GDP). (accessed 7 April 2024).

Rogne, O., Corell., R. W., Kotlyakov, V. M. (2015). Initiation of the Institutional Arctic Science Committee (IASC). In Rogne, O., Rachold, V., Haquebord, L., Corell, R. W. (eds.) *25 Years of International Arctic Research Cooperation: IASC after 25 Years.* International Arctic Science Committee (IASC).

Rudd, K. (2023). *USA-Cina. Una guerra che dobbiamo evitare.* Milano: Rizzoli.

Russell, M. (2022). *Western Sanction on Russia. What Are They? Do They Work?. In-Depth Analysis.* European Parliamentary Research Service: Brussels.

Saxena, A. (2024). *75 Years of China-Russia Relations: Indeed a 'No Limits' Partnership.* Institute for Security and Development Policy. Available at: https://www.isdp.eu/75-years-of-china-russia-relations-indeed-a-no-limits-partnership/ (accessed 5 April 2024).

SERDP-ESTCP. (2024). *About Us.* US Department of Defense. Available at: https://serdp-estcp.mil/about (accessed 10 April 2024).

SERDP-ESTCP. (2023). *Understanding the Impacts of Climate Change on Military Training Lands in Alaska.* Available at: https://www.serdp-estcp.mil/newsitems/details/4b1dde09-1fce-4d5b-9def-32f2fab7f52e/understanding-the-impacts-of-climate-change-on-military-training-lands-in-alaska (accessed 10 April 2024).

SIPRI. (2001). *Military Expenditure and Arms Production.* SIPRI Yearbook 2001. Available at: https://www.sipri.org/yearbook/2001/04 (accessed 7 April 2024).

SIPRI. (2015). *Russia and the Arctic: An End to Cooperation?.* Available at: https://www.sipri.org/commentary/essay/2015/russia-and-arctic-end-cooperation (accessed 14 September 2023).

SIPRI. (2024). *Global Military Spending Surges Amid War, Rising Tensions and Insecurity.* Available at: https://www.sipri.org/media/press-release/2024/global-military-spending-surges-amid-war-rising-tensions-and-insecurity (accessed 7 April 2024).

Smieszek, M. (2022). What Effects Has the Ukraine war Had on the Arctic Council?. *High North News*, 30 March 2023. Available at: https://www.highnorthnews.com/en/what-effects-has-ukraine-war-had-arctic-council (accessed 10 October 2023).

Speak, D. (2023). *The Melting Arctic Gets a U.S. Ambassador and an Influx of Military Cash.* National Public Radio. Available at: https://www.npr.org/2023/03/22/1164315952/the-melting-arctic-gets-a-u-s-ambassador-and-an-influx-of-military-cash (accessed 8 April 2024).

Staalesen, A. (2022). *Hundreds of Russian Arctic Troops Believed to Be Involved in War Crimes in Ukraine.* The Barents Observer. Available at: https://thebarentsobserver.com/en/security/2022/03/hundreds-russian-arctic-troops-believed-be-involved-war-crimes-ukraine (accessed 8 April 2022).

Statista. (2024). *Countries with the Highest Military Spending Worldwide in 2023.* Available at: https://www.statista.com/statistics/262742/countries-with-the-highest-military-spending/#:~:text=The%20United%20States%20led%20the,to%202.4%20trillion%20U.S.%20dollars. (accessed 8 April 2024).

Sun, K. (2014). Beyond the Dragon and the Panda: Understanding China's Engagement in the Arctic. *Asia Policy,* 18: 46–51.

Teeple, N. (2021). *The Impact of the Post-Arms Control Context and Great Power Competition in the Arctic.* The Arctic Institute. Available at: https://www.thearcticinstitute.org/impact-post-arms-control-context-great-power-competition-arctic/ (accessed 6 April 2024).

The Arctic Institute. (2024). *Active Polar Icebreakers.* Available at: https://www.thearcticinstitute.org/country-backgrounders/singapore/ (accessed 7 May 2024).

The Arctic Institute. (2024a). *Active Polar Icebreakers.* Available at: https://www.thearcticinstitute.org/country-backgrounders/japan/ (accessed 7 May 2024).

The Canadian Encyclopedia. (2023). *Indigenous Peoples in Canada.* Available at: https://www.thecanadianencyclopedia.ca/en/article/aboriginal-people#:~:text=There%20are%20three%20categories%20of,contained%20in%20the%20Arctic%20region. (accessed 20 May 2024).

The Economist. (2017). *The Arctic as it is Known Today Is Almost Certainly Gone.* Available at: https://www.economist.com/leaders/2017/04/29/the-arctic-as-it-is-known-today-is-almost-certainly-gone

The Moscow Time. (2024). *Moscow Vows Response to Sweden's NATO Accession.* Available at: https://www.themoscowtimes.com/2024/02/28/moscow-vows-response-to-swedens-nato-accession-a84280 (accessed 27 April 2024).

The State Council of China. (2018). *China's Arctic Policy. The State Council Information Office of the People's Republic of China.* Available at: https://english.www.gov.cn/archive/white_paper/2018/01/26/content_281476026660336.htm (accessed 5 April 2024).

The White House. (2022). *National Strategy for the Arctic Region.* Washington: The White House.

Tómas, R. (2022). *Iceland to Increase Defence Spending, PM Announces.* Available at: https://www.icelandreview.com/news/iceland-to-increase-defence-spending-pm-announces/ (accessed 7 April 2024).

Trenin, D. (2019). *20 Years of Vladimir Putin: How Russian Foreign Policy Has Changed.* Carnegie Moscow Centre. Available at: https://carnegieendowment.org/posts/2019/08/20-years-of-vladimir-putin-how-russian-foreign-policy-has-changed?lang=en&center=russia-eurasia (accessed 9 April 2024).

Tsui, E. (2019). *A Commentary on the Agreement on Enhancing International Arctic Scientific Co-operation: Legal and Practical Consequences.* Available at: https://arcticyearbook.com/arctic-yearbook/2019/2019-briefing-notes/333-a-commentary-on-the-agreement-on-enhancing-international-arctic-scientific-co-operation-legal-and-practical-consequences (accessed 29 April 2024).

United Nations. (1982). *United Nations Convention on the Law of the Sea.* Montego Bay.

UN. (1972). *Report of the United Nations Conference on the Human Environment.* Stockholm.

UN. (2024a). *Sustainability.* Available at: https://www.un.org/en/academic-impact/sustainability (accessed 21 April 2024).

UN. (2024b). *The UN and the War in Ukraine: Key Information.* Available at: https://unric.org/en/the-un-and-the-war-in-ukraine-key-information/ (accessed 5 April 2024).

UN. (no date). *Current Members.* Available at: https://www.un.org/securitycouncil/content/current-members#:~:text=Five%20permanent%20members%3A%20China%2C%20France,Algeria%20(2025) (accessed 5 April 2024).

UN Stockholm Convention. (2019). *Overview.* Available at: https://www.pops.int/TheConvention/Overview/tabid/3351/Default.aspx (accessed 2 May 2024).

UNEP. (2021). *About us.* Available at: https://minamataconvention.org/en/about (accessed 2 May 2024).

United States Environmental Protection Agency. Climate Change Indicators. Permafrost: (2022). Available at: https://www.epa.gov/climate-indicators/climate-change-indicators permafrost#:~:text=Permafrost%20is%20defined%20as%20rock,with%20seasonal%20changes%20in%20temperature.

US Army. (2021). *Regaining Arctic Dominance. The US Army in the Arctic.* Washington: Department of the Army.

US Department of Defense. (2021). *Climate Adaptation Plan.* Washington: US Department of Defense.

US Department of Defense. (2016). *Dod Directive 4715.21 Climate Change Adaptation and Resilience.* Washington: US Department of Defense.

US Department of Homeland Security. (2024). *US Coast Guard. Fiscal year 2025.* Available at: chrome-extension://efaidnbmnnnibpcajpcglclefindmkaj/https://www.uscg.mil/Portals/0/documents/budget/2025/USCG%20FY%202025%20Congressional%20Justification.pdf (accessed 8 April 2025).

Vigeland Rottem, S., Folkestad Soltvedt, I. (2020). *Arctic Governance: Law and Politics.* London: I.B.Tauris.

Walsh, N. P., Dean, S. (2022). *Russia's Militarization of the Arctic Shows no Sign of Slowing Down.* CNN. Available at: https://edition.cnn.com/2022/12/21/europe/russia-arctic-military-intl/index.html

Walt, S. (2022). *Does Anyone Still Understand the 'Security Dilemma'?.* Foreign Policy. Available at: https://foreignpolicy.com/2022/07/26/misperception-security-dilemma-ir-theory-russia-ukraine/ (accessed 5 December 2024).

Waltz (1979) *Theory of International Politics.* Addison-Wesley Publishing Company: Reading.

Wandenfels, V., Williams, M. (2024). *The Environmental Impacts of the War in Ukraine in the Arctic, Belfer Center for Science and International Affairs, Harvard Kennedy School.* Available at: https://www.belfercenter.org/publication/environmental-impacts-war-ukraine-arctic (accessed 11 May 2024).

Weir, D. (2024). *The Climate Costs of War and Militaries Can no Longer Be Ignored. The Guardian.* Available at: https://www.theguardian.com/commentisfree/2024/jan/09/emission-from-war-military-gaza-ukraine-climate-change (accessed 21 April 2024).

Winkle, J. (2023). *The Impact of the Ukraine War on the Arctic.* AIES. Available at: https://www.aies.at/download/2023/AIES-Fokus-2023-05.pdf (accessed 8 April 2024).

Yaxin, W. (2020). *China's Participation in the International Scientific Cooperation in the Arctic.* IOP Conference Series: Earth and Environmental Science. Available at: https://iopscience.iop.org/article/10.1088/1755-1315/539/1/012044 (accessed 3 May 2024).
Yu Lin, Y. (2023). *What Is Russia Teaching China in Military Drills?.* The Diplomat. Available at: https://thediplomat.com/2023/08/what-is-russia-teaching-china-in-military-drills/ (accessed 5 April 2023).
Zachary, P. (2023). The War in Ukraine and the Dawn of Russian Revisionism: An English School Approach. *International Journal,* 78(4): 539–555.

3 The scramble for natural resources

Introduction

This chapter discusses the geopolitical and legal complexities of the Arctic with a focus on its natural resources that, together with transportation routes (discussed in the fourth chapter), are the element 'responsible' for the increasing interest of states both inside and outside the region. It is necessary to stress here that, as argued in the previous chapter, the Arctic is not the only region where natural resources attract the geopolitical and economic interests of states. The Antarctic, the Third Pole, and Africa as well are excellent examples. All these regions are embedded within the global economic and political system. This is why it is necessary to study the scramble for the natural resources of these regions in the broader international context. For instance, the Arctic has a long history of 'global convergence and economic integration' (Dodds and Nuttall, 2016, 33). An example is the fur trade that is documented back to the ninth century in the Eurasian north and that brought northern people into contact with southern people like the Egyptians and the Chinese (Dodds and Nuttall, 2016, 33).

Furthermore, in an interesting book titled *The Race for What's Left: The Global Scramble for the World's Last Resources*, Michael Klare (2012, 3), professor of Peace and World Security Studies at Hampshire College in Massachusetts (US), discusses how the world economy has entered a period of 'tough' extraction for energy, minerals, and other natural resources due to the fact that those places that are easy to reach have been depleted, thus pushing states to turn to resources in the planet's most remote regions like the Arctic. Climate change, causing ice-melting, is making exploring and exploiting these remote regions possible although this might have dramatic environmental consequences for fragile ecosystems like the one of the Arctic. At the same time, the scramble for natural resources unleashed by climate change is accompanied by another factor, the war in Ukraine, which has increased tensions and competition among states in the region.

In order to analyse how these two variables impact on the geopolitical dynamics in the Arctic, this chapter takes into consideration the cases of water, energy, minerals, and fisheries, to which four separate sections are dedicated, one for each case. These sectors are of utmost importance in the economy of the Arctic states but are also targeted by states and actors (e.g., the EU) outside the region because of their economic and geopolitical relevance.

DOI: 10.4324/9781032633008-4

The 'blue gold' of the Arctic

Water is the 'blue gold' of the Arctic. As it is essential for the survival of human beings, plants, and animals, it is extremely important. Also, water 'lies at the heart of a nexus of social, economic, and political issues – agriculture, energy, cities, trade, finance, national security, and human livelihoods, within rich and poor countries alike' (World Economic Forum Water Initiative, 2011, 10). In spite of this, demographic surge, the consequent growth in consumption, anthropogenic factors (e.g., pollution), and climate-related phenomena (e.g., the increase in temperature, the scarcity of rainfall especially in summer, and reduced snowfall) are all factors that contribute to making water a scarce and thus precious resource.

Over time, the need of water has been increasing. Since the Industrial Revolution of the 18th century, which meant the transition from an agrarian and handicraft economy to an industrial one, the utilisation of water has increased much faster than the world's population (Dionet-Grivet, 2012, 6). As with the Industrial Revolution, life conditions have improved and the need for water has grown (Dionet-Grivet, 2012, 8). As a result, 1.1 billion people worldwide lack access to water, and about 2.7 billion find water scarce for at least one month of the year (WWF, 2024). In many regions, people are using more water than the rivers and groundwater can sustain to irrigate crops, operate factories and power plants, or for household needs (National Geographic, 2024). Furthermore, climate change exacerbates this situation because it reduces water availability in some regions of the world like in sub-Saharan Africa, Eastern and Southeastern Asia, and Central and South Asia (Dionet-Grivet, 2012, 8; Cassivi et al., 2023). South Asia and sub-Saharan Africa are the areas where the largest percentage of people lack access to safe drinking water (National Geographic, 2024a), which has been recognised as a fundamental human right by the UN General Assembly since 2010 (UN Committee on Economic Social and Cultural Rights, 2010) and is the sixth of the UN Sustainable Development Goals.[1] Very significantly, Article 1 of the Council of Europe Water Resources Management Directive (EU/60/2000//EU) stipulates that 'water is not a commercial product like any other but, rather, a heritage which must be protected, defended and treated as such' (Eur-Lex, no date).

Also, in 2020, the World Health Organisation/UN Children's Fund (WHO/UNICEF) Joint Monitoring Programme (JMP) for Water Supply, Sanitation, and Hygiene reported that 26% of the world population did not have access to safely managed drinking water services (WHO/UNICEF, 2021).

Although the same year the JMP reported that in the Arctic there is nearly universal access to safely managed drinking water (99% in Canada; >99% in the

1 The 17 UN Sustainable Development Goals are: 1) no poverty; 2) zero hunger; 3) good health and well-being; 4) quality education; 5) gender equality; 6) clean water and sanitation; 7) affordable and clean energy; 8) decent work and economic growth; 9) industry, innovation, and infrastructure; 10) reduced inequalities; 11) sustainable cities and communities; 12) responsible consumption and production; 13) climate action; 14) life below water; 15) life on land; 16) peace, justice, and strong institutions; 17) partnerships for the goals (UN, 2023).

Kingdom of Denmark, Finland, Iceland, Norway, and the US, and 76% in the Russian Federation) (WHO/UNICEF, 2021; Cassivi et al., 2023, 1), the crisis also affects this region where some people suffer from water and sanitation challenges (National Geographic, 2024a). For instance, the US (Alaska), Russia, and Greenland contain rural areas that lack safe in-house water and sanitation facilities so that some people must not only carry their own water into their homes but they must also remove human waste themselves, collecting it and hauling it out of their home (National Geographic, 2024a). In the Arctic, 'climate change is having an impact on water availability by melting glaciers, decreasing seasonal rates of precipitation, increasing evapotranspiration and drying lakes and rivers existing in permafrost grounds' (Evengard et al., 2011, 1). Degradation of permafrost could cause drainage of ponds (Evengard et al., 2011, 2). In Siberia and Alaska, lakes in permafrost regions are undergoing rapid change as some are increasing in size and number while some others have decreased, and in some cases have disappeared (Evengard et al., 2011, 2). Rivers have increased winter discharge even in non-dammed tributaries (Evengard et al., 2011, 2). In the Russian Arctic, vast territories of the tundra may be replaced by taiga (the difference between tundra and taiga is that tundra is characterised by the absence of trees because it's colder than taiga) (Evengard et al., 2011, 2).

Surface water is abundant in summer when it is necessary for breeding grounds for birds, fish, and mammals, many of which are obliged to migrate out of the Arctic in winter when the surface is frozen and only lakes deeper than 2 metres and rivers with significant flow retain liquid water (Arctic Centre, 2024a). Many people in the Arctic rely on surface water, thus when conditions change and access to water diminishes, the prerequisites for human survival are negatively affected (Evengard et al., 2011, 2). One-quarter of settlements in Chukotka and half of settlements in Yakutia have no regular water supply and lack centralised sewerage (Dudarev, 2018). Moreover, when access to water is limited, there are consequences for health causing two–three times higher hospitalisation rates especially among children less than three years old for pneumonia, influenza, and respiratory syncytial virus infections as well as higher rates of skin infections in people of all ages (Evengard et al., 2011, 3).

Additionally, pollution is jeopardising the quality of water in the Arctic with consequences for health (Evengard et al., 2011, 1). Sources of aquatic pollution in the Arctic include wastewater and waste from settlements, riverine nutrient inputs caused by thawing permafrost and erosion (Tank et al., 2012; Brioni et al., 2022), emissions from increasing tourism and shipping, long-range atmospheric and oceanic pollution, commercial fisheries, and chemical and waste emissions from resource exploitation including mining, minerals, and oil and gas extraction (AMAP, 2018; Brioni et al., 2022). These anthropogenic activities are exacerbated by climate change that has affected the Arctic much more severely than many other regions. For instance, a study of the impact of drinking water sources on the risks to human health and well-being in the remote territories of the Russian Yamal Nenets Autonomous Okrug (YNAO) in 2012, 2014 to 2019, and 2022, conducted by researchers from various Russian universities and funded by the Tomsk State

University Development Program (Priority-2030) demonstrated that the availability of high-quality drinking water is limited for local residents due to climatic and anthropogenic risks, despite the abundant water resources (freshwater, snow, ice, lakes, and rivers) (Bogdanova et al., 2023). The YNAO is an economically important region located in the northwest of western Siberia in Russia where almost half of the minority indigenous population of the Russian Arctic (about 45,000 people) reside (Bogdanova et al., 2023). Local people are experiencing an insufficient supply of high-quality drinking water due to anthropogenic pollution of water bodies with heavy metals due to the prevalence of extracting industries such as mining and oil and gas extraction, the distribution of harmful trace elements in surface waters, and the violation of sanitary and hygienic conditions for the extraction and transportation of water to the population (Bogdanova et al., 2023). In addition to this, climate change also negatively affects water availability. Since the beginning of the 21st century, higher temperatures have been recorded in almost all territories of western Siberia causing a shortage of snow in western Siberia and negative anomalies in the water supply from the snow (Bogdanova et al., 2023).

Another problem coming from Arctic warming concerns water infrastructures as thawing permafrost is impacting not only source water coming from groundwater, rivers, and lake, but also piped water, water storage, and purification systems often built on permafrost (Evengard et al., 2011, 3). An example of the problems stemming from the Arctic warming is the damage caused by the floods that have affected Yakutia more than any other region in Russia (Evengard et al., 2011, 3). For instance, in 2001, a flood occurred in the city of Lensk causing the water level to rise by 2.0–2.5 metres, which resulted in the destruction of city infrastructures and in the increase of hepatitis A (Evengard et al., 2011, 3).

Infrastructure in the Arctic is a topic that is growing in importance because it is crucial for local people's lives and also for economic development and the modernisation of those areas. Its scarcity and, in some cases, poor conditions is a problem common to all eight Arctic states. An example is the precarity of Canada's Arctic infrastructure that was recently highlighted by the case of the contamination of Iqaluit's water supply in 2021 (The Arctic Institute, 2022). In October that year, the city of Iqaluit in Nunavut (the homeland of the Inuit people) decided to test the city's water supply after it received an official complaint from citizens that had noticed a foul taste and smell coming from the tap water that had been typically safe to drink (The Arctic Institute, 2022). The tests on the water supply revealed the presence of fuel in the water, making it unsafe for drinking, due to a 60-year-old fuel tank that was buried next to the water treatment plant (The Arctic Institute, 2022). It took two months to bring the situation back to normal (The Arctic Institute, 2022). The problem is that the drinking water infrastructure in the territorial capital of Iqaluit is old and limited and is below Canadian national standards (The Arctic Institute, 2022).

In spite of the problems that it is encountering in relation to water, the Arctic remains one of the few regions where 'blue gold' is abundant. The Arctic Ocean, which covers an area of 15.558 million square kilometres, is 1.4% of the World Ocean total volume and includes the Barents Sea, Beaufort Sea, Chukchi Sea, East

Siberian Sea, Greenland Sea, Kara Sea, Laptev Sea, Northwest Passage, Norwegian Sea, and other tributary water bodies (CIA, 2024). It is the smallest of the world's five ocean basins after the Pacific Ocean, Atlantic Ocean, Indian Ocean, and the Southern Ocean (CIA, 2024). The Arctic is one of the main places where Earth's freshwater is stored. In fact, 68.7% of freshwater is locked up in ice and glaciers while 30% is groundwater (aquifers, soil moisture, marshes, permafrost), 0.3% is lake and river water, and a very small amount of water is in the atmosphere where it exists as water vapour (CIA, 2024). In spite of this, water is incredibly rare. Indeed, although about 70% of the Earth is covered by water, only 3% of the world's water is fresh water (WWF, 2024; USGS, 2019). Also, over two-thirds of global fresh-water resources are stored in the form of ice, of which over 90% is located in the Antarctic. The Arctic and the Antarctic contain iceberg water, which is one of the purest sources of water (Karimidastenaei et al., 2021, 1).

The utilisation of icebergs has a long history as the first to use an iceberg as a source of freshwater was English explorer James Cook in 1773.[2] In the 1850s, initial attempts at larger-scale iceberg transport were done when sailing boats were used to tow small icebergs from Chile to supply ice to the emerging ice market in Peru over 4,000 kilometres away (Karimidastenaei et al., 2021, 2; Weeks and Campbell, 1973, 210). In the same decade, ice was transported from Alaska to California as a commercial commodity (Karimidastenaei et al., 2021, 2). In the 1950s, polar exploration ships were considered the most practical vehicle for iceberg transportation and the idea of transporting icebergs to arid regions of the globe came up (Karimidastenaei et al., 2021, 2). A few years later, the feasibility of using icebergs to supply freshwater to the northern hemisphere was assessed (Ostrander and Hult, 2001, 45). In 1977, Prince Mohammad al-Faisal of Saudi Arabia asked the French explorer Paul-Emile Victor to tow an iceberg from Antarctica to Saudi Arabia (De Villiers, 2001, 76). That same year, Prince al-Faisal organised the first conference on iceberg use as a freshwater supply, the International Conference and Workshops on Iceberg Utilisation for Fresh Water Production, Weather Modification, and Other Applications, in Ames, Iowa (US) (Lewis, 2015, 443). The conference identified and discussed the technological, economic, political, legal, and practical obstacles of iceberg harvesting in order to turn the arid desert lands of Saudi Arabia into arable and fertile lands (Lewis, 2015, 443). The result of the conference was disagreement among experts about the possibility of towing icebergs especially because of the enormous costs (Lewis, 2015, 443). Furthermore, another problem concerns the legal vacuum in which the practice of iceberg towing and harvesting

2 James Cook (born in Marton, Yorkshire, 1728, died Hawai'i 1779) was an English explorer who conducted several expeditions for the Royal Society. For instance, in 1770 he discovered the Strait that was named after him in New Zealand. He also explored the eastern coasts of Australia discovering the Cook Islands in 1777 and Hawai'i (that he called Sandwich Islands) in 1778. He also travelled to Alaska where he navigated the strait later called Cook Inlet, but he could not continue his exploration because of ice. Thus, he came back to the Sandwich Islands where he was killed by the indigenous people. His explorations can be considered the foundations of British colonial power (Enciclopedia Treccani, no date).

would operate if it became feasible (Lewis, 2015, 442). Indeed, neither the international community nor any nation has promulgated laws or regulations expressly designed to regulate this practice because a towing and harvesting market does not exist (Lewis, 2015, 442).

In 1986 the first ever efforts at commercial iceberg utilisation for the production of bottled freshwater were made in Canada (Karimidastenaei et al., 2021, 2). Also, in 1995 Canada was the first state where vodka production using iceberg water started (Herlihy, 2012, 87). More recently, some industries have established factories to use icebergs as the primary material to produce beer, vodka, cosmetics, and luxury bottled water (Karimidastenaei et al., 2021, 3).

In 2020, an interesting study based on a systematic literature review (SLR) in three databases (Scopus, Web of Science, and ProQuest) was conducted by the University of Oulu (Finland) and the University of Boise (US) (Karimidastenaei et al., 2021, 1). It analysed 47 separate studies from 1973 to 2019 that highlighted how harvesting iceberg water offers several benefits such as supplying fresh water, creating new jobs, avoiding iceberg damage to offshore structures, and reducing the rate of sea-level rise due to global warming before icebergs melt into the ocean although the magnitude of this effect is quite small (Karimidastenaei et al., 2021, 1). The SLR found that most studies considered iceberg transport to water-deficient regions as a solution to supplying freshwater to some regions suffering from water scarcity (Karimidastenaei et al., 2021, 5). However, some studies highlighted that the major limitations to iceberg utilisation are the economic costs and risks associated with iceberg towing (Karimidastenaei et al., 2021, 5). In spite of this, some studies stressed the fact that the economic feasibility of the iceberg water harvesting depends on the location of the icebergs and the distance of the target location (Karimidastenaei et al., 2021, 5). More specifically, the technical practicability of towing an iceberg constitutes four parts: 1) 'locating a suitable source and supply'; 2) 'calculating the necessary towing power requirements'; 3) 'accurately predicting and accounting for in-transit melt'; 4) 'estimating the economic feasibility of the entire endeavor' (Lewis, 2015, 445). However, not all icebergs can be towed and harvested because there is a high risk that they would roll over while being towed given their weight, density, and massive size (Lewis, 2015, 445). In fact, rectangular icebergs with tabular shapes with a similar draft or underwater shape to that of a ship are the most desirable (Lewis, 2015, 445). As the Arctic produces less tabular icebergs, the main source of suitable icebergs is the Antarctic (Lewis, 2015, 446).

Moreover, the SLR identified both environmental disadvantages and advantages. On the one hand, environmental impacts were identified as the main challenge to exploiting this resource, but they were not given enough attention in the literature, while on the other hand, the utilisation of icebergs as a freshwater resource has limited environmental impacts both near the ice source area and the destination (Karimidaseinaei et al., 2021, 8).

Although the richest reserve of freshwater is the Antarctic, which is estimated to hold 70% of the fresh water of the entire planet (Antarcticland, 2024), it is very probable that in the future the Arctic will be one of the regions richest in water together with the Antarctic and the Third Pole. According to some scholars, water will be at the centre of conflicts in the 21st century as it will become increasingly scarce (Dunn, 2013, 46). For instance, in 2013, the US News and World Report published an article in which the author foresaw that 'the water-war surprises will come, perhaps not in one year, perhaps not in four, but soon, and long into the future' (Judge, 2013). This assumption echoed World Bank Vice President Ismail Serageldin's 1995 statement that 'the wars of the next century will be about water' (Wolf et al., 2006). Nevertheless, at present there is consensus in the academic literature that no wars have or will be fought over water (Hall, 2023). In fact, mismanagement of water rarely causes wars, but it exacerbates tensions and undermines cooperation (Hall, 2023). For instance, in an article published by the Woodrow Wilson International Center for Scholars in 2006, the authors argue that until that point, no states had gone to war specifically for water resources and that international water disputes have always been solved peacefully (Wolf et al., 2006). They argued that instances of cooperation between riparian states outnumbered conflicts by more than two to one between 1945 and 1999 because states can't afford to fight for water as it is crucial for survival (Wolf et al., 2006). Also, they argue that water fosters interdependence between states that can build trust and prevent conflicts through cooperation (Wolf et al., 2006). At the same time, water can be used for negotiations because it can offer 'a communication lifeline connecting countries in the midst of the crisis' (Wolf et al., 2006).

Furthermore, in an interesting article entitled 'Water Conflicts: From Ancient to Modern Times and in the Future' published in the *Sustainability Journal* in 2021, the authors explain that historically water has contributed to increase tensions in conflicts that had begun for other reasons and, in some cases, it has been used as a weapon to cause damage through deprivation or erosion of water resources of enemy populations and their army (Angelakis et al., 2021, 1). They also point out that the main reasons for water conflicts concern territorial disputes, fighting for resources, and strategic advantage, both in ancient and modern times (Angelakis et al., 2021, 1). Additionally, water conflicts often arise around delimitation of boundaries, waterlogging (e.g., dams and lakes), diversion of river flow, running water, and food and political distresses (Angelakis et al., 2021, 1). Also, the concept of water resource sustainability is an important component of water conflicts (Angelakis et al., 2021, 1). It is defined as

> the ability to use water in sufficient quantities and quality from the local to the global scale to meet the needs of humans and ecosystems for the present and the future to sustain life and to protect humans from the damages brought about by natural and human-caused disasters that affect sustaining life.
>
> (Angelakis et al., 2021, 1)

Today there is a focus on the sustainable use of water by reducing its use and increasing its production, which will become increasingly important in the future.

In short, the Arctic plays a key role in water supply as it is one of the regions richest in water on Earth, which will increase its geopolitical and economic importance in the future. In spite of this, some problems concerning access to safe water, essentially due to climate change, affects indigenous people living in the Arctic.

Energy: between economic opportunities and geopolitical challenges

The fact that the Arctic is considered a region rich in energy resources is very well known. The assessment of the energy resources contained in the Arctic, which was completed by the US Geological Survey (USGS) in 2008, is very well known as well. According to the USGS, the region is estimated to contain about 30% of undiscovered gas resources and about 13% of undiscovered oil resources. More specifically, more than 70% of the undiscovered oil resources is estimated to occur in five provinces: Arctic Alaska, Amerasia Basin, East Greenland Rift Basins, East Barents Basins, and West Greenland–East Canada. Also, more than 70% of the undiscovered natural gas is estimated to occur in three provinces, namely the West Siberian Basin, the East Barents Basins, and Arctic Alaska (USGS, 2008, 4). Additionally, the USGS further estimates that approximately 84% of the undiscovered oil and gas occurs offshore (USGS, 2008, 4). More specifically, 22% and 69% of the offshore oil and gas, respectively, are located in the Russian Arctic; 40% and 12% in the US Arctic; 21% and 10% in the Greenland Arctic; 13% and 5% in the Canadian Arctic; and 4% and 4% in the Norwegian Arctic (Zhang et al., 2024). However, these numbers only represent an estimate of the potential reserves held by the Arctic, thus they are based on geological probability rather than on drilling results (Pelodeix and Basse, 2021, 2).

Nevertheless, the exploration for and exploitation of hydrocarbons in the Arctic began in the 1970s in Russia, Norway, Canada, and Denmark/Greenland (in this last case the activities ceased in the 1980s and resumed in 2000) (Pelodeix and Basse, 2021, 1). Additionally, although offshore oil and gas exploitation started around the world more than a century ago, it was only in a few years that greater depths (over 152 metres) have been targeted because reserves of oil and gas are depleted in shallow waters (Pelodeix and Basse, 2021, 1). In the case of the Arctic, offshore oil and gas exploitation is due to the combination of several conditions: 1) between 2004 and 2008 the high prices of oil and gas were an incentive to invest in offshore exploitation. In fact, as offshore exploration and exploitation are extremely expensive, it is convenient to invest in such activity only if the price of hydrocarbons on the international market is high in order to fund the costs (for example, the dramatic financial crisis of 2008 drove oil prices up to about 150 dollars per barrel increasing interest in Arctic energy resources (AC Sustainable Development WG, 2009; OECD Library, 2014); 2) When gas supplies to European states were cut off due to the 2006 gas crisis between Russia and Ukraine,[3] energy

3 The origins of the gas crisis between Russia and Ukraine of 2006 are found in 2004 with the dramatic political events leading to the elections of President Viktor Yushchenko (2005–2010). This was followed by dramatic developments in relation to Ukrainian–Russian gas supplies. In particular, Russia and Ukraine clashed over the price of natural gas supplied and the cost of transit. The new Ukrainian administration refused to allow Gazprom, the Russian energy company, any ownership in

security was a top priority on the political agenda and directed attention to the Arctic. For instance, this was one of the reasons why the EU developed its first Arctic policy in 2008; 3) Oil and gas reserves are depleted in conventional fields such as the onshore Prudhoe Bay Oil Field in Alaska and in the North Atlantic; and 4) remote fossil-fuel fields are being targeted as a result of the increasing demand of energy especially from emerging powers such as China and India (Pelodeix and Basse, 2021, 1).

Apart from these specific conditions, climate change plays a key role in offshore oil and gas exploitation in the Arctic because ice-melting makes those resources more accessible. This is highlighted by the AC's Arctic Climate Impact Assessment (ACIA), a scientific report that focuses on the impacts of climate change on oil and gas activities that was released at the ACIA International Scientific Symposium held in Reykjavik, Iceland, in 2004 (Mikkelsen and Langhelle, 2011, 33). The conclusions of this report highlighted not only that the reduced extent of ice and thinner sea ice would also 'allow construction and operation of more economical offshore platforms', but also that 'increasing movement of ice in some areas initially could hamper oil and gas operations offshore, and that thawing ground could disrupt oil and gas extraction on land, affecting travel, buildings, pipelines, and industrial facilities' (Mikkelsen and Langhelle, 2011, 33; ACIA, 2005). Also, the report defined damage to oil and gas transmissions lines in the permafrost zone as 'a particularly serious situation' that would require an increase in the cost of maintaining these structures (Mikkelsen and Langhelle, 2011, 33; ACIA, 2005). Moreover, some offshore activities could be hindered by increased wave action in Siberia and adjacent seas and reduced sea ice could 'hamper winter seismic work on shore-fast ice' (Mikkelsen and Langhelle, 2011, 33; ACIA, 2005).

Furthermore, another study based on the Coupled Model Intercomparison Project, whose objective is 'to better understand past, present and future climate changes arising from natural, unforced variability or in response to changes in radiative forcing in a multi-model context' (World Climate Research Programme, 2024), suggests that the reduction of Arctic sea ice thickness due to warming caused by climate change will increase Arctic offshore oil production but that it is likely to remain a small portion of total global oil production until it will be possible to exploit resources onshore elsewhere in the world where costs are lower (Zhang et al., 2024). According to the study, changes in sea ice thickness are likely to have the largest impacts on US Arctic offshore oil production, especially in the case of the Alaskan Platform Assessment Unit level, which is 'a sub-unit of hydrocarbon basins with similar geological properties' (Zhang et al., 2024). The study explores the impact of the interaction between energy market forces

---

the country's gas transportation and storage assets, as well as moving significantly towards market prices for gas, namely the prices paid by the EU. Russia cut off Ukraine from its natural gas exports, jeopardising gas supplies to the EU (that passed through Ukraine), and dramatically increased prices for Ukraine. Nevertheless, Russia and Ukraine managed to achieve an agreement on the prices that Ukraine should pay to Russia and the crisis was overcome (Seitz and Zazzaro, 2019, 12).

and climate change (including the consideration of human efforts to reach a low-carbon future) on the relative attractiveness of exploiting oil and gas resources (Zhang et al., 2024). In the short term (until 2030), neither climate change causing sea ice thinning nor low-carbon transition scenarios are likely to cause expansion of Arctic offshore oil production into new assessment unit levels, and future Arctic offshore oil and gas extraction is not likely to affect prices or production in the broader global oil and gas markets (Zhang et al., 2024). In the long term, the effects of human efforts to achieve a low carbon future might increase Arctic offshore oil production due to the simultaneous effect of reduction in unconventional oil production and the gradual depletion of non-Arctic crude oil over the century (Zhang et al., 2024). Nevertheless, this study also highlights the fact that the two factors that it takes into consideration are not the only ones shaping future Arctic offshore oil and gas extraction (Zhang et al., 2024). Other forces include technology barriers and advancements, public policies, environmental and safety concerns, and other externalities related to Arctic offshore extraction (Zhang et al., 2024). Technology is of the utmost importance in order to drill in the Arctic. However, not all Arctic states own the necessary modern technology and expertise to conduct offshore drilling in the Arctic (Zhang et al., 2024). Thus, they are obliged to import those capabilities or cooperate with international energy companies (Zhang et al., 2024). The fact that this is contingent upon international relationships can greatly affect the feasibility of extracting offshore oil and gas resources from the Arctic (Zhang et al., 2024). For instance, Russia's drilling operation in the Kara Sea, which in 2014 revealed oil resources of more than 130 million tons, was halted because of Western sanctions imposed on Russia because of its illegal annexation of Crimea with the aim of restricting one of the Kremlin's largest revenue sources (Zhang et al., 2024; Trainer et al., 2024). Indeed, in July 2014 the EU, as well as the US, decided that 'the sale, supply, transfer or export of certain sensitive goods and technologies should be prohibited when they are destined for deep water oil exploration and production, arctic oil exploration and production or shale oil projects' (Official Journal of the European Union, 2014). In September of the same year, the EU and the US strengthened restrictions on Russia by implementing a series of sanctions on individuals and entities in the Russian energy sector, including the heads of major Russian energy companies (Zhang et al., 2024). Also, these sanctions consisted of asset freezes and travel bans on specific individuals (Trainer et al., 2024). Additionally, the US placed six major companies (Gazprom, Rosneft Oil Company, Novatek, Lukoil, Surgutneftegas, and Transneft) on the Sectoral Sanctions Identifications (SSI) List, which is at the lower end of the US sanctions escalation ladder because it does not fully block the target from US dollar financial services, but it solely prohibits US citizens from 'transacting in, providing financing for, or otherwise dealing in debt of specified tenors or equity if that debt or equity was or is issued on or after the relevant sanctions effective date' by, for the benefit of, or on the behalf of persons operating in Russia's financial and energy sectors (Trainer et al., 2024). Interestingly, of the targeted companies, only Gazprom and Surgutneftegas published statements in response to these sanctions, while Lukoil, Novatek, Rosneft, and Transneft did not publicly comment on increased restrictions (Trainer et al., 2024).

In 2022, Western sanctions were even stricter. For instance, the EU issued minimal sanctions in 2014 but implemented expansive sanctions in correlation with the 2022 invasion of Ukraine (Trainer et al., 2024). In 2022, the EU imposed an embargo on the import of crude oil followed in 2023 by one on oil products, including petrol and diesel (McWilliams et al., 2024). In 2024, the EU decided to impose sanctions on Russian gas as well, which didn't hit the majority of Russia's liquid natural gas (LNG) exports to the EU, but they banned EU ports from reselling Russian LNG after it arrived and blocked financing for Russia's planned Arctic and Baltic LNG terminals (Zimmermann et al., 2024). The US has progressively imposed stringent sanctions on Russia's energy export pipelines with restrictions on imports of crude oil, petroleum, petroleum fuels, oils, and products of their distillation, liquefied natural gas, coal, and coal products of Russian origin (Office of Foreign Assets Control, 2022; Trainer et al., 2024). It has imposed a ban on Russia's LNG exports (in 2023 Russia was the fourth largest LNG exporter in the world after the US, Qatar, and Australia), including Russian and international entities involved in the Russian energy company Novatek's Arctic LNG 2[4] and transshipment facilities (Aliyev, 2024; Statista, 2024). The main problem of Arctic LNG 2 is the shortage of tankers equipped with icebreakers, as Russia's Deputy Prime Minister Alexander Novak has argued (Dell'Aguzzo, 2024). Western sanctions have slowed down Russia's plans to develop Arctic LNG 2 (Aliyev, 2024). For instance, Novatek's plan to lease a floating power plant from the Turkish company Karpowership was not implemented because the terms of the lease were subject to change every month (Aliyev, 2024). Nevertheless, Novatek is confident that the completion of Arctic LNG 2 will be completed in spite of Western sanctions (Aliyev, 2024). In fact, 'Novatek expects to tow the 3rd and final production line of Arctic LNG 2 from the construction yard near Murmansk to the Gydan peninsula during July 2026' (Humpert, 2024).

Furthermore, Western sanctions affect other Russian companies as well such as Gazprom Nedra, one of Russia's major oil and gas service companies operating several rigs for the exploration of the Arctic shelf and Asian companies like the Singaporean shipping operator Red Box that has continued delivering modules from China to Russia throughout 2023 and into 2024 (Aliyev, 2024). Additionally, US sanctions also target the planned Obsky LNG, Arctic LNG 1, and Arctic LNG 3 projects, as well as companies building pipeline infrastructure for Murmansk LNG and Vostok Oil (Aliyev, 2024).

Nevertheless, the Arctic is a geopolitical and economic region of utmost importance to Russia as its immense natural resources, which are crucial for the economic development and the modernisation of the whole state, are functional to

4 Novatek owns a 60% share of the Arctic LNG while French company TotalEnergies, Chinese companies CNPC and CNOOC, and the Japanese consortium Japan Arctic LNG owning 10% each (Dell'Aguzzo, 2024).

its aim to keep its great power status both regionally and internationally. This is why Russia has reacted to Western sanctions by finding other trade partners for its energy resources in order to substitute the EU market that had been its major energy trading partner until then. Thus, Russia has turned to the East and, in particular, to China with which it has strengthened closer economic relations. According to some analysts, the growing economic interdependence between Russia and China, which concerns especially energy and other resources sectors, is the very reason driving their relationship (Larin, 2020, 12; Røseth, 2017, 27; Wachtmeister, 2023, 6). Indeed, Russia's abundant energy resources and China's ever-growing energy demand make their cooperation and trade in the sector 'a natural fit' (Wachtmeister, 2023, 6). A good example of the Russia–China economic relations is the Yamal LNG project, located on the Russian Yamal Peninsula. It is one of the largest and complex LNG projects in the world and one of the most competitive because it manages the immense onshore gas resources of the Yamal Peninsula that are sold to Europe and Asia. Yamal was initially a French–Russian project as French Total and Russian Novatek were the main shareholders, but in 2013 the China National Petroleum Corporation (CNPC) signed a memorandum to join the consortium and purchased a 20% equity share in Yamal LNG (Bros and Mitrova, 2016). At present, Novatek owns 50.1%, Total and CNPC 20% each, and the Chinese Silk Road Fund[5] 9.9% (Hydrocarbons Technology, 2024). If, on the one hand, the involvement of China in the project gives it the possibility to access Russia's energy resources while also being involved in such a huge LNG project, on the other hand, it is part of Russia's geopolitical strategy to diversify its energy markets. China's participation in the Yamal LNG project is an example of the advantages of the strengthened Russia–China energy relations as China's investments have secured the development of the project in spite of Western sanctions. The project was successfully completed on budget (27 billion dollars) and on time as it became operational in 2017 (LNG Prime Staff, 2023).

Very interestingly, in an article titled 'EU Receives 100 Shipments of LNG and Gas Condensate from Yamal LNG Project', published on the High North News, Malte Humpert (2024a), senior fellow and founder of The Arctic Institute, points out that Russia sends most of the Yamal LNG project production to Europe. Indeed, during the first 120 days of 2024, EU Member States received almost 100 shipments (Humpert, 2024a). In particular, between 1 January and 30 April EU Member States (primarily France, Belgium, and Spain) took delivery of 89 shipments, which is an increase compared to the 82 shipments received during the same period in 2023 (Humpert, 2024a). Additionally, the Netherlands received nine shiploads of gas condensate from Yamal as the import of condensates (hydrocarbon liquids produced from natural gas fields, accounting for around 10% of Yamal

5 The Silk Road Fund is a medium- and long-term equity investment fund committed to the development of the Belt and Road Initiative by investing in a number of sectors like infrastructure, energy, and resources, industrial cooperation, financial cooperation, and sustainable development (Silk Road Fund Co. Ltd., 2024).

LNG's overall production) was unsanctioned (Humpert, 2024a). Nevertheless, at the end of June 2024 the EU imposed new sanctions on Russia that introduced a number of targeted measures on the Russian LNG sector (Forwood et al., 2024). More specifically,

> to prevent EU facilities from transshipping Russian LNG to third countries, and thereby reducing Russia's revenues from LNG sale and transport, it is now prohibited to provide reloading services in the EU territory for transshipment operations relating to LNG originating in or exported from Russia, as well as the provision of related technical assistance, brokering services, financing and financial assistance.
>
> (Forwood et al., 2024)

Nevertheless, 'a derogation is available for transshipment operations of LNG [...] originating in Russia or exported from Russia, if such reloading is necessary for its transport to a Member State which has confirmed that the transshipment is used to ensure the energy supply in that Member State' (Forwood et al., 2024). Additionally, 'the restrictions do not apply to reloading services necessary for the bunkering of liquified natural gas fuelled vessels. There is a wind-down period until 26 March 2025 for the execution of contracts concluded before 25 June 2024' (Forwood et al., 2024). By prohibiting the use of its terminals for reloading of LNG, the EU obliges Russia to redesign its logistic networks (Humpert, 2024b).

In the same period, the EU decided to make available the first payment of €1.5 billion generated from immobilised Russian assets in support of Ukraine (European Commission, 2024b). Iceland and Norway, which are members of the European Economic Area (EEA), have aligned themselves with the EU's package of sanctions against Russia by also imposing sanctions, such as assets freezing, in accordance with EU legislation that 'allows for extraordinary revenues generated by immobilised Central Bank of Russia assets to be used to support Ukraine' (Government of Iceland, 2024; Government of Norway, 2024). On the website of the Norwegian government, it is possible to read that although the Central Bank of Russia has no assets in Norway, it is important that Norway 'supports measures introduced by our allies that can help Ukraine in its fight to defend itself, and in due course help to rebuild a free Ukraine' (Government of Norway, 2024).

Furthermore, in order to phase out Russian fossil fuel imports, in 2022 the EU adopted the REPowerEU Plan aiming at saving energy, diversifying energy supplies, and producing clean energy.[6] As for saving energy, it seems that this plan is quite successful. For instance, natural gas demand declined by 18% between August 2022 and March 2024 (European Commission, 2024). Additionally, the EU now has a system in place to fill up gas storage ahead of every winter that

6 The REPowerEU Plan is mainly funded through the Recovery and Resilience Fund (300 billion euro), which is a temporary instrument through which 'the Commission raises funds by borrowing on the capital markets' (issuing bonds on behalf of the EU) (European Commission, 2024; European Commission, 2024a).

enables it to avoid blackouts and energy shortages (European Commission, 2024). As for diversifying energy supplies, the share of EU gas imports coming from Russia diminished from 45% to 15% (European Commission, 2024). As for producing clean energy, since 2022 the EU has managed to increase its production and capacity by 'reaching a record of almost 96 GW of new solar energy capacity installed, increasing wind capacity by 33 GW, and ensuring 46% of our electricity now comes from renewables' (European Commission, 2024).

In this context, the economic ties between the EU and the Nordic region (including both EU and non-EU members, namely Denmark, Finland, Iceland, Norway, and Sweden) plays a crucial role as the Nordic states are at the forefront of renewable energy production. Iceland, whose natural energy reserves include hydro and geothermal power, is one of the world's leading countries in renewable energy, with almost 100% of its electricity produced from renewable sources (Arctic Portal, 2024). In particular, roughly 73% of its electricity comes from hydroelectric dams powered with runoff water from the country's melting glaciers (Seidel, 2024). Norway, whose economy is largely based on petroleum and natural gas production, is very much committed to promoting renewable energy production with almost 90% of its electricity generated from hydropower (Arctic Portal, 2024; European Parliament, 2023). Also, the government is trying to develop green energy in the northern provinces of Nordland, Troms, and Finnmark where hydropower is the main source of energy, but usage of wind and tidal current energy are increasing (Arctic Portal, 2024). For instance, in 2022 the government presented an initiative aimed at promoting offshore wind power to generate electricity (European Parliament, 2023). Like in Norway, also in Sweden most electricity is generated from hydropower, but wind power has been increasing during the last few decades becoming the second source of electricity (European Parliament, 2023). Denmark's technology leadership is important in the areas of offshore wind, biomethane, and district heating (International Energy Agency, 2023). Denmark has a very high share of wind electricity, which, together with bioenergy and solar photovoltaic, makes up over 80% of the electricity mix (International Energy Agency, 2023). Finland is one of the world leaders in the utilisation of renewable sources of energy, especially bioenergy, and renewable energy sources represent about 40% of energy end-consumption (Ministry of Economic Affairs and Employment of Finland, 2023). Per capita, the Nordic states together consume four times as much renewable energy for heat as the EU (Nordic Energy Research, 2021). Across the region, transport is becoming increasing renewable as more electricity is adopted on road and rail, driven by a surge of electric vehicles in Norway (Nordic Energy Research, 2021).

Moreover, according to the Renewable Energy in the Nordics, a report published by Nordic Energy Research in 2021, that year all the Nordic states had met the 2020 targets set in the EU Renewable Energy Directive while only half of the EU members were on track (Nordic Energy Research, 2021).

In general terms, the renewables share of Nordic energy consumption is almost five times the EU average (Nordic Energy Research, 2021). Given the advantage of the Nordic states in the energy sector and the necessity to speed up its green transition, the EU is strengthening its relations with Iceland and Norway, which are however EEA members. Iceland and Norway are implementing EU energy legislation covering the Third Energy Package of 2009,[7] which entered into force in the EEA states in 2019 (EFTA Surveillance Authority, 2020). Moreover, the case of cooperation between the EU and Norway is particularly interesting as they have recently increased their ties (Delivorias and De Martini, 2023, 4). In fact, in 2022 they signed a joint statement with the very aim to secure their energy independence and improve the EU's resilience (Delivorias and De Martini, 2023, 1). The statement focuses on developing cooperation on renewable energy, carbon capture research, and hydrogen as well as on gas supply from Norway to EU members (Delivorias and De Martini, 2023, 1). Also, in 2024 they signed the Green Alliance 'to strengthen their joint climate action, environmental protection efforts, and cooperation on the clean energy and industrial transition' (European Commission, 2023). The Green Alliance is 'the most comprehensive form of bilateral engagement established under the European Green Deal, with both parties committing to climate neutrality and to aligning their domestic and international climate policies to pursue this goal' (European Commission, 2023). It is interesting to note that during the negotiations Norway tried to pressure the EU into supporting an increase in oil and gas exploration and extraction, but the EU responded by pushing Norway to consider 'the precautionary principle and a more rapid transition away from fossil energy in the Arctic' (Walstad, 2023). Thus, the EU has been coherent with its pledge included in its 2021 Arctic policy to keep oil, coal, and gas in the ground (European Commission, 2021).

Generally speaking, in the Arctic there is a growing interest in the development of renewable energy and the green economy essentially for three reasons: 1) the need to tackle climate change and other environmental problems; 2) the desire to strengthen energy security by reducing dependence on imported oil and gas; and 3) the need to stimulate job creation in many rural areas, particularly in the aftermath of the 2008 economic and financial crisis (Arctic Portal, 2024).

In this context, an important issue concerns the impact of renewable energy production development on indigenous peoples that are very vulnerable to environmental changes because their livelihood depends on the nature surrounding them. In fact, renewable energy technology has a negative impact on vulnerable communities. An example is the case of the development of wind turbines in the Fosen region of central Norway. In 2023, the Saami community, an indigenous group whose traditional lands stretch across Norway, Sweden, Finland, and western Russia, demonstrated to pressure the Norwegian government to turn down two wind farms (Storheia and Roan) constituted of 151 turbines in the Fosen region and belonging to Norwegian energy companies Statkraft and TrønderEnergi, German

7 Currently, only the gas part of the Third Energy Package, which is a set of laws regulating the internal gas and electricity market of the EU adopted in 2009, is still in force as the electricity market rules were adopted as part of the Clean Energy for All Europeans package in 2019 (European Commission, no date).

utility Stadtwerke Muenchen, and Denmark's Nordic Wind Power DA (Nugent, 2023). The two wind farms, whose construction was completed in 2020, are part of Europe's largest onshore wind development leading Norway to triple its onshore wind capacity since 2018 (Nugent, 2023). The protesters argue that reindeer are terrified by the noise and sight of the turbines, making the lands unsuitable for grazing and in jeopardising the Saami's livelihood (Nugent, 2023). They also claim that Norway is breaking the law by keeping the turbines running, especially because in October 2021 Norway's Supreme Court ruled that their construction violated the Saami's protected cultural rights under a UN treaty and that the energy ministry's decision to license them was 'invalid' (Nugent, 2023). At the end of 2023, the Norwegian government reached an agreement with the south Fosen group of reindeer herders (Reuters, 2024; Nugent, 2023). The agreement includes an annual compensation of 7 million Norwegian crowns to herders that allows the turbines to stand, the procurement of an additional winter grazing area from 2026 to 2027, and veto right for any plans to extend the wind farm's operating licences past 2045 (Reuters, 2024). Nevertheless, the dispute continues as an agreement has not been reached with the north Fosen group of reindeer herders (Reuters, 2024).

At the same time, the implementation of oil and gas extraction and exploitation activities also has a negative impact on indigenous people. The case of the Yamal LNG project mentioned above is a case in point. Olga Murashko, researcher at the Research Institute and Museum of Anthropology of Moscow State University, said there is 'substantial risks to the future survival of the Nenets, their rights and their existence as a distinct group' (Morgounova Schwalbe, 2016, 7). The area licensed for the Yamal LNG project is of utmost importance for herders who live and migrate with their herds in the tundra (Morgounova Schwalbe, 2016, 7). During their seasonal migration, the reindeer herders also use the area for hunting, gathering, and subsistence fishing (Morgounova Schwalbe, 2016, 6). Moreover, the development of gas and oil industries has a negative impact on the environment, which is vital to the livelihood of the Nenets (Morgounova Schwalbe, 2016, 6).

Furthermore, different from the oil and gas extraction and exploitation activities, renewable energy technology has a double impact on indigenous people. If on the one hand, they negatively affect indigenous communities, on the other hand, it could be a step forward in the self-governance of indigenous people since remote Arctic communities depend on diesel (80%) as the primary energy source, which is imported (de Witt et al., 2019). Imports can come by sea on barges during the summertime or by truck over frozen rivers during winter time and in exceptional cases or in case of emergency, fuel has to be flown in (de Witt et al., 2019). Consequently, fuel transportation is very critical and very expensive (de Witt et al., 2019). Therefore, the use of local energy sources (e.g., hydropower and wind power) can increase the energy security of indigenous communities and lower the cost of energy (de Witt et al., 2019). This is why the use of renewable energy in the Arctic is increasing and states are implementing national policies aimed at developing its technology in their northernmost areas. For instance, Canada has introduced several programs to support renewable projects in order to achieve the aim of reducing carbon dioxide emissions by 30% until the year 2030 (de Witt et al., 2019). An example is the Energy Innovation Program, set up to support innovations for clean energy (de Witt et al., 2019). Greenland has passed from fossil fuels, which historically have been its main source of energy, to renewables in a few decades (Mikkola et al., 2016). In 2008, Alaska set up a Renewable Energy Fund (REF) to reduce the cost of energy and increase energy security (de Witt et al., 2019) and the Rural Power System Upgrades program to help rural communities with less than 2,000 inhabitants to increase the efficiency of their generators (de Witt et al., 2019). Furthermore, Russia is also trying to develop renewable energy in its Arctic territories. In fact, it has established the Kolskaya Wind Farm, the world's largest wind farm beyond the Arctic Circle, located in the Murmansk Oblast on the Kola Peninsula and began production in 2023 (PJSC EL5-Energo, 2024). Very significantly, on the website of Russian company Lukoil, which was in charge of the construction of the wind power plant (WPP), it is possible to read that 'the majority of the equipment installed at the WPP was made in Russia' and that 'the Kolskaya plant was constructed under the state support programme for renewable energy generation and the agreement with the government of the Murmansk region on renewable energy development' (Lukoil, 2023). Indeed, in 2021 the plant was named 'a strategic investment project in the region' as it is supposed to prevent greenhouse gas emissions of up to 600 thousand tonnes of carbon dioxide equivalent (Lukoil, 2023). Additionally, the Kola Peninsula is the area where most resources and projects are concentrated and where clean energy such as hydroelectricity is already available (Russian International Affairs Council, 2021). Indeed, as Inger Johanne Wiese, chair of the Arctic Contaminants Action Program (ACAP) of the AC, said, there are some 'success stories' in the renewables field (Arctic Council, 2024). An example is the ACAP project at the Polmos Tundra Reindeer Farm on the Kola Peninsula, which 'was based on a switch from old diesel generators to a hybrid wind/diesel power system based on modern energy efficient technologies' (Arctic Council, 2024). Another successful AC project is the Karelia Valday Cluster that, like the Polmos Tundra, was 'intended to demonstrate the viability of renewable energy sources in the Arctic as well as highlight the health, environmental, and long-term economic benefits associated with a shift to renewables' (ACAP, 2017). The Karelia Valday Cluster has implemented concrete action toward pollution prevention, abatement, and elimination with measurable positive effects on the environment of the Arctic (ACAP, 2017). These projects were financed by the Project Support Instrument, a financing instrument 'for the purpose of mobilising and channelling financing for prioritised Arctic Council projects responding to the Declaration of the Fourth Ministerial meeting of the Arctic Council in Reykjavik 2004', that, inter alia, 'emphasized the need for reinforcing efforts to finance circumpolar cooperation, supported the Project Support Instrument (PSI) concept as a mechanism to enhance the process of identifying, mobilizing and transferring financing for specific priority Arctic Council projects' (Huber and Rystedt, 2016, 2).

Therefore, the energy sector is strongly affected by both climate change and the war in Ukraine. Climate change is making oil and gas resources increasingly accessible, but the Arctic states are trying to become independent from them by developing renewable energy technologies, which is crucial also to fight climate change. At the same time, the war in Ukraine has interrupted cooperation between the West and Russia in the sector pushing Russia to turn to the East.

The geopolitics of minerals

A combination of ice-melting due to climate change and advances in mining technology is reducing the cost of extracting critical minerals in the Arctic. Like in the case of energy, it is difficult to get precise data about the amount of minerals present in the Arctic. Thus, the available data are estimated figures according to which the region holds about 90% of the world's reserves of nickel and cobalt, 60% of copper, and 96% of platinum, mainly in Russia and northern Canada, but also partly in Alaska (Laruelle, 2019, 152). Other minerals that it is possible to find in the region are coal, iron ore, zinc, lead, diamonds, and gemstones (Middlebury Institute of International Studies at Monterey, 2022).

Russia has a mining history of almost 300 years, beginning in the 18th century with the mining of gold and silver while in the 20th century it became one of the world's most important sources of metals and diamonds – today Russia is the largest producer of diamonds (Statista, 2024a). Russian company Alrosa is the largest producer of diamonds in the world, and Russia is the second-largest seller of diamonds after South Africa (Laruelle, 2019, 152). Moreover, Russia is one of the largest producers of steel and its company Norilsk Nickel is one of the world's largest producers of nickel, platinum, and palladium and is located in northern Siberia (Boyd et al., 2016, 9; Arctic Economic Council, 2024, 8). The most abundant mineral resources are located on the Kola Peninsula because of its geological peculiarities (Laruelle, 2019, 152). Here, the Murmansk Oblast is rich in reserves of nickel-copper ores, alumina, rare metals, titanium, construction materials, and semi-precious and precious stones like amazonite and amethyst (Jørgensen-Dahl, 2010; Laruelle, 2019, 152). Also, there are bauxite reserves in the Arkhangelsk Oblast and the north Onezhsky bauxite mine is the largest in Europe (Jørgensen-Dahl, 2010). Gold and silver can be found near the Taimyr Peninsula and in the northern part of Yakutia, while nickel and copper can be found around Noril'sk and the Kola Peninsula (Laruelle, 2019, 152). Today, in the Russian Arctic there are more than 25 centres of mining activity of which Norilsk-Talnakh is the largest nickel-copper-palladium complex in the world (Laruelle, 2019, 152). Norilsk-Talnakh is also important for agriculture because three-quarters of the phosphate fertiliser used in Russia is manufactured from apatite concentrate located in the Khibiny deposit in the Kola Peninsula (Laruelle, 2019, 152).

Alaska and Canada also have major mining industries (Boyd et al., 2016, 9). For instance, the Red Dog group of mines in northwestern Alaska is one of the world's largest zinc mines (Teck Alaska, 2024). The Red Dog group was established in 1982 through an operating agreement between the operator Teck and NANA, a regional Alaska Native corporation owned by the Iñupiat people of northwest Alaska (Arctic Economic Council, 2024, 8). Additionally, Alaska is a major producer of gold and also produces gemstones, construction sand and gravel, crushed stone, lead, and silver (USGS, 2024). Metals contribute over 90% of the value of minerals mined in the state (USGS, 2024). A report published by the University of Alaska in December 2022 highlights the fact that interest in Alaska's mining potential has gained national attention since the passing of the climate law called the Inflation Reduction Act (University of Alaska, 2022, 4). This law has marked 'the most significant action Congress has taken on clean energy and climate change in the nation's history' (The White House, 2023). The goal of the law is to implement the green transition by making fossil fuels more expensive and less attractive than alternatives (Waldhols, 2023). In order to do so, the law finances 'incentives for nearly every sector of the economy to adopt renewable energy and other low-carbon technologies' (Waldhols, 2023).

Like Alaska, Canada also adopted a mineral strategy in 2022 with the goal to 'increase the supply of responsibly sourced critical minerals and support the development of domestic and global value chains for the green and digital economy' (Government of Canada, 2022). Canada's mining industry is the leading global producer of potash and a major producer of aluminium, cobalt, diamonds, fluorspar, gemstones, gold, indium, niobium, palladium, platinum, tellurium, titanium concentrate, and uranium (Government of Canada, 2024). Also, the Cantung Mine in the northwest territories of Canada is one of the world's largest producers of tungsten (Alvarez & Marsal Canada Inc., 2024). Commercial discoveries are especially found in the northwest territories, Ontario and Nunavet (Boyd et al., 2016, 9).

The Norwegian continental shelf contains copper, zinc, cobalt, gold, iron, and manganese (International Energy Agency, 2023a). Norway's Svalbard islands are rich in coal, copper, zinc, gold, and silver (Jones, 2023). The Trælen graphite mine in north Norway is the most important producer of natural crystalline graphite in Europe and the highest-grade flake graphite producer in the world (Geological Survey of Norway, no date). Also, nepheline syenite (feldspar minerals) is produced on the island of Senja off the coast of northernmost Norway (Geological Survey of Norway, no date). In addition, Norway extracts high-purity quartz, which is needed for the production of silicon, and titanium minerals, which can be used for the production of titanium metal (Geological Survey of Norway, no date). In June 2023, the Minister of Trade and Industry presented Norway's Mineral Strategy with the stated goal of developing the mineral industry as the most sustainable in the world (International Energy Agency, 2023a). In its Mineral Strategy, the Norwegian government highlights that

> for extraction to be sustainable, considerations of human rights, the environment, waste management, climate footprint and local communities must be sufficiently addressed. We therefore need a Norwegian mineral industry that continuously works to improve sustainability by reducing its environmental impact and land use, ensuring maximum resource utilisation, reducing greenhouse gas emissions and points of conflict, and aligning its activities with the respective local communities.
>
> (Norwegian Ministry of Trade, Industry and Fisheries, 2023, 9)

Additionally, Greenland's subsoil contains a variety of valuable minerals such as gold, silver, copper, lead, zinc, graphite, olivine, cryolite, lithium, and marble (Hardy et al., 2024; Greenland Institute of Natural Resources, 2024). In particular, Greenland contains one of the largest sources of nickel and cobalt (Arctic Economic Council, 2024, 8). However, a number of mines have closed in the past few years, including the Seqi olivine mine near Maniitsoq, which was shut down in 2011, and the Nalunaq gold mine near Nanortalik, which was decommissioned in 2013 (Greenland Institute of Natural Resources, 2024). In spite of this, new mining projects have been launched such as a ruby mine near Qeqertarsuatsiaat (Fiskenæsset) (Greenland Institute of Natural Resources, 2024). Also, Kvanefjeld,[8] an area in southern Greenland, 'has the potential to become one of the world's largest producers of rare earth magnet metals, creating significant wealth for this impoverished and often forgotten area of the Nordic hemisphere' (Hartmann et al., 2024). This should be seen in the context of the Greenland Mineral Strategy 2020–2024, which was issued by the government in 2020. The document's overall vision 'is to differentiate the economy, create new jobs, skills and business for existing enterprises and contribute with revenue to the treasury and contribute to the economic development to the benefit of all of Greenland' (Government of Greenland, 2020, 5). Some scholars define Greenland's resources as 'the most important strategic resource of the 21st century' and 'one of Greenland's most important strategic assets' (Andersson et al., 2018, 2). Also, natural resources revenue (e.g., minerals and petroleum) are considered a necessary economic prerequisite to obtain independence from Denmark (Spohr et al., 2020, 125). Furthermore, in 2021, the Greenland parliament passed the so-called Uranium Act, which 'creates a ban against the prospecting, exploration and exploitation of uranium, providing that the Government might issue rules to restrict or revoke prospecting, exploration or exploitation licences' (Hartmann et al., 2024). Moreover, since US President Donald Trump came to power for the second time in January 2025, Greenland's mineral wealth has been at the centre of international attention. President Trump has expressed several times its desire 'to get Greenland' (Kardon and Gabuev, 2025), pointing to 'economic security' (Murray, 2025) as well as to 'national security' (Cook, 2025) given the growing geopolitical and military relevance of the Arctic. In March 2025, President Trump stated the possibility to use military force to assert control over Greenland (Cook, 2025). However, in a visit to Greenland touring the US' Pituffik Space Base in the northwest part of the island, US Vice President James David Vance stated that he did not believe that 'military force is ever going to be necessary' and that the US would be able 'to cut

8 The Kvanefjeld field is at the centre of a dispute initiated in 2023 between Greenland Minerals (GM), a wholly-owned subsidiary of the Australian mining company Energy Transition Minerals, and the governments of Denmark and Greenland. The issue central to the dispute is 'whether GM is or should be permitted to mine uranium and the extent to which this is covered by its licence'. The main point underlying the contention is that the extraction of rare earth elements inevitably involves the simultaneous mining of radioactive materials, such as uranium and thorium, because uranium and rare earth metals coexist within the same mineral deposits in Kvanefjeld (Hartmann et al., 2024).

a deal, Donald Trump-style, to ensure the security of this territory' (Cook, 2025). President Trumps' aims on Greenland have inevitably led to a confrontation with Mette Frederiksen, Denmark's Prime Minister at the time of writing. Nevertheless, Prime Minister Frederiksen tried to downplay tensions arguing in an interview at her office in Copenhagen's Christiansborg Palace that 'I have tried to de-escalate the situation, because in this world, with a very aggressive Russia, with a closer cooperation between Iran, North Korea and Russia, helped by China, I will do what I can to ensure that nothing goes wrong between allies and good friends and partners. But at the same time, we have to stick to the most important values and principles' (Tostevin, 2025).

Iceland is poor in metals but rich in crystallised minerals such as zeolite and Iceland spar due to volcanic activity (Natural History Museum, no date). According to the 2019 Minerals Yearbook of the USGS, aluminium and ferrosilicon are the leading mineral commodities produced in Iceland (USGS, 2019).

Finland is rich in copper, iron ore, nickel, cobalt, and chromium (World Atlas, 2024). Finnish bedrock contains significant known deposits of many critical metals and minerals, and has considerable potential for discovery of new resources such as platinum, rare earth metals, and zinc (Government of Finland, 2022). Thus, Finland has good potential for battery minerals (in particular cobalt, nickel, lithium, and graphite) as it has expertise in the whole production chain of these minerals from the mining industry to the further processing of battery raw materials, the technology related to the manufacture, use, and charging of batteries, and recycling (Chambers and Partners, 2024). Also, Finland is the only producer of cobalt in the EU and a major producer of copper, which is essential to the energy transition (Chambers and Partners, 2024).

Sweden is the largest iron ore producer in the EU and is also among the foremost producers of base and precious metals (Geological Survey of Sweden, 2020). In particular, the state-owned mining company LKAB is responsible for about 80% of the iron ore in the EU (Preve, 2024). Most mines are located in the regions of Norrbotten, Skelleftefältet, and Bergslagen (Geological Survey of Sweden, 2020). Sweden produces zinc, copper, and lead, whose production has decreased over the last few years, while the production of gold and silver has increased (Geological Survey of Sweden, 2020). Sweden's Mineral Strategy aims to strengthen the position of the state as the 'EU's leading mining and mineral nation' by increasing the competitiveness of its mining and minerals industry (Swedish Ministry of Enterprise Energy and Communications, 2013, 4). In order to achieve this goal, Sweden has identified five 'strategic objectives': 1) a mining and minerals industry in harmony with the environment, cultural values, and other business activities; 2) dialogue and cooperation to promote innovation and growth; 3) a clear and effective regulatory framework and infrastructure for competitiveness and growth; 4) an innovative mining and minerals industry with an excellent knowledge base; and 5) an internationally renowned, active, and attractive mining and minerals industry (Swedish Ministry of Enterprise Energy and Communications, 2013, 5). In doing so, Sweden could profitably contribute to reducing the amount of critical minerals from Russia and China 'where they may have been produced under poor environmental and social conditions, and due to geopolitical circumstances linked to risks with supply', as it is possible to read on the LKAB's website (LKAB, 2022).

Furthermore, the Arctic also contains rare earth elements (REEs)[9] that are present in Greenland, Canada, and northern Scandinavia (Meja Hernandez, 2024). REEs are an essential part of many high-tech devices (American Geosciences Institute, 2024). In its news release 'Going Critical', the USGS explains that

> REEs are necessary components of more than 200 products across a wide range of applications, especially high-tech consumer products, such as cellular telephones, computer hard drives, electric and hybrid vehicles, and flat-screen monitors and televisions. Significant defense applications include electronic displays, guidance systems, lasers, and radar and sonar systems. Although the amount of REE used in a product may not be a significant part of that product by weight, value, or volume, the REE can be necessary for the device to function. For example, magnets made of REE often represent only a small fraction of the total weight, but without them, the spindle motors and voice coils of desktops and laptops would not be possible.
>
> (American Geosciences Institute, 2024)

Also, graphite and cobalt are essential manufacturing materials contained in electric vehicles; tin and indium are used in high-tech devices, such as touchscreens and solar panels; and zinc is used to prevent corrosion in renewable energy technologies, such as wind turbines. Thus, energy transition is not possible without critical minerals. This is why the production of critical minerals has geopolitical implications, especially considering that China is the leader in mineral production with 4.6 billion tons per year in total, followed by the US with 2.2 billion tons and Russia with roughly 1.7 billion tons (World Population Review, 2024). In the 1980s, China was the first to understand the importance of rare metals (Laruelle, 2019, 155). Thus, it decided to increase its production in spite of the environmental problems this creates (Laruelle, 2019, 155). Today, China produces around 60% of the world's rare earth metals, and is the source of around 90% of refined rare earth metals on the market (Gavin, 2024). More specifically, China controls the majority of essential mining refineries and raw materials, including 73% of cobalt refineries, 68% of nickel refineries, 59% of lithium refineries, and 40% of copper refineries (Khurshid et al., 2023, 2). As the development of China's economy is advancing at a rapid pace, China's demand for resources continues to increase. This is why China is interested in Arctic resources. In the case of minerals, Greenland is of particular strategic importance for China that has expressed its interest in funding Greenland-based projects while the US and other states 'are positioning

9 The 17 rare earth elements are: lanthanum (La), cerium (Ce), praseodymium (Pr), neodymium (Nd), promethium (Pm), samarium (Sm), europium (Eu), gadolinium (Gd), terbium (Tb), dysprosium (Dy), holmium (Ho), erbium (Er), thulium (Tm), ytterbium (Yb), lutetium (Lu), scandium (Sc), and yttrium (Y) (The Northern Miner Group, 2024).

themselves to take advantage of Greenland's resource potential, rare earth elements, markets, and geostrategic location' (Nuttall, 2021, 1674). Nevertheless, Chinese involvement in Greenland's mineral sector has generated disagreements between Denmark and Greenland. Denmark fears that China might seize control of Greenland's vast mineral riches and that its investments hide political and military objectives (Andersson et al., 2018, 2). By contrast, Greenland considers the involvement of China in its mining sector as a feasible way to achieve economic independence, while for China to be involved in Greenland's mineral sector means the possibility to be more involved in Arctic affairs (Andersson et al., 2018, 2).

Furthermore, the 'Greenland and Iceland in the New Arctic' report released by Iceland's Ministry of Foreign Affairs in 2020 points out that 'a major supply of rare earth metals have put Greenland in a new and unique position. Several overlapping factors indicate that the 21st century will be prosperous for the Greenlandic mining industry' (Nuttall, 2021, 1675). Very interestingly, in 2023 Greenland signed the Paris Agreement (United Nations, 2024), which means that 'it does not wish to be bound by Denmark's commitments to the treaty, especially as restrictions on CO_2 emissions would hinder the development of mines' (Nuttall, 2021, 1675). In addition, in 2021 Greenland joined the European Raw Materials Alliance, which was established as part of the Action Plan on Critical Raw Materials aiming 'to reduce Europe's raw materials' dependency on third countries [especially China], diversifying supply from both primary and secondary sources and improving resource efficiency and circularity while promoting responsible sourcing worldwide' (European Commission, 2022). Greenland is considered by the EU as a major supplier for most of the critical minerals it needs, including its rare earth metals (Nuttall, 2021, 1675).

Additionally, the war in Ukraine is another variable affecting the critical minerals market (Khurshid et al., 2023, 2). For instance, the decrease of Russian exports of gold, copper, cobalt, and other precious metals and mining goods by 35.5% due to the invasion of Ukraine has shaken the Russian economy and mineral markets and has affected the global renewables market (Khurshid et al., 2023, 2). Also, Russia is the main nickel and cobalt producer, while Ukraine supplies rare earth metals to Europe (Khurshid et al., 2023, 8). For example, Ukraine exports ores, slag, and ash (8.3%), and iron and steel (7.9%) to the EU (European Commission, no date-a). The Russia–Ukraine conflict has caused an increase in the price of nickel by 36% and cobalt by 2% on the global market (Khurshid et al., 2023, 8). In a study conducted on the impact of the Russia–Ukraine conflict on the prices of critical metals, Khurshid et al. show that this conflict has interrupted critical metals supply routes, raising concerns about accessibility and pricing (Khurshid et al., 2023, 8). This has created uncertainty, which has raised prices (Khurshid et al., 2023, 8). Similarly, mining disruption has reduced production and supply causing uncertainty and interruptions to the global supply chain for essential metals (Khurshid et al., 2023, 8). This has happened because the international supply chain for critical metals is inter-related and supported by an extensive network of producers, processors, and suppliers (Khurshid et al., 2023, 8). Consequently, disruptions in one area can affect other parts of the supply chain (Khurshid et al., 2023, 8). Additionally, the

Russia–Ukraine conflict has created speculation and anxiety over the future prices of critical metals negatively impacting the global supply chain (Khurshid et al., 2023, 8). From a geopolitical perspective, 'supply disruptions can exacerbate tensions and lead to conflicts over access to essential metal reserves' (Khurshid et al., 2023, 9). In the case of the Arctic more specifically, there are no territorial conflicts (there are a few territorial disputes though over shipping routes as discussed in the following chapter) but the growing tensions between the Western Arctic states and Russia is increasing the significance of the mining sector as sanctions and scarcity have affected natural supplies, including minerals (Jones, 2023). The Svalbard archipelago (also known as Spitsbergen) is a good example. It has a considerable mineral wealth including copper, zinc, gold, silver, and non-metallic minerals such as sand, gravel, limestone, and fertiliser minerals (Natural History Museum, 2022; Eurostat, 2023). Also, coal reserves are the cornerstone of its economy (Natural History Museum, 2022). The 1920 Svalbard Treaty gave Norway sovereignty over the archipelago but with some limitations.[10] All signatories of the treaty had the right to engage in mining activities but since 2012 Russia and Norway have been the only nations with a presence on Svalbard (Jones, 2023). Furthermore, the Russia–Ukraine war has increased the importance of minerals that are essential to energy transition thus making the natural resources of the Svalbard archipelago geopolitically more relevant. As Dr Elizabeth Buchanan, head of navy research at the Sea Power Centre in Australia, has argued, 'geostrategically, Svalbard is significant. But geopolitically it is increasingly gaining significance too, particularly given the Ukraine-Russia War' (Jones, 2023).

Therefore, both climate change and the war in Ukraine have increased the geopolitical relevance of minerals in the Arctic (but also globally) as they are essential for technology and energy transition. If on the one hand, technology and energy transition are crucial to fight climate change, on the other hand, energy transition is fundamental to reduce the relevance of Russia as an energy supplier by diversifying energy supplies.

The geopolitics of fisheries

Commercial fishery is one of the most important economic activities in the Arctic. For instance, in terms of percentage contribution to GDP, the seafood industry contributes to 16.53% in Greenland (FAO, 2020, 2), 2.3% in Norway (Fishfarming Expert, 2023), 2% in Canada (Government of Canada, 2023), 8.1% in Iceland (Business Iceland, 2021, 1), 0.1% in Sweden (European Commission, no date-b),

10 The Treaty of Paris envisages that Norway has 'the full and absolute sovereignty' over the archipelago of Svalbard, including land masses and territorial waters, but it also stipulates that sovereignty is subject to several conditions. In particular, the limitations imposed by the treaty concern not only fiscal and military constraints but also the application of the principle of non-discrimination to the nationals of all the contracting parties, namely equal rights of fishing and hunting, equal freedom of access and entry, and equal exercise and practice of all maritime, industrial, mining, and commercial enterprises (Conde and Iglesias Sánchez, 2019, 76).

0.3% in Russia (FAO, 2007, 9), and 0.1% Finland (FAO, 2017, 2). Alaska 'is the top US seafood producer, producing more wild seafood than all other states combined' (60%) (Alaska Seafood, 2024).

There are important fishing grounds in the Barents Sea[11] and the Bering Sea[12] that provide the bulk of the landings from northern fisheries (Hoel, 2020, 2). However, the Norwegian Sea, located south of the Barents Sea,[13] and the waters between Iceland and Greenland,[14] and in the northwest Atlantic[15] are productive fishing grounds as well (Hoel, 2020, 2). It is estimated that the Arctic is home to about 240 fish species, mostly sculpins, snailfishes, eelpouts, and cod (Norkross and Iken, 2016). One of the most numerous fish species in the Arctic is probably the Arctic cod, which holds 'a central role in linking the sea ice-associated and water column food webs to higher level consumers' (Norkross and Iken, 2016). In fact, a large array of seabirds, seals, and whales all depend heavily on Arctic cod (Norkross and Iken, 2016). At the regional level, Norway is by far the dominant producer in the Arctic (especially due to salmon farming) as it produces more than half of the world's total output (Arctic Group, 2024), but aquaculture is also present in the other Arctic states although at a small scale (Øystein and Max, 2012). Additionally, the waters of the Arctic supply over 15% of the world's marine fish catch (Mueter, 2021, 3024) and Arctic aquaculture contributes 2% of global production (Øystein and Max, 2012). At the international level, Russia, the state with the longest coast in the region (but produces fish in other parts of the country like the east), is the fourth leading fishing state worldwide with 5.2 million metric tonnes of fish after China (13.14 million metric tonnes), Indonesia (7.2 million metric tonnes) and Peru (6.58 million metric tonnes) (data for the year 2021 – Statista, 2023).

Nevertheless, the productivity of a number of fish species is expected to change in the near future due to climate change, which poses serious threats to both capture fisheries and aquaculture (Brander, 2007, 1). Researchers have studied the nexus between Arctic fisheries and climate change concluding that changes in Arctic fisheries can occur according to two phenomena. The first one is tropicalisation consisting of the poleward shift of species that prefer warm temperatures that leave areas that have become too warm for them (Baily and Snook, 2021, 1677). The second phenomenon is deborealisation consisting in the decrease of cold water species

11 The most important fish species are cod, haddock, and capelin but there are also other species like saithe (pollock), redfish, Greenland halibut, and the crustaceans: deepwater prawns, king crab, and snow crab (Staby, 2020).

12 The most important species are salmon, halibut, and shellfish fisheries. Other fisheries are Pacific cod, king crab, halibut, rockfish, sable fish, and Atka mackerel (Alaska Department of Fish and Game, no date).

13 The most important fish species are mackerel, herring, and blue whiting (Hoel, 2020, 2).

14 The most important fish species are cod, haddock, saithe (pollock), redfish, Greenland halibut, and various other flatfish, wolffish, tusk, and ling (International Council for the Exploration of the Sea, no date).

15 The most important fish species are Atlantic cod, redfish, American plaice, witch flounder, yellowtail flounder, Greenland halibut, white hake, thorny skate, capelin, shortfinned squid, northern shrimp, splendid alfonsino (Northwest Atlantic Fisheries Organization, 2024).

that could suffer in the transition to warmer marine ecosystems (Baily and Snook, 2021, 1677). Additionally, researchers have found that fished species generally decline more than unfished ones, especially in the context of deborealisation (Baily and Snook, 2021, 1677). Thus, 'there are strong interactions between the effects of fishing and the effects of climate because fishing reduces the age, size, and geographic diversity of populations and the biodiversity of marine ecosystems, making both more sensitive to additional stresses such as climate change' (Brander, 2007). This can be particularly problematic because fish, seafood, and marine mammals are vital in the diets and livelihoods of indigenous people (Baily and Snook, 2021, 1677).

Furthermore, climate change, which leads to increasing accessibility to ice waters and the consequent opportunity to access fish more easily, also has important geopolitical implications that translate into two effects. If on the one hand it pushes states to cooperate, on the other hand it fosters pre-existing political tensions among states.

When it comes to the first effect, it is clear that states are more likely to cooperate in order to protect their geopolitical and economic interests in the region by participating in the decision-making processes concerning the fishery sector. An illuminating example is the Agreement to Prevent the Unregulated High Seas Fisheries in the Central Arctic Ocean[16] (CAOFA) signed by Canada, Denmark/Greenland, Norway, Russia, and the US – the Arctic 5 (the coastal states) – together with China, the EU, Iceland, Japan, and the Republic of Korea (therefore also called the Arctic 5+5 Agreement) in Ilulissat (Greenland) in 2018. The CAOFA, which aims to prevent commercial fishing by the signatory states, entered into force in 2021 and will remain in effect for 16 years until 2037 (Arctic Council, 2021; European Commission, 2021b). During this period of time, the parties will study the ecosystem emerging from below a retreating sea ice cover in order to decide whether to renew the CAOFA in increments of five years (Arctic Council, 2021; Shibata et al., 2019, 34). Indeed, the CAOFA envisages a joint scientific program aiming to identify species, their abundance, predator-prey relationships, and the factors that jeopardise them such as climate change (Hoag, 2017, 14). The collected information will help the parties decide whether one or more additional regional fisheries management organisations or arrangements should be established for the CAO (European Commission, 2021b; Shibata, 2019, 139). The CAOFA followed the legally non-binding Declaration concerning the Prevention of Unregulated High Seas Fishing in the Central Arctic Ocean (Oslo Declaration), which was adopted by the Arctic 5 in 2015, and reflected the conclusions of the Nuuk (Greenland) meeting of 2014 (Shibata, 2019, 140; Liu, 2017, 1). The Oslo Declaration posed

16 The CAO is beyond the national jurisdiction of the coastal states. It is the largest high seas enclave in the Arctic, an area of roughly 2.8 million kilometres squared totally enclosed by the EEZs of the five coastal states. It is unique both because it is unusually large and still covered by ice for most of the year and because there has not been any significant commercial activity for centuries in this area (Vylegzhanin, 2020, 2).

the basis for the legally binding CAOFA and provided two key elements that are included in this, namely the 'geographical scope', which refers to the high seas portion of the central Arctic Ocean, and the 'qualified abstention from commercial high seas fishing' (Shibata, 2019, 140). These two elements are particularly relevant because they create different interests for the Arctic 5, on the one hand, and the Other Five, on the other hand (Shibata, 2019, 140). The fishing interests of the Arctic 5 'are derived from their sovereignty, sovereign rights and jurisdiction over fisheries resources in their adjacent coastal state maritime zones as well as from their right to fish on the high seas', as Articles 2(1), 49(1), 56(1)(a), 77(4), and 116 of the United Nations Convention on the Law of the Sea (UNCLOS) stipulates (Shibata, 2019, 140). The fishing rights of the Other Five derive instead from the right to fish on the high seas only (Shibata, 2019, 140). This means that if there will be a fish stock in the high seas portion of the CAO allowing for the commencement of a commercially viable fishery, it is very probable that the Other Five will support such a commencement (Shibata, 2019, 140). Conversely, the Arctic 5 will support this possibility only if they intend to participate in the fishery themselves, otherwise they will oppose if it conflicts with their coastal state interests, which can be predominantly utilisation-oriented or conservation-oriented (Shibata, 2019, 141). Conflict with utilisation-oriented coastal state interests can, for instance, arise when there is a 'straddling fish stock' that is a fish stock occurring in one or more exclusive economic zones (EEZs) and the adjacent high seas (Shibata, 2019, 141). Those of the Arctic 5 that are allowed to fish in their own maritime zone adjacent to the CAOFA area have a clear interest to withhold their support to the commencement of fishing in the high seas 'component' of the stock because the high seas 'would then act as a reserve for the replenishment of the stock's coastal component' (Shibata, 2019, 141). Moreover, as the fish stock has to cross the adjacent coastal state maritime zones in order to expand northward, the Arctic 5 could be in a position to 'stifle this northward expansion by increasing fishing effort in their own maritime zones' (Shibata, 2019, 141). Conflict with conservation-oriented coastal states interests of the Arctic 5 can arise in relation to a straddling fish stock (Shibata, 2019, 141). Those of the Arctic 5 that prohibit fishing in their own maritime zone adjacent to the CAOFA area have a clear interest to oppose the commencement of fishing in the high seas component (Shibata, 2019, 141). Also, those of the Arctic 5 that prohibit fishing more generally in their maritime zones may oppose the commencement of fishing in the high seas for stocks that do not occur in their maritime zones (Shibata, 2019, 141). Additionally, the Arctic 5 also have utilisation-oriented and conservation-oriented interests in relation to the natural resources of their outer continental shelves underlying the high seas portion of the CAO (Shibata, 2019, 141). In this case, three elements can be identified: 1) sedentary species like the snow crab are excluded from the CAOFA because the definition of fish does not apply to them; 2) the Arctic 5 have the right to 'impose restrictions on high seas bottom fisheries that have significant adverse impacts on these sedentary species or other benthic organisms (e.g. sponge beds or cold-water coral reefs), provided that the exercise of this entitlement does not infringe or result in any unjustifiable interference with the right to fish on the high sea'; 3) a coastal state can still be concerned with predator-prey relationships between non-sedentary species targeted by high seas fisheries, on the one hand, and sedentary species and other benthic organisms belonging to its continental shelf, on the other hand, even in case 'fishing does not target sedentary species on the outer continental shelf and also does not make direct physical contact with sedentary species or the seabed' (Shibata, 2019, 141). Furthermore, it is very interesting to note that these fishing interests of the CAOFA parties are related to their broader interests in the domains of international fisheries law, the international law of the sea, and the international law relating to the Arctic (Shibata, 2019, 142). This means that a state acts as a coastal state in its region but may also act as a distant water fishing state in other regions (Shibata, 2019, 142). Thus, this could lead to a situation in which, in its capacity as a distant water fishing state, 'it could agree to concessions to coastal states in their region, and use these concessions – in its capacity as a coastal state – as a precedent for similar concessions in its own region' (Shibata, 2019, 142).

Furthermore, it is important to stress two relevant factors that help explain the role that climate change plays in the redefinition of the relations among states. The first sector is the inclusion of non-Arctic states in the CAOFA agreement, which shows the increasing geopolitical importance of the region at the international level, but also the geopolitical significance of Arctic fish at the same time. In fact, for non-Arctic states being involved in such an agreement means a step into Arctic affairs. The second factor is the involvement of the EU as a party in the CAOFA, which deserves special attention not only because it is a major consumer of Arctic fish importing 30%–40% of seafood from the region, especially from Iceland and Norway,[17] (Raspotinik and Stępień, 2020, 135) but also because the initiatives taken in the context of its Common Fishery Policy[18] (CFP) serve its purpose to deepen its geopolitical and economic engagement in the Arctic. The CAOFA is defined as a 'key deliverable under the EU's International Ocean Governance agenda and the EU's Arctic policy' (European Commission, 2021b). This is why the EU has been a strong supporter of such an agreement since its very beginning and was the second signatory to ratify the agreement in 2019 (European Commission, 2021b). Furthermore, CAOFA is a clear example of the importance of fisheries in the EU's foreign policy. As Raspotnik and Østhagen (2020) argue, fisheries are 'one of the EU's common policies that has always had a strong external dimension', which is particularly important for the CFP not only because it contributes to the supply of the EU markets, it is a major source of economic activity and jobs, but it also makes the EU a legitimate actor in multilateral fishing governance globally (Raspotnik and Østhagen, 2020, 261). This is why in 2015, the European Parliament claimed that the EU has to be 'a leader in the prevention of unregulated fishing in the Arctic' arguing that the EU has 'every right to do so' due to its involvement in all

17 The EU's main Arctic suppliers of fish are Norway (26.5%), Iceland (4.2%), US (3.55%), Greenland (2.6%), and Russia (2.4%) (European Commission, 2020).

18 The importance of the Common Fishery Policy has grown over time leading the EU to separate it from the Common Agriculture Policy in the 1970s (European Commission, 2021a).

levels of Arctic governance (Raspotnik and Østhagen, 2020, 262). The European Commission also took a similar stance in 2016 (Raspotnik and Østhagen, 2020, 262).

Very significantly, the EU has included commercial fishery in its Arctic policy since 2008. It is interesting to note here that the complexity of the EU's approach to the fishery sector in the Arctic has been growing over time. The 2008 Arctic Policy identifies the 'exploitation of Arctic fisheries resources at sustainable levels whilst respecting the rights of local coastal communities' as its main objective (European Commission, 2008, 7). The 2012 Arctic Policy stresses not only the necessity of the sustainable exploitation of marine biological resources and a precautionary approach, but also that the EU 'is keen to ensure good cooperation with Arctic states' in order to set up an effective 'international conservation and management system' (European Commission, 2008, 10). Cooperation is also identified in the 2016 Arctic Policy, which stresses that 'the EU should welcome the recent declaration signed by five Arctic coastal states [Oslo Declaration] on Arctic fisheries and the need to obtain more information on ecosystems in the Arctic Ocean before opening up this region to commercial fishing' (European Commission, 2008, 16). In its 2021 Arctic Policy, the EU has included the necessity of sustainable exploitation of marine biological resources in the broader context of the 'sustainable blue economy', which is defined as 'all economic activities related to oceans, seas and coasts' (European Commission, 2018) and was adopted in 2021. In this context, it is interesting to note that the 2013 CFP stresses that 'the sustainable exploitation of marine biological resources should be based on the precautionary approach, which derives from the precautionary principle[19] (Official Journal of the European Union, 2013).

As for the second effect of climate change, namely the exacerbation of pre-existing political tensions and competition among states, a good example is the potential conflict between Russia and Norway over the Svalbard Fisheries Protection Zone (FPZ)[20] in the Barents Sea, which is quite acute 'given Russian fishing interests in the FPZ and the wider security relations between the two countries' (Østhagen, 2020, 4). Climate change is exacerbating the situation as it is making the fish stocks in the region shift northwards into the FPZ (Østhagen, 2020, 4). For the Russian fleet, access to the FPZ and to the Norwegian EEZ is of utmost importance because

19 The precautionary principle is contained in Article 191(2) of the Treaty on the Functioning of the EU. Although it is not defined anywhere in the Treaties, in the 2000 Communication on the Precautionary Principle, the European Commission defined it as a risk management strategy to be employed 'where scientific evidence is insufficient, inconclusive or uncertain and there are indications through preliminary objective scientific evaluation that there are reasonable grounds for concern that the potential dangerous effects on the environment, human, animal or plant health may be inconsistent with the chosen level of protection' (Eur-lex, 2016).

20 The FPZ was created in 1977 by the Norwegian Department for Foreign Policy's Regulation no. 6 for the conservation of living marine resources by regulating fishing and hunting activities. This regulation 'ensures that the outer limits for this protected marine area is at a distance of 200 nautical miles from the established baselines connecting the outermost points of the archipelago' (FAO, 2023).

Russia takes a relatively small share of its catches in the Russian EEZ, where fish are predominantly young and small, and weather and ice conditions are quite harsh (Østhagen, 2020, 4).

In order to understand the Svalbard dispute between Russia and Norway, it is necessary to go back to 1976 when Norway declared an EEZ of 200 nautical miles off its coast (Østhagen et al., 2020, 5). According to Norway, it was entitled to establish an EEZ around the archipelago as it was the coastal state of Svalbard and 'the non-discriminatory provision in the Treaty [signed in Paris in 1920] referred only, and explicitly, to the islands themselves and their territorial waters' (Østhagen, 2020, 7; Østhagen et al., 2020, 5). Nevertheless, some states disagreed with this view (Østhagen, 2020, 4; Østhagen et al., 2020, 5). Thus, in order to avoid recourse to legal proceedings, Norway established the FPZ, which satisfied several states, in particular the UK, the Netherlands, and Denmark (Østhagen, 2020, 7; Østhagen et al., 2020, 7; Pedersen and Henriksen, 2009, 146). By contrast, other states with extensive fishing rights like Russia, Spain, and Iceland were quite critical although they had different positions (Østhagen et al., 2020, 7). Russia expressed its position, which is still the current one, in diplomatic notes stating that Norway had no right to unilaterally establish a FPZ and that it should have negotiated fisheries in the waters around Svalbard with Russia (Østhagen, 2020, 7; Østhagen et al., 2020, 7; Pedersen and Henriksen, 2009, 146).

Andreas Østhagen, Anne-Kristin Jørgensen, and Arild Moe analysed the dispute between Russia and Norway over the FPZ in the Barents Sea outlining interesting findings. While since 1977, when the FPZ was established, there was no confrontation between Russia and Norway, since 1998, Norway began enforcing the regulations causing Russia's disappointment (Østhagen, 2020, 7; Østhagen et al., 2020, 7; Pedersen and Henriksen, 2009, 146). Many experts from the Russian side considered this change of behaviour as a breach of contract as the two states had stipulated a 'gentlemen's agreement', whose existence had never been acknowledged by Norway (Østhagen, 2020, 7; Østhagen et al., 2020, 7; Pedersen and Henriksen, 2009, 146). Østhagen, Jørgensen, and Moe identify three phases of the Norway–Russia dispute over Svalbard. The first phase, corresponding to the years between 1998 and 2005, is characterised by Russia's criticism of Norway's new line (Østhagen, 2020, 7; Østhagen et al., 2020, 7; Pedersen and Henriksen, 2009, 146). In this period, Norway arrested a Russian trawler, the *Novokuybyshevsk*, fishing in a closed area in the FPZ. This caused a tough reaction in Russia where a core narrative was that Norway was trying to take advantage of Russia's temporary weakness in order to expel its fishers from the Svalbard zone (Østhagen, 2020, 7; Østhagen et al., 2020, 7; Pedersen and Henriksen, 2009, 146). Since then, Norwegian–Russian fisheries cooperation was characterised by disagreement on several important management issues, including the size of the annual total allowable catch (Østhagen, 2020, 7; Østhagen et al., 2020, 7; Pedersen and Henriksen, 2009, 146). However, between 2001, when the trawler *Chernigov* was arrested, prosecuted, and fined for serious violations, and 2005 there were no arrests (Østhagen, 2020, 7; Østhagen et al., 2020, 7; Pedersen and Henriksen, 2009, 146). The controversy emerged again with force in 2005, when the second phase started as a consequence of the unsuccessful arrest of the Russian trawler *Elektron* (Østhagen et al., 2020, 9). The case was very much discussed both in Russia and in Norway but in 2009/2010, they reached an agreement on common rules for mesh size in trawls, minimum size limits for fish, and regulations concerning closing/opening of fishing grounds (Østhagen et al., 2020, 9). In spite of this, the controversy between them reached its peak in 2011 when the trawler *Sapfir-2* was seized for discarding fish (Østhagen et al., 2020, 9). That year Russia and Norway ratified (signed in 2010) a maritime boundary treaty that defined the boundary between the Norwegian and the Russian EEZs, which was strongly contested by fishers (Østhagen et al., 2020, 9). According to the Chairman of the Coordination Council for Northern Fisheries (Sevryba) Vyacheslav Zilanov, the fact that sometimes the texts in Russian and Norwegian do not always coincide in meaning might be the source of conflict when it comes to the application of the treaty (Zilanov, 2017, 30). This second phase lasted until 2012 (Østhagen et al., 2020, 11).

The third phase, which lasted from 2012 until 2018, was characterised by disagreement but also by 'attenuated reactions' (Østhagen et al., 2020, 11). Norway arrested some Russian trawlers while Russia arrested the Norwegian trawler *Remøy* in the Russian Economic Zone (REZ), which was considered by Norway as revenge (Østhagen et al., 2020, 11: Østhagen, 2020, 10). On its side, in an interview in 2016, Vyacheslav Zilanov claimed that inspections of Russian vessels have 'a humiliating character' (Østhagen et al., 2020, 11). Nevertheless, the joint commission initiated a process to solve the disagreement between the two states (Østhagen et al., 2020, 11). Negotiations were difficult but 'the atmosphere in the Joint Fisheries Commission and its subsidiary bodies has improved in recent years'. Very interestingly, Østhagen et al. state that 'interviews also indicate that the deterioration in government-level Norwegian–Russian relations after 2014 [the year of Russia's annexation of Crimea] has not affected the Commission's work' (Østhagen et al., 2020, 15). In spite of this, Russia's criticism of Norway continues as the letter sent by Minister for Foreign Affairs Sergey Lavrov to his Norwegian counterpart lists Russian complaints, including 'the unlawfulness of Norway's fisheries protection zone' demonstrates (Østhagen et al., 2020, 15).

Østhagen et al. stress that the dispute over the FPZ has not only legal implications, as Russia has economic and military interests in the area, but the Arctic also has a strong historical value for the state (Østhagen et al., 2020, 15). They argue that Russian observers usually refer to fishing history and to the fact that Russia's early marine scientists have given an enormous contribution to exploration and mapping the stocks around Svalbard (Østhagen et al., 2020, 15; Vylegzhanin et al., 2020, 5; Zilanov, 2017, 32). According to Østhagen et al., 'there is also much to indicate that feelings of historical injustices continue to shape Russia's perceptions of its legitimate role in the area' (Østhagen et al., 2020, 17). Additionally, the fact that Russia was excluded from participation in the negotiations on the Svalbard Treaty has determined the way Russia perceives the Svalbard issues 'in retrospect' and 'this narrative of the "weakened superpower" was reactivated in the Russian Svalbard debate after the dissolution of the Soviet Union' (Østhagen et al., 2020, 17; Zilanov, 2017, 33).

Østhagen et al. found two turning points (Østhagen et al., 2020, 18). The first one in 2005 when Russia went from protest to dialogue (Østhagen et al., 2020, 18). In 2005, the *Elektron* case showed that Russia emerged as a more unified power internationally as a consequence of Putin's power consolidation (Østhagen et al., 2020, 18). The central power decided how to handle the situation preferring dialogue to confrontation. Østhagen et al. argue that 'several analyses have indicated that centralization under Putin helped the Norwegian–Russian fisheries cooperation to develop in a positive direction in those years' (Østhagen et al., 2020, 18). The second turning point was in 2011 when criticism quieted. Jørgensen has pointed out that 'the absence of official protests against the arrest of Russian vessels in the FPZ could be interpreted as tacit acceptance of Norway's right to exercise jurisdiction there' (Østhagen et al., 2020, 18). At the same time, Russia sent signals that its rights would not be infringed and, following the same line of the Soviet Union, it exerted pressure on Norway to have a special position in the region, for instance by proposing joint arrangements and by sending Russian fisheries inspection vessels to the FPZ (Breum, 2022). This is in line with the neorealism assumption that states are very careful regarding relative gains and that cooperation is possible only when it is convenient for them.

Moreover, another important conclusion that the authors draw from their analysis is that Russia does not formally recognise Norwegian jurisdiction because 'this would be a step too far, as it would collide with overarching Russian priorities and ambitions in the region' (Breum, 2022). Russia uses UNCLOS as a basis for its foreign policy in the Arctic (Østhagen et al., 2020, 18; Caitlyn, 2010, 24). Also, Russia's policies in the FPZ have been a 'balancing act' aimed at outlining its official position and demonstrating that Norwegian enforcement can be accepted only to a certain extent while ensuring the survival of the enforcement regime, for example, by accepting that Russian vessels are inspected onboard by Norway (Østhagen et al., 2020, 18).

Furthermore, the other variable impacting the Arctic fisheries sector is the war in Ukraine. In 2022, the US imposed a ban on fresh fish imports from Russia although Russian fish continued entering the market via China (McBride, 2024). In 2023, the US expanded its ban on Russian seafood in order to include imports of seafood that originated in Russia and that had been processed in third countries, including China (McBride, 2024). At the time of writing, the EU is also considering to extend sanctions to include Russian fish that has remained unaffected until now (McBride, 2024). More specifically, the EU began considering the possibility of imposing fish bans after the meeting of the Group of Seven (G7 – Canada, Italy, France, Germany, Japan, UK, and US) nations held in Apulia, a region in southern Italy, in June 2024 (Chace, 2024). On that occasion, the G7 nations issued a lengthy communiqué in which, inter alia, they criticised Russia's seafood-trading practices[21] (Chace, 2024).

21 The communiqué of the G7 nations included a number of issues such as support to Ukraine against Russia, African development, and the achievement of the UN Sustainable Development Goals. The document also stressed the necessity to reinforce global food security and enhance climate resil-

In 2022, the EU sanctions only included crustaceans, caviar, and caviar substitutes as part of the fifth package of economic and individual sanctions in 2022 (McBride, 2024). Other species like pollock, which is commonly used in fast-food outlets as a substitute for cod, are instead still allowed (Chace, 2024; McBride, 2024). The importance of pollock in the food chain is, for instance, clearly demonstrated by the case of Germany where 85% of the consumed Alaska pollock comes from Russia (McBride, 2024). Stefan Meyer, managing director of the Federal Association of the German Fishing Industry and Fish Wholesalers, stated that 'if supplies from Russian pollock fishing in Alaska were to stop completely due to sanctions, there would be no replacement for them at the moment' (McBride, 2024). The main problem is that Germany relies on imported fish because it has only six deep-sea trawlers and does not engage in deep-sea fishing (McBride, 2024). In addition, it seems that over-reliance on imported fish has been institutionalised across the EU as the European Commission is willing to reduce national fishing fleets to facilitate more imported fish to obtain greater profit margins on resale (McBride, 2024).

Moreover, another issue that the EU has been discussing concerns the fact that Russian vessels are prohibited from landing in the ports of EU Member States, which has not significantly reduced the amount of Russian fish entering the EU market via Norway and the Faroe Islands (McBride, 2024).

Furthermore, the war in Ukraine has also had a negative impact on the relations between Russia and other Arctic states in the fisheries sector although in some cases strong economic interests have prevented states from totally interrupting their exchanges with Russia in the sector. This is the case, for instance, in the relations between Norway and Russia that have a long history of cooperation in the fisheries sector, which is due to geographical proximity and strong economic interests. Their cooperation started in the 1900s when two prominent researchers, Norwegian Fridtjof Nansen and Russian Nikolaj Knipovitsj met to discuss their views on research into fish stocks in the Barents Sea laying the foundations for the future development of the relationship between the two neighbouring nations bordering the Barents Sea (Joint Norwegian–Russian Fisheries Commission, no date). In the post-war period, when Norway and the Soviet Union began to develop their fishing activities in the Barents Sea, researchers from both states developed closer cooperation in order to discover the reasons for the fluctuations in catch volumes of cod, haddock, capelin, herring, and other fish species, and to lay down measures for regulations of fishing (Joint Norwegian–Russian Fisheries Commission, no date). This initiative led to joint research that was carried out on a regular basis from 1968, involving annual meetings.[22] In 1975, Norway and the Soviet Union

ience, to take concrete steps to address the triple crisis of climate change, pollution, and biodiversity loss and to act together to promote economic resilience. Moreover, it reaffirmed their commitment to gender equality (The White House, 2024).

22 Joint cooperation was established on the occasion of a joint research session that was organised in Murmansk in the summer of 1957. This session involved researchers from the Institute of Marine Research in Norway and the Knipovich Polar Research Institute of Marine Fisheries and Oceanography in Russia (Murmansk). They decided to compile a joint program for surveillance of the

established the Joint Norwegian–Russian Fisheries Commission (JNRFC), which became an essential instrument to solve the problems that emerged in the sector, approved programs for joint research on the most important fish stocks (e.g., cod, haddock, and capelin) in the Barents Sea and, on this basis, adopted a proper approach to fisheries management for all catch areas (Joint Norwegian–Russian Fisheries Commission, no date). At the beginning of the 1980s, the fundamental elements of the bilateral management regime had been put in place and in the 1990s the JNRFC adopted a number of important regulation initiatives like the implementation of satellite monitoring of fishing vessels (Joint Norwegian–Russian Fisheries Commission, no date). In the 2000s, Norway and Russia intensified their cooperation by continuing to exchange information on quotas and landings per vessel as well as inspectors on each other's vessels and joint control of landings in third countries (Joint Norwegian–Russian Fisheries Commission, no date).

Furthermore, the Treaty Concerning Maritime Delimitation and Cooperation in the Barents Sea and the Arctic Ocean (signed in 2010 and entered into force in 2011) is another example of the importance that cooperation in the fisheries sector has for both Norway and Russia. It applies to Norway's and Russia's respective EEZs (in addition to the Fisheries Protection Zone around Svalbard) and the continental shelf within and beyond 200 nautical miles (Jensen, 2011, 151). The agreement delimits the frontier between Norway and Russia in the Barents Sea and the Arctic Ocean (Jensen, 2011, 151; FAOLEX, 2020a). In particular, it

> includes a special provision for the area east of the maritime delimitation line and within 200 nautical miles of the baselines from which the breadth of the territorial sea of mainland Norway is measured, but beyond 200 nautical miles of the baselines from which the breadth of the territorial sea of the Russian Federation is measured. It is referred to as the 'Special Area' in Article 3 of the Treaty.
>
> (Jensen, 2011, 151)

According to Article 3, Russia 'shall exercises the sovereign rights or jurisdiction in the Special Area as provided for in this Agreement. Such exercise of sovereign rights or jurisdiction derives from the agreement of the Parties and does not constitute an extension of its exclusive economic zone' (FAOLEX, 2020a). The agreement also concerns fishing opportunities of both parties and cooperation in the sphere of fisheries. For instance, it stipulates that the Joint Norwegian–Russian Fisheries Commission shall continue to assess improvements to surveillance and control measures for jointly managed fish stocks (Joint Norwegian–Russian Fisheries Commission, no date). Also, Article 4 stipulates that 'the Parties shall pursue close cooperation in the sphere of fisheries, with a view to maintain their existing respective shares of total allowable catch volumes and to ensure relative stability of their fishing activities for each of the stocks concerned' and that 'they

condition of fish stocks and the environment in the Barents Sea (Joint Norwegian-Russian Fisheries Commission, no date).

shall apply the precautionary approach widely to conservation, management and exploitation of shared fish stocks, including straddling fish stocks, in order to protect the living marine resources and preserve the marine environment' (FAOLEX, 2020a). Furthermore, it is very interesting to highlight the three factors underlying this agreement as outlined by Øystein Jensen, research professor at the Fridtjof Nansens Institute in Oslo. First, the regulatory framework under international law has provided the legal principles for a delimitation solution (Jensen, 2011, 158). Second, Norway and Russia have achieved an agreement because both were willing to make concessions as they were going through a period in which they were 'foreign policy actors with good relations that manage to unify the various power interests and achieve mutual, long-term solutions' (Jensen, 2011, 158). At the same time, economic reasons can also play a role in the decision to agree on a border because this can enable activities related to the oil and gas industry not only in the disputed area but in the wider Barents Sea as well (Jensen, 2011, 158). Third, in the 2000s, relations between Norway and Russia were characterised by mutual trust and respect (Jensen, 2011, 158). By contrast, at the time of writing, relations between them have worsened due to the war in Ukraine but their economic interests and common interest of effectively managing fishing resources have led them to stipulate a fishery agreement both for 2024 and 2025 (McBride, 2024a; Bye, 2023; Edvardsen, 2023). The 'fisheries cooperation is one of the few still existing areas of interaction between Norway and Russia after the Ukraine War' (Edvardsen, 2023). As Norwegian Minister of Fisheries and Ocean Policy Cecilie Myrseth said in 2023,

> it is good that we have entered into a fisheries agreement with Russia, despite also this year being in an extraordinary situation. The agreement ensures long-term and sustainable ocean management in the High North and is crucial for us to protect the cod stock and the other species in the Barents Sea.
> (Edvardsen, 2023)

In 2024, Norway and Russia agreed a fishery agreement for the following year through digital negotiations (Bye, 2024). However, the two parties decided that the total 2025 quota for cod will be 25% lower than the quota for 2024, which means that it will be the lowest since 1991 (Bye, 2024). The reason is that Norway and Russia want to try to stop negative stock development due to the negative impact of climate change on biodiversity (Bye, 2024).

Nevertheless, the fact that Norway and Russia have found an agreement does not exclude security concerns. In particular, three kinds of concerns can be identified. First, in 2023 the Norwegian naval academy claimed that 'between 50 and 100 of those [fishing vessels] operating in Norwegian waters could be linked to intelligence gathering activities and pose a potential security threat' (Østhagen and Evans, 2023). At the same time, there are concerns over critical infrastructure such as subsea cables, which are quite vulnerable, and the way in which fishing vessels could be used in possible disruptive action (Østhagen and Evans, 2023). Second, the relatively high level of military exercise activities in the North Atlantic jeopardises the lives of fishers (Østhagen and Evans, 2023). Third, a potential source of unintentional escalation is due to the fact that the Norwegian coastguard inspects and occasionally fines Russian fishers in the Norwegian EEZ or the Fish Protection Zone around Svalbard, which could cause unintentional escalation taking a state–state dimension (Østhagen and Evans, 2023).

Furthermore, another example of the prevalence of economic interests over political reasons is the case of the Faroe Islands as an agreement was reached with Russia over mutual fishing rights for 2024 (McBride, 2023). Like in the case of the agreement between Norway and Russia, also in this case the catch quotas for fish (e.g., for Atlantic mackerel and Atlanto-Scandian herring) were adjusted in accordance with reductions recommended for 2024 by the International Council for the Exploration of the Seas (McBride, 2023). Additionally, the negotiations also envisage a 20% decrease in the cod quota and an 18% reduction in haddock (McBride, 2023).

In an analysis in the Danish newspaper *Altinget* published in 2022, editor Andreas Krog explained that the Faroe Islands decided to maintain trade with Russia because 'the business interests are so great that the idea of a fishery agreement with Russia has not yet been rejected' (McBride, 2023). The government, which was criticised for working against the goal of the Western sanctions, responded that the Western sanctions do not cover the export of fish to Russia and that a break with Russia on fisheries would endanger Russia's commitment to sustainable fishing in the entire North Atlantic (Breum, 2022). Nevertheless, when Russia invaded Ukraine in 2022, the Faroe Islands aquaculture industry private enterprises spontaneously stopped almost all exports to Russia (Bye, 2024). By contrast, when Russia illegally annexed Crimea in 2014, the Faroe Islands decided not only not to interrupt its relations with Russia in the sector but also to boost their exports of fish from aquaculture, salmon in particular, to the Russian market (Bye, 2024).

In addition, like Norway, the Faroe Islands' government has decided to introduce a port ban against Russian ships, with the exception of Russian fishing vessels in order to preserve the bilateral fishery cooperation with Russia and the management of the fish stocks between the two countries (Breum, 2022). Thus, the relations between the Faroe Islands and Russia, which were established in 1977 when they signed their first fisheries agreement, have not been interrupted (Bye, 2024).

Additionally, the case of Greenland is slightly different as political reasons might be at the basis of the government's decision to halt fisheries quotas with Russia although the explanation did not include any reference to the war in Ukraine (Breum, 2022). By contrast, the message to Moscow was only that the fish stocks in Greenland's water are presently not sufficient to allow for the usual quota swapping with Russia thus not breaching the agreement they stipulated in 1992 (Breum, 2022). Nevertheless, Greenland has expressed its condemnation of the war initiated by Russia in Ukraine on several occasions (Breum, 2022). For instance, at the very beginning of the war in 2022, Greenland Premier Mute B. Egede stated 'I forcefully condemn Russia's acts against the Ukrainian people. They are senseless and for that reason we want to demonstrate our solidarity with the people of Ukraine with our adherence to the international sanctions on Russia' (Breum, 2022).

However, the decision to halt fisheries quota swaps with Russia was made in a closed meeting of Naalakkersuisut, Greenland's government, and no public announcement was made (Breum, 2022). The reason behind this discretion might be the fact that Greenland has 'an interest in preserving a workable relationship with Russia within the ongoing multilateral and difficult negotiations on fishing quotas in the greater North Atlantic' (Breum, 2022). In these negotiations, 'representatives from Greenland, Norway, Iceland, the Faroe Islands and others are face-to-face with Russian counterparts in negotiations over fish that are of serious economic importance to all involved' (Breum, 2022). Thus, Greenland might not want to break up its bilateral relations with Russia completely, hoping to come back to cooperate again as soon as possible.

Nevertheless, Russia has also responded to the West's reaction to the war in Ukraine, as in the case of Alaska, which is the major producer of seafood in the US as stated above, clearly demonstrates. Russia imposed a ban on US food in 2014 while the US imposed a ban on Russian goods in 2022 (Venua, 2024). The main problem for Alaska is that Russian seafood is processed in China and exported to the US where it is sold with a Chinese label, not Russian (Strout, 2023). Senator for Alaska Dan Sullivan, said that 'Russia is the No. 1 problem when it comes to our fishing industry. Right now, the Russians have essentially admitted they're not just at war in Ukraine, they're at war with the American fishing industry' (Brooks, 2024). This is why the Alaskan delegation introduced the US–Russian Federation Seafood Reciprocity Act of 2023 in both the US House and Senate (Strout, 2023). This bill, which was approved, 'prohibits the importation of seafood and seafood products from Russia. This prohibition applies to seafood products of Russian origin, including any such product that is incorporated into another product or that is substantially transformed in a country other than Russia' (US Congress, 2023). In support of this bill, Senator Sullivan pointed out on the Senate floor that 'if you're against this bill, you're for Russian oligarchs who are still avoiding sanctions on seafood, you're against the American fishermen whether in Alaska or Massachusetts – because they're getting screwed by this uneven trade relationship – and you're helping the Chinese. I can't imagine anyone being against this' (Strout, 2023). Nevertheless, Japan and the European states, which are major markets for Alaskan fish, are still allowing Russian seafood imports, thus weakening the impact of the US bill (Yozel, 2024).

All in all, commercial fisheries are another sector that is becoming increasingly sensitive in the context of the geopolitical dynamics of the Arctic because of climate change and the war in Ukraine. These two variables have different effects on the relations among states both inside and outside the region. Climate change has a double impact as in some cases it pushes states to cooperate while in some others it fosters tensions and competition. The war in Ukraine has also made relations among states more difficult although economic interests are sometimes stronger than political reasons when it comes to continued cooperation in some ways.

Conclusion

Water, energy, minerals, and fisheries are of utmost importance for people and the economic development of states. This is why they are sectors that are very sensitive to geopolitical variables such as climate change and the war in Ukraine. The growing need for those resources due to the increase in the world's population and technological development have made the Arctic a region whose geopolitical and economic importance is steadily increasing.

The results of the analysis show that in the case of water, climate change is the only variable (the other one being the war in Ukraine, taken into consideration in this book) with a geopolitical impact on the sector. An explanation can be the fact that a huge trade in Arctic water does not exist, yet. Nevertheless, the fact that the Arctic is one of the places richest in water, in addition to the Antarctic and the Third Pole, makes it a region with a great potential to become one of the most important sources of 'blue gold' in the future. Paradoxically, the Arctic is facing serious problems of access to water in some areas as climate change is reducing water availability due to the increase of temperatures that is causing a shortage of snow. However, there are also other reasons for this, namely anthropogenic pollution and the precarity of infrastructures that are jeopardised by ice-melting.

Furthermore, in the case of the other natural resources discussed in this chapter, namely energy, minerals, and fishery, the analysis has demonstrated that both climate change and the war in Ukraine play a key role in the definition of the Arctic as a geopolitically sensitive and important region. It is possible to argue that the sectors of energy and minerals are strictly intertwined since minerals are essential for technology and energy transition. The intersection of these two sectors is perhaps the clearest example of the complementarity of climate change and the war in Ukraine as variables with a huge impact on geopolitics in the Arctic. The reason is that energy transition, which definitely needs minerals, has become necessary not only for environmental reasons, namely to fight climate change, but also for political reasons, that is to say that the EU aims to become independent from Russia's energy resources. The war in Ukraine has revealed more than ever before the vulnerability of the EU in the energy sector while also highlighting that the partnership between Russia and China, both in the Arctic and internationally, is more dictated by the necessity to fight against the US adversary than by a true alliance (which it is not).

Finally, the sector of fisheries has also been deeply affected by both climate change and the war in Ukraine. Climate change has a double impact on this sector because it pushes states (both inside and outside the region) to cooperate while also exacerbating previous tensions and competition. The war in Ukraine increases tensions among states and actors (e.g., the EU) also in the fisheries sector leading to interrupted relations in the sector. However, in some cases such as the Faroe Islands, Greenland, and Norway, economic interests have prevented states from breaking previous agreements.

References

AC Sustainable Development WG. (2009). *SDWG Report on Arctic Energy*. Available at: chrome-extension://efaidnbmnnnibpcajpcglclefindmkaj/https://core.ac.uk/download/pdf/236379602.pdf (accessed 17 September 2024).

ACAP. (2017). *Reduction of Black Carbon from Diesel Sources in the Russian Arctic. Tundra Reindeer Farm*. Arctic Council.

ACIA. (2005). *Arctic Climate Impact Assessment*. Cambridge: Cambridge University Press.

Alaska Department of Fish and Game. (no date). *Bering Sea / Aleutian Islands Area Subsistence Fishing*. Available at: https://www.adfg.alaska.gov/index.cfm?adfg=ByAreaSubsistenceBeringAleutians.main#:~:text=Important%20subsistence%20fisheries%20in%20the,and%20processed%20in%20local%20facilities. (accessed 25 October 2024).

Alaska Seafood. (2024). *Economic Impact*. Available at: https://www.alaskaseafood.org/industry/economic-impact/#economic-impact-report (accessed 25 October 2024).

Aliyev. N. (2024). *Moscow's Arctic Projects Amidst the War: Sanctions, LNG Projects, Icebreakers and the Northern Sea Route*. Available at: https://www.ispionline.it/en/publication/moscows-arctic-projects-amidst-the-war-sanctions-lng-projects-icebreakers-and-the-northern-sea-route-178452 (accessed 18 September 2024).

Alvarez & Marsal Canada Inc. (2024). *Introduction*. Available at: https://www.alvarezandmarsal.com/northamerican (accessed 12 October 2024).

AMAP. (2018). *AMAP Assessment 2018: Biological Effects of Contaminants on Arctic Wildlife and Fish*, vol. VII. Arctic Council.

American Geosciences Institute. (2024). *What Are Rare Earth Elements, and Why Are They Important?*. Available at: https://www.americangeosciences.org/critical-issues/faq/what-are-rare-earth-elements-and-why-are-they-important#:~:text=The%20rare%20earth%20elements%20(REE,of%20many%20high%2Dtech%20devices. (accessed 14 October 2024).

Andersson, P., Zeuthen, J., Kalvig, P. (2018). Chinese Mining in Greenland: Arctic Access or Access to Minerals?. *Arctic Yearbook*.

Angelakis, A., Valipour, M., Ahmed, A., Tzanakakis, V., Paranychianakis, N. V., Krasilnikoff, J., Drusiani, R., Mays, L., El Gohary, F., Koutsoyiannis, D., Khan, S., Del Giacco, L. J. (2021). Water Conflicts: From Ancient to Modern Times and in the Future, *Sustainability Journal*, 13: 1–31.

Antarcticland. (2024). *Antarctica Is the Largest Freshwater Reserve*. Available at: https://antarcticlands.org/antarctica-is-the-largest-freshwater-reserve/ (accessed 5 August 2024).

Arctic Centre. (2024a). *How Is the Arctic Region Changing?*. Available at: https://www.arcticcentre.org/EN/arcticregion/climatechange (accessed 29 April 2024).

Arctic Council. (2021). *An Introduction to: The International Agreement to Prevent Unregulated Fishing in the High Seas of the Central Arctic Ocean*. Available at: https://arctic-council.org/news/introduction-to-international-agreement-to-prevent-unregulated-fishing-in-the-high-seas-of-the-central-arctic-ocean/ (accessed 25 October 2024).

Arctic Council. (2024). *Green Energy Shift in the Arctic*. Arctic Council. Available at: https://arctic-council.org/www/ru/news/green-energy-shift-in-the-arctic/ (accessed 10 October 2024).

Arctic Economic Council. (2024). *Arctic Mining Report 2024*. Available at: https://www.arctictoday.com/new-report-arctic-could-be-vital-supplier-of-critical-minerals-for-global-green-transition/ (accessed 20 October 2024).

Arctic Group. (2024). *Aquaculture*. Available at: https://www.arctic.com/sectors/aquaculture (accessed 25 October 2024).

Arctic Portal. (2024). *Energy Portlet. Future Development*. Available at: https://arcticportal.org/energy-portlet/renewable-energy/energy-renewable-future-development (accessed 8 October 2024).

Arruda, G. (2020). *Renewable Energy for the Arctic.* Oxford and New York.
Baily, M., Snook, J. (2021). Warming-Driven Changes in Arctic Fish Communities Must Not Leave Local Indigenous Communities Out in the Cold. *One Earth*, 4: 1676–1677.
Bogdanova, E., Lobanov, A., Andronov, S., Soromotin, A., Popov, A., Skalny, A., Shaduyko, O., Callaghan, T. (2023). Challenges of Changing Water Sources for Human Wellbeing in the Arctic Zone of Western Siberia. *Water Journal, Special Issue Climate Change and Anthropogenic Impacts on Wetland Ecosystems in Siberia: Past, Present, and Future,* 15(8): 1–20.
Boone, C. (2021). *Renewable Energy in the Russian Arctic and Beyond: Can a Region Dominated by Oil and Gas Contribute to Russia's Paris Agreement Targets?.* Russian International Affairs Council. Available at: https://russiancouncil.ru/en/blogs/carter-boone/renewable-energy-in-the-russian-arctic-and-beyond-can-a-region-dominat/#:~:text=The%20Russian%20Arctic%2C%20indeed%2C%20has,harness%20the%20power%20of%20renewables (accessed 10 October 2024).
Boyd, R., Bjerkgård, T., Nordahl, B., Schiellerup, H. (2016). *Mineral Resources in the Arctic. An Introduction.* Geological Survey of Norway.
Brander, K. M. (2007). *Global Fish Production and Climate Change.* Pennsylvania State University.
Breum, M. (2022). Greenland Halts Fisheries Quota Swaps with Russia. *Arctic Today.* Available at: https://www.arctictoday.com/greenland-halts-cooperation-on-fish-with-russia/?utm_source=rss&utm_medium=rss&utm_campaign=greenland-halts-cooperation-on-fish-with-russia (accessed 30 October 2024).
Brioni, L. T., Reppas-Chrysovitsinos, E., Sühring, R., Halsall, C. J., Mengo, E., Sanders, T. K., Crabeck, O., Kaiser, J., Birchenough, S. N. R. (2022). Pollution in the Arctic Ocean: An Overview of Multiple Pressures and Implications for Ecosystem Services. *Ambio,* 51(2): 471–483.
Brooks, J. (2024). *Fishers, City Officials Seek Broader Russia Seafood Boycott to Benefit Ukraine and Alaska. Now that the United States Has Banned Russian-Sourced Products, Alaskans Want American Allies to Follow Suit.* Alaska Bacon. Available at: https://alaskabeacon.com/2024/05/23/fishers-city-officials-seek-broader-russia-seafood-boycott-to-benefit-ukraine-and-alaska/ (accessed 20 October 2024).
Bros, A., Mitrova, T. (2016). *Yamal LNG: An Economic Project under Political Pressure.* Fondation pour la Recherche Stratégique, 17. Available at: https://www.frstrategie.org/en/publications/notes/yamal-lng-economic-project-under-political-pressure-2016 (accessed 30 September 2024).
Business Iceland. (2021). *Icelandic Fisheries.* Available at: chrome-extension://efaidnbmnnnibpcajpcglclefindmkaj/https://www.responsiblefisheries.is/media/1/icelandic-fisheries-press-kit-mai-2021-enska.pdf (accessed 23 October 2024).
Bye, H. G. (2024). Norway and Russia Decrease Cod Quotas By 25 Percent Next Year. *The High North News.* Available at: https://www.highnorthnews.com/en/norway-and-russia-decrease-cod-quotas-25-percent-next-year (accessed 30 October 2024).
Bye, H. G. (2023). Norway and Russia Reached a Fishery Agreement for 2024. The High North News. Available at: https://www.highnorthnews.com/en/norway-and-russia-reached-fisheries-agreement-2024
CAFF. (2013). *Arctic Biodiversity Assessment: Status and Trends in Arctic Biodiversity.* Conservation of Arctic Flora and Fauna, Arctic Council.
Caitlyn, A. (2010). The Next Geographical Pivot: The Russian Arctic in the Twenty-first Century. *Naval War College Review*, 63(3): 15–38.
Cassivi, A., Covey, A., Rodriguez, M. J., Guilherme, S. (2023). Domestic Water Security in the Arctic: A Scoping Review. *International Journal of Hygiene and Environmental Health*, 247: 1–12.
Chace, C. (2024). *EU Considering Sanctions Against Russian Seafood; Russia Plans to Denounce, Potentially Leave ICES.* SeafoodSource. Available at: https://www

.seafoodsource.com/news/supply-trade/eu-considering-sanctions-against-russian-seafood-while-russia-plans-to-denounce-and-potentially-leave-ices (accessed 30 October 2024).

Chambers and Partners. (2024). *Mining 2024. Finland.* Available at: https://practiceguides.chambers.com/practice-guides/mining-2024/finland/trends-and-developments (accessed 6 December).

Chambers, C., Henke, T., Barr, B., Cook, D., Costa Pierce, B., Einarsson, N., Kaiser, B., Ögmundur, K., Kokorsch, M., Sutton, T. (2021). Marine Fisheries and Aquaculture in the Arctic. In Natcher, D., Koivurova, T. (eds.) *Renewable Economies in the Arctic.* New York: Routledge.

CIA. (2024). *Arctic Ocean.* Available at: https://www.cia.gov/the-world-factbook/oceans/arctic-ocean/ (accessed 31 July 2024).

Conde, E., Iglesias Sánchez, S. (2019). *Global Challenges in the Arctic Region. Sovereignty, Environment and Geopolitical Balance.* New York: Routledge.

Cook, E. (2025). Trump Doesn't Rule Out Military Force to Take Greenland. Newsweek. Available at: https://www.newsweek.com/donald-trump-military-force-greenland-denmark-jd-vance-2052718

Dell'Aguzzo, M. (2024*). Le sanzioni gelano i sogni della Russia sul Gnl nell'Artico.* Startmag. Available at: https://www.startmag.it/energia/russia-novatek-sospensione-arctic-lng-2/ (accessed 18 September 2024).

De Villiers, M. (2001). *Water: The Fate of Our Most Precious Resource.* Boston: Houghton Mifflin Harcourt.

de Witt, M., Stefánsson, H., Valfells, Á. (2019). Energy Security in the Arctic: Policies and Technologies for Integration of Renewable Energy. *Arctic Yearbook.* Available at: https://arcticyearbook.com/arctic-yearbook/2019/2019-briefing-notes/329-energy-security-in-the-arctic-policies-and-technologies-for-integration-of-renewable-energy (accessed 10 October 2024).

Dionet-Grivet, S. (2012). *Géopolitique de l'eau.* Paris: Ellipses.

Dodds, C., Nuttall, M. (2016). *The Scrumble for the Poles.* Cambridge: Polity Press.

Dudarev, A. (2018). Public Health Practice Report: Water Supply and Sanitation in Chukotka and Yakutia, Russian Arctic. *Internation Journal of Circumpolar Health,* 77(1): 1–7.

Dunn, G. (2013). Water Wars. A Surprisingly Rare Source of Conflict. The Politics of Water. *Harvard International Review*, Fall 2013: 46–49.

Edvardsen, A. (2023). Norway and Russia Reached a Fisheries Agreement for 2024. *The High North News.* Available at: https://www.highnorthnews.com/en/norway-and-russia-reached-fisheries-agreement-2024 (accessed 30 October 2024).

EFTA surveillance Authority. (2020). *Energy.* Available at: https://www.eftasurv.int/internal-market/environment-and-energy/energy (accessed 1 October 2024).

Enciclopedia Treccani. *Cook, James.* Istituto Della Enciclopedia Italiana Fondata da Giovanni Treccani. Available at: https://www.treccani.it/enciclopedia/james-cook/ (accessed 27 July 2024).

Eur-Lex. (2016). *The Precautionary Principle.* European Union. Available at: https://eur-lex.europa.eu/EN/legal-content/summary/the-precautionary-principle.html (accessed 28 October 2024).

Eur-Lex. (no date). *Directive 2000/60/EC of the European Parliament and of the Council of 23 October 2000 Establishing a Framework for Community Action in the Field of Water Policy.* European Union. Available at: https://eur-lex.europa.eu/eli/dir/2000/60/oj (accessed 19 July 2024).

European Commission. (2008). *Communication from the Commission to the European Parliament and the Council. The European Union and the Arctic Region.* COM(2008) 763 Final, Brussels.

European Commission. (2012). *Joint Communication to the European Parliament and the Council. Developing a European Union Policy towards the Arctic Region: Progress since 2008 and Next Steps*. JOIN(2012) 19 Final, Brussels.

European Commission. (2016). *Joint Communication to the European Parliament and the Council. An Integrated European Union Policy for the Arctic Region.* JOIN(2012) 19 Final, Brussels.
European Commission. (2020). *External Trade.* Available at: https://oceans-and-fisheries.ec.europa.eu/facts-and-figures/facts-and-figures-common-fisheries-policy/external-trade_en (accessed 30 October 2024).
European Commission. (2018). *What Is the Blue Economy?.* Available at: *https://blueindicators.ec.europa.eu/sites/default/files/blue_economy_2018_infographic_.pdf*
European Commission. (2021). *Joint Communication to the European Parliament, the Council, the European Economic and Social Committee and the Committee of the Regions. A Stronger EU Engagement for a Peaceful, Sustainable and Prosperous Arctic.* Join (2021) 27 final. Brussels.
European Commission. (2021a). *Common Fisheries Policy.* Available at: https://oceans-and-fisheries.ec.europa.eu/policy/common-fisheries-policy-cfp_en (accessed 25 October 2024).
European Commission. (2021b). *Arctic: Agreement to Prevent Unregulated Fishing Enters into Force.* Available at: https://oceans-and-fisheries.ec.europa.eu/news/arctic-agreement-prevent-unregulated-fishing-enters-force-2021-06-25_en#:~:text=The%20agreement%20applies%20a%20precautionary,the%20ecosystems%20and%20potential%20fisheries.
European Commission. (2022). *European Raw Materials Alliance.* Available at: https://erma.eu/about-us/ (accessed 20 October 2020).
European Commission. (2023). *European Green Deal: New EU-Norway Green Alliance to Deepen Cooperation on Climate, Environment, Energy and Clean Industry.* Available at: https://ec.europa.eu/commission/presscorner/detail/en/ip_23_2391 (accessed 30 September 2024).
European Commission. (2024). *REPowerEU.* Available at: https://commission.europa.eu/strategy-and-policy/priorities-2019-2024/european-green-deal/repowereu-affordable-secure-and-sustainable-energy-europe_en (accessed 30 September 2024).
European Commission. (2024a). *The Recovery and Resilience Facility.* Available at: https://commission.europa.eu/business-economy-euro/economic-recovery/recovery-and-resilience-facility_en (accessed 30 September 2024).
European Commission. (2024b). *First Transfer of €1.5 billion of Proceeds from Immobilised Russian Assets Made Available in Support of Ukraine Today.* Available at: https://neighbourhood-enlargement.ec.europa.eu/news/first-transfer-eu15-billion-proceeds-immobilised-russian-assets-made-available-support-ukraine-today-2024-07-26_en (accessed 30 September 2024).
European Commission. (no date). *Third Energy Package.* Available at: https://energy.ec.europa.eu/topics/markets-and-consumers/market-legislation/third-energy-package_en (accessed 30 September 2024).
European Commission. (no date-a). *Ukraine. Trade Picture.* Available at: https://policy.trade.ec.europa.eu/eu-trade-relationships-country-and-region/countries-and-regions/ukraine_en#:~:text=Ukraine's%20main%20exports%20to%20the,EU%20agrifood%20imports%20by%20value. (accessed 15 October 2024).
European Commission. (no date-b). *Sweden.* European Maritime and Fisheries Fund. Available at: chrome-extension://efaidnbmnnnibpcajpcglclefindmkaj/https://oceans-and-fisheries.ec.europa.eu/system/files/2016-09/op-sweden-fact-sheet_en.pdf (accessed 25 October 2024).
European Parliament. (2023). *EU Energy Partnerships: Norway. Energy Cooperation with non-EU Countries.* Briefing. Brussels.
Eurostat. (2023). *Glossary: Non-Metallic Minerals.* Available at: https://ec.europa.eu/eurostat/statistics-explained/index.php?title=Glossary:Non-metallic_minerals (accessed 20 October 2024).

Delivorias, A., De Martini, A. (2023). *EU Energy Partnerships. Energy Cooperation with Non-EU Countries.* European Parliamentary Research Service.

Evengard, B., Berner, J., Brubaker, M., Mulvad, G., Revich, B. (2011). Climate Change and Water Security with a Focus on the Arctic. *Global Health Action,* 4: 1–4.

FAO. (2007). *National Fishery Sector Overview. The Russian Federation.* Fishery and Aquaculture Country Profile. Available at: chrome-extension://efaidnbmnnnibpcajpcglclefindmkaj/https://www.fao.org/fishery/docs/DOCUMENT/fcp/en/FI_CP_RU.pdf (accessed 20 October 2024).

FAO. (2017). *The Republic of Finland.* Fisheries and Aquaculture Department. Available at: file:///C:/Users/Tiziana/Downloads/FAO%20Fisheries%20&%20Aquaculture%20-%20Fishery%20and%20Aquaculture%20Country%20Profiles%20-.pdf (accessed 25 October 2024).

FAO. (2020a). *Treaty between Norway and the Russian Federation Concerning Maritime Delimitation and Cooperation in the Barents Sea and the Arctic Ocean.* FAOLEX Database. Available at: https://www.fao.org/faolex/results/details/en/c/LEX-FAOC159673/ (accessed 31 October 2024).

FAO. (2020b). *Greenland.* Globefish Market Profile. Available at: chrome-extension://efaidnbmnnnibpcajpcglclefindmkaj/https://openknowledge.fao.org/server/api/core/bitstreams/50fcd3ed-abd4-493e-ba04-2db84ab95911/content (accessed 25 October 2024).

FAO. (2023). *Regulation No. 6 on Fishery Protection Zone Around Svalbard.* FAOLEX Database. Available at: https://www.fao.org/faolex/results/details/en/c/LEX-FAOC118326/ (accessed 26 October 2024).

Fishfarming Expert. (2023). *Seafood Industry Accounted for 2.3% of Norway's GDP Last Year.* Available at: https://www.fishfarmingexpert.com/nofima-norway-seafood-industry-value-creation/seafood-industry-accounted-for-23-of-norways-gdp-last-year/1593971 (accessed 24 October 2024).

Forwood, G., Nordin, S., Zuber, T., Marssola, J., Crowe, P. (2024). *14th EU Sanctions Package Targets Russian LNG and Political Donations, Expands Import and Export Bans and Closes Loopholes.* White & Case. Available at: https://www.whitecase.com/insight-alert/14th-eu-sanctions-package-targets-russian-lng-and-political-donations-expands-import (accessed 30 September 2024).

Gavin, G. (2024). *Precious Rare Earth Metals Belong to the State, China Declares.* Politico. Available at: https://www.politico.eu/article/precious-rare-earth-metals-belong-to-the-state-china-declares/ (accesse 15 October 2024).

Geologycal Survey of Norway. (no date). *Critical Raw Materials.* Available at: https://www.ngu.no/en/geological-resources/critical-raw-materials#:~:text=Nepheline%20syenite%20(feldspar%20minerals)%20is,the%20production%20of%20titanium%20metal. (accessed 12 October 2024).

Geological Survey of Sweden. (2020). *Swedish Mines.* Available at: https://www.sgu.se/en/mineral-resources/swedish-mines/#:~:text=Sweden%20is%20by%20far%20the,%2C%20Norrbotten%2C%20Skelleftef%C3%A4ltet%20and%20Bergslagen. (accessed 14 October 2024).

Government of Canada. (2022). *The Canadian Critical Minerals Strategy.* Available at: https://www.canada.ca/en/campaign/critical-minerals-in-canada/canadian-critical-minerals-strategy.html (accessed 14 October 2024).

Government of Canada. (2023). *Canada's Fisheries Fast Facts 2023.* Available at: https://www.dfo-mpo.gc.ca/stats/publications/fast-facts-info-eclair/2023/index-eng.html (accessed 24 October 2024).

Government of Canada. (2024). *Canadian Mineral Production.* Available at: https://natural-resources.canada.ca/maps-tools-and-publications/publications/minerals-mining-publications/canadian-mineral-production/17722 (accessed 12 October 2024).

Government of Finland. (2022). *Finland's Minerals Strategy.* Helsinki.

Government of Greenland. (2020). *Greenland's Mineral Strategy 2020–2024.* Nuuk.
Government of Iceland. (2024). *War in Ukraine - Iceland's Response.* Available at: https://www.government.is/topics/foreign-affairs/war-in-ukraine/ (accessed 30 September 2024).
Government of Norway. (2024). *Norway Aligns Itself with New Sanctions against Russia.* Available at: https://www.regjeringen.no/en/aktuelt/norway-aligns-itself-with-new-sanctions-against-russia/id3047474/ (accessed 30 September 2024).
Greenland Institute of Natural Resources. (2024). *Minerals.* Available at: https://natur.gl/guidance/miljoe/?lang=en#:~:text=Greenland%20has%20been%20a%20mining,%2C%20olivine%2C%20cryolite%20and%20marble. (accessed 13 October 2024).
Hall, N. (2023). *No Water Wars?.* Center for Strategic and International Studies. Available at: https://www.csis.org/analysis/no-water-wars (accessed 23 July 2024).
Hardy, E., Helmeci, D., Westgaard, K. (2024). *Don't Buy Greenland, Buy Its Minerals.* Internationale Politik Quarterly. Available at: https://ip-quarterly.com/en/dont-buy-greenland-buy-its-minerals (accessed 12 October 2024).
Hartmann, J., Bastida, A. E., Daza-Clark, A. M. (2024). *Transition Minerals: A Cautionary Tale from Greenland.* Available at: https://www.ejiltalk.org/transition-minerals-a-cautionary-tale-from-greenland/ (accessed 20 October 2024).
Herlihy, P. (2012). *Vodka: A Global History.* Clerkenwell: Reaktion Books.
Hoag, H. (2017). Nations Put Science Before Fishing in the Arctic. *Science*, 358(6368).
Hoel, A. H. (2020). *The Geopolitics of Fish in the Arctic.* Policy Brief 11. NUPI.
Huber, P., Rystedt, M. (2016). *Arctic Council Project Support Instrument.* Arctic Council.
Hult, J. L., Ostrander, N. C. (2001). *Antarctic Icebergs as a Global Freshwater Resource.* Santa Monica: RAND.
Humpert, M. (2024). Russia's Novatek to Complete Arctic LNG 2 by 2026 Despite Sanctions. *The High North News.* Available at: https://www.highnorthnews.com/en/russias-novatek-complete-arctic-lng-2-2026-despite-sanctions (accessed 18 September 2024).
Humpert, M. (2024a). EU Receives 100 Shipments of LNG and Gas Condensate from Yamal LNG Project. *The High North News.* Available at: https://www.highnorthnews.com/en/eu-receives-100-shipments-lng-and-gas-condensate-yamal-lng-project (accessed 30 September 2024).
Humpert, M. (2024b). EU Looking to Pass 14th Sanctions Package End of June, Including Partial Ban on Russian LNG. *The High North News.* Available at: https://www.highnorthnews.com/en/eu-looking-pass-14th-sanctions-package-end-june-including-partial-ban-russian-lng (accessed 30 September 2024).
Hydrocarbons Technology. (2024). *Yamal LNG Project, Sabetta.* Available at: https://www.hydrocarbons-technology.com/projects/yamal-lng-project-russia/ (accessed 30 September 2024).
International Council for the Exploration of the Sea. (no date). *Icelandic Waters.* Available at: https://www.ices.dk/advice/ESD/Pages/Icelandic-Waters-Fish.aspx#:~:text=The%20main%20demersal%20species%20include,%2Dspawning%20herring%2C%20and%20mackerel. (accessed 25 October 2024).
International Energy Agency. (2023a). *Norwegian Mineral Strategy.* Available at: https://www.iea.org/policies/17656-norwegian-mineral-strategy (accessed 12 October 2024).
International Energy Agency. (2023b). *Denmark.* Available at: https://www.iea.org/countries/denmark (accessed 9 October 2024).
Jensen, O. (2011). Current Legal Developments the Barents Sea. Treaty between Norway and the Russian Federation Concerning Maritime Delimitation and Cooperation in the Barents Sea and the Arctic Ocean. *International Journal of Marine and Coastal Law*, 26(1): 151–168.
Joint Norwegian-Russian Fisheries Commission. (no date). *History.* Available at: https://www.jointfish.com/eng/THE-FISHERIES-COMMISSION/HISTORY.html (accessed 30 October 2024).

Jones, F. (2023). "A 'Frozen' Geopolitical Issue": Svalbard and the Geopolitics of Arctic Mining. *Mining Technology*. Available at: https://www.mining-technology.com/features/arctic-mining-svalbard-russia/?cf-view (accessed 12 October 2024).

Jørgensen-Dahl, A. (2010). *Arctic Mineral Resources*. Available at: http://www.arctis-search.com/Arctic+Mineral+Resources (accessed 12 October 2024).

Judge, C. (2013). *The Coming Water Wars*. Available at: https://www.usnews.com/opinion/blogs/clark-judge/2013/02/19/the-next-big-wars-will-be-fought-over-water (accessed 31 July 2024).

Kardon, I.B., Gabuev, A. (2025). Trump's Greenland Obsession Will Not Secure America. Foreign Policy. Available at: https://foreignpolicy.com/2025/05/26/trump-greenland-arctic-russia-china-nato-strategy-geopolitics-security/

Karimidastenaei, Z., Klöve, B., Sadegh, M., Haghighi, A. T. (2021). Polar Ice as an Unconventional Water Resource: Opportunities and Challenges. *Water, Special Issue: Water Scarcity: From Ancient to Modern Times and the Future,* 13(22): 1–14.

Khurshid, A., Chen, Y., Rauf, A., Khan, K. (2023). Critical Metals in Uncertainty: How Russia-Ukraine Conflict Drives Their Prices. *Resources Policy,* 85: 1–10.

Klare, M. (2012). *The Race for What's Left: The Global Scramble for the World's Last Resources*. New York: Metropolitan Books.

Larin, V. (2020). Russia–China Economic Relations in the 21st Century: Unrealized Potential or Predetermined Outcome? *Chinese Journal of International Review*, 2(1): 1–26.

Laruelle, M. (2019). *Russia's Arctic Strategies and the Future of the Far North*. New York: Routledge.

Lewis, C. (2015). Iceberg Harvesting: Suggesting a Federal Regulatory Regime for a New Freshwater Source. *Boston College Environmental Affairs Law, 2014–2015*, 42: 439–472.

Liu, Dan. (2017). *The 2015 Oslo Declaration on Arctic High Seas Fisheries: The Starting Point Towards Future Fisheries Management in the Central Arctic Ocean*. Arctic Yearbook.

LKAB. (2022). *LKAB's Four Considerations for the Critical Raw Materials Act*. Available at: https://lkab.com/en/news/lkabs-four-considerations-for-the-critical-raw-materials-act/ (accesse 20 October 2024).

LNG Prime Staff. (2023). *Novatek's Yamal Project Produces 100 Million Tons of LNG*. LNG Prime. Available at: https://lngprime.com/asia/novateks-yamal-project-produces-100-million-tons-of-lng/91290/ (accessed 30 September 2024).

Lukoil. (2023). *Lukoil Commissions the Second Stage of Kolskaya Wind Power Plant*. Available at: https://www.lukoil.com/PressCenter/Pressreleases/Pressrelease/lukoil-commissions-the-second-stage-of-kolskaya-w (accessed 10 October 2024).

McBride, O. (2024). EU Faces Dilemma Over Further Sanctions on Russian Fish Imports. *The Fishing Daily*. Available at: https://thefishingdaily.com/featured-news/eu-faces-dilemma-over-further-sanctions-on-russian-fish-imports/ (accessed 27 October 2024).

McBride, O. (2024a). *Norway and Russia Agree on 2025 Fisheries Management Plan*. The Fishing Daily. Available at: https://thefishingdaily.com/latest-news/norway-and-russia-agree-on-2025-fisheries-management-plan/ (accessed 30 October 2024).

McBride, O. (2023). Faroese-Russian Fisheries Agreement: Quota Adjustments for 2024. *The Fishing Daily*. Available at: https://thefishingdaily.com/european-fishing-industry-news/faroese-russian-fisheries-agreement-quota-adjustments-for-2024/#:~:text=The%20Faroe%20Islands%20and%20Russia%20reached%20an%20agreement%20on%20their,the%20Faroe%20Islands%20and%20Britain. (accessed 30 October 2024).

McWilliams, B., Sgaravatti, G., Tagliapietra, S., Zachmann, G. (2024). *The European Union-Russia Energy Divorce: State of Play*. Bruegel. Available at: https://www.bruegel.org/analysis/european-union-russia-energy-divorce-state-play (accessed 15 September 2024).

Meja Hernandez. (2024). *Polar Plunder: Extractivism in the Arctic.* European Environmental Bureau. Available at: https://meta.eeb.org/2024/07/17/the-race-for-critical-minerals-heats-up-the-arctic/ (accessed 11 October 2024).

Middlebury Institute of International Studies at Monterey. (2022). *Arctic Minerals.* Center for the Blue Economy. Monterey.

Mikkelsen, A., Langhelle, O. (eds). (2011). *Arctic Oil and Gas. Sustainability at Risk?.* Oxon: Routledge.

Mikkola, N., Randall, L., Hagberg, A. (2016). *Green Growth in Nordics Regions. 50 Ways to Make it Happen.* NORDREGIO. Stockholm.

Ministry of Economic Affairs and Employment of Finland. (2023). *Renewable Energy in Finland.* Available at: https://tem.fi/en/renewable-energy (accessed 8 October 2024).

Morgounova Schwalbe, D. (2016). *The Yamal LNG Project and the Nenets Reindeer Nomads Impacts, Survival and Indigenous Opposition to Gas Exploitation in Russia's Arctic.* Köln: GegenStrömung – CounterCurrent.

Mueter, F., Planque, B., Hunt, G., Alabia, I., Hirawak, T., Eisner, L., Dalpadado, P., Chierici, M., Drinkwater, K., Harada, N., Arneberg, P., Saitoh, S. (2021). Possible Future Scenarios in the Gateways to the Arctic for Subarctic and Arctic Marine Systems: II. prey Resources, Food Webs, Fish, and Fisheries. *ICES Journal of Marine Science*, 78(9): 3017–3045.

Murray, A. (2025). Inside the race for Greenland's mineral wealth. BBC. Available at: https://www.bbc.com/news/articles/c9d5jwvw9nlo (accessed 30 May 2025).

National Geographic. (2024). *World Water Map.* Available at: https://education.nationalgeographic.org/resource/world-water-map/ (accessed 4 July 2024).

National Geographic. (2024a). *Water Inequality.* Available at: https://education.nationalgeographic.org/resource/water-inequality/ (accessed 4 July 2024).

Natural History Museum. (2022). *Mineral Resources on Svalbard.* University of Oslo. Available at: https://www.nhm.uio.no/english/research/themes/arctic/min-geo/min-res-1.html (accessed 20 October 2024).

Natural History Museum. (no date). *Geology.* Available at: https://natkop.kopavogur.is/en/safnkostur/jardfraedi/#:~:text=The%20majority%20of%20Icelandic%20rocks,such%20as%20granite%20are%20rare.&text=Iceland%20is%20very%20poor%20of,as%20zeolits%20and%20Iceland%20spar. (accessed 14 October 2024).

Nordic Energy Research. (2021). *Nordics Lead Europe in Renewables.* Available at: https://www.nordicenergy.org/article/nordics-lead-europe-in-renewables/ (accessed 1 October 2024).

Norkross, B., Iken, K. (2016). *Fishes in the Arctic.* Ocean Exploration. Available at: https://oceanexplorer.noaa.gov/explorations/16arctic/background/fishes/fishes.html#:~:text=A%20recent%20census%20estimates%20there,webs%20to%20higher%20level%20consumers. (accessed 25 October 2024).

Northwest Atlantic Fisheries Organization. (2024). *Species.* Available at: https://www.nafo.int/Science/Science-Advice/Species (accessed 25 October 2024).

Norwegian Ministry of Trade, Industry and Fisheries. (2023). *Norwegian Mineral Strategy.* Government of Norway. Available at: chrome-extension://efaidnbmnnnibpcajpcglclefindmkaj/https://www.regjeringen.no/contentassets/1614eb7b10cd4a7cb58fa6245159a547/norges-mineralstrategi_engelsk_uu.pdf (accessed 12 October 2024).

Nugent. (2023). *Why Greta Thunberg and Other Climate Activists Are Protesting Wind Farms in Norway.* Time. Available at: https://time.com/6259144/greta-thunberg-norway-protests-climate-activists/ (accessed 10 October 2024).

Nuttall, M. (2021). Greenland and the Geopolitics of Critical Minerals. *One Earth,* 4(12): 1674–1675.

OECD Library. (2014). *Oil Prices.* Available at: https://www.oecd-ilibrary.org/docserver/factbook-2014-48-en.pdf?expires=1727371863&id=id&accname=guest&checksum=00FC0B5AABCAA86F10FCC6E7430F3E5A (accessed 17 September 2024).

Office of Foreign Assets Control. (2022). *Russian Harmful Foreign Activities Sanctions.* Available at: https://ofac.treasury.gov/faqs/1014#:~:text=No%2C%20only%20imports%20of%20crude,Investments%20With%20Respect%20to%20Continued (accessed 28 September 2024).
Official Journal of the European Union. (2013). *Regulation No 1380/2013 of the European Parliament and of the Council of 11 December 2013 on the Common Fisheries Policy, Amending Council Regulations (EC) No 1954/2003 and (EC) No 1224/2009 and Repealing Council Regulations (EC) No 2371/2002 and (EC) No 639/2004 and Council Decision 2004/585/EC.* Available at: https://eur-lex.europa.eu/eli/reg/2013/1380/oj (accessed 28 October 2024).
Official Journal of the European Union. (2014). *Council Decision 2014/512/CFSP of 31 July 2014 Concerning Restrictive Measures in View of Russia's Actions Destabilising the Situation in Ukraine.* Available at: https://eur-lex.europa.eu/legal-content/EN/TXT/?uri=CELEX:32014D0512 (accessed 13 September 2024).
Østhagen, A. (2020). Fish, Not Oil, at the Heart of (Future) Arctic Resource Conflicts. *Arctic Yearbook 2020, 1-17.*
Østhagen, A., Evans, G. (2023). *In Hot Water: Arctic Fisheries as a Proxy for Geopolitical Tensions.* The Royal United Services Institute for Defence and Security Studies. Available at: https://rusi.org/explore-our-research/publications/commentary/hot-water-arctic-fisheries-proxy-geopolitical-tensions (accessed 30 November 2024).
Østhagen, A., Jørgensen, A. K., Moe, A. (2020). The Svalbard Fisheries Protection Zone: How Russia and Norway Manage an Arctic Dispute. *Arctic and North,* 40.
Øystein, H., Max, T. (2012). *Aquaculture in the Arctic.* Nofima AS. Available at: https://nofima.com/publication/1154618/ (accessed 25 October 2024).
Pedersen, T., Henriksen, T. (2009). Svalbard's Maritime Zones: The End of Legal Uncertainty?. *The International Journal of Marine and Coastal Law,* 24(1): 141–161.
Pelodeix, C., Basse, E. M. (2021). *Governance of Offshore Oil and Gas in the Arctic. Between Diversity and Coexistence.* New York: Routledge.
Preve, C. (2024). *What Does Finland and Sweden's Membership to NATO Mean for Race to Arm the Arctic?.* Euronews. Available at: https://www.euronews.com/my-europe/2024/05/31/what-does-finland-and-swedens-membership-to-nato-mean-for-race-to-arm-the-arctic#:~:text=Their%20accession%20into%20NATO%20%E2%80%94%20in,are%20in%20the%20military%20alliance. (accessed 20 October 2024).
PJSC EL5-Energo. (2024). *Kola Wind Farm.* Available at: https://www.el5-energo.ru/en/about-us/kola-wind-farm/ (accessed 10 October 2024).
Raspotnik, A., Østhagen, A, (2020). How Much Is the Fish? When Foreign Policy Meets Fishing Interests in the EU's Arctic Endeavour. *International Relations,* 35(2): 256–276.
Raspotnik, A., Stępień, A. (2020). The European Union and the Arctic: A Decade into Finding Its Arcticness. In Weber, J. (ed.) *Handbook on Geopolitics and Security in the Arctic. The High North between Cooperation and Confrontation.* Springer, pp. 131–146.
Reuters. (2024). Norway ends dispute with reindeer herders over wind farm. Available at: https://www.reuters.com/sustainability/norway-ends-fosen-wind-farm-dispute-2024-03-06/
Røseth, T. (2017). Russia's Energy Relations with China: Passing the Strategic Threshold? *Eurasian Geography and Economics*, 58(1): 23–55.
Seidel, M. (2024). *From Ice to Fire: Climate Change and Iceland's Sustainable Energy.* Planet Forward. Available at: https://planetforward.org/story/iceland-renewable-energy/#:~:text=Iceland%20is%20one%20of%20the,from%20the%20country's%20melting%20glaciers. (accessed 8 October 2024).
Seitz, W., Zazzaro, W. (2019). *Sanctions and Public Opinion: The Case of the Russia-Ukraine Gas Disputes.* Working Paper 529. Centre for Studies in Economics and Finance.
Shibata, A., Zou, L., Sellheim, N., Scopelliti, M. (2019). *Emerging Legal Orders in the Arctic.* London and New York: Routledge.

Silk Road Fund Co. Ltd. (2024). *Silk Road Fund.* Available at: https://www.silkroadfund.com.cn/enweb/ (accessed 30 September 2024).
Spohr, K., Hamilton, D. S., Moyer, J.C. (2020). *The Arctic and World Order.* Johns Hopkins University SAIS: Washington.
Staby, A. (2020). C4 – *Barents Sea. Poleward Moving Fish Species Entering the Arctic.* Climefish. Available at: https://climefish.eu/c4f-barents-sea/#:~:text=This%20area%20supports%20three%20main,king%20crab%20and%20snow%20crab. (accessed 20 October 2024).
Statista. (2023). *Top 10 Fishing Nations Worldwide in 2020.* Available at: https://www.statista.com/statistics/240225/leading-fishing-nations-worldwide-2008/
Statista. (2024). *Leading Exporting Countries of Liquefied Natural Gas Worldwide in 2023.* Available at: https://www.statista.com/statistics/274528/major-exporting-countries-of-lng/#:~:text=The%20world's%20largest%20exporter%20of,for%20shipping%20and%20storage%20purposes. (accessed 18 September 2024).
Statista. (2024a). *Production Volume of Diamonds Worldwide in 2023, by Country.* Available at: https://www.statista.com/statistics/449683/global-mined-diamond-production-by-country/ (accessed 12 October 2024).
Strout, N. (2023). *Alaska Lawmakers Want to Expand US Ban on Russian Seafood Imports.* Available at: https://www.seafoodsource.com/news/supply-trade/alaska-lawmakers-want-to-expand-ban-on-russian-seafood-imports (accessed 27 October 2024).
Swedish Ministry of Enterprise Energy and Communications. (2013). *Sweden's Minerals Strategy.* Available at: chrome-extension://efaidnbmnnnibpcajpcglclefindmkaj/https://rmis.jrc.ec.europa.eu/uploads/legislation/Sweden_MineralsStrategy_ENGLISH.pdf (accessed 14 October 2024).
Tank, S. E., Manizza, M., Holmes, R. M., McClelland, J. W., Peterson, B. J. (2012). The Processing and Impact of Dissolved Riverine Nitrogen in the Arctic Ocean. *Estuaries and Coasts*, 35: 401–415.
Teck Alaska. (2024). *Red Dog.* Available at: https://www.teck.com/operations/united-states/operations/red-dog/ (accessed 12 October 2024).
The Arctic Institute. (2022). *Iqaluit's Water Crisis Highlights Deeper Issues with Arctic Infrastructure.* Available at: https://www.thearcticinstitute.org/iqaluits-water-crisis-highlights-deeper-issues-arctic-infrastructure/ (accessed 10 July 2024).
The Northern Miner Group. (2024). *Rare Earth Elements: Where in the World Are They?.* Available at: https://www.mining.com/web/rare-earth-elements-where-in-the-world-are-they/ (accessed 12 October 2024).
The White House. (2023). *Inflation Reduction Act Guidebook.* Washington. Available at: https://www.whitehouse.gov/cleanenergy/inflation-reduction-act-guidebook/ (accessed 14 October 2024).
The White House. (2024). *G7 Apulia Leaders' Communiqué.* Available at: https://www.whitehouse.gov/briefing-room/statements-releases/2024/06/14/g7-leaders-statement-8/ (accessed 30 October 2024).
Tostevin, M. (2025). Trumpposing 's Greenland Bid Poses Global Dangers, Says the Woman Facing Him Down, Newsweek. Available at: https://www.newsweek.com/trump-greenland-denmark-mette-frederiksen-nato-russia-china-2077596 (accessed 30 May 2025).
Trainer, J., Lokker, N., Taylor, K., Certain, U. (2024). *Sanctions by The Numbers: The Russian Energy Sector.* Center for a New American Security. Available at: https://www.cnas.org/publications/reports/sanctions-by-the-numbers-the-russian-energy-sector (accessed 14 September 2024).
UN. (2023). *The 17 Goals.* Available at: https://sdgs.un.org/goals (accessed 25 July 2024).
UN Committee on Economic Social and Cultural Rights. (2010). *General Comment No.15 the Right to Water.* New York: United Nations General Assembly.
United Nations. (2024). *Greenland Signs up for Paris Agreement.* Available at: https://unric.org/en/greenland-signs-up-for-paris-agreement/ (accessed 21 October 2024).

United States Environmental Protection Agency. (2022). *Climate Change Indicators: Permafrost.* Available at: https://www.epa.gov/climate-indicators/climate-change-indicators-permafrost#:~:text=A%20warming%20climate%20has%20brought,many%20locations%20around%20the%20world. (accessed 4 July 2024).
University of Alaska. (2022). *Alaska's Minerals. A Strategic National Imperative. Summary and Next Steps.* Alaska.
US Congress. (2023). *S.2011 - United States-Russian Federation Seafood Reciprocity Act of 2023.* Available at: https://www.congress.gov/bill/118th-congress/senate-bill/2011 (accessed 31 October 2024).
USGS. (2008). *Circum-Arctic Resource Appraisal: Estimates of Undiscovered Oil and Gas North of the Arctic Circle.* Available at: https://pubs.usgs.gov/fs/2008/3049/ (accessed 11 September 2024)
USGS. (2019). *2019 Minerals Yearbook. Iceland.* US Department of the Interior. Available at: chrome-extension://efaidnbmnnnibpcajpcglclefindmkaj/https://pubs.usgs.gov/myb/vol3/2019/myb3-2019-iceland.pdf (accessed 20 October 2024).
USGS. (2024). *The Mineral Industry of Alaska.* Available at: https://www.usgs.gov/centers/national-minerals-information-center/mineral-industry-alaska#:~:text=Alaska%20leads%20in%20zinc%20production,minerals%20mined%20in%20the%20State. (accessed 12 October 2024).
Venua, B. (2024). *Alaska's Seafood Industry Is in Trouble.* Processors and Policymakers Blame Russia.
Vylegzhanin, A. N., Young, O., Berkman, P. A. (2020). The Central Arctic Ocean Fisheries Agreement as an Element in the Evolving Arctic Ocean Governance Complex, *Marine Policy*, 118: 1–10.
Wachtmeister, H. (2023). *Russia-China Energy Relations since 24 February: Consequences and Options for Europe.* Report. Swedish National China Centre.
Waldhols, R. (2023). *A Year in, Landmark U.S. Climate Policy Drives Energy Transition But Hurdles Remain.* National Public Radio. Available at: https://www.npr.org/2023/08/16/1193726242/a-year-in-landmark-u-s-climate-policy-drives-energy-transition-but-hurdles-remai (accessed 14 October 2024).
Walstad, A. (2023). *EU-Norway Green Alliance: Hype or Hope?.* Available at: https://gasoutlook.com/analysis/eu-norway-green-alliance-hype-or-hope/ (accessed 8 October 2024).
Weeks, W. F., Campbell, W.J. (1973). Icebergs as a Fresh-water Source: An Appraisal. *Journal of Glaciology,* 12(65): 207–233.
WHO/UNICEF. (2021). *Progress on Household Drinking Water, Sanitation and Hygiene 2000-2020: Five Years into the SDGs World Health Organization (WHO) and the United Nations Children's Fund (UNICEF).* Geneva: WHO/UNICEF.
Wolf, A., Kramer, A., Carius, A., Dabelko, G. (2006). *Water Can Be a Pathway to Peace, Not War.* Navigating Peace, 1. Woodrow Wilson International Center for Scholars.
World Atlas. (2024). *What Are The Major Natural Resources Of Finland?.* Available at: https://www.worldatlas.com/articles/what-are-the-major-natural-resources-of-finland.html (accessed 14 October 2024).
World Climate Research Programme. (2024). *WCRP Coupled Model Intercomparison Project (CMIP).* Available at: https://www.wcrp-climate.org/wgcm-cmip (accessed 13 September 2024).
World Economic Forum Water Initiative. (2011). *Water Security, The Water-Food-Energy-Climate Nexus.* London: Island Press.
World Population Review. (2024). *Mineral Production by Country.* Available at: https://worldpopulationreview.com/country-rankings/mineral-production-by-country (accessed 15 October 2024).

WWF. (2024). *Overview.* Available at: https://www.worldwildlife.org/threats/water-scarcity/#:~:text=Only%203%25%20of%20the%20world's,one%20month%20of%20the%20year. (accessed 1 July 2024).

Yozel, Sally. (2024). *Is the US Ban on Russian Seafood Working?.* Stimson. Available at: https://www.stimson.org/2024/is-the-us-ban-on-russian-seafood-working/ (accessed 31 October 2024).

Zhang, Y., Msangi, S., Edmonds, J., Waldhoff, S. (2024). Limited Increases in Arctic Offshore Oil and Gas Production with Climate Change and the Implications for Energy Markets. *Scientific Reports*, 14. Available at: https://www.nature.com/articles/s41598-024-54007-x (accessed 13 September 2024).

Zilanov, V. (2017). Delimitation between Russia and Norway in the Arctic: New Challenges and Cooperation. *Arctic and North* 29: 24–49.

Zimmermann, A., Gljs, C., Jack, V., Verhelst, K. (2024). *EU Approves First-Ever Sanctions on Russian Gas.* Politico. Available at: https://www.politico.eu/article/eu-approves-first-ever-sanctions-russian-gas-lng-vladimir-putin-ukraine-invasion/ (accessed 17 September 2024).

4 Shipping and infrastructure in the Arctic

Introduction

This chapter analyses the impact of climate change and the war in Ukraine on Arctic geopolitics in the sectors of shipping, ports, and Outer Space. Shipping, which is the other element that strongly contributes to the increase in the importance of the Arctic for actors inside and outside the region, together with natural resources, is obviously very closely linked to the sector of ports. They are discussed separately in two different sections in order to clearly explain how states pursue their geopolitical and economic interests in the broader shipping domain and in the case of ports more specifically. Also, the reason why Outer Space has been included in this chapter is that it is part of the Arctic infrastructures together with ports.

Shipping routes, which are becoming increasingly accessible because of climate change, are making the geopolitical and economic relevance of the Arctic grow exponentially. In fact, regional and world trade mainly depend on shipping. Moreover, the increasing accessibility of shipping routes also has legal implications given the fact that states are very interested in free navigation in the Arctic. This is true especially for the Northeast Passage (NEP) and the Northwest Passage (NWP) that are under Russian and Canadian jurisdictions, respectively. The case of the Transpolar Route (TSR) is different because it is still frozen and there are no territorial claims at the moment. In this context, ports play a crucial role because they provide the necessary infrastructure that makes navigation possible. However, the small number of ports and the difficulties in developing them due to a number of reasons, such as high costs, make navigation quite problematic.

The other infrastructure that is relevant from a geopolitical perspective is those relating to Outer Space. The Arctic states are developing space infrastructure that, through satellites, is useful for many aims such as monitoring climate change, search and rescue, and military use. Although the 1967 Treaty on Principles Governing the Activities of States in the Exploration and Use of Outer Space, including the Moon and Other Celestial Bodies (also called the Outer Space Treaty) stipulates that 'Outer Space is not subject to national appropriation by claim of sovereignty,

DOI: 10.4324/9781032633008-5

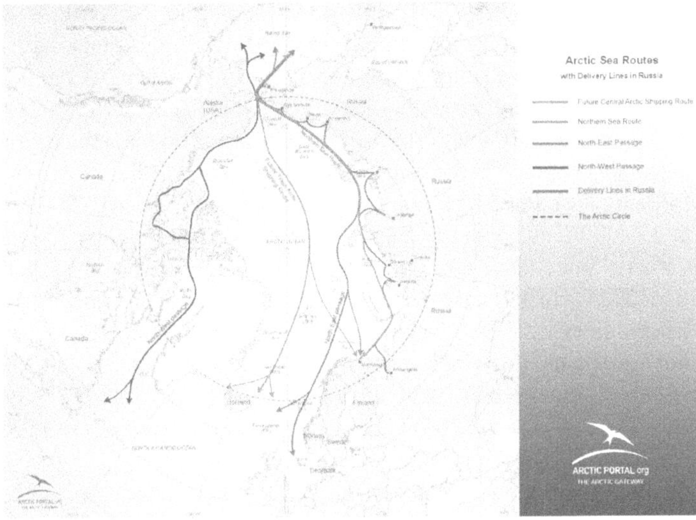

Figure 4.1 Arctic shipping routes

by means of use or occupation, or by any other means',[1] states still compete to develop the necessary technology to 'conquer' Outer Space and have an advantage over other states that translates into geopolitical competition.

Shipping routes and climate change

Shipping is a very important component of the world maritime industry as it is responsible for around 90% of world trade (International Chamber of Shipping, 2023). This is why the Arctic shipping routes – the NEP, the NWP, and the TSR, (Figure 4.1) which are about 40% shorter in distance than traditional routes (the Suez and the Panama canals) – meaning considerable savings in time, fuel, and emissions (Huang et al., 2019) and offer great economic opportunities. As Megan et al. (2018) put it, 'if the Arctic routes become an integral component of the world maritime transport system, the countries with ports along the associated coastline can expect an upgrade of the economic activity as well as an increased level of influence in the arena of geo-economics'. In spite of this, Arctic shipping is also quite challenging because navigation in icy waters (especially in winter) is risky and the fragile environment is jeopardised. Indeed, if on the one hand shorter sea routes have the potential to reduce global shipping emissions, on the other hand the risk of increasing high-latitude black carbon deposition is quite high (Melia et al.,

1 The Outer Space Treaty was signed in 1967 by Great Britain, the Soviet Union, and the US and entered into force in the same year. It now includes 115 parties (United Nations Office for Outer Space Affairs, 2024).

2016, 9720; Theocharis, 2020, 23). However, shipping in the Arctic is supposed to continue intensifying as ice melting due to global warming is making it increasingly feasible in the foreseeable future. For instance, between 2013 and 2019 the number of vessels entering the region increased by 25% (Lasserre, 2021). This is especially true for the NEP and NWP as the TSR is still frozen, although it is supposed to become navigable in the near future (Bennett et al., 2020, 116). In the case of the NEP, a total of 36.254 million tons of cargo was shipped in 2023, which is more than 250,000 tons above the target set in the Russian project, Development of the Northern Sea Route, and implemented by the energy company Rosatom (Chaudhury, 2024). In the case of the NWP, 'the growth in traffic was mainly driven by fishing vessels (+106.2 percent between 2009 and 2019) and cargo ships (+122 percent) of which dry bulk experienced the fastest expansion (+288.9 percent), driven by mining activities, and general cargo (+156.5 percent), driven by community supply' (Lasserre, 2021). Consequently, the geopolitical and economic significance of Arctic shipping routes is increasing enormously.

Historically, 'alterations in transport routes have been associated with seismic shifts in the balance of economic and political power' (Blunden, 2012, 116). For instance, the oceanic voyages of the Spanish and Portuguese during the Age of Discovery (from the 15th to mid-16th centuries) to search for new trade routes to the Indies 'shifted the power away from the Mediterranean' (Blunden, 2012, 117). This reflected and accelerated the gradual decline of Venice and the rise in wealth and power of the Iberian states (Blunden, 2012, 117). The Spanish and Portuguese voyages were followed by the those of the French, Dutch, and English that created new economic and political opportunities 'which allowed Europeans in due course to acquire the greatest concentration of wealth and power in human history' (Blunden, 2012, 117). Thus, as Margaret Blunden (2012), professor and director of International Security Studies at the London Academy of Diplomacy at the University of East Anglia, puts it, 'it may not be entirely fanciful to compare the potential significance of a new Arctic sea lane, in economic, geopolitical and security terms, with that of the opening of the new sea routes to the Indies during the Age of Discovery'. Furthermore, Professor Blunden also correctly points out that the emergence of new sea lines does not depend only on changing climate and maritime conditions, but also on other factors such as a surge of innovation and political problems (Blunden, 2012, 117). Professor Blunden argues that these two factors played a key role in the case of the new trade routes to the Indies (Blunden, 2012, 117). She adds that nowadays, the trade routes connecting Europe and Asia, which carry a volume of trade that was unimaginable before, pass through choke points like the Suez Canal and the Strait of Malacca that are highly vulnerable to congestion and deliberate or accidental disruption (Blunden, 2012, 117). Congestion is also due to the fact that the number and the size of vessels are expected to increase because the booming trade between China and the West requires the use of larger container ships (Laruelle, 2014, 177). Data show that in 2023 more than 106,700 merchant ships were sailing around the world (over 11% of them carrying oil) ,while in 2008 the world fleet counted only 77,500 vessels in operation (Atlas Magasin, 2024; Blunden, 2012, 117). Additionally, the

Suez Canal is vulnerable also because of current conflicts in the Middle East (e.g., Palestine and Israel, extending to the whole region). For instance, the 2024 Iran-backed Houthi rebels in Yemen caused a dramatic decrease in commercial vessel traffic in the Red Sea by 60% and the cost of insurance for Western ships transiting the Bab el-Mandab Strait has skyrocketed (Detsch, 2024). Another reason increasing the vulnerability of choke points is climate change. This is evident, for instance, in the case of the Panama Canal as the level of Gatún Lake, which holds the water supply for the canal, continues to drop (Ruiz and Shintani, 2024). All these factors can alter the balance of commercial advantage, accelerate advanced technologies of shipbuilding and navigation facilitating the opening up of Arctic shipping routes (Blunden, 2012, 117).

For instance, these factors have led to an increase in voyages along the NSR over time.

In the 1990s, only six voyages along the NSR were accomplished, each of about 25 days (Laruelle, 2014, 175). In particular, in 1997 two ships sailed the entire NSR with a cargo mainly consisting of fertilisers, metal, and timber exported from Finland and Sweden to Japan as well as agricultural products transported to Europe from China and Thailand (Laruelle, 2014, 175). In the 2000s, experimental voyages tested the possibilities of navigation along the NEP (Laruelle, 2014, 175; Blunden, 2012, 118). One example was accomplished by two ships belonging to Beluga Shipping, a German company that is a major European heavy-lift exporter, that in August and September 2009 made the first non-Russian commercial transit voyage from Ulsan in South Korea to Rotterdam through the NEP, shaving 3,000 nautical miles off the Suez Canal route and saving about 300,000 dollars for each of the two vessels involved (Blunden, 2012, 118). They were the first foreign ships not to use icebreakers (Laruelle, 2014, 174). In 2011, *Polarcus Alima*, a United Arab Emirates research vessel, went from Hammerfest in Norway to the Bering Strait giving a demonstration of the potential of the Arctic Sea routes as it saved 13 days compared to the Suez Canal route (Blunden, 2012, 118). Moreover, ice melting will very probably make the transit from Russia to the North American continent shorter, both eastward along the NSR and westward (Murmask is 9,600 kilometres from Vancouver, Canada, via the Bering Strait, and 16,000 kilometres via the Panama Canal) (Laruelle, 2014, 174). In 2007, concept of the 'Arctic Bridge' emerged that is quite interesting as it unites the two historical enemies in the region, namely Russia and the US, intending a connection between the port of Churchill in Manitoba (Canada) and Murmansk (Russia) through Iceland–Greenland (Laruelle, 2014, 175).

Moreover, the NSR is relevant from a geopolitical perspective because of two elements. First, it is expected to be the first Arctic shipping route to be free from ice that is receding more quickly for shipping routes off Siberia (Blunden, 2012). Indeed, compared with the NWP it has lighter sea ice conditions and a more developed navigation infrastructure (Zhang et al., 2023, 2). This makes the NSR the Arctic shipping route with the highest commercial potential as the melting ice would make it crucial for the transportation of goods and natural resources (Wegge and Keil, 2018; Intesa San Paolo, 2020; Megan et al., 2018). During the

Cold War, 'all shipping in the Arctic Ocean consisted of either the movement of military or strategic cargo or transport for political or administrative purposes' (Kitagawa, 2001). The Soviet Union invested enormous resources in NSR navigation (Kitagawa, 2001). For instance, in December 1972 and January 1973 the icebreaker *Indigirka* pioneered winter NSR navigation by voyaging from Murmansk to Dudinka in 12 days (Kitagawa, 2001). NSR traffic reached its peak in 1987 but declined because of the deterioration of infrastructures following the collapse of the Soviet Union (Blunden, 2012, 118). It was formally opened for foreign vessels in 1991 with the collapse of the Soviet Union, as at that time commercial considerations prevailed over national security (Blunden, 2012, 118). Nowadays, 'the use of this route during the six-month navigation provided by the icebreaker fleet of Russia reduces travel time by two weeks and costs by 20%' (Makarov et al., 2022, 1114). Shipping along the NSR can be destinational, which means regional or trans-Arctic as it has an entry or arrival port along the NSR, or transitory, which means that it crosses two points outside the NSR (Laruelle, 2014, 174). The importance of this distinction lies in the fact that these two types of shipping need two different kinds of ships (Laruelle, 2014, 174). Transit shipping involves very large tonnage tankers in order to be profitable and invokes different commercial strategies and logistical challenges (Laruelle, 2014, 174).

The NSR is considered of utmost importance by Russia in order to achieve its geopolitical and economic objectives, both internationally and regionally. Indeed, the Decree on the Russian Arctic Policy of March 2020 stresses the fact that the NSR is 'the strategic backbone of Russia's economic future and vital to Arctic maritime shipping' (Meade, 2020). The decree defines the development of the NSR as 'a competitive national transport line of the Russian Federation in the global market' (Meade, 2020), which is one of the most important national priorities of Russia (President of the Russian Federation, 2020). Importantly, this document states that the development of the Arctic as a strategic resource base and its rational use to accelerate national economic growth are crucial goals of Russia (Meade, 2020). The economic development of the Arctic serves the geopolitical objective of Russia to keep its role of a great power at both the international and regional levels because its natural resources (especially energy) are key to developing and modernising the whole country. Therefore, the construction of infrastructure along the NSR is crucial. The decree states that Russia considers as essential the 'construction of a sufficient number of icebreaker, rescue, and auxiliary fleets with the capabilities necessary to ensure year-round, safe, uninterrupted, and cost-effective navigation in the waters of the NSR and other maritime transportation passages' (President of the Russian Federation 2020).

Nevertheless, travelling along the NSR poses a number of challenges. Climate change does not make navigation easier because, in spite of ice melting, especially in summer, ice does not disappear as icebergs will always be present making the danger of collision considerable, thus reducing the predictability of the journey (Laruelle, 2014, 176). Travel in an extreme climate is expensive. Straits have the tendency to accumulate large ice masses that may block the progress of vessels (Laruelle, 2014, 176). From a financial perspective, the administrative procedure of transiting the NSR is time-consuming and fees are required by Russia for chartering icebreakers and obtaining weather and ice reports in addition to the obligation to hire two Russian pilots to guide ships in the straits and pay for clean-up after accidents (Laruelle, 2014, 177). Moreover, the requisite insurance for the Arctic trip, which is among the most expensive in the world, as in the Antarctic, increases the costs (Laruelle, 2014, 177). From an environmental perspective, maritime traffic is likely to increase accidents as the case of two oil tankers belonging to the Murmansk Shipping Company demonstrates (Laruelle, 2014, 177). In 2010, they collided along the NSR, fortunately without causing too much damage, but the accident could have had more serious consequences (Laruelle, 2014, 177).

Second, the NSR is under the jurisdiction of Russia, which is one of the major powers regionally and internationally. Russia considers its sovereign rights over the NSR as vital to its geopolitical and economic interests, as the Basic Principles of the State Policy of the Russian Federation in the Arctic Zone Until 2035 (referred to as the Basic Principles in this book) clearly demonstrates. This document, which was approved by President Putin in 2020, updates the one adopted by previous President Dmitrij Medvedev in 2008. It is interesting to note that Russia adopted this document 'at a time [when] tensions between Russia and its Arctic neighbors are increasing and just ahead of Russia chairing the Arctic Council in 2021' (Meade, 2020; Klimenko, 2020). This document defines Russia's goals and necessary actions to develop its Arctic territory (Meade, 2020; Klimenko, 2020). In particular, it identifies six national interests, two of which are new if compared to the 2008 version (Meade, 2020; Klimenko, 2020). The two new national interests are: '1) to ensure Russia's sovereignty and territorial integrity and to guarantee high living standards; and 2) prosperity for people of the Russian Arctic zone' (Meade, 2020). The other four national interests are:

> 3) to preserve the Arctic as a world territory, with stable and mutually beneficial partnerships; 4) to develop the Russian Arctic as a strategic resource base and its rational use to accelerate national economic growth; 5) to develop the NSR as a competitive national transport line of the Russian Federation in the global market; 6) to protect the Arctic environment, the primordial homeland, and the traditional way of life of the indigenous minorities in the Russian Arctic.
>
> (Meade, 2020; Klimenko, 2020)

The first and the fifth national interests identified concern the NSR in particular. Although it was introduced in the 2020 document, the first national interest is in reality a continuation of Russia's strategy in the Arctic as it's Russia's long-term goal to enforce its sovereignty over Arctic territories and waters (Meade, 2020; Klimenko, 2020). This is one of the reasons why, for instance, Russia increased its military capabilities in the region (like all the other Arctic states, as discussed in Chapter 3) and demonstrates this force through air and navy patrols and military drills (Klimenko, 2020). The Basic Principles identify Russia's main military goal as the 'prevention of the use of military force against Russia, protection of its sovereignty and territorial integrity' (Meade, 2020). This goal aligns with 'Russia's claim that it exercises sovereign control over the NSR' (Meade, 2020).

Nevertheless, the NSR is a contested waterway as Russia claims sovereignty rights over it, while the US (supported by the EU) argues that it passes through international straits (Blunden, 2012). The NSR consists of maritime areas with different legal status, in most of which Russia enjoys sovereignty or sovereign rights as they are internal waters, territorial seas, or exclusive economic zones (EEZs), but the NSR also includes parts of the high seas that Article 87 of the United Nations Convention on the Law of the Sea (UNCLOS) defines as 'open to all states' (Todorov, 2017, 63; United Nations, 1982).

It is internationally recognised that the first document by which the Soviet Union exercised special rights to regulate navigation along the NSR is the 1971 Statute on the Administration of the Northern Sea Route Attached to the Ministry of the Maritime Fleet (Shibata et al., 2019, 190). In the 1990s, Russia issued other legal provisions to better regulate NSR navigation (Shibata et al., 2019, 190). The USSR Minister of Merchant Marine approved the Regulations for Navigation on the Seaways of the Northern Sea Route, which provided the legal framework for access to and navigation of the NSR for vessels of all states (Shibata et al., 2019, 192). A particularly interesting aspect of the regulations is the fact that it defines the NSR as the 'national transport route of the USSR, which is situated within the inland waters, territorial sea (territorial waters), or exclusive economic zone adjoining the USSR northern coast, and includes seaways suitable for guiding ships in ice' (Shibata et al., 2019, 192). This caused the opposition of the international community claiming that some of the Arctic high seas that the regulations consider as part of the NSR fell under USSR jurisdiction (Shibata et al., 2019, 192). In particular, the legal status of the NSR has been at the centre of a dispute between Russia and the US since the 1960s (Todorov, 2017, 62). In 1963, the US Coast Guard Cutter *Northwind* collected data in the Laptev Sea without prior permission from Soviet authorities, which led to a diplomatic incident between the two superpowers (Todorov, 2017, 62). In 1967, the US planned a navigation trip of the US Coast Guard icebreakers *Edisto* and *East Wind* in the waters off the coast of Novaya Zemlya and Severnaya Zemlya and in the Laptev Sea and the East Siberian Sea (Todorov, 2017, 62). However, severe ice conditions obliged the two icebreakers to pass through the Karsky Sea and to proceed towards the Vilkitsky Straits, causing protest by the Soviet Union that considered these actions as a violation of its regulations (Todorov, 2017, 63). As a consequence, the US cancelled the planned navigation (Todorov, 2017, 63). Over time, Russia has issued legislation aiming at affirming its sovereign rights over all areas of the NSR. For instance, in 1996 Russia adopted the Guide to Navigating through the Northern Sea Route, which served as a supplement for the 1990 Regulations, and the Regulations for Icebreaker and Pilot Guiding of Vessels Through the Northern Sea Route, which contained detailed regulations on the requirement for prior application to access the NSR (Shibata et al., 2019, 192).

However, the acceleration of climate change has pushed Russia to take the chance to 'make the NSR a potentially competitive commercial route of global significance' (Shibata et al., 2019, 195). In order to achieve this aim, Russia developed new legislation that significantly amended the previous laws (Shibata et al., 2019, 195). The 2013 new Rules of Navigation on the Water Area of the Northern Sea Route concerning icebreaker assistance and pilotage, which suspended the 1990 regulations on this matter, is an example (Shibata et al., 2019, 193). Very importantly, the 2013 amendments also consisted of a new definition of the NSR included in the Merchant Marine Code (Shibata et al., 2019, 193). In this regard, an interesting comparative study has been conducted on the definition of the NSR between the 1990 Regulations and the updated Merchant Marine Code (Shibata et al., 2019, 193; Zhang et al., 2015, 139). This study had two important results, both of which supported the idea that Russia 'has taken up an accommodating attitude towards international use of the NSR' (Shibata et al., 2019, 194; Zhang et al., 2015, 139). The first finding is that the new definition of the eastern boundary of the NSR (that was confined within the Line of Maritime Demarcation with the US and Cape Dezhnev parallel to the Bering Strait) has avoided disputes with the US in the East (Shibata et al., 2019, 194; Zhang et al., 2015, 139). The second finding concerns the northern boundary of the NSR, which eliminated the ambiguity of the 1990 Regulation (that allowed Russia to exercise its jurisdiction beyond the EEZ in order to organise NSR navigation) by acknowledging the northern boundary to coincide with that of Russia's Arctic EEZ (Shibata et al., 2019, 194; Zhang et al., 2015, 139).

Furthermore, another interesting study comparing the 1990 Regulations and the 2013 Rules has revealed that another significant change concerns the regulations on icebreaker assistance (Shibata et al., 2019, 194; Zhang et al., 2015, 139). More specifically, differently from the 1990 Regulations, which requested arbitrary and mandatory icebreaker guiding, the 2013 Rules had no such wording and included an annex on the 'criteria of the admission of ships to the NSR' (Shibata et al., 2019, 194; Zhang et al., 2015, 139).

These findings demonstrate a change in Russia's strategy towards the Arctic in the 2000s. Russia was prone to cooperate for geopolitical and economic interests and its cooperative attitude was 'indicative of Russia's departure from the widespread stereotype as a revisionist power in the high north' (Shibata et al., 2019, 197). Russia has been a member of the AC since its establishment in 1996 and played a crucial role together with Canada in the International Maritime Organisation's (IMO) development of the Polar Code, which aims to enhance the safety of ships navigating in polar waters and the protection of the polar marine environment, which is becoming increasingly necessary due to climate change. It was developed by the IMO and entered into force in 2017. It is an add-on to the International Convention for the Safety of Life at Sea (SOLAS) and the International Convention for the Prevention of Pollution from Ships (MARPOL) (Bognar-Lahr, 2020, 3), which were also adopted by the IMO.

Canada and Russia dominated the discussions about the Polar Code as they are the states that have the longest coasts facing the Arctic and that control two crucial shipping routes in the region, namely the NWP (Canada) and the NSR (Russia). For this reason, Russia and Canada were the two states with the strongest interests in trying to regulate the relationship between the Polar Code and Article 234 of UNCLOS, which was the legal basis to nationally regulate shipping in the Arctic (Bognar-Lahr, 2020, 3). Article 234 is also called the 'Arctic exception' because it regulates navigation on ice-covered areas.[2] It stipulates that

> Coastal States have the right to adopt and enforce non-discriminatory laws and regulations for the prevention, reduction and control of marine pollution from vessels in ice-covered areas within the limits of the exclusive economic zone [that extends to 200 nautical miles from the baseline, Article 57 of UNCLOS], where particularly severe climatic conditions and the presence of ice covering such areas for most of the year create obstructions or exceptional hazards to navigation, and pollution of the marine environment could cause major harm to or irreversible disturbance of the ecological balance. Such laws and regulations shall have due regard to navigation and the protection and preservation of the marine environment based on the best available scientific evidence.
>
> (United Nations, 1982)

Both Canada and Russia relied upon Article 234 to support national regulations for Arctic shipping that might have been impacted by the International Code for Ships Operating in Polar Waters (commonly called the Polar Code) (Bognar-Lahr, 2020, 4). They also tried to shape the content of the new legal provision in such a way that it mirrored their respective national regulations especially in relation to the operational and access limitation of ships and control by coastal states (Bognar-Lahr, 2020, 4). They particularly focused their arguments on the rights of coastal states envisaged by Article 234 (Bognar-Lahr, 2020, 4). One difference between them was that while Russia explicitly referred to Article 234, Canada spoke more generally of international law applicable to the Arctic (Bognar-Lahr, 2020, 4).

Additionally, Canada and Russia had different positions on and approaches to the Polar Code (Bognar-Lahr, 2020, 4). This was mainly due to their differences in terms of capabilities and economic realities as well as geopolitical positions (Bognar-Lahr, 2020, 4). In terms of capabilities and economic realities, an example of the divergences between the two states is their different position on the oil discharge ban (Bognar-Lahr, 2020, 4). While Canada supported a complete prohibition of oil and oily mixture discharges in the Polar Code, Russia contrasted it because those requirements were already applicable in the International Convention for the Prevention of Pollution from Ships's (MARPOL) special areas in which the Arctic was not included (Bognar-Lahr, 2020, 4). Additionally, Russia stressed that special areas require adequate and specific port reception facilities for vessel-sources waste that it considers 'time consuming' (Bognar-Lahr, 2020, 4). This difference

2 It has been described as 'a textbook example of finding a compromise in international treaty negotiations' as it was the result of multilateral and bilateral negotiations between Canada, the Soviet Union, and the US during the UNCLOS III (the third UNCLOS conference was held between 1973 and 1982, the second one in 1960, and the first one in 1958) (Bartenstein, 2011, 23).

was mainly due to the fact that in Russia the development of the Arctic has required more infrastructure than in Canada, which would have required huge economic investment as most of them came from Soviet times (Bognar-Lahr, 2020, 4).

Furthermore, another element that has made the two positions different is geopolitics. Canada was more committed than Russia to ensuring that as much international legal bases was added to the measures adopted to regulate its Arctic waters (Bognar-Lahr, 2020, 4). By contrast, Russia, which is a great power, has a different attitude towards international law and multilateralism (Bognar-Lahr, 2020, 6). Although it recognises the necessity of multilateral cooperation allowing participation in decision-making processes, Russia prefers unilateralism especially when it serves its national interests and is more likely to disregard challenges to its actions and regulations. Additionally, Canada's and Russia's understanding of sovereignty is very different. Russia's sovereignty in the Arctic is instead based on strategic military considerations and on the control of the NSR that it defines as a 'national transportation route' (Bognar-Lahr, 2020, 8). The strategic military interests of Russia are not affected by the Polar Code because it does not apply to warships but control over the Arctic waters could be influenced by it because it applies to icebreakers (Bognar-Lahr, 2020, 8). Instead, Canada understands sovereignty as very much linked to environmental protection (Bognar-Lahr, 2020, 8). This is clearly demonstrated by two cases that are strictly intertwined, namely the 1970 Arctic Water Pollution Protection Act (AWPPA) and the NWP (that is constituted of a series of passageways through the waters of the Canadian Arctic Archipelago, a group of Canadian islands north of the Canadian mainland connecting the Atlantic and Pacific Oceans). In 1968, the US tanker the *SS Manhattan* crossed the NWP without Canadian permission with the aim to test the commercial feasibility of a shipping route passing through the NWP to transport oil discovered in the area of Prudhoe Bay (Alaska) by tankers instead of by pipelines (Solski, 2021, 4). During the voyage, the tanker had to be accompanied by US and Canadian icebreakers that freed it from ice several times. Additionally, the tanker also suffered some structural damage (Solski, 2021, 4). The *SS Manhattan* case soon became the subject of many domestic debates in Canada over the necessity of protecting the waters of the NWP from the unauthorised passage of foreign vessels (Solski, 2021, 4). However, the real focus of domestic debates were the possible challenges posed to Canadian sovereignty over the NWP rather than on environmental ones although the *SS Manhattan* case was officially downplayed because it was not a threat to Canadian sovereignty (Solski, 2021, 5). The environmental concerns became more important only one year later in 1969 when the government highlighted the importance of protecting the Arctic environment from human activity (Solski, 2021, 6). At the same time, stressing the environmental concerns turned out to be a more successful strategy than openly claiming sovereignty rights (Solski, 2021, 6). The AWPPA reflects this reasoning. While the official aim of the AWPPA is to protect the waters under its sovereignty, Canada's real goal was to defend its control over the NWP. The AWPPA, which introduced a complete ban on the discharge of waste in Arctic waters (McRae and Goundrey, 1982, 211), extended the jurisdiction of Canada over foreign vessels to an area of 100 kilometres from land and gave it the right to regulate navigation (McRae and Goundrey, 1982, 211; Solski, 2021, 7). In this context, the extension of sovereignty is an expression of Canada's geopolitical interests in controlling the NWP, which also has strong economic value because it is an important commercial shipping route in the Arctic. It is indeed a crucial way of transporting energy resources. Consequently, control over shipping routes has both geopolitical and economic significance. Therefore, sovereignty over shipping routes increases the power of a state ensuring its ability of influence geopolitical dynamics regionally and eventually internationally.

Furthermore, the NWP raises a number of environmental and legal concerns, mirroring those of the NSR. Indeed, in both cases there is a high risk of increasing pollution and environmental disasters especially because of increasing traffic, as well as sovereignty issues at stake. In fact, Canada has claimed for a long time that the NWP belongs to its internal territorial waters on the basis of two arguments. First, legal arguments stemming from decades-old cases settled by the International Court of Justice (ICJ) (Steinfield, 2020). A good example is the so-called Fisheries Case of 1951, in which the ICJ decided that 'Norway had the right to draw straight baselines to encase a large region of its northern waters and designate them as Norwegian waters despite this not being the standard procedure of drawing coastal baselines' (Burke, 2018). By taking this ruling into account, Canada argues that, like Norway, 'it too has the right to implement straight baselines, which it did in 1985, around the outer limit of the Arctic Archipelago making waters landward of these baselines internal waters' (Burke, 2018). Second, a long history of native Inuit use of the waters. According to Carl Söderbergh, Director of Policy and Communications at Minority Rights Group International, 'lacing the Northwest Passage outside national jurisdiction risks leading to a free-for-all, unless a proper regulatory framework is put in place' (Fuller, 2020). He also argues that considering the waters around the Arctic Archipelago as international also 'risks weakening current indigenous governance structures, as these are generally operating within national legal frameworks and with national governments answerable to them' (Fuller, 2020).

The NWP is at the centre of controversy between Canada and its historical ally, the US. During the Cold War, given the military alliance between them, the NWP had become a geostrategically important route as it was used as a launching point for American nuclear submarines and a passage for American merchant ships, warships, and submarines with no contentions (Hong, 2020, 102). Nevertheless, the US have always countered Canada's claim that the NWP was entirely under its jurisdiction on the basis of its interpretation of UNCLOS, a treaty that it accepts as international law but that it has never ratified (Steinfield, 2020). On the basis of this interpretation, the US sees the NWP as an international strait (a view shared by the EU), which is a designation usually only used in cases where there is a large volume of traffic transiting the strait (Steinfield, 2020). In 1988, Canada and the US stipulated the Canada–US Arctic Cooperation Agreement in 1988, with which the two parties declared to maintain their respective positions on the legal status of the NWP (meaning that they agreed to disagree on the issue) and agreed that the US would ask Canada for permission to transit in the region (Government of Canada,

2024; Fuller, 2020). Also, they recognised 'that it is desirable to cooperate in order to advance their shared interests in Arctic development and security' and agreed 'to take advantage of their icebreaker navigation to develop and share research information, in accordance with generally accepted principles of international law, in order to advance their understanding of the marine environment of the area' (Government of Canada, 2024). This agreement made the dispute 'dormant' and, more recently, renewed international interest in the NWP due to the economic opportunities opened up by climate change has made it clear that the dispute is not bilateral anymore (Burke, 2018). A clear example of this is the statement contained in China's 2018 Arctic Policy, according to which

> China maintains that the management of the Arctic shipping routes should be conducted in accordance with treaties including the UNCLOS and general international law and that the freedom of navigation enjoyed by all countries in accordance with the law and their rights to use the Arctic shipping routes should be ensured.
>
> (University of Alaska Fairbanks, 2018)

Thus, China holds the same position both on the NWP and the NSR (as well as the TR), which is of utmost importance for its geopolitical and economic interests especially in relation to its Polar Silk Road (PSR), initiated in 2013 as part of its broader Belt and Road Initiative (BRI), which is a very ambitious infrastructure project launched in 2013 by President Xi Jinping (McBride et al., 2023). Originally, the BRI was devised to link East Asia and Europe through physical infrastructure, but in the last decade it has expanded to include Africa, Oceania, and Latin America, thus 'significantly broadening China's economic and political influence' (McBride et al., 2023). Moreover, China's initial plan was called the One Belt, One Road initiative and constituted two parts, namely the overland Silk Road Economic Belt and the Maritime Silk Road, which later became the BRI (McBride et al., 2023). Some analysts consider the BRI as an 'unsettling extension of China's rising power', thus leading some states to oppose to it (McBride et al., 2023). This is the case of the US, for instance, raising 'the concern that the BRI could be a Trojan horse for China-led regional development and military expansion' (McBride et al., 2023). Currently, the BRI includes 147 states that have already signed the project or have expressed their willingness to participate in it, thus accounting for two-thirds of the world's population and 40% of global GDP (McBride et al., 2023). The BRI would create a vast network of railways, energy pipelines, and highways, and would expand both westward through the mountainous former Soviet republics and southward, to Pakistan, India, and the rest of Southeast Asia (McBride, 2023). In so doing, China would expand the international use of Chinese currency, the Renminbi, and 'break the bottleneck in Asian connectivity', as President Xi Jinping has declared (McBride, 2023). Consequently, it is clear that strong geopolitical and economic interests are the engine of the BRI and the PSR is functional to the achievement of the overall aim of the project to shape a more assertive China by promoting 'unity at home and influence abroad' (McBride et al., 2023; Economy, 2014).

The PSR is commonly considered a joint Russian–Chinese initiative because it was jointly announced and defined in 2017 by President Xi Jinping and President Vladimir Putin as a potential area of cooperation between Russia and China (Lamazhapov et al., 2023). In reality, the PSR originated from a Russian invitation to China to get more involved in Arctic shipping. More specifically, during the Belt and Road Forum held in Beijing in May 2017, President Putin expressed his hope that 'China will utilize Arctic shipping routes and connect them to the Belt and Road' (Hong, 2020, 128). Two months later, during a visit of the Chinese President to Moscow, the two Presidents announced that Russia and China would 'launch cooperation on Arctic shipping routes and jointly develop a Polar Silk Road' (Hong, 2020, 128). The same year, Vice Prime Minister Dmitrij Medvedev reiterated the two leaders' desire to develop Arctic shipping routes and the Polar Silk Road (Hong, 2020, 128). Since then, the term 'Polar Silk Road' has been included in China's Arctic White Paper and used by the two leaders (Hong, 2020, 128).

Furthermore, the PSR should be seen as an expression of the pragmatism that characterises the strategic partnership between Russia and China. Indeed, Dr Sergey Sukhankin, senior fellow at The Jamestown Foundation and an advisor at Gulf State Analytics (Washington, DC), argues that Russia's approach to the PSR is essentially based on three premises (Hong, 2020, 131; Sukhankin, 2018). First, it sees China's involvement as 'a remedy for [the] long-lasting structural problems' that it faces in the High North bringing new economic opportunities (e.g. creation of new work sites and large infrastructure projects) contributing to the socioeconomic development of the Russian Arctic (Hong, 2020, 131; Sukhankin, 2018). Second, cooperating with Russia is the only opportunity that Chinese vessels have to travel to and from Europe given the bad relations it has with the US and Canada due to the war in Ukraine (Hong, 2020, 131; Sukhankin, 2018). Third, China will not be able to 'sideline' Russia not only because Russia has a dominant position in the Arctic but also because of the nature of their relations (Hong, 2020, 131; Sukhankin, 2018).

Nevertheless, Dr Sukhankin questions Russia's assumptions for four reasons. First, China does not consider Russia its only potential partner in the Arctic because it considers its involvement in Arctic affairs as a multilateral issue, not a bilateral one (Hong, 2020, 131; Sukhankin, 2018). Indeed, China's White Paper states that

> China will work with all other countries to build a community with a shared future for mankind in the Arctic region. While pursuing its own interests, China will pay due regard to the interests of other countries and the broader international community, bear in mind the importance of the protection and development of the Arctic, and of keeping in proper balance its current and long-term interests, so as to promote the sustainable development of the Arctic.
>
> (The State Council of the People's Republic of China, 2018)

Second, China's interest is to maintain ties with all Arctic states through multinational platforms for dialogue and cooperation (Hong, 2020, 131; Sukhankin, 2018). Third, relations between Russia and China are characterised by a balance between competition and cooperation 'lingering mistrust on both sides, be it in Central Asia, the Russian Far East or the Arctic', and are based more on mutual economic benefits than on a strategic pact (Hong, 2020, 131; Sukhankin, 2018). Four, Russia will always be cautious about China's ambitions in the Arctic because it is a coastal state that is keen to protect its sovereign rights in the region (Hong, 2020, 131; Sukhankin, 2018).

At the same time, China's cooperation with Russia both internationally and in the Arctic is an important component of the BRI because the use of the NSR for the realisation of the PSR is functional to its national strategy, inspired by the ideas of the 'Chinese dream' (that can be summarised as being a strong nation) and the 'Belt and Road'. As Mariia Kobzeva, researcher at the Arctic University of Norway argues,

> according to the 18th Party Congress' decisions, China should take advantage of the 'period of strategic opportunities', achieve economic prosperity and globally play the role of 'major responsible country'.[8] This message applies to all significant policy directions, including the Arctic, and is reflected in the theses of the White Paper.
>
> (Kobzeva, 2019, 96)

Furthermore, another factor that has determined the rapprochement between Russia and China is the war in Ukraine that has, in fact, pushed Russia to make the NSR 'turn to the East', especially to China (and India) 'to get its Arctic energy projects off the ground' (Eiterjord, 2022). Indeed, the NSR 'is solidifying into an energy corridor' (Eiterjord, 2022). For instance, in 2020, 64% of the total cargo volume transported on the NSR came from the Yamal liquid natural gas (LNG) project located along the NSR and another 20% of oil exports came from the nearby Novoportovskoye oil field, exported through the Arctic Gate terminal (Eiterjord, 2022). Generally speaking, the driver for Arctic transit shipping traffic on the NSR is traffic between Russia and China, as a report by the Centre for High North Logistics shows (Humpert, 2024). In particular, crude oil, coal, and iron are transported from Russia to China while container shipping travels in both directions (Humpert, 2024). During the first two months of the 2024 summer and autumn navigation season, 30 transit voyages carrying around 1.3 million tons of cargo travelled from Russia to China along the NSR, as Norway's Centre for High North Logistics has reported (Humpert, 2024). In addition, Russia's state nuclear agency, Rosatom, and China's, Hainan Yangpu Newnew Shipping Co Ltd, signed an agreement at the annual St Petersburg International Economic Forum (SPIEF-2024) held on 6th June 2024 with the aim to establish a year-round container shipping line along the NSR (Riviera News, 2024). This agreement is part of the Russian strategy to find alternative shipping routes, especially in light of Western sanctions imposed on Russia due to the war in Ukraine (Riviera News,

2024). Rosatom's special representative for Arctic development, Vladimir Panov, said that 'Russia expects a record transit cargo flow along the NSR of up to 3M tonnes in 2024' (Riviera News, 2024).

Moreover, the case of the TSR is different from that of the NSR and NWP because it is still frozen and it is not at the centre of any territorial dispute. It stretches from the Atlantic to the Pacific Ocean from the centre of the Arctic Ocean and is shorter and deeper than the other two Arctic routes. Scientific models forecast an ice-free Central Arctic Ocean (CAO) at least in summer by the mid-21st century thus making the TSR navigable offering a third and faster Arctic shipping route (Bennett et al., 2020, 2). As Bennett et al. (2020a) argue, 'with its direct routing, deeper bathymetry, and lack of Russian tariffs and jurisdiction, the TSR may eventually attract Europe-Asia transit shipping away from the NSR'. Nevertheless, they also point out that 'the TSR's ability to compete with the NSR [...] faces several obstacles' (Bennett et al., 2020a, 164). More specifically, the potential of the TSR's container shipping remains limited by the lack of intermediate markets (Bennett et al., 2020a). Also, the fact that the TSR is ice-covered throughout most of the year poses a problem for 'just-in-time container shipping' (Bennett et al., 2020a, 164). Moreover, due to the lack of hydrographical knowledge about the TSR and its unpredictability, insurance costs will be higher than for the NSR and NWP, at least in the near term (Bennett et al., 2020a, 164). Another problem concerns the fact that the TSR crosses the CAO without passing any natural resource extraction sites or communities requiring resupply with the exception of the Bering and Fram Strait entrances (Bennett et al., 2020a, 164). By contrast, Arctic shipping is mainly destinational as it involves the transportation of cargo to Arctic locations and resources out of the region, rather than transit or using Arctic waters to transport cargo from one Arctic port to another (Bennett et al., 2020a, 165).

From a legal perspective, the TSR, which crosses the high seas, is regulated by UNCLOS. In particular, Article 87 allows all states to use the high seas for free navigation, overflight, laying submarine cables and pipelines, the construction of artificial islands and other installations permitted under international law, and conducting scientific research (United Nations, 1982). The TSR began being used only in the second half of the 20th century for occasional military, scientific, and, more recently, tourist purposes (Bennett et al., 2020a, 162). Ice-melting might allow also fishing, which is also envisaged by Article 87, but the 2018 Central Arctic Ocean Fisheries Agreement forbids fishing there (Bennett et al., 2020a, 165). Also, the TSR passes through the Bering Strait, which is the only marine gateway between the icy Arctic and the Pacific Ocean (Ocean Conservancy, 2024). Here shipping regulations are more complex (Bennett et al., 2020a, 171). Generally speaking, it is used for international navigation, 'defined as connecting one part of the high seas or a state's Exclusive Economic Zone (EEZ), which extends up to 200 nautical miles out from a country's baseline, with another part of the high seas or an EEZ' (Bennett et al., 2020a, 171). Thus, states enjoy the right to transit passage according to Article 37 of UNCLOS (Bennett et al., 2020a, 171). The Bering Strait has two navigational channels passing through the territorial seas of Russia and the US (Bennett et al., 2020a, 171). As Article 42 of UNCLOS allows states bordering straits to 'adopt laws and regulations relating to transit passage through straits'[3] in relation to maritime traffic and pollution prevention (United Nations, 1982), vessels crossing the US and Russian waters may be subject to different regulations (Bennett et al., 2020a, 171). The war in Ukraine has determined a sharp increase in transport of Russian oil to China through the Bering Strait jeopardising the fish and wildlife harvests of the isolated villages on the American side of the border (Herz, 2023). Increased traffic increases the risk of oil spill that in the Arctic would be particularly catastrophic given the fragility of the environment. Consequently, the livelihood of the people living in the villages located in the area of the Bering Strait would be dramatically damaged given that foods harvested from the ocean (e.g., fish, whales, seals, walrus) are essential for subsistence (Herz, 2023). Indeed, Ben Pungowiyi, the president of the tribal government in the 800-person village of Savoonga, said in an interview that Bering Sea food is the main source of food security for the people living there (Herz, 2023).

Furthermore, another potential legal issue concerning the TSR is if and how climate change might affect the applicability of Article 234, which allows coastal states 'to adopt and enforce non-discriminatory laws and regulations for the prevention, reduction and control of marine pollution from vessels' in areas that are covered by ice for most of the year within their EEZ (Bennett et al., 2020a). In case Article 234 will continue being applied, ships navigating along the TSR would have to adhere to various environmental regulations depending on the EEZ (Bennett et al., 2020a). Moreover, the Polar Code, which also applies to the TSR and comprises a series of amendments to existing IMO conventions including the International Convention on the Safety of Life at Sea (SOLAS – signed in 1974 and ratified in 1988) and the Convention for the Prevention of Pollution from Ships (MARPOL – signed in 1973 and ratified in 1978), 'underscores the standardization and formalization of polar shipping and the expansion of the sector's "pluralistic governance" involving both Arctic coastal/port states and flag states' (Bennett et al., 2020a).

From a geopolitical perspective, it is interesting to note that, as Bennett et al. (2020a) argue, Russia 'might attempt to influence regulation of the TSR or, in what would be a highly controversial move, consider enforcing national transit regulations in the high seas north of their EEZ through which parts of the route run' (Bennett et al., 2020a). In fact, the TSR is situated farther north than the northernmost extent of the NSR, which Russian federal law considers as falling entirely within the Russian EEZ, territorial waters, and internal waters (Bennett et al., 2020a). Also, Russia is very well positioned to offer expertise and services along the NSR given its well-established legal framework developed for the NSR and its

3 In particular, Article 42 'adopt laws and regulations relating to transit passage through straits' in respect of the safety of navigation and the regulation of maritime traffic; of the prevention, reduction and control of pollution; the prevention of fishing in respect of vessels; and the loading or unloading of any commodity, currency, or person in contravention of the customs, fiscal, immigration, or sanitary laws and regulations of states bordering straits (United Nations, 1982).

fleet of icebreakers (Bennett et al., 2020a). Russia owns the only nuclear icebreaker fleet in the world, which it has built to meet maritime transportation requirements in the Arctic through modern nuclear technology (Nadig, 2023). Also, Russia's icebreaker fleet is the largest in the world with around 30 diesel-powered icebreakers, four nuclear-powered icebreakers, and the largest and currently the only nuclear-powered cargo ship, the *Sevmorput* LASH carrier (as of 2019) (Investment Portal of the Arctic Zone of the Russian Federation, 2020). In 2023, Russia's Rosatom signed contracts for two new icebreakers (Humpert, 2023). The main tasks of icebreakers are to ensure continuous passability of the NSR and to enable the development of natural resources of the Arctic (Investment Portal of the Arctic Zone of the Russian Federation, 2020). Over the last few years, the Russian shipbuilding industry has been growing, as Alexey Rakhmanov, president of Russia's United Shipbuilding Corporation, argued in 2023 (Nadig, 2023). He added that 'this has especially happened in specific market segments, such as research vessels and nuclear-powered icebreakers, and niches such as the ice-resistant, self-propelled research platform North Pole' (Nadig, 2023).

By contrast, the US does not own a strong fleet of icebreakers. The US Coast Guard has postponed the completion of its first new icebreaker in 25 years by four years (Humpert, 2023). However, in a joint statement made during a NATO summit in Washington in July 2024, the US, Canada, and Finland announced a trilateral pact to build icebreakers for the Arctic region (Brewster, 2024). The agreement also includes the sharing of expertise, information, and capabilities and is open to the participation of other states and stipulates that the utility of icebreakers is not limited to the Far North (Brewster, 2024). The joint statement said that 'this partnership will strengthen the shipbuilding industries in each nation with the goal of creating good-paying jobs in shipyards, marine equipment manufacturers and many other related services across all three countries' (Brewster, 2024).

Building new icebreakers has not only an economic value but also a geopolitical one. In a background briefing in Washington, a senior American security official said that building new icebreakers 'is a strategic imperative' and that

> this will help build out our industrial capacity but also provide benefits to our allies, consistent with the message you've been hearing this week at the NATO summit. There's also a signalling benefit. The ice pact will reinforce the message to Russia and China that the United States and its allies intend to be present in the polar regions.
>
> (Brewster, 2024)

Thus, the US and its NATO allies are in a weaker position compared to Russia when it comes to Arctic navigation. Indeed, in a press release, the Davie Shipyard, based in Lévis, Quebec, said that 'while adversaries' shipbuilding industries operate on an effective war footing, Western allies markedly lack sufficient icebreakers and other specialized ships. No single nation can solve this challenge alone, but trusted allies with common goals and advanced shipbuilding can' (Brewster, 2024). Therefore, building new icebreakers is a challenge that is costly and time-consuming but that it is necessary to face. For instance, in January 2024, the US Coast Guard warned the government that it needs new icebreakers as soon as possible and that it is necessary to build between eight and ten new icebreakers to replace its aging fleet (Brewster, 2024). This is even more urgent since China is increasing its physical presence in the Arctic. In fact, in summer 2024 China sent three icebreakers to the Arctic, which is 'a clear signal' that Beijing is seriously 'pursuing its great power ambitions commercially, scientifically, diplomatically and militarily in the polar regions' (Grady, 2024). Additionally, China will begin the construction of a fourth icebreaker in 2025 (Grady, 2024). In an interview to Chinese newspaper *Global Times* (that is pro-government), the ship's designer said that when the icebreaker enters into operation 'China will have the ability to operate year-round in polar environments for in-depth scientific research missions and obtain the capabilities of full-area and all-time entry' (Grady, 2024).

In addition to this, in a shipping forum held in Saint Petersburg in 2024, China announced together with Russia a plan to build high ice-class containerships to begin year-round shipments on the NSR (Humpert, 2024a). The vessels will be deployed on the Arctic Express route connecting the Chinese ports of Shanghai and Ningbo with those of St. Petersburg and Arkhangelsk in Russia (Humpert, 2024a).

In conclusion, the geopolitical importance of the Arctic shipping routes has been increasing over the last few decades both at the regional and international level. At the moment, this is true for the NSR and the NWP, but it is expected that the TSR will challenge the geopolitical importance of the other two shipping routes when it becomes navigable.

Geopolitics of the Arctic ports

Ports play a key role as they are crucial transportation hubs facilitating trade and logistics and are at 'the core of the Arctic development' (Lasserre and Faury, 2020, 162; Ragner, 2000). As Frédéric Lasserre, professor in the Geography Department at Laval University, and Olivier Faury, assistant professor at EM Normandie in Le Havre (France), argue, 'ports are one of the main pillars of Arctic development, since they serve the triple purpose of safety, economic development and maintenance of national sovereignty' (Lasserre and Faury, 2020, 161). In fact, ports provide a refuge for vessels in times of need, facilitate cargo exports and the supply of goods to the population, and help states maintain their sovereignty over disputed areas (Lasserre and Faury, 2020, 162). Consequently, ports have a strong geopolitical value because 'they are the nodes that enable a country to exert economic and political influence beyond its territory' (Noorali et al., 2022). Indeed, ports are geopolitical and economic tools in the globalisation of international trade (Lasserre and Faury, 2020, 162).

Nevertheless, Lasserre and Faury point out that 'their [of ports] low number and density has not secured navigation and has not provided a place for vessels damaged by the ice' and that the remoteness of the location of natural resources like oil, gas, and minerals makes the modernisation, maintenance, building, and profitability of ports a challenge (Lasserre and Faury, 2020, 162). The Arctic presents a variety of ports depending on regional diversity due to differences in population density, climate conditions, economic development, and geography constraints (Lasserre and Faury, 2020; Gritsenko and Kiiski, 2016, 145). Nordregio, a leading Nordic research institute within the broad research fields of regional development, policy, and planning, has conducted a study on the Arctic ports taking as a point of departure the World Port Index's (WPI) database published by the US National Geospatial-Intelligence Agency, which provides the ports' location and physical characteristics as well as the facilities and services offered by major ports and terminals worldwide (Nordregio, 2019). The WPI includes 350 ports in the Arctic (Nordregio, 2019). Nordregio has categorised the ports by size and ice conditions by using several factors, including area, facilities, and wharf space (Nordregio, 2019). Based on this classification, Nordregio has found that the port of Murmansk is the only large port in the Arctic, several others are medium sized, and almost 200 ports in the Arctic are ice-free year-round (Nordregio, 2019).

Furthermore, different from what happens in the temperate maritime areas, in the Arctic region deepwater ports, places of refuge, marine salvage, adequate port reception facilities for ship-generated waste, and towing services are rarely available (Arctic Knowledge Hub, 2009). The availability of infrastructure, which strongly influences the level of risk associated with transiting a particular waterway, is strongly linked to the levels of marine insurance rates (Arctic Knowledge Hub, 2009). Another crucial factor is remoteness, which is related to the geography of the Arctic and 'has a negative impact on the building and maintenance cost of port infrastructures', thus questioning the profitability of certain ports and the implementation of infrastructures (Lasserre and Faury, 2020, 163).

Also, deepwater ports are crucial in the global supply chain because they facilitate the movement of food and cargo between land and sea transport (Hamburg Port Consulting, 2024). In the Arctic, there are essentially no deepwater ports along the North Slope of Alaska or throughout the Canadian Archipelago, except for that of Tuktoyaktuk (Canada), while there are few deepwater ports in US and Russian waters near the Bering Strait (Arctic Knowledge Hub, 2009). More specifically, on the US side of the Bering Strait there is Dutch Harbor, while on the Russian side there are the ports of Provideniya, Egvekinot, Anadyr, and Beringovsky (Arctic Knowledge Hub, 2009). Moreover, the US is developing its first deepwater Arctic port in Nome that could support US Coast Guard operations in the area (Herz, 2023). By contrast, there are a number of deepwater ports along the west coast of Greenland (Arctic Knowledge Hub, 2009). In Canada, the Port of Churchill is the only northern deepwater seaport with well sheltered, along-side berthing facilities (Arctic Knowledge Hub, 2009). The Port of Churchill forms the so-called 'Arctic Bridge' previously mentioned, together with the Murmansk port, because 'it requires sea and rail systems to complete the transport of goods to North American destinations' (Arctic Knowledge Hub, 2009). The use of icebreakers could significantly lengthen the shipping season that goes from mid-July to the beginning of November (Arctic Knowledge Hub, 2009). Another significant port in the eastern Canadian Arctic is Iqaluit that 'features some of the highest tides on the planet as well as one of the largest tidal ranges in existence' (Arctic Knowledge Hub, 2009).

Here ships have to anchor and use barges to land their cargo (Arctic Knowledge Hub, 2009).

If the ports' facilities along the NSR and the NWP are compared, it is clear that there are few deepwater ports along the NWP, which is a limiting factor in the development of the route (Eger, 2010). Nevertheless, in spite of several obstacles related to trans-Arctic shipping in the near future (e.g., ice conditions, refuge, seasonality, geographical complexity, draft restrictions, choke points, insurance limitations, and other costs), it is expected that there will be an increase in the shipping sector along the NWP in the near future, but the shipping will be to destinations in the Arctic and intra-Arctic and mostly resource based (Eger, 2010). A significant element that will contribute to the NWP is the increasing Arctic population and increasing demand for consumer goods, community construction, and industrial shipments (Eger, 2010). Consequently, these factors imply significant port improvements (Eger, 2010). This is why Canada has built a deep sea port in Iqaluit, in the Nunavut region, which is rich in gold, diamonds, iron ore, uranium, rare earth materials, natural gas, and oil (Eger, 2010). The Iqaluit Deep Sea Port Project was completed in September 2022 (Wenger, 2022). On that occasion, the Minister of Intergovernmental Affairs, Infrastructure, and Communities said that 'safe and efficient marine transportation is critical for the North's economic and social development – and that is exactly what the Iqaluit Deep Sea Port will deliver' (Wenger, 2022). Iqaluit's people had wanted a port since the 1970s, when the first project was discussed, because the previous solution with barges was complex, costly, and dangerous (Wenger, 2022).

Additionally, another Arctic state that is investing in the development of its ports is Iceland. In 2019, the Icelandic consulting company ELFA and the communities of Vopnafjarðarhreppur and Langanesbyggð partnered with the German port operator Bremenport to create the Finnafjord Port Development Company (Humpert, 2019). The project envisaged the construction of a deep-water port in Finnafjord in northeastern Iceland close to the community of Langanesbyggð, an associated industrial park, and the connection of the new infrastructure to road networks and supply of electricity and water (Humpert, 2019). The very aim of the project is twofold. On the one hand, it aims to serve as a transit hub for traffic entering and exiting Russia's NSR, while on the other one, it aims to serve as a search and rescue base as traffic volume throughout the region increases (Humpert, 2019). Elia Peturson, mayor of Langanesbyggð, argued that they 'have worked more than a decade towards this milestone. This port will become a new gateway to the world and create new opportunities for north-eastern Iceland' (Humpert, 2019). Þór Steinarsson, mayor of Vopnafjarðarhreppur, agreed with this view and considered the Finnafjord project as an essential economic step for Iceland (Humpert, 2019). Indeed, the construction of this port has geopolitical and economic implications for Iceland as its relevance as a shipping hub in the Arctic would increase. However, Iceland is not the only state that wants a port that could serve as a potential shipping hub in the region. For instance, Russian company Novatek announced the creation of a regional hub for the trans-shipment of LNG produced on the Yamal Peninsula in the subarctic port of Bechevinka in the Kamchatka Peninsula in eastern Russia (Lasserre and Faury, 2020, 167). Moreover, Norway has successfully managed to create a trans-shipment hub in a Norwegian fjord managed by Tschudi, the owner of the Port of Kirkenes (Lasserre and Faury, 2020, 167).

Moreover, a study on the Arctic ports conducted by Professor Lasserre and Assistant Professor Faury has identified three groups of ports. One group is constituted of ports focused on the export of raw materials, managed by both state and private stakeholders like the port of Sabetta that was constructed from scratch to export the products of the LNG plant located in the Yamal Peninsula (Lasserre and Faury, 2020). Another group of ports supplies local communities with goods necessary for their survival (Lasserre and Faury, 2020). Finally, a third group includes regional hubs with the aim to 'transship the cargo via a shuttle to a bigger vessel that will reach the final consumer' (Lasserre and Faury, 2020). These ports are located in the Arctic or at its frontier and links smaller ports within the region with foreign ports (Lasserre and Faury, 2020). The Murmansk Commercial Seaport is the only existing case of this kind (Lasserre and Faury, 2020). It is located on the eastern shore of Kola Bay in the Barents Sea and is ice-free on a yearly basis (Lasserre and Faury, 2020). It is the world's largest port located north of the polar circle and the main home of Russia's icebreaker fleet (Grid Arendal, 2023). The Murmansk Commercial Seaport is located in the Murmansk Oblast, which is the biggest Arctic shipping hub according to statistics (Arctic Portal, 2023). Additionally, it has geopolitical significance because it is important for oil and gas transport from northwest Russian Arctic fields as it is strategically located near natural resources including oil, gas, and minerals as well as railroads, pipelines, and roads (Grid Arendal, 2023). In this context, it is necessary to stress that 80% of Russia's natural gas and 20% of its crude oil are produced in the Arctic (International Energy Agency, 2022). The Norwegian Petroleum Directorate estimates that the Barents Sea has an undiscovered resource of 2.4 billion cubic metres of oil equivalent comprising 1.3 billion cubic metres of liquid and 1.1 trillion cubic metres of gas (Searancke, 2023). Additionally, in its annual review, the Norwegian Petroleum Directorate highlighted that the largest gas field was discovered in the Barents Sea in 2022 (Searancke, 2023).

Before the war in Ukraine, the EU could have taken advantage of this discovery as until 2021, Russia was the main EU supplier of crude oil, natural gas, and solid fossil fuels (Eurostat, 2021) and the EU was Russia's first energy export destination globally (EEAS, 2021). Since the beginning of the war in Ukraine in 2022, the EU has been reducing its gas imports from Russia (European Council, 2023) while trying to diversify its energy supplies and speed up its green energy transition. Also, the EU (and the West more broadly) has imposed economic sanctions on Russia that have seriously deteriorated their political and economic relations. As these sanctions have jeopardised its trade, Russia is turning to China where it exports gas from the Arctic and is becoming the main destination of its trade (Lipsky and Graham, 2023). As a representative of Rosatom, a Russian nuclear energy state corporation, explained at a meeting of NSR stakeholders in 2022, 'external pressure of the sanctions [...] the reorientation of cargo flows to the east has become an obvious fact. Both consumers of our products and potential investors in the development of the Arctic are concentrated in the East' (Eiterjord, 2022).

Furthermore, the EU has imposed a port ban on tankers engaging in ship-to-ship (STS) transfers of Russian oil at sea (Riviera News, 2023). In May 2024, the EU decided to impose a ban on trans-shipments of Russian LNG to European ports in order to 'hamper the logistics of Russian gas exports from the Arctic [especially from the Yamal LNG project], which during the winter months requires the use of ice-breaking LNG carriers' (Urbados Arbeloa, 2024). Trans-shipment services are essential for Russian LNG logistics because they take place mainly in Zeebrugge (Belgium) and Montoir-de-Bretagne (France) in order to access the Asian market (Urbados Arbeloa, 2024). This happens in winter when permanent darkness and ice in the Arctic Ocean makes it impossible for LNG tankers and even icebreakers to reach Asian markets through the Bering Strait (Urbados Arbeloa, 2024). The EU's measure aims to reduce Russia's export revenues and prepare the ground for a ban on Russian LNG imports to the EU by 2027, in line with REPowerEU (Urbados Arbeloa, 2024).

Like the EU, Norway has imposed bans on its ports. In particular, in 2022, Norway decided that Russian fishing vessels are permitted access only to three Norwegian ports and that all Russian vessels arriving at these ports would be subject to inspection (Government of Norway, 2022). These ports are Tromsø, Kirkenes, and Båtsfjord, which are located in the Barents Euro-Arctic Region (BEAR) and are the ports with the highest number of calls by Russian fishing vessels (Government of Norway, 2022). Additionally, Minister of Foreign Affairs Anniken Huitfeldt explained that Norway has 'been closely monitoring Russian activities in Norwegian waters and ports to ensure that Norway is not used as a transit country for the illegal transport of goods to Russia' (Government of Norway, 2022). She added that Norway has 'information that indicates there is a need to increase restrictions relating to Russian fishing vessels' (Government of Norway, 2022). Nevertheless, as Norway manages a number of fish stocks together with Russia, it has granted Russian fishing vessels certain exemptions to the ban on port access (Government of Norway, 2022). Indeed, Minister Huitfeldt stressed that this is necessary in order to ensure that the successful 50-year fishing cooperation between Norway and Russia continues (Government of Norway, 2022). This is important not only to let the fishing sector flourish but also to have stability in the Arctic. Another reason why the Norwegian government made that decision is its responsibility of protecting the cod stock in the Barents Sea (Bye, 2023). Interestingly, State Secretary of the Norwegian Ministry of Trade, Industry, and Fisheries Vidar Ulriksen (Labor) stated that Norway has 'responsibility for the resource management to be carried out also after the war in Ukraine is over' because Norway shares important fish stocks in the Arctic with Russia (Bye, 2023). This is why he considered that 'it is wise to be calm about what is happening in the High North so that we can return more quickly to a more normal situation in regard to resource management in our northern areas' (Bye, 2023).

However, the port ban has created uncertainty in the shipping sector. This is for instance the case of the port of Kimek, in Norway, which has based itself on trade and cooperation with Russia (Bye, 2023). Greger Mannsvek, the chief executive officer of the port of Kimek, said, in fact, that Russian fishing vessels have always been the main customers of the port thus constituting its main market (Bye, 2023). He argued that 'the constant pestering creates uncertainty for our operation, for all my employees, and for the community here' (Bye, 2023). In 2022, the government of Norway also pointed out that the sanctions on Russia negatively affect the shipping sector in the region that is very much connected to the Russian market (Bye, 2023).

In short, ports play a role of utmost importance in the geopolitical and economic strategies of the Arctic states. However, their development is quite problematic mainly because of the harsh weather of the Arctic and the consequent high costs. Additionally, the ports ban imposed by the EU and Norway is quite problematic as it is seriously damaging the successful cooperation between Russia and the EU as well as between Russia and Norway.

The Arctic and Outer Space

The Arctic and Outer Space are essentially intertwined in two ways. First, the 'Arctic climate is a consequence of Earth's orbital mechanics, most notably the tilt of the planet, which leads to the absence of sunlight in winter and to 24-hour sunlight in summer' (Byers, 2020). Sunlight is the most impacting factor influencing the Arctic climate (National Snow and Ice Data Center, 2024). In winter, there is little or no solar energy leaving the region dark and cold, while in summer the sun shines for many hours or around the clock, bringing warmth and light (National Snow and Ice Data Center, 2024). Second, the Arctic is linked to Outer Space through satellites that are of utmost importance to 'Arctic communications, surveillance, navigation, search and rescue, weather forecasting, sea-ice monitoring, fishing, prospecting, and environmental research' (Byers, 2020).

Satellites are used to study the impact of climate change on the region. For instance, the National Environmental Satellite, Data, and Information Service of the US Department of Commerce has been observing ice, ocean, and atmosphere properties from satellites for 30 years (National Oceanic and Atmospheric Administration – NOAA, 2024). As it is possible to read on NOAA's website, 'real-time satellite data are critical for accurate forecasting and warning of events, such as rapid sea ice formation and frequent storms that pose major hazards to life, property, and economic activities in the Arctic' (NOAA, 2024). Indeed, sea-ice forecast is crucial for the activities of many stakeholders operating in the marine environment, including the coast guard, the Arctic coastal communities living in the Arctic, the oil and gas and fishing industries, the first responders to emergencies, and scientific researchers (NOAA, 2024). Also, in August 2024, the Arctic Weather Satellite was launched from Vandenberg, in California, with the aim 'to show how a potential polar-orbiting constellation of satellites could provide data for very short-term weather forecasts and nowcasts in the Arctic, and around the world' (European Space Agency, 2024).

Furthermore, the EU European Space Agency (ESA) launched the Climate Change Initiative (CCI), which is a major research program aiming to generate 'global, decades-long satellite data records to track and understand key aspects of the Earth climate system, and known as Essential Climate Variables'[4] (European Space Agency, 2024a). The CCI program involves more than 500 experts from across Europe that are in charge of analysing the data from the satellites. It will contribute to and strengthen the scientific understanding of the climate and allow ESA member states to adopt necessary measures on climate action in support of the Paris Agreement goals (European Space Agency, 2024a). Additionally, from 2023 to 2029, the CCI program will support the UN Framework Convention on Climate Change (UNFCCC) Global Stocktake[5] by continuing to expand the Essential Climate Variables, supporting progression towards national and global implementation of the Paris Agreement, and providing research and development for an operational climate service (European Space Agency, 2024a).

Moreover, satellite data, together with weather observations, are used by artificial intelligence (AI) systems. This is, for instance, the case of IceNet, a cutting-edge project conducted by the British Antarctic Survey and The Alan Turing Institute 'to address the impact of climate change on the Arctic using an AI sea ice forecasting system' (British Antarctic Survey, 2024). This AI system observes pan-Arctic 25 kilometres square of sea ice concentration on a daily timescale up to several months ahead in order to help Arctic residents prepare and adapt to changing conditions (British Antarctic Survey, 2024). In the Arctic there is an increasing trend to use AI, which is very useful for gathering physical data about the Arctic that is very difficult to collect otherwise. In fact, scientists would need a long-term monitoring presence in order to understand the Arctic climate and its environment, but this is not possible due to the fact that 'the environment of the Arctic Ocean is too harsh, too logistically challenging, and too expensive for a continued year-round human presence' (Hosking, 2024). AI allows scientists to deploy autonomous robotic platforms that are able to collect data from the atmosphere, ocean, and sea ice right across the Arctic Ocean, but their number is still insufficient (Hosking, 2024). However, these systems can't take all kinds of measurements (Hosking, 2024). This is why in 2019 an international partnership launched the Multidisciplinary drifting Observatory for the Study of Arctic Climate (MOSAIC) campaign, the largest polar expedition in history and the first of its kind (Hosking, 2024). Thus, the German research icebreaker *Polarstern* set sail from Tromsø, Norway, to spend a year drifting in the Arctic Ocean, trapped in ice (Hosking, 2024). The team constituted researchers from 20 states with the aim to 'take the closest look ever at the Arctic as the epicenter of global warming and to gain fundamental insights that are key to better understand global climate change' (Hosking,

4 An Essential Climate Variable is a physical, chemical, or biological variable or a group of linked variables that critically contribute to the characterisation of Earth's climate (ESA, 2024b).

5 'According to the Paris Agreement, Parties shall periodically take stock of its implementation to assess the collective progress towards achieving the purpose of the Agreement and its long-term goals' (UNFCCC, 2024).

2024). The data gathered were supposed to be transmitted to scientists around the globe (Hosking, 2024).

In this context, satellite technology is a crucial tool to tackle climate change by observing the environment and by tracking things like atmospheric gases, sea levels, and weather patterns (Smithsonian Institution, 2024). Satellites can also help to adapt to climate change by providing real-time data for disaster management, thus allowing scientists to predict and monitor events like hurricanes and wildfires (Smithsonian Institution, 2024). Additionally, farmers can take advantage of satellite data to provide farmers with information about soil and crop conditions, which helps them adjust to new climate realities (Smithsonian Institution, 2024). This will become increasingly important in the Arctic due to the fact that climate change will make the region warmer thus making it suitable for the cultivation of a number of crops (Universal-Sci Weekly, 2024). This is an issue that is being increasingly researched as is evident from the many peer-reviewed articles that have been published on this topic over the last few years. Two examples support this statement. The first article is titled 'Wilderness areas under threat from global redistribution of agriculture' and was published in the *Current Biology* in November 2023. This article discusses a study based on the Food and Agricultural Organization (FAO) Ecocrop model (high-resolution climate data) of climate suitability for 1,708 crop varieties (Gardner et al., 2023, 4721). The authors conclude that over the next 40 years '2.7 million km^2 of land within wilderness will become newly suitable for agriculture, equivalent to 7% of the total wilderness area outside Antarctica' (Gardner et al., 2023, 4721). A substantial portion of the land that will become cultivable lies within the high-latitude regions of the northern hemisphere, including the Arctic (Gardner et al., 2023, 4721). The authors also find that globally 72% of currently cultivable land will probably suffer from a net loss in total crop diversity while wild land like in the Arctic will experience an unprecedented agricultural expansion (Gardner et al., 2023, 4721). The second article is titled 'The challenges fraught opportunity of agriculture expansion into boreal and Arctic regions' and was published by *Agricultural Systems* in September 2022. In 2021, the authors organised a United Nations Summit dialogue on 'Local and global food security shaped by northern agriculture' with the aim to complement a 2019 survey of the scientific community on boreal and Arctic agriculture (Klöffel et al., 2022, 203). The 33 attendees concluded that 'climate change might offer significant agricultural opportunities in boreal and Arctic communities such as increased food security, sovereignty, and economic development, this should not be considered lightly and without strong support for environmental sustainability as carbon and biodiversity losses are main risks' (Klöffel et al., 2022, 203). Yet, no research studies the link between the use of satellites and the development of agriculture in the Arctic.

Moreover, satellites are becoming increasingly important for communicating effectively due to the fact that shipping traffic in the Arctic is growing. This will pose big challenges to communication in the Arctic because 'communications satellites operating in geostationary Earth orbit do not cover the area of the Arctic' (European Space Agency, 2024c). Indeed, although satellite technology is advancing at a very fast pace, 'there are still significant spatio-temporal gaps in global communications and earth observations, especially as these apply to high latitude regions' (Garand et al., 2014, 247). The reason is that satellites are not able to cover the entire area of the Earth, yet (Garand et al., 2014, 247). There are various reasons for this: 1) the space industry is relatively young; 2) economic constraints impose limitations on the number of low Earth orbiting (LEO) meteorological satellites, which are the only ones that at present observe the polar regions (Garand et al., 2014, 247). Additionally, the link between satellites and the Arctic can be disrupted because of ice on antennas or heavy seas (European Space Agency, 2024c). Nevertheless, the Iridium satellite constellation, which is in low-earth orbit (approximately 780 kilometres above the earth),[6] is able to supply communications services to the Arctic, but some cases of interruptions to the service lasting several minutes have been recorded (European Space Agency, 2024c). Another problem is that the Iridium satellite constellation does not provide the broadband communication necessary to the development of human activities in the region, thus posing a challenge for the coming years (European Space Agency, 2024c). Canada has tried to find a solution as much of its territory lies in the Arctic (European Space Agency, 2024c). More specifically, the Canadian Space Agency has been developing the Polar Communications and Weather satellite mission since 2007 (European Space Agency, 2024c; Garand et al., 2014, 247). The project, which is still being developed, comprises two satellites that should serve Canada's communication needs and that should collect information for the global research community on Arctic weather and climate (European Space Agency, 2024c). Also, in 1962, Canada launched its first satellite, Alouette-I, becoming the third state to have a satellite in orbit after the Soviet Union and the US that launched Sputnik I in 1957 and Explorer 1 in 1958, respectively (Byers, 2024, 9). Alouette-I was designed to study the ionosphere, a layer of the upper atmosphere, to understand why Arctic radio communications are disrupted by solar storms (Byers, 2024, 9). In 1972, Canada launched Anik (that means 'little brother' in Inuktitut), which is the world's first domestic communications satellite (Byers, 2024, 9). Nunavut, the largest of Canada's three northern territories (Yukon, Northwest Territories, and Nunavut), is entirely dependent on satellites for communications; they facilitate healthcare, education, economic development, and governance (Byers, 2024, 9). However, communications satellites have some limitations because connectivity with the rest of the territory, country, and world is expensive, unreliable, and slow (Byers, 2024, 9). Furthermore, the use of satellites can contribute to the advancement of healthcare, education, and commerce as they foster the Canadian Arctic economy allowing the Inuit and First Nations youth to work for global tech companies or create start-ups of their own (Byers, 2024, 9). For instance, the American SpaceX Starlink is the current market leader and its terminals are appearing outside homes and businesses across the North (Byers, 2024, 9; Charron-Leclerc, 2023). SpaceX Starlink has a competitor, OneWeb, which originally was a British

6 The Iridium constellation is able to provide stronger signals and faster connections through smaller antennae with lower power requirements (Iridium Communications, 2024).

company that is now part of the French company Eutelsat, with a constellation of more than 600 satellites (Byers, 2024, 9). In 2023, Eutelsat contracted the Canadian Ontario-based Galaxy Broadband Communications company to provide connectivity across Canada, including 25 communities in Nunavut (Eutelsat OneWeb, 2023). Moreover, the Icelandic government also contracted OneWeb. More specifically, it initiated a program of partnership with OneWeb to assess the suitability of LEO space-based connectivity across the Arctic nation (Satellite Evolution Group, 2023). Both Iceland and Canada have included the relevance of and the necessity for satellites in their Arctic policies, although from different perspectives. With its 2021 'Policy on Matters Concerning the Arctic Region', the Icelandic government aimed to enhance the welfare of its inhabitants by 'ensuring access to digital communications, education and health care services by telecommunications and satellite navigation systems, amongst other technologies' (Satellite Evolution Group, 2023). Instead, Canada's 2024 defence policy stresses the importance of satellites in enhancing the communication capabilities of its armed forces (Byers, 2024, 9). In order to achieve this aim, Canada's government will enable its armed forces to communicate securely and reliably with its deployed forces, allies, and partners by acquiring 'a comprehensive worldwide satellite communication capability' and working with its allies to jointly 'develop updated access to the satellite constellations that enable the military to operate effectively around the world, including by better defending its communications against jamming or disruptions by adversaries while deployed' (Byers, 2024, 9).

Another essential space-based service is the Global Positioning System (GPS) that is owned and operated by the US military, but it is also widely used by civilians because it provides a highly accurate position, navigation, and timing service from a constellation of 32 satellites in mid-Earth orbit (Byers, 2024, 9). However, it is not the only existing global positioning, navigation, and timing satellite system as Russia, the EU, and China have their own, namely GLONASS, Galileo, and BeiDou, respectively (Byers, 2024, 9). Also, GPS is very useful for search and rescue operations. To this aim, the US, the Soviet Union, and France created the International Cospas-Sarsat program in 1979 (Byers, 2024, 10; Cospas-Sarsat, 2024). It works with the Cospas-Sarsat beacon, also called a distress radio beacon or emergency beacon, 'a radio transmitter that can be activated in a life-threatening emergency to summon assistance from government authorities' (Cospas-Sarsat, 2024). The satellites supporting the Cospas-Sarsat program are owned and operated by Russia, the US, Canada, France, the EU, and the European Organisation for the Exploitation of Meteorological Satellites (EUMETSAT), the European operational satellite agency for monitoring weather, climate, and the environment from space[7] (Cospas-Sarsat, 2024; Byers, 2024, 10). The Cospas-Sarsat program is an

7 EUMETSAT is an intergovernmental organisation with 30 member states and is based in Darmstadt, Germany. It operates the geostationary satellites Meteosat-10 and Meteosat-11 over Europe and Africa, and Meteosat-9 over the Indian Ocean (EUMETSAT, 2024).

international cooperative of 43 states and agencies and 200 states benefit from it (Cospas-Sarsat, 2024).

Furthermore, satellites are used by powers to compete in the technological and military domains. This has already been evident during the Cold War when the US and the Soviet Union competed in the so-called space race. The Soviet Union was the first state to launch a satellite, Sputnik (that means travel companion), on the 4th October 1957. This shocked the US not only because the Soviet Union had come first in the race but also because its security was jeopardised by the technological progresses made by the Soviet Union in the missile sector (Di Nolfo, 2015, 404). The space race has appeared again on the international scene over the last few decades as the rivalry between the US, China, and Russia has worsened. In fact, 'As China has become deeply enmeshed in strategic competition with the US – while edging towards outright hostilities with other regional neighbours – Washington's alarm at the pace of its advancement in space is growing ever-louder' (Davidson, 2024). In 2024, China launched a robotic spacecraft, Chang'e-6, on a round trip to the moon's far side with the aim to accomplish a mission that will pave the way for an inaugural Chinese-crewed landing and a base on the lunar south pole (Davidson, 2024). During the same week, China launched Shenzhou-18, Beijing's latest staffed spacecraft mission to the Tiangong space station, which it developed after having been excluded from the International Space Station (ISS) in 2011 when Congress passed a law prohibiting any official American contact with the Chinese space program due to concerns about national security (Davidson, 2024; Kluger, 2015).

Moreover, Russia is also very interested in developing its capabilities in the space. The Russian Federal Space Agency (ROSCOSMOS), which has regrouped the space industries and organisations inherited from the Soviet Union, is 'the coordinating hub for space activities, serving both civilian and military needs' (Kim, 2020). ROSCOSMOS has always been an important and reliable partner for the ISS, manufacturing component modules and providing transportation (Kim, 2020). In 2021, Russia launched Arktika-M N1, the first of two satellites, part of the Arktika-M mission, operated by ROSCOSMOS and assisted by the Russian Federal Service for Hydrometeorology and Environmental Monitoring (ROSHYDROMET) (eoPortal, 2022). The entire constellation of the Arktika-M mission is planned to be fully operational by 2025 and aims to monitor the Earth's atmosphere and surface in the Arctic, collect and relay information from Arctic facilities, monitor cosmic rays, and assist the Cospas-Sarsat program (eoPortal, 2022). However, the war in Ukraine has had serious consequences for the Russian space industry because a number of factors have made the sustainable development of the Russian space program impossible (Jones, 2023). Some factors that have negatively affected Russia's space sector are sanctions, the embargo on advanced industrial equipment, workforce shortages, limited financial resources spread among too many projects, and the economic inefficiency of the Russian space industry (Jones, 2023). Also, another important factor is the cancellation of space cooperation with Western partners, except operations on the ISS (Luzin, 2024). Thus, Russia has identified two priorities to pursue by 2030, namely to maintain the presence of Russian astronauts in Outer Space, in spite of the end of cooperation on the ISS and without any significant scientific outcomes, and to switch satellite manufacturing from space-grade electronics to relatively simple and cheap consumer-grade electronics (Luzin, 2024). Therefore, like in the case of shipping, Russia's space sector has also turned to the East. At the beginning of 2024, Yuri Borisov, Head of ROSCOSMOS, announced plans for Russia and China to build an automated nuclear power plant on the Moon between 2033 and 2035 (Suess and Crawford, 2024). This project aims to strengthen space cooperation between the two partners, which already began in 2021 with the introduction of the International Lunar Research Station (ILRS), which is

> a complex experimental research facilities to be constructed with a possible attraction of partners on the surface and/or in the orbit of the Moon designed for multi-discipline and multi-purpose scientific research activities, including exploration and use of the Moon, moon-based observation, fundamental research experiments and technology verification, with capability of long-term unmanned operation with the prospect of subsequent human presence.
> (Suess and Crawford, 2024; China National Space Administration, 2021)

Furthermore, in April 2024, Russia vetoed a US-drafted UN Security Council resolution calling on states to prevent an arms race in Outer Space (Nichols, 2024). The US proposal was due to the fact that it accused Russia of developing an anti-satellite nuclear weapon to put in space, which Russia denied (Nichols, 2024). However, the use of the Moon and other celestial bodies for weapon use of any kind is against the Outer Space Treaty stipulating that they 'shall be used exclusively for peaceful purposes' (United Nations Office for Outer Space Affairs, 2024).

Moreover, the EU has an orbital satellite launch complex called Esrange, which is located in the very north of Sweden, above the Arctic Circle, and has been in operation since 1966 (Preve, 2024; Swedish Space Corporation, 2021). It is used by the international scientific community to launch sounding rockets for microgravity and atmospheric research, high altitude balloons for astronomy, as well as for atmospheric research, and drop tests of space and aerial vehicles. It also has a new infrastructure offering reusable rocket tests, engine and fuel tests, and satellite launches, thus being the first site on EU territory with orbital launch capability (Swedish Space Corporation, 2021). Esrange also includes one of the world's largest civilian satellite ground stations and acts as a hub in our satellite station network (Swedish Space Corporation, 2021). In this way, Esrange 'brings the European bloc closer to competing in the space race between the United States, China, and Russia. Sweden is creating a major data centre hub in the northern part of the country' (Preve, 2024).

In conclusion, the development of the space sector is stimulated by climate change, and offers many possible solutions to the challenges that climate change poses. At the same time, the war in Ukraine is affecting space cooperation among states while also contributing to the definition of 'space geopolitics' as Russia's turning to the East in this sector clearly demonstrates.

Conclusion

Shipping routes and infrastructure are a central element in the geopolitical dynamics of the Arctic. Climate change, which is making shipping routes increasingly accessible, and political issues (e.g., the current conflict in the Middle East between Israel and Palestine, which is extending to the whole region) are making the NSR, the NWP, and TSR very important economically and geopolitically because they are supposed to become the most important navigation routes substituting traditional ones in the near future. However, as specified in the first section, at the moment of writing only the NSR and the TSR are navigable since the TSR is still frozen although it is expected to be ice-free in the next few decades. Furthermore, in the case of the NSR, the war in Ukraine is turning navigation towards the East because Russia has been moving its trade target from Europe to Asia, in particular to China. Additionally, both the NSR and the NWP are at the centre of legal disputes internationally as Russia and Canada, which have jurisdiction over the NSR and the NWP, respectively, claim that they are part of their national territory while other states have an interest in considering them international waters. Instead, the case of the TSR is a bit different because it is still frozen but legal and geopolitical issues could emerge when it would become ice-free, which is expected to happen in the near future.

In this context, ports play a role of utmost importance for the development of shipping routes because they provide vital support to vessels. However, there are still very few deepwater ports and they need to be developed, but high costs due also to the harsh weather make it quite problematic. Additionally, the ban imposed by the West contributes to making the fishery trade quite difficult and has created economic problems for Western ports as well like in the case of the Norwegian ports where trade is strictly intertwined with that of the Russian ports.

Finally, the development of space infrastructure is also an important factor from a geopolitical perspective because it represents a technological advancement of states in a sector that is becoming increasingly relevant. Indeed, satellites have multiple uses such as monitoring climate change, which is useful for agriculture, search and rescue, and military operations. Arctic states are trying to develop their space infrastructure in order to use satellites for a number of issues, thereby giving birth to a 'new space race'. However, the war in Ukraine is negatively affecting cooperation between the West and Russia in the Outer Space sector thus leading Russia and China to cooperate on joint projects that are essential to developing their respective space programs.

References

Arctic Knowledge Hub. (2009). *Arctic Ports. AMSA Report 2009.* Available at: http://www.arctis-search.com/Arctic+Ports (accessed 16 November 2024).

Arctic Portal. (2023) *Shipping.* Available at: https://portlets.arcticportal.org/hub-ports/92-hub-ports (accessed 6 September 2023).

Atlas Magasine. (2024). *The World Merchant Fleet.* Available at: https://www.atlas-mag.net/en/category/tags/focus/the-world-merchant-fleet (accessed 11 November 2024).

Bartenstein, K. (2011). The "Arctic Exception" in the Law of the Sea Convention: A Contribution to Safer Navigation in the Northwest Passage?. *Ocean Development & International Law,* 42(1–2): 22–52.

Bennett, M., Stephenson, S., Yang, K., Bravo, M., De Jonghe, B. (2020a). Climate Change and the Opening of the Transpolar Sea Route: Logistics, Governance, and Wider Geo-economic, Societal and Environmental Impacts. In Spohr, K., Hamilton, D. (eds.) *The Arctic and World Order.* Washington: Johns Hopkins University.

Bennett, M., Stephenson, S., Yang, K., Bravo, M., De Jonghe, B. (2020b). The Opening of the Transpolar Route: Logistical, Geopolitical, Environmental, and Socioeconomic Impacts. *Marine Policy,* 121: 1–15.

Blunden, M. (2012). Geopolitics and the Northern Sea Route. *International Affairs,* 88(1): 115–129.

Bognar-Lahr, D. (2020). In the Same Boat? A Comparative Analysis of the Approaches of Russia and Canada in the Negotiation of the IMO's Mandatory Polar Code. *Ocean Development and International Journal,* 51(2): 1–19.

Brewster, M. (2024). Canada, U.S. and Finland form Pact to Build Icebreakers for Arctic. Canada and the U.S. Have Been Struggling to Rebuild Their Icebreaking Fleets. *CBC News.* Available at: https://www.cbc.ca/news/politics/canada-us-finland-icebreakers-1.7260460 (accessed 16 November 2024).

British Antarctic Survey. (2024). *November 2023: How Is AI Being Used for Good in the Arctic?.* Available at: https://www.bas.ac.uk/media/beyondtheice/november-2023-how-is-ai-being-used-for-good-in-the-arctic/#:~:text=The%20IceNet%20AI%20uses%20satellite,and%20adapt%20to%20changing%20conditions. (accessed 12 December 2024).

Burke, D. C. (2018). *The Northwest Passage Dispute.* Oxford Research Group. Available at: https://www.oxfordresearchgroup.org.uk/blog/the-northwest-passage-dispute (accessed 13 November 2024).

Bye, H.-G. (2023). *The Constant Calls for Port Bans Causes Great Uncertainty for Our Operations.* Available at: https://www.highnorthnews.com/en/constant-calls-port-bans-causes-great-uncertainty-our-operations (accessed 6 September 2023).

Byers, M. (2020). Arctic Security and Outer Space. *Scandinavian Journal of Military Studies,* 3(1): 183–196.

Byers, M. (2024). *Outer Space and the Arctic: Connections, Opportunities, Challenges.* Working Papers. CIGI Papers, n. 303. Provided in Cooperation with: Centre for International Governance Innovation (CIGI), Waterloo, Ontario.

Charron-Leclerc, F. (2023). Starlink Getting the Bugs Out: Nunavummiut Share Their Experience with the Service Online. *Nunavut News.* Available at: https://www.nunavutnews.com/news/starlink-getting-the-bugs-out-7282336 (accessed 22 November 2024).

Chaudhury, D. (2024). Russia's Northern Sea Route Emerges as Key Connectivity Initiative in Indo-Pacific Region. *The Economic Times.* Available at: https://economictimes.indiatimes.com/industry/transportation/shipping-/-transport/russias-northern-sea-route-emerges-as-key-connectivity-initiative-in-indo-pacific-region/articleshow/106869625.cms (accessed 12 November 2024).

China National Space Administration. (2021). *International Lunar Research Station (ILRS) Guide for Partnership.* Available at: https://www.cnsa.gov.cn/english/n6465652/n6465653/c6812150/content.html (accessed 25 November 2024).

Cospas-Sarsat. (2024). *What Is a Cospas-Sarsat Beacon?.* Available at: https://cospas-sarsat.int/en/ (accessed 24 November 2024).

Davidson, H. (2024). The New 'Space Race': What Are China's Ambitions and Why Is the US so Concerned?. *The Guardian.* Available at: https://www.theguardian.com/world/article/2024/may/05/the-new-space-race-what-are-chinas-ambitions-and-why-is-the-us-so-concerned (accessed 25 November 2024).

Detsch, J. (2024). The Geopolitics of New Arctic Shipping Lanes. Turmoil in the Middle East Makes the Northern Route More Attractive, if Still Treacherous. *Foreign Policy*. Available at: https://foreignpolicy.com/2024/05/30/arctic-geopolitics-russia-china-maritime-trade-northern-sea-route/ (accessed 14 November 2024).

Di Nolfo, E. (2015). *Storia Delle Relazioni Internazionali. Gli Anni Della Guerra Fredda 1946–1990*. Bari: Laterza.

Economy, E. (2014). China's Imperial President. Xi Jinping Tightens His Grip. *Foreign Affairs*, November/December 2014. Available at: https://www.foreignaffairs.com/articles/china/2014-10-20/chinas-imperial-president?_gl=1%2Awbjkju%2A_gcl_au%2AMTc3MjI5MjYwNy4xNzI3MjcxMjIw%2A_ga%2AMTI4ODEwNzI5Ni4xNzI3MjcxMjIw%2A_ga_24W5E70YKH%2AMTczMTk2NTc3Mi45LjEuMTczMTk2NjQxMS42MC4wLjA.%2A_ga_N9V4J2JY26%2AMTczMTk2NTc3Mi45LjEuMTczMTk2NjQxMS42MC4wLjA. (accessed 12 November 2024).

EEAS. (2021). *Facts and Figures about EU – Russia Relations*. Available at: https://www.eeas.europa.eu/sites/default/files/eeas-eu-russia_relation-en_2021-07.pdf (accessed 6 September 2023).

Eger, K. M. (2010). *Canadian Ports on the Northwest Passage*. Available at: http://www.arctis-search.com/Canadian+Ports+on+the+Northwest+Passage (accessed 17 November 2024).

Eiterjord, T. (2022). Amid Ukraine War, Russia's Northern Sea Route Turns East. *The Diplomat*. Available at: https://thediplomat.com/2022/12/amid-ukraine-war-russias-northern-sea-route-turns-east/ (accessed 6 September 2023/14 November 2024).

eoPortal. (2022). *Arktika-M*. Available at: https://www.eoportal.org/satellite-missions/arktika-m#References (accessed 25 November 2024).

EUMETSAT. (2024). *Who We Are*. Available at: https://www.eumetsat.int/about-us/who-we-are (accessed 24 November 2024).

European Council. (2023). *Infographic - Where Does the EU's Gas Come from?*. Available at: https://www.consilium.europa.eu/en/infographics/eu-gas-supply/ (accessed 6 September 2023).

European Space Agency. (2024). *The Mission*. Available at: https://www.esa.int/Applications/Observing_the_Earth/Meteorological_missions/Arctic_Weather_Satellite#:~:text=The%20mission,Arctic%2C%20and%20around%20the%20world. (accessed 20 November 2024).

European Space Agency. (2024a). *The Climate Change Initiative*. Available at: https://climate.esa.int/en/about-us-new/climate-change-initiative/ (accessed 20 November 2024).

European Space Agency. (2024b). *Essential Climate Variable*. Available at: https://climate.esa.int/en/about-us-new/climate-change-initiative/essential-climate-variables/ (accessed 20 November 2024).

European Space Agency. (2024c). *Arctic Poses Communication Challenges*. Available at: https://www.esa.int/Enabling_Support/Preparing_for_the_Future/Space_for_Earth/Arctic/Arctic_poses_communications_challenges (accessed 20 November 2024).

Eurostat. (2021). *From Where Do We Import Energy?*. Available at: https://ec.europa.eu/eurostat/cache/infographs/energy/bloc-2c.html (accessed 6 September 2023).

Eutelsat OneWeb. (2023). *Galaxy Broadband Secures OneWeb Capacity for Canada*. Press release. Available at: https://oneweb.net/resources/galaxy-broadband-secures-oneweb-capacity-canada#:~:text=Galaxy%20Broadband%20signs%20US%2450,northern%20Canadian%20territory%20of%20Nunavut. (accessed 23 November 2024).

Fuller, S. (2020). *The Climate Emergency and Global Security. The International Bar Association, the Global Voice of Legal Association*. Available at: https://www.ibanet.org/article/2994759e-bccb-436b-80fd-65274530b7c4 (accessed 12 November 2024).

Garand, L., Trishchenko, A. P., Trichtchenko, L. D., Nassar, R. (2014). The Polar Communications and Weather Mission: Addressing remaining gaps in the Earth Observing System. *Physics in Canada*, 50(27): 247–254.

Gardner, A., Trew, B., Maclean, I. M. D., Sharma, M. D., Gaston, K. (2023). Wilderness Areas under Threat from Global Redistribution of Agriculture. *Current Biology*, 33(21): 4721–4726.

Government of Canada. (2024). *Agreement Between the Government of Canada and the Government of the United States of America on Arctic Cooperation E101701 - CTS No. 1988/29*. Available at: https://www.treaty-accord.gc.ca/text-texte.aspx?id=101701 (accessed 12 November 2024).

Government of Norway. (2022). *Norway Tightens Restrictions on Russian Fishing Vessels*. Available at: https://www.regjeringen.no/en/aktuelt/tightens_restrictions/id2933272/ (accessed 6 September 2023).

Grady, J. (2024). *Chinese Icebreaker Mission to Arctic 'Clear Signal' of Beijing's Polar Ambitions, Says Expert*. US Naval Institute. Available at: https://news.usni.org/2024/09/03/chinese-icebreaker-mission-to-arctic-clear-signal-of-beijings-polar-ambitions-says-expert (accessed 17 November 2024).

Grid Arendal. (2023). Nuclear Icebreaker , Murmansk, "Arctica", Russia. Available at: https://www.grida.no/resources/3641 (accessed 29 May 2025).

Gritsenko, D., Kiiski, T. (2016). A Review of Russia Ice-Breaking Tariff Policy on the Northern Sea Route 1991–2014. *Polar Record*, 52(2): 144–158.

Hamburg Port Consulting. (2024). *DEE Sea Ports*. Available at: https://www.hamburgportconsulting.com/sectors/ports/deep-sea-ports/#:~:text=Deep%20sea%20ports%20are%20critical,between%20land%20and%20sea%20transport. (accessed 17 November).

Herz, N. (2023). Alaska Watches, Nervously, as Ukraine War Pushes More Russian Oil through Bering Strait. *Alaska Public Media*. Available at: https://alaskapublic.org/2023/09/05/alaska-watches-nervously-as-ukraine-war-pushes-more-russian-oil-through-bering-strait/ (accessed 25 November 2024).

Hong, N. (2020). *China's Role in the Arctic. Observing and Being Observed*. Routledge: New York.

Hosking, S. (2024). *Ships, Submarines and Satellites - A Brief History of Sea Ice Measurements*. The Alan Turing Institute. Available at: https://www.turing.ac.uk/blog/new-age-arctic-science-discovery-ai-way (accessed 12 December 2024).

Huang, L., Minghao, L., Igrec, B., Cardiff, P., Stagonas, D., Thomas, G. (2019). *Simulation of a Ship Advancing in Floating Ice Floes*. Proceedings of the 25th International Conference on Port and Ocean Engineering under Arctic Conditions, 9–13 June, Delft, The Netherlands.

Humpert, M. (2019). Iceland Invests in Arctic Shipping With Development of Finnafjord Deep-Water Port. *The High North News*. Available at: https://www.highnorthnews.com/en/iceland-invests-arctic-shipping-development-finnafjord-deep-water-port (accessed 18 November 2024).

Humpert, M. (2023). New US Icebreaker Delayed Until 2027, Russia Orders 6th and 7th Nuclear Icebreaker. *The High North News*. Available at: https://www.highnorthnews.com/en/new-us-icebreaker-delayed-until-2027-russia-orders-6th-and-7th-nuclear-icebreaker (accessed 16 November 2024).

Humpert, M. (2024a). China-Russia Announce Plans for Five Ice-Capable Containerships for Year Round Arctic Service. *The High North News*. Available at: https://www.highnorthnews.com/en/china-russia-announce-plans-five-ice-capable-containerships-year-round-arctic-service (accessed 17 November 2024).

Humpert, M. (2024b). New Report: Busy Summer for Arctic Shipping on Russia's Northern Sea Route. *The High North News*. Available at: https://www.highnorthnews.com/en/new-report-busy-summer-arctic-shipping-russias-northern-sea-route (accessed 14 November 2024).

International Chamber of Shipping. (2023). *Shipping and World Trade: World Seaborne Trade*. Available at: https://www.ics-shipping.org/shipping-fact/shipping-and-world-trade-world-seaborne-trade/#:~:text=The%20international%20shipping%20industry%20is,would%20simply%20not%20be%20possible (accessed 3 September 2023).

International Energy Agency. (2022). *Energy Fact Sheet: Why Does Russian Oil and Gas Matter?.* Available at: https://www.iea.org/articles/energy-fact-sheet-why-does-russian-oil-and-gas-matter (accessed 6 September 2024).

Intesa San Paolo. (2020). The Arctic Route. Climate Change Impact, Maritime and Economic Scenario, Geo-strategic Analysis and Perspectives. SRM Services.

Investment Portal of the Arctic Zone of the Russian Federation. (2020). *Icebreakers in the Arctic: The World's Most Powerful Icebreaker Fleet.* Available at: https://arctic-russia.ru/en/article/icebreakers-in-the-arctic-the-world-s-most-powerful-icebreaker-fleet/ (accessed 15 November 2024).

Iridium Communications. (2024). *Perfectly in Sync, While Traveling More Than 30,000 Kilometers Per Hours.* Available at: https://www.iridium.com/network/ (accessed 20 November 2024).

Jones, A. (2023). Russia's War on Ukraine Has Caused Lasting Damage to International Spaceflight Cooperation. *Space*. Available at: https://www.space.com/russia-war-ukraine-damage-international-spaceflight-cooperation (accessed 25 November 2024).

Kim, S. (2020). *Russia. SPARC Brief.* University of Washington. Available at: https://www.sparc.uw.edu/russia/ (accessed 20 November 2024).

Kitagawa, H. (2001). The Northern Sea Route. The shortest sea route linking East Asia and Europe. Tokyo>Ship and Ocean Foundation.

Klimenko, E. (2020). *Russia's New Arctic Policy Document Signals Continuity Rather Than Change.* Stockholm International Peace Research Institute. Available at: https://www.sipri.org/commentary/essay/2020/russias-new-arctic-policy-document-signals-continuity-rather-change (accessed 11 November 2024).

Kluger, J. (2015). The Silly Reason the Chinese Aren't Allowed on the Space Station. *Time*. Available at: https://time.com/3901419/space-station-no-chinese/ (accessed 25 November 2024).

Kobzeva, M. (2019). China's Arctic Policy: Present and Future. *The Polar Journal*, 9(1): 94–112.

Lamazhapov, E., Stensdal, I., Heggelund, G. (2023). *China's Polar Silk Road: Long Game or Failed Strategy?.* The Arctic Institute. Available at: https://www.thearcticinstitute.org/china-polar-silk-road-long-game-failed-strategy/ (accessed 13 November 2024).

Laruelle, M. (2014). *Russia's Arctic Strategies and the Future of the Far North.* Routledge: New York.

Lasserre, F. (2021). *The Future of the Arctic Route for Maritime Trade: A Geopolitical Revolution?.* Italian Institute for International Political Studies. Available at: https://www.ispionline.it/en/publication/future-arctic-route-maritime-trade-geopolitical-revolution-32054 (accessed 14 November 2024).

Lasserre, F., Faury, O. (2020). *Arctic Shipping. Climate Change, Commercial Traffic and Port Development. Routledge Studies in Transport Analysis.* London and New York: Routledge.

Lipsky, J, Graham, N. (2023). *China Is Trading More with Russia—but So Are Many US Allies and Partners.* Available at: https://www.atlanticcouncil.org/blogs/new-atlanticist/china-is-trading-more-with-russia-but-so-are-many-us-allies-and-partners/ (accessed 6 September 2023).

Luzin, P. (2024). *Russia's Space Program After 2024. Report.* Foreign Policy Research Institute. Available at: https://www.fpri.org/article/2024/07/russias-space-program-after-2024/ (accessed 26 November 2024).

Makarov, D., Makarova O., Mayurov, N., Mayurov, P., Turova, V. (2022). Development Prospects and Importance of the Northern Sea Route. X International Scientific Siberian Transport Forum. *Transportation Research Procedia*, 63: 1114–1120.

McBride, J., Berman, N., Chatzky, A. (2023). *China's Massive Belt and Road Initiative.* Council on Foreign Relations. Available at: https://www.cfr.org/backgrounder/chinas-massive-belt-and-road-initiative (accessed 12 November 2024).

McRae, D. M., Goundrey, D. J. (1982). Environmental Jurisdiction in Arctic Waters: The Extent of Article 234. *University of British Columbia Law Review,* 16(2): 197–298.

Meade, J. (2020). *Russia's New Arctic Policy 2035: Implications for Great Power Tension Over the Northern Sea Route. Research Short.* National Intelligence University.

Megan, D., Dalaklis, D., Kitada, M., Ölçer, A., Ballini, F. (2018). Geopolitics of Arctic Shipping: The State of Icebreakers and Future Needs. *Polar Geography,* 41(2): 107–125.

Melia, N., Haines, K., Hawkins, E. (2016). Sea Ice Decline and 21st Century Trans-Arctic Shipping Routes. *Geophysical Research Letters. Special section: The Arctic: An AGU Joint Special Collection,* 43: 9720–9728.

Nadig, S. (2023). *The Nuclear Icebreakers Enabling Drilling in Russia's Arctic. Mining Technology.* Available at: https://www.mining-technology.com/features/the-nuclear-icebreakers-enabling-drilling-in-russias-arctic/?cf-view (accessed 15 November 2024).

National Snow and Ice Data Center. (2024). *What Is the Arctic Climate.* Available at: https://nsidc.org/learn/parts-cryosphere/arctic-weather-and-climate (accessed 19 November 2024).

National Oceanic and Atmospheric Administration. (2024). *Our Mission, Values and Vision.* Available at: https://www.noaa.gov/our-mission-values-and-vision#:~:text=Climate%2C%20weather%20and%20water%20affect,America's%20coastal%20and%20marine%20resources. (accessed 19 November 2024).

Nichols, M. (2024). Russia, US Clash at UN Over Nuclear Weapons in Space. *Reuters.* Available at: https://www.reuters.com/science/russia-blocks-us-move-un-nuclear-weapons-space-2024-04-24/ (accessed 25 November 2024).

Noorali, H., Flint, C., Ahmadi, S. (2022). Port Power: Towards a New Geopolitical World Order. *Journal of Transport Geography,* 105: 1–12.

Nordregio. (2019). *Sea Routes and Ports in the Arctic.* Available at: https://nordregio.org/maps/sea-routes-and-ports-in-the-arctic/ (accessed 16 November 2024).

Ocean Conservancy. (2024). *Protecting the Arctic.* Available at: https://oceanconservancy.org/protecting-the-arctic/take-deep-dive/bering-strait-gateway-arctic/ (accessed 14 November 2024).

President of the Russian Federation. (2020). *Указ об основах государственной политики Российской Федерации в Арктике на период до 2035 года [Decree on the Foundations of the Russian Federation State Policy in the Arctic for the period up to 2035].* Moscow: Government of the Russian Federation.

Preve, C. (2024). What Does Finland and Sweden's Membership to NATO Mean for Race to Arm the Arctic?. *Euronews.* Available at: https://www.euronews.com/my-europe/2024/05/31/what-does-finland-and-swedens-membership-to-nato-mean-for-race-to-arm-the-arctic#:~:text=Their%20accession%20into%20NATO%20%E2%80%94%20in,are%20in%20the%20military%20alliance. (accessed 25 November 2024).

Ragner, C.L. (2000). Northern Sea Route Cargo Flows and Infrastructure - Present State and Future Potential.The Fridtjof Nansen Institute, FNI Report13-2000.

Riviera News. (2024). Russia and China look to use Northern Sea Route year-route. Available at: https://www.rivieramm.com/news-content-hub/news-content-hub/russia-and-china-to-introduce-shipping-route-through-the-arctic-81137 (accessed 29 May 2025)

Riviera News. (2023). *EU Sanctions Target Russian STS Transfers and Ships That Turn off AIS.* Available at: https://www.rivieramm.com/news-content-hub/news-content-hub/eu-sanctions-russian-ship-to-ship-oil-transfers-in-a-bid-to-dent-profiteering-76720 (accessed 6 September 2023).

Ruiz, S., Shintani, C. (2024). *Drought in Panama Is Disrupting Global Shipping. These 7 Graphics Show How.* Woodwell Climate Research Center. Available at: https://www.woodwellclimate.org/drought-panama-canal-7-graphics/ (accessed 11 November 2024).

Satellite Evolution Group. (2023). *Space- Based Internet Programme Puts Iceland on Front Foot for 'High North' Satcomms Connectivity.* Available at: https://www

.satelliteevolution.com/post/space-based-internet-programme-puts-iceland-on-front-foot-for-high-north-satcomms-connectivity (accessed 23 November 2024).

Searancke, R. (2023). Meet the Barents: Momentum Builds in Norway's Far North. *Upstream*. Available at: https://www.upstreamonline.com/exploration/meet-the-barents-momentum-builds-in-norway-s-far-north/2-1-1391342 (accessed 29 September 2023).

Shibata, A., Zou, L., Sellheim, N., Scopelliti, M. (2019). *Emerging Legal Orders in the Arctic*. New York: Routledge.

Smithsonian Institution. (2024). *In the Air. New Science for Cleaner Air*. Available at: https://science.si.edu/in-the-air/#:~:text=These%20satellites%20track%20things%20like,the%20effects%20of%20climate%20change (accessed 21 November 2024).

Solski, J. (2021). The Genesis of Article 234 of the UNCLOS. *Ocean Development and International Law*, 52(1): 1–19.

Steinfield, D. (2020). *The U.S. – Canada Northwest Passage Dispute*. Brown Political Review. Available at: https://brownpoliticalreview.org/2020/04/the-u-s-canada-northwest-passage-dispute/ (accessed 12 November 2024).

Suess, J., Crawford, J. (2024). *Russia and China Reaffirm Their Space Partnership*. The Royal United Services Institute for Defence and Security Studies. Available at: https://rusi.org/explore-our-research/publications/commentary/russia-and-china-reaffirm-their-space-partnership (accessed 25 November 2024).

Sukhankin, S. (2018). China's 'Polar Silk Road' Versus Russia's Arctic Dilemmas. *Eurasia Daily Monitor*, 15(159). Available at: https://jamestown.org/program/chinas-polar-silk-road-versus-russias-arctic-dilemmas/ (accessed 13 November 2024).

Swedish Space Corporation. (2021). *Esrange*. Available at: https://sscspace.com/esrange/ (accessed 25 November 2024).

The State Council of the People's Republic of China. (2018). *China's Arctic Policy*. Available at: chrome-extension://efaidnbmnnnibpcajpcglclefindmkaj/https://www.uaf.edu/caps/resources/policy-documents/china-arctic-policy-2018.pdf (accessed 14 November 2024).

Theocharis, D. (2020). Approaches of the Profitability of Arctic Shipping in the Literature. In Lasserre, F., Faury, O. (eds.) *Arctic Shipping. Climate Change, Commercial Traffic and Port Development*. New York: Routledge.

Todorov, A. (2017). The Russia-USA legal dispute over the straits of the Northern Sea Route and similar case of the Northwest Passage. *Arctic and North*, 29: 62–75.

UNFCCC. (2024). *Global Stocktake*. Available at: https://unfccc.int/topics/global-stocktake (accessed 20 November 2024).

United Nations. (1982). *United Nations Convention on the Law of the Sea*. Montego Bay.

United Nations Office for Outer Space Affairs. (2024). *Treaty on Principles Governing the Activities of States in the Exploration and Use of Outer Space, Including the Moon and Other Celestial Bodies*. Available at: https://www.unoosa.org/oosa/en/ourwork/spacelaw/treaties/introouterspacetreaty.html (accessed 27 November 2024).

Universal-Sci Weekly. (2024). *Farming in the Arctic: It's Closer Than You Think*. Available at: https://www.universal-sci.com/article/farming-in-the-arctic-is-closer-than-you-think?utm_content=cmp-true (accessed 20 November 2024).

University of Alaska Fairbanks. (2018). *Full Text: China's Arctic Policy*. Available at: chrome-extension://efaidnbmnnnibpcajpcglclefindmkaj/https://www.uaf.edu/caps/resources/policy-documents/china-arctic-policy-2018.pdf (accessed 13 November 2024).

Urbados Arbeloa, I. (2024). *Banning Russian LNG Transhipment in European Ports: A Pragmatic and Effective Measure*. Elcano Royal Institute. Available at: https://www.realinstitutoelcano.org/en/commentaries/banning-russian-lng-transhipment-in-european-ports-a-pragmatic-and-effective-measure/ (accessed 18 November 2024).

Wegge, N. Keil, K. (2018). Between classical and critical geopolitics in a changing Arctic. Polar Geography, 41(2), 87–106.

Wenger, M. (2022). Nunavut's Capital Gets Its Deep Sea Port. *Polar Journal*. Available at: https://polarjournal.ch/en/2022/11/17/nunavuts-capital-gets-its-deep-sea-port/ (accessed 18 November 2024).

Zhang, X., Zou, L., Jingfang, T. (2015). From Mandatory Icebreaker Guiding to a Permission Regime: Changes to the New Russian Legislation of the Northern Sea Route. *Advances in Polar Science,* 25(3): 138–146.

Zhang, Y., Sun, X., Zha, Y., Wang, K., Chen, C. (2023). Changing Arctic Northern Sea Routeand Transpolar Sea Route: A Prediction of Route Changes and Navigation Potential before Mid-21st Century. *Journal of Marine Science and Engineering,* 11(2340): 1–20.

Conclusion

The Arctic is becoming increasingly important for many states after having been at the margins of international politics for several decades. The very first reason is that its harsh climate is becoming increasingly less harsh, and its ice is expected to reduce in the near future. Thus, the possibility of participating in the exploitation of natural resources and shipping routes has pushed several states and actors external to the region to strengthen their links with internal states making the Arctic less regional and more international. This is especially the case of China and the EU, to which so much space has been dedicated in this book. China is an emerging power on the international scene with an economy that is developing at a very fast pace, thus challenging the geopolitical influence of the US. This is why the Arctic is an excellent opportunity for China to get other resources especially since it has established close relations with Russia, the largest state in the Arctic with the longest coast and the largest amount of natural resources. However, this is not the only reason underpinning the rapprochement between Russia and China. The other reason is that the war in Ukraine has had a double impact on their relations. On the one hand, it has pushed Russia to 'turn to the East' because Western sanctions have dramatically diminished trade relations with the EU, which was its main trade partner. The rapprochement between Russia and China in energy relations is perhaps one of the most illuminating examples of the geopolitical consequences of the war in Ukraine. The partnership with Russia allows China to access its energy resources and participate in Russian energy projects like the Yamal liquid natural gas (LNG) project, one of the largest and most complex LNG projects in the world. At the same time, Russia can diversify its energy markets and reduce economic losses. On the other hand, the war in Ukraine has strongly contributed to a partnership of convenience between Russia and China because they have the same adversary, the US, but it is not an alliance because their relations have been historically quite complicated. They have been marked by alternating of periods of cooperation and fierce strategic rivalry.

The EU is another important actor that is trying to find its place in the region through a deeper involvement in Arctic affairs to which it is closely tied geopolitically, economically, socially, and environmentally. Climate change has played a key role in raising the interest of the EU in the region as well as in the definition of its strategy towards the region. In fact, ice-melting has pushed the EU to adopt its first Arctic policy in 2008 in which it highlights its links with the Arctic in

DOI: 10.4324/9781032633008-6

various sectors (e.g., energy, fisheries, environment, transport, climate change, and research) and its support for cooperation in the region. Since then, the EU has tried to affirm itself as a geopolitical actor in the Arctic as the 'evolution' of the language used in its following Arctic policies clearly demonstrates. In order to achieve this aim, the EU applied for observer status in the AC several times, but its applications have been rejected for geopolitical and economic reasons because of Russia's and Canada's opposition, respectively. In spite of this, the EU has managed to be an Arctic Circle ad hoc observer giving it the possibility of participating in a number of projects that it contributes to financially. This is particularly evident in the cases of environmental protection and the fight against climate change, which are the engine behind its Arctic policy. This is consistent with the fact that it is a leader in these two sectors internationally. Therefore, the commitment to contribute to the protection of the Arctic environment and to the fight against climate change in the region is an excellent opportunity for the EU to be more deeply involved in Arctic affairs.

Furthermore, the war in Ukraine has inevitably affected the relations of the EU and the West more broadly with Russia also in the Arctic. In fact, the necessity to become less dependent on Russian energy resources is pushing the EU and the West to accelerate the energy transition. This has an impact on the minerals market whose importance is growing because they are crucial for achieving energy transition. Climate change is increasing their accessibility because of ice-melting but the war in Ukraine has caused market uncertainty.

Moreover, fishery, which is traditionally a vital sector for the economy of the Arctic states, is also heavily affected by climate change and the war in Ukraine. However, these have contradictory consequences for the fishery sector. Climate change has pushed states and international actors to cooperate, but in some cases it fosters pre-existing tensions and competition. Two examples are the Central Arctic Ocean Fisheries Agreement and the potential conflict between Russia and Norway over the Svalbard Fisheries Protection Zone, respectively. The war in Ukraine has also created tension among states but some cases (e.g., the Faroe Islands) demonstrate that economic interests can prevail over politics.

Moreover, different from the results obtained in the case of other sectors, the analysis has shown that the water sector is only affected by climate change, not by the war in Ukraine. The reason might be that the Arctic trade of water is not very much developed yet, but it can develop in the future because of ice-melting.

Furthermore, apart from natural resources, shipping routes are the other factor that is crucial to the geopolitical dynamics in the Arctic while also having relevant legal implications. The Northern Sea Route is certainly the shipping route most affected by both climate change and the war in Ukraine. Indeed, it is becoming ice-free more quickly than the Northwest Passage while the Transpolar Route is still frozen. Additionally, the war in Ukraine is 'turning it to the East' and in particular to China. In this context, ports have a huge geopolitical value because they play a key role in the economic development of the Arctic. This is why the West has imposed bans that however risk damaging its ports' economy, like in the case of the Norwegian ports. In the case of Norway, in fact, the government has decided to leave the ports of Tromsø, Kirkenes, and Båtsfjord, which are located in the Barents Euro-Arctic Region (BEAR), accessible to Russian vessels although it has imposed some limitations.

Another sector that is suffering from the consequences of the war in Ukraine is the scientific sector, which is suffering very much from the halt of cooperation between the West and Russia. Worsened relations and the imposed sanctions have obliged the West to stop joint research projects with Russia, thus preventing scientists from accessing scientific data that are crucial for environmental protection and the fight against climate change. In fact, most data about the Arctic environment can be collected in Russia given the fact that it is the largest state with the longest coast in the region.

The war in Ukraine has, in fact, destroyed the valuable cooperative links among the states in the region that had been constructed since the very end of the Cold War and had been fostered by the necessity of protecting the Arctic environment and fighting against climate change. However, as this book has tried to demonstrate, climate change has also had another important consequence for Arctic geopolitical dynamics. It has not only fostered pre-existing tensions as said above, but it has also created new tensions as in the case of the 2008 Ilulissat Declaration. This is the clear expression of the fact that geopolitical and economic interests prevail over cooperation and good relations. The coastal states' priority is to protect their sovereignty over their territories while non-coastal states, which are a minority in the region, aim not to be excluded from the decision-making processes. This is the main reason why the political importance of the Arctic Council (AC) has increased over time. It has provided a valuable platform where states can discuss and exchange knowledge, best practices, lesson learned, and information. The AC has the great merit to have strengthened the relations among the Arctic states and foster their cooperation while also giving states and organisations external to the region a platform on which to have their voice heard and to bring their experience to the High North. Nevertheless, the war in Ukraine has also halted cooperation within the AC by excluding Russia, a key player both regionally and internationally. The recent NATO membership of Finland and Sweden, which is perhaps one of the major geopolitical results of the war in Ukraine, has contributed to divide the AC and the Arctic more broadly between NATO members and Russia, further worsening relations between them. However, the importance of the AC in the geopolitical dynamics of the region is so high that it has survived in such a difficult historical period although Russia is currently excluded from its work.

Finally, the geopolitical and legal implications of climate change and the war in Ukraine in the High North that have been discussed in this book clearly show that 'Arctic exceptionalism' is the wrong image. Even if compared with the other two regions of ice, the Antarctic and the Third Pole, it is evident that the Arctic is not exceptional. Also, the spirit of Gorbachev's Murmansk Speech of 1987, which was at the basis of the 'Arctic exceptionalism' concept, has been completely lost as soon as relations among powers at the international level worsened, demonstrating that the Arctic is the reflection of the international order.

Index

FSC
www.fsc.org
MIX
Papier | Fördert gute Waldnutzung
FSC® C083411

Kolibri 360 GmbH
Ferdinand-Jühlke-Straße 7
99095 Erfurt, Deutschland
produktsicherheit@kolibri360.de